THE AGE
OF BOWIE

Also by Paul Morley

Ask: The Chatter of Pop

Nothing

Words and Music:
A History of Pop in the Shape of a City

Joy Division: Piece by Piece

Earthbound

The North:
(And Almost Everything In It)

WITH GRACE JONES

I'll Never Write My Memoirs

THE AGE OF BOWIE

How David Bowie Made a World of Difference

Paul Morley

**SIMON &
SCHUSTER**

London · New York · Sydney · Toronto · New Delhi

A CBS COMPANY

First published in Great Britain by Simon & Schuster UK Ltd, 2016
A CBS COMPANY

Picture credits: Getty Images, pp.1 (bottom), 2 (bottom left, bottom right),
3 (top, middle right), 4, 5 (top left, top right, middle left, middle right),
6 (top left, top right), 7; Alamy pp.1 (top left, top right), 2 (top left, top right),
3 (middle left, bottom left), 5 (bottom), 6 (middle bottom), 8.

1 3 5 7 9 10 8 6 4 2

Simon & Schuster UK Ltd
1st Floor
222 Gray's Inn Road
London WC1X 8HB

www.simonandschuster.co.uk

Simon & Schuster Australia, Sydney
Simon & Schuster India, New Delhi

The author and publishers have made all reasonable efforts to contact
copyright-holders for permission, and apologise for any omissions or errors
in the form of credits given. Corrections may be made to future printings.

A CIP catalogue record for this book
is available from the British Library

Hardback ISBN: 978-1-4711-4808-8
Trade paperback ISBN: 978-1-4711-4809-5
eBook ISBN: 978-1-4711-4810-1

Typeset in the UK by M Rules
Printed and bound by CPI Group (UK) Ltd, Croydon, CR0 4YY

Simon & Schuster UK Ltd are committed to sourcing paper
that is made from wood grown in sustainable forests and support the Forest
Stewardship Council, the leading international forest certification organisation.
Our books displaying the FSC logo are printed on FSC certified paper.

e.s.p.

CONTENTS

David Bowie's 1970s in 140 scenes featuring certain deletions, omissions and oversights

PREFACE

When I was a schoolboy aged around thirteen, one of the punishments my temperamental, wild-eyed physics teacher would hand out when faced with some act of insubordination was to force the badly behaved to write out the preface to the thick, indecipherable science textbook we had been given for the year. 'Preface,' he would thunder at me after I had failed to impress him once more or talked behind his back or on one particularly rebellious occasion flicked ink from my pen at the back of his jacket, and yet again I would have to copy out two pages of dense text that I didn't understand and never would.

Forty-five years later, the world has reached a stage where you would hope that a new subject being made available in more enlightened schools would be 'David Bowie'. A subject that could help explain how much the world has changed between the 1950s and the second decade of the twenty-first century by working through his extraordinary, unique life, by following how much he changed, as a performer, and as a human being. He reflects how different the world is after over sixty years of changes many of which occurred because of the popular culture he both loved as an obsessive fan and then made his life. He became a kind of one-man song-and-dance index to the entire history of pop culture.

And if anyone studying the rich, varied history, geography, biology, art, religion and music of David Bowie found their attention wandering or a sudden need to provoke their teacher and they were told to write out the preface to their Bowie textbook, then perhaps this would be the preface they'd be writing out. Hopefully, the disobedient child might enjoy writing out the preface so much they'd decide to carry on, copying more and more of the book to come, learning more not only about Bowie's life but how the world changed so dramatically over fifty years often because of a pop song and a pop singer.

I've definitely not written this book like a textbook, because writing out all those physics prefaces put me off those sorts of books for life; but the subject – David Bowie – needs detailed explanation and exploring, not least because everyone has their own David Bowie. So many Bowies: how do you keep up with them in a book, and try to keep him inside the pages as he constantly, provocatively moves somewhere else and becomes someone else?

Sometimes you have to take things very seriously, as he did, and sometimes as much as the book is exploring a beloved, wildly charming entertainer who made millions of people believe through his songs that he intimately understood their emotions, even loved them, this book also studies a tempestuous, wily avant-garde spirit who achieved popularity by rejecting, or completely rearranging, show-business clichés. He generated a radically different way of appealing to the masses, introducing them to different, surprising, often quite intimidating ways of thinking. To keep up with Bowie, and understand what he was doing and why he was doing it, the audience itself had to be as much a genius as Bowie.

A lot changes as he changes, and the changes keep coming now he has died, and writing this book I found that to properly interpret those changes the book itself needed to move through transformations. The Bowie in the 1950s as he begins his life as energetic, extremely curious and sensitive south Londoner Davie Jones, becomes another frantic, ambitious Davie Jones altogether in the early 1960s as he begins with spectacular purpose a musical and theatrical life that he soon begins to think of as an artistic life.

As the 1950s collided into the 1960s, reality shifted shape and colour as profoundly as Bowie himself, and I wanted to record the transformation in how I told the story, a different style for a different decade or a different stage in his life.

By the 1970s, when Davie Jones has become the internationally famous David Bowie, life, culture, society are accelerating towards a dangerous, deeply unpredictable future. Pop music and rock and roll has become a seductive, influential force, one taking over the minds of most thirteen-year-olds seriously doubting the sanity of their physics teachers. It takes another sort of writing, almost from a different book, to reflect those fractured, shattering 1970s, and the fragmenting, speeding mind and body of David Bowie as he finds the stardom he desperately craved and then struggles to deal with the catastrophic and challenging fallout.

Bowie becomes a different Bowie virtually by the day, until he almost loses control, and so it seems necessary to explain that by placing him in a near science-fiction setting. The most honest way of writing about David Bowie and all the David Bowies he became in the 1970s as he turned his entire existence and his musical technique into a collage of impressions, memories and experiences is to create a collage in response, to exaggerate the exaggerations and the excess.

He becomes yet more Bowies throughout the 1980s and 1990s and beyond, and the whole idea of the chronology of Bowie begins to break down even further. As much as I know there is a need to follow a life in a certain order, as one thing follows another in an apparently relatively straightforward procession, there comes a point with Bowie when that is impossible to do, because of the way his mind works, because of how he constructed his own life and his work and reacted to the chaos, and delights, and mystery, of the world around him.

In a real sense, obviously Friday would become Saturday and then Sunday, but he was such an illusionist, such a magician, that he could make it seem as though he was playing around with time, and making it run in his own order for his own means. He relished imagining new ways of juxtaposing different elements to produce new, fresh associations, and a book about Bowie needs to be in that spirit; sometimes he is doing something in 1998 as though he is following up something he did in 1977, and he manipulates time in a perpetual search for artistic freedom and therefore personal freedom.

It does make more sense to make sense of Bowie, and all of the Bowies that he became, by accepting that his life didn't always follow a straightforward trajectory. Trying to straighten it out, to make it all go in one direction, is not only impossible to do, but it doesn't help explain who he was, how he thought and how he found inspiration.

And where do you begin to tell the story of something and someone that was always beginning? There is no one real 'in the beginning' for someone who was visibly and purposefully constantly changing. It is not easy with someone like Bowie to find an actual beginning, a defining central moment. Because everyone has their own Bowie the best way to begin is to begin with your personal Bowie, when he came into your own life. The first contact. That's how I decided to begin, with the moment he leapt into my mind, so I could leap into his.

Paul Morley, May 2016

INTRODUCTION: STRANGE FASCINATION

He is backing into a dark forbidding wardrobe and closing the door on himself at the end of the video to 'Lazarus', a tranquil story of life and death, told in reverse ... The idea had been suggested to him by someone on the shoot. At first, he is not sure whether it is something he wants to do. Then he smiles and decides, yes. I'll do that. 'That will keep them guessing,' he says, always a kidder. It will look like a final exit. The very end of a true story. Of the journey of a man whose alternate selves took him on a fantastic adventure through space, time and sexuality. Everybody knows him now, and he is going somewhere else.

He hides himself ... Inside the cupboard, there's a tomblike darkness. There is nothing much to do. He pulls off his wig with a sigh of relief, pleased to be momentarily relinquishing the burden of playing someone else. His mind starts to race as he stands there, in the dark, wondering about what in fact people might think, about the agitated way he moves backwards, the way his eyes are obscured in the video, and how he only sort of breathes. It feels like he's fallen out of history. While I'm here waiting, he thinks, it's a good job that there is a lot to think about. A lot to remember, if I haven't forgotten. A lot of things that I've done. A lot of books I've read. A lot of places I've visited. The people I've known. The strangeness of the world. It makes my brain whirl. I could think about my life for a thousand years.

He patiently stands in the quiet dark and shuts his eyes. He imagines he is alone on a stage, and about to sing a song to an audience in front of him, anticipating his next move, his every move, reading so much into every gesture and word, into every thought, because some believe they can hear him think. He thinks about what he will sing, about what the opening line will be . . . he takes a deep breath . . . he opens his eyes and it seems to be darker inside than when he first climbed in . . . he hears a voice . . .

It is 1970, I am thirteen, and at some point during the year I hear the name David Bowie spoken for the very first time. I come to realise that someone called David Bowie is alive. I knew nothing about him, but I began to notice that there was someone on the planet with that name. The name seemed very ordinary, but something about it meant it cut right through to where I was, and cut deep. The surname made an everyday David seem much sharper. Somehow you caught sight of your own reflection in the name, and something else, which you couldn't yet make out.

When I heard him sing for the first time, not long after I had heard someone say his name – 'here's "The Supermen" by David Bowie, *when all the world was very young*' – he had a voice that felt made up of unusual things, one that pierced straight to the heart of me. It was something that my brain was clearly missing. The sound of him put me on high alert, and I thought here was definitely someone I should get to know. I didn't know much about anything at the time, and was at the very early stages of working out who I was and what on earth I was going to do with myself, but he really caught my attention.

I found him, and at the same time, he found me; he was, I was soon to understand as I discovered more about him, on an almost desperate, conquistadorial mission to find as many listeners and fans as he could, to fill in the blanks inside him he felt were blotting out his soul, which meant *he* needed to be found. To find some fans, and at the beginning just a few would be fine, he was devising new sorts of ways he could be found and once found never ignored.

During the 1999 commencement address he delivered at Berklee College of Music in Boston after receiving an honorary doctorate, he would say that as a musician he had been 'on a crusade to change the kind of information that rock music contained'. He confided that growing up he adored John Coltrane, Harry Partch, Eric Dolphy, the Velvet Underground, John Cage and Sonny Stitt. 'Unfortunately, I also loved Anthony Newley, Florence Foster Jenkins, Johnnie Ray, Julie London, Legendary Stardust Cowboy, Edith Piaf and Shirley Bassey,' he went on, referring to that part of him that would consistently disrupt his enduring, probing curiosity for the obscure and transitional.

Music, he discovered, was a great game of 'what if'. 'What happens if you combined Brecht/Weill musical drama with rhythm and blues? What happens if you transplant the French chanson with the Philly sound? Will Little Richard lie comfortably with Schoenberg? Can you put haggis and snails on the same plate? Well, no, but some of these ideas worked out very well.'

As a boy without then knowing who any of these people were – except Shirley Bassey, mostly for singing 'Goldfinger', contributing appreciable glamour to the provisional myth of James Bond – what first pulled me in was his potentially deranged blend of something warped and deeply thoughtful with a definite, kinky show-business flourish. The mixing and merging of the strange with the familiar, mortal grossness with the airy spirit, sounded like nothing else I'd heard – and ultimately ever would hear – because there were few others so drawn to both the offbeat *and* the ostentatious. It's very rare for a performer to cross so easily from the experimental to the opulent and the embellished, infatuated with artifice and excess but possessing an inquisitive, militant spirit. Both ends of the spectrum, the freely chaotic or the defiantly melodic, the so-called good or bad taste, could make the mind spin through very interesting changes and make constant new discoveries.

To find Bowie as a teenager, and be found by him, was incredible, and, perhaps, inevitable. At that point, those of us becoming teen-agers in the early 1970s needed something of our own, having been too young to catch the 1960s. We'd missed the Beatles, we'd missed the Stones – as something that belonged and spoke directly to us. Bowie wasn't, though, that easy to find in the early 1970s, when music was not everywhere, all the time, instantly available with a swipe or a jab, where every day was yet to be packed with endlessly available event, product and entertainment.

Nothing was then easy to find when you were in your early teenage years hemmed in by parents, school and a solid set of very fixed expectations. There were few places to find the new, and what places there were tended to be hard to find, out of sight, needing some form of permission or disobedience to access. Difference was hidden; you had to work hard to get there.

I had heard Bowie in the background the year before I started to develop an insatiable interest in pop music, thinking of his hit song 'Space Oddity', but that had been one of those songs that just appeared, closely harnessed to the climax of the 1960s space race, and then disappeared, as though it wasn't actually by anyone. It was conceived by committee especially for the occasion. Men landed on the moon, and occasionally as the astonishing footage was shown, you could hear the song, as though the man on the moon and the singer of the song was called Major Tom.

I first heard his name said across the airwaves on self-proclaimed 'wonderful' BBC Radio 1. This was the central place where you came across pop music at the time; one of the only places, especially when you were too young to go out, to clubs and concerts. The one place to actually see pop was the weekly half-hour *Top of the Pops*, a family show where smuggled into its wholesome midst were stunning signs and sightings of the mysterious underground you heard tantalising rumours about at school, whispered through names of groups and seen on album sleeves that had a touch of witchcraft about them. *Top of the Pops* would feature dramatically deranged-looking rock musicians using lively, immediate pop songs to sing about lust, paranoia, fear, anger, rebellion, mystery, because if it was in the charts, it would be broadcast. That was the rule.

It didn't matter how long the hair of the male lead singer, how outlandish and dubious the clothes, how obviously stoned-seeming the drummer, how subversive the lyrics, being a hit gave it a free pass directly into the home of millions of viewers courtesy of a relatively generous BBC policy.

Even the Who, demanding that you all f-f-f-fade away, a classic, unholy four-letter word teetering on the lippy tip of flailing singer Roger Daltrey's tongue, had made it through onto what was essentially a souped-up variety show. A programme generally watched after a shared teatime in the same room by parents and their children, silently appraising a random parade of performances that meant very different things to the different generations in the empty spaces of their mind waiting to be filled, or emptied further.

These occasional insubordinate cameos by groups wearing the clothes and expressions of revolutionary spirits gave the whole procedure the edge of something that challenged the apparently secure nature of the relationship between child and adult, between teenager and the everlasting normal society they were expected to enter without a second thought. There was a general sense as these occasional surreal bombs exploded in the middle of ordinary British houses on ordinary British streets that it wasn't really happening, and even if it was, it would all soon be over and normal service would be resumed.

Bowie, though, in 1970 was more in that distantly rumbling underground, his travels then limited to the smaller, dirtier venues and mundane local halls and clubs across the land, separated from any possible appearance on *Top of the Pops*. He was out there somewhere, but I could never find him. I would discover that once in the late 1960s after a late-night folk club performance in

Stockport where I lived he missed the last train and had to sleep on the platform overnight. This meant we were to an extent sleeping together, under the same clouds, or sleeping only separated by a couple of miles. It took me forty years to learn that. At the time he might as well have been orbiting Saturn for all I knew.

A young, naive teenager didn't yet possess the understanding of how to break into that impenetrable seeming underground. What clothes were necessary, how long should your hair be, did you need special words, a knowledge of arcane symbols? Pop music cliques then by their very nature contained a rarefied inner elite that seemed impossible to join.

Bowie wasn't then getting much if any play on the radio. Except to a few loyal followers, he wasn't that well known, despite having had the surprise top 10 song the year before, quickly forgotten in the way things were back then, because life seemed to be moving fast into the future and a few months could make the difference between having your hit and being forgotten.

His hit might even have cost him his few hard-core fans, as they were the sort of discriminating, or snobby, music lovers who viewed commercial hits as a sign of artistic worthlessness. The world then was clearly divided between the album and the single. Rock already had its own equivalent of the highbrow versus lowbrow battle. One side, it had been decided, had more value than the other. Albums were serious; singles were trivial. Those of us that slipped naturally between the two worlds were viewed at the time as extremely weak-minded. For those that did slip more easily between the two worlds, it seemed a very good way to locate the future.

Constructing an idea of the future – any future within reason, even if it had its own problems – was vital at the time, a pushing away from a disorientating war that your parents and their parents were still suffering from, the gloom, conflicts, monotony and general effects that were hard to escape. Mainstream society and culture was committed to maintaining itself as it was for its own security but coming under pressure.

An alternative future was slowly taking shape around life in the 1950s, so that the basic, dreary flatness of the nation was showing the first electric signs of the shapes, colours and attitudes about to dominate the world, and propel it into a very different age altogether. A storm of progress was brewing. This was pop culture beginning to make its way to the centre of everything, and introducing a global informality, a new world order of noise and image.

Rock music, a warning sign in the mid-Fifties, an invading force by the mid-Sixties, was helping the young escape the pressure from elsewhere, its exponents and fans relishing and celebrating not just the new possibilities of personal freedom and independent thinking. They were also keeping a vigilant eye on those freedoms and independence being interfered with by those who tended to be responsible for wars and miscellaneous national and international crack-ups. In the grander scheme of things, to transcend the effects of the war, incite a galvanising sense of optimism, it was needing something outrageous and difficult to believe, like the Americans flying to the moon, and walking on it, and beaming the evidence back to earth and the television sets that were themselves an invading force.

Rock and pop could supply equivalent capsule moments of adventure and wonder, with images that in their own way were as vividly of the moment as an astronaut planted in a moonscape. Sometimes the incongruous impact of pop could seem as strange to a young mind separated from wider, more poetic and artistic influences as the classic image Karlheinz Stockhausen had used when he described his 1955 work *Gesang der Jünglinge* ('Song of the Youths') mixing up human voice with electronics as being like 'finding an apple on the moon' – an ordinary thing being transplanted into an extraordinary place. (Oddly enough the moon landing itself in 1969 as shown on television had the quality of being an apple found on the moon. There were no apples. The astronauts were the apples. When Jethro Tull appeared on *Top of the Pops*, like frugal New Age farmers from Narnia, they were the apples, and *Top of the Pops* was the moon.)

The future arrived down on earth through music, which could then take you to another planet. Bowie symbolised the future first of all when you heard the sound of his voice, and then when you saw him, in a photograph, or, eventually, on the TV, his appearance sealed the deal. You could see it in his eyes; mixed in with his own sense of amusement, anxiety and engagement, there was something else, perhaps the weirdly attained wisdom of the ages, reflected straight back at you.

Your mind was rearranged, as it turned out it needed to be, even if it hadn't been when you had only heard him. When I first saw him – and everyone remembers the first time they laid eyes on him performing, and what Bowie, at what period of time – I'm not sure it was something I actually explicitly thought or spoke out loud, but there was definitely a feeling of, in the middle of all the everyday gloom, tension and endless school routine ... I could be like that. I could go there, or somewhere close. Not that I would dye my hair, brighten my face with cosmetics, trace mystical shapes with my fingers, wear flowing robes and Turkish shoes, matter-of-factly claim to be from out there to fulfil a special mission through music, to recreate the cosmic order, but in my own way, I could find my own way.

Because his music wasn't specifically cheerful enough, or straightforward and conventionally comforting, I will have heard his name said for the first time in a low, deliberately unexcited monotone by John Peel. That was David Bowie, 'The Supermen', *strange mad celebration*, and very little else. The first time ever I heard his name. One of the few times anyone said it on the BBC in 1970.

Peel was the late-night disc jockey who first played some of the most exciting music I would hear, and music I still listen to today. It turns out that this music wasn't about postponing the process of growing up, which was one view at the time. It was there to become a part of your whole life, and often make more sense the older you were.

Peel wasn't a fake friend, the sort of disc jockey who was going to pretend to be happy with life and burst with mock delight at the music he was playing like his daytime colleagues. It wasn't his job to perkily wake you up in the morning and put a spring in your step, or keep you chuckling through the day as you got on with your dull routine, at work, or doing the housework. He wasn't playing at being social tranquilliser or stimulant. As a gentle-seeming, quite amiable eccentric, he was actually more of a social irritant, opening up channels to pioneering, racy new music that had, or gallantly pretended to have, a greater meaning. His motives were difficult to work out, although it was clear he was not in favour of romantic claptrap. He didn't appear to have a purpose at all in what he was doing, but in a way that was the highest purpose of all.

His job as he saw it was to play music, the loveliest, strangest he came across. It was up to the listener to work out for themselves what they liked or didn't like of all the music he played, and whether it was meant to calm them down or psych them up, or whatever else, and for what reason. You were given few direct cues about the value or importance of the music by the legendarily sardonic Peel. He would unfussily open a gate, usher you forward, and leave you to work out whether you were in a muddy field or an unforgettable new world, perhaps under stars that would stretch forever.

He was treating his listeners as people who knew their own minds, or why would they be listening to him, and the often eerie and extreme music he was interested in. If you were a Peel listener, you were definitely taking music more seriously than those that weren't. You had come to some specific decision that would take time to articulate about how hearing other voices through the music they played was going to stop you going mad; listening only to the sound of your own voice was definitely going to challenge your senses, and you wanted these other thoughts in your head, to help get a perspective on the reality unravelling around you. You weren't alone, even as you were on your own.

Listening to Peel scouting the far, unmapped frontiers of music, through constant crackles of static on a tiny transistor radio that smelled of plastic and excitement, in bed, usually under the blankets because it was school tomorrow, was a forbidden activity that added an extra layer of thrill to the tantalising, unusual sounds you were hearing. You shouldn't have been doing it. It was a secret venture. And you found secret hiding places that contained the difference you were craving. It also seemed, as it is with the great broadcasters, that Peel was only talking to you; there was no one else.

I found Bowie all on my own, as far as I could tell, bravely tracking John Peel late at night, coming across the living, breathing Bowie and feeling as though he, like Peel, was only for me. He was right next to me. So close he could hear me breathe, in my bedroom cocoon, and be very knowing when my breathing got faster. Even before he actually sang it on 'Rock 'n' Roll Suicide', quoting one of *his* memorable, one-of-a-kind finds, Jacques Brel, he was getting right inside your mind and making it clear, imploring that oh no love I wasn't alone and we were in this together, and he was getting inside my head, and I was getting inside his. I could hear him thinking. *Give me your hands* ...

Bowie was calling to me that year, gathering me in. During the next few months when I began to concentrate on the depth and intrigue of pop music I started to think about him all the time, falling for him in a rush with what you could call love.

I started to read the music magazines, especially the *New Musical Express*. By 1972, the year of his real breakthrough, relieved that a recent lull in proceedings was not permanent, determined not to ever lose his grip again, he was all over the music papers. This was at a time when the sole source of information about the activity and attitude of pop stars was through music papers, and the writing about pop stars contributed to their image and impact often by constructing a riveting, semi-fictional framework around them. Reality and fantasy were being mixed up. The nature and meaning of pop and rock stars were being invented, on the understanding that the importance of what they were doing needed to be exaggerated, articulated and celebrated. There was a sense of mission in these new sights and sounds, and the writing set out to reflect and enhance that idealistic and/or self-serving velocity.

Growing up, Bowie had been an avid reader of music papers, and he recognised the importance of their role. However famous and apparently remote he became, he only stopped making himself available for interviews in the last few years of his life, when the idea of silence had a greater resonance in the middle of a now over-saturated non-stop talking pop culture, where more and more people were blankly demanding 'look at me'. He found other equivalents of the interview and the profile, other ways of drawing attention and expressing, or protecting, himself.

He was brilliant to interview, with his own sense of how to make things up and invent new truths and doctrines; he always had something to say, taking the whole idea of himself very seriously and yet also as a game he was inventing as he went along, writing himself into being, escaping both from and into reality. Music paper interviews were a great way for musicians with something to say to talk about themselves, and he clearly loved doing this. He used them as therapy, a chance to brainstorm new ideas, make new plans, boast about his prowess, blur boundaries, and generally sell himself and his rapidly forming worldview, on the hunt for kindred spirits ready to join his campaign and surrender to his ways.

Along with the interview there would always be photographs. In all these photos, there was that secret thing about his eyes that suggested that however serious, or not, he was being, in how he appeared, and arranged himself, it was coming with a suggestive, confident wink. Come and try me. Come and buy my records. If you dare . . .

I started buying records during 1970 and 1971, slowly at first, because they cost more than my pocket money got anywhere near. Every bit of money I managed to muster went on books or records. The records I got hold of one by one became precious things, at first mainly singles by T. Rex, who were having their breakthrough year; they were the first things I owned apart from toys and comics that I could truly call my own. Bit by bit, month by month, my collection of mostly singles grew, some bought in a bargain bin at my local record shop, cheap because they had been pre-used in jukeboxes, but still carefully chosen and cared for like nothing else in my life.

Among my first records bought at full price, or asked for as birthday and Christmas gifts, alongside Roxy Music, Mott the Hoople and Jimi Hendrix, were singles and albums by David Bowie that started to be released at the end of 1971 into early 1972. They each had an RCA label in bright space-age orange and a futuristic label logo that suggested both *A Clockwork Orange* and *2001: A Space Odyssey*. The intense future world orange along with the enigmatically plain title and songwriting information on the label would become inextricably mixed up in my mind with the world, and the name, of David Bowie. If I see that orange now, I still feel an internal blood-tingling swoon, a moment of delicious pause knowing that there will soon be magic, and a whole new set of clues about what to think next.

News announcing their release in the music papers updating rock every seven days would mean weeks of build-up before the moment I could actually hold the record in my hands, stare at it like it was something sacred, and play it, A-side and B-side, side one and side two, over and over again, until it was completely a part of me. The anticipation, the run up and the space around a record, allowing your mind to roam free dreaming up what was about to happen, became as much a part of the music as the song itself.

The cliffhanging wait, the dreamy fantasising, the intense

hope, amplified the feeling of excitement as you slid the record you had finally managed to get out of its sleeve, having saved up for weeks, because buying a record then was more like going on holiday than simply deciding to listen to something and instantly making it so. It was an event, often an occasion, and usually inextricably linked with those moments of relief – holidays, Christmas, birthdays – in a year where school and routine were most of the time slammed into your being. Mostly, you had no choice: with a record you had managed to buy, suddenly, you did.

The orange label would appear, the gleaming black plastic with grooves that gave you a first sense of what you were about to receive, in terms of how tightly, or loosely packed, they were etched into the vinyl, how many gaps there were between tracks, and you would catch your breath at the sight of the title on the label, as though it had been sealed in place by Bowie himself. The titles alone, often giving language a new twist, a novel tug, because of how the words now sounded taken over by Bowie for his specific use, released a torrent of new associations and possibilities.

At the beginning of 1972, using timely Christmas money, I owned David Bowie's *Hunky Dory* album, a single taken from it, 'Changes' with 'Andy Warhol' on the B-side, the first intro-duction for many of us to not just the artist but art itself, and an anomalous collection of his early, pre-'Space Oddity' songs that had been released to cash in on his brief chart status in 1970 on a budget-priced album called *The World of David Bowie*.

From the very beginning of my experience with David Bowie, things didn't go in chronological order: re-releases, deletions, compilations, radio sessions and television shows featuring songs from albums not released for months, all threw time into a mixer, producing bits and pieces of Bowie from different periods that were more raw material for the personal collage you were making out of David Bowie, in the way he made collages of sound and vision from what he found and felt.

The World of David Bowie featured a cover where an angelic but slightly shocked-looking Bowie stared out under lit-up golden curls that made him look like a close, puckish hippie cousin of his old friend Marc Bolan of T. Rex, fast becoming a spellbinding *Top of the Pops* regular, increasing Bowie's burning need to make it onto the show.

The songs on *The World of David Bowie* were only a few years old, but compared to the songs on *Hunky Dory*, they seemed to come from a very old-fashioned, hare-brained world. It made me think of live-action Disney movies, Danny Kaye, the movie *Chitty Chitty Bang Bang* and the 'Little White Bull' of Tommy Steele. Here was Bowie as a cheeky, cheery-seeming chap giving away how much he wanted to win friends and impress people. It filled in some details about where he had come from, as an entertainer, but it wasn't exactly the Bowie I'd first come across under the bedclothes taking me by surprise with suggestive, fleeting thoughts about the energy of his mind.

I could sense, even though it was not something I understood, that the sound of the songs were not as rich, as unconventionally enchanting as the songs on *Hunky Dory*. I responded to a sound on *Hunky Dory* that suited more that look in his eyes, the shapes he would throw in photos using his limbs, mouth and the tips of his fingers.

The comedy was subtler, the tragedy deeper, the cuteness more cosmic, the love songs not as bouncy. And on the fantasy cover, a freeze-frame from a dream, his hair was brushed long and blond, and his obsessions were clearly more with the deeper truths of existence. I couldn't have explained it like that to myself at the time, but I sensed it. I sensed that the earlier Bowie was not the same as the later Bowie, and that no matter how many times Mick Jagger or John Lennon changed their appearance, or their music, they were still staying where they were. Bowie wasn't.

Thinking of Bowie's ability even in those early days to generate gorgeous, blooming but unorthodox melodies, even on songs that otherwise meandered to cryptic, pseudo-anthemic conclusions, it was as though between that late Sixties period, when he was imagining appearing in charming if off-beat musicals, and *Hunky Dory*, when he had lived through experimental theatre, the Velvet Underground, the Stooges, he had distilled out the sugar candy. Even his sweet songs where he lingered inside some metaphysical cabaret club were less cloying.

I had a small collection of David Bowie, but I wanted more. He was ready to hand out more. In the first months of 1972, with *Hunky Dory* at best a cult success, a music paper hit but a mainstream miss, there was a sudden surge of activity, an acceleration away from the atmospheric night-time woodland of John Peel towards the shining lights, tacky delights and semi-naked dancing girls of *Top of the Pops*.

The fans were tangled up in the middle of this, helping to cause it, because we were more or less doing what Bowie told us to do, looking where he said to look, leading us on, having us on, with the conniving force of someone who knew what we were thinking, as fans, because he had been, and still was, exactly that type of fan. There was a building sense of togetherness. He knew exactly how to manipulate and stimulate the fan's desire for some form of permission to be different and to turn the ordinary idea of buying records into something positively greater.

In the early 1970s, he became a kind of teacher, so much more inspiring and motivating than my real teachers at school. In the middle of a lifeless provincial world that severely limited possibility and gave you very few options, his explosive mind and the way he represented it through astonishing, changeable appearance and vivid otherness suggested you didn't have to be so stuck. You didn't have to be so deferential.

Bowie had made use of things he had been taught as a fan by the artists, entertainers and performers he'd found, and passed on this information with the added extras of his imaginative input. 'When I heard someone say something intelligent, I used it later as if it were my own ... It's just like a car, replacing parts.'

He sang that he had no inspiration on 'Soul Love', a lucid song about love, and death, from his 1972 album, *The Rise and Fall of Ziggy Stardust and the Spiders from Mars*, but of course he absorbed so many influences – 'You nick a touch of this, you nick a touch of that. Then you do it better simply by using Scotch tape, sawdust and a little imagination' – and passed on his secrets, advice and techniques for others to use. His intention was to gather others in the search for the flaming dove. The more people looking, swapping clues, suggesting routes, stumbling across treasure, believing in the presence and ultimate meaning of the flaming dove, the more likely it would happen. It might be a futile project, but it should never stop.

That Bowie is referring to 'the flaming dove' on a relatively unheralded song from *The Rise and Fall of Ziggy Stardust and the Spiders from Mars*, the album that finally lifted him to fame in 1972, is itself a sign of how far his reading roamed in the constant quest for learning, and material, how wherever you looked in his songs there were words, lines, phrases, images, quotes that could set you off on a wild trail of your own learning.

'The flaming dove' is a definite clue he had been reading, or reading someone who had been reading, T. S. Eliot, and noticing Eliot's own endless recycling and reframing. Eliot refers in the fourth section of 'Little Gidding', the last poem in *Four Quartets*, to the dynamic symbolism of the dove in the Bible. The dove represented the Holy Spirit, and there are many passages in the Bible where doves are descending, symbolising the descent of the Holy Spirit. A bright dove descends on Christ at his baptism.

In the flaming sense, it was the dove being sacrificed as an offering to God of something with great spiritual value, a symbol of peace, and the flaming dove is an allusion to the phoenix, born out of flames symbolising birth and the immortality of the spirit. The flaming dove to Bowie was freedom; later, much later, he would use 'that bluebird' to express the same feeling, but at a very different stage of life.

Flames are constant through the war poem 'Little Gidding'. The dove is both destructive – breaking the air with flames of transcendent terror, German planes dropping fire-bombs above a stricken, very vulnerable London a few years before Bowie is born in the city – and purifying – discharging us from sin and error by fighting the fire of war with the fire of the Holy Spirit.

At fifteen, I had no idea of any of this, and it's probably simply another way of interpreting what Bowie might have been up to, leaving everything wide open, which was part of his skill; but the way he sang the words, and how the words themselves powered out of an electric pop song, had such force you sensed, you felt, that he was bringing with him a tremendous amount of knowledge and energy.

In the same way as a reader of Eliot's *Four Quartets* might not know all – or any – of the other writers, myths and references Eliot is placing into a brand-new context, but can feel that he is building his living, breathing, weeping world from so many other places, listeners to Bowie do not know the exact details of the borrowing, thieving and rewriting, the nicking of word and sound, but can feel the intoxicating intensity.

Every Bowie line seemed like its own artwork, filled with detail waiting to be understood. The flaming dove perhaps meant nothing outside the fact that it sounded wonderful when he sang it – perhaps all he thought about at the time, finding unusual words to sing with brassy style – but what made the difference was that he had the type of mind that thought of putting the flaming dove into a pop song. Maybe it was just a response to how often he had heard 'Oh for the Wings of a Dove' on Sunday radio when he was a child, a transforming of a dull, monotonous time into a fiery piece of showing-off. He was setting his boring past on fire, dropping bombs on a previous life, moving on as fast as he could.

You might interpret 'the flaming dove' as being a sign of how obsessed Bowie was with the reality of evil, and how often his songs longed for transcendence. Once you start following a trail inspired by Bowie on a song like 'Soul Love', and who he had been inspired by, you can begin with a search for the poetry of salvation, with Eliot's description of Charles Baudelaire as a 'deformed Dante' and take it from there. Or you can simply consider the song to be part of the greatest masterpiece of the glam rock era, with little meaning beyond that, but who needs any more meaning than that.

According to the legend, glam rock emerged in Britain in the very early 1970s largely as a consequence of the arrival of colour television, which encouraged madcap male dressing up in satin and lipstick on *Top of the Pops*, and from a need to spray gaudy, intoxicating colour over a nation that seemed made up of black, white, grey and depressed red brick.

The glitter and colour might have been gaudy, but it also implied a certain rough but welcoming luxury in a narrowed, monochrome world. With Bowie, it also seemed he was embracing extravagant costume and radical rainbow colours – appropriated from underground clubs, hippie loungewear, drag bars, Hollywood movies, avant-garde haute couture, bohemian vagabonds, experimental art laboratories and an idiosyncratic history of theatre – in order to express the luminous brightness of his mind.

He flooded ordinary everyday reality with exotic information, and made intellectual discovery seem incredibly glamorous and accessible. Those indifferent to his ways would probably have just seen grotesque sexualised pantomime, heard noisy, repetitive, overheated nursery rhymes and a narcissistic, half-naked, fidgety, goofy, effeminate singer wearing hobgoblin hair trying far too hard to impress. To those who got it, he was at ease exhibiting his mind and body in the public glare so fantastically, and if you had cracked the code, he was dramatically splitting reality wide open and penetrating time itself. The perfect role model for a teenager.

He communicated like little else at the time an abundant sense of confidence. A confidence that there would always be a future, and because there always would be, why shouldn't the dreamers, stargazers and prophets take hold of it? And if there wasn't going to be a future – and he faced up to that eventuality with a defiant sometimes nihilistic relish – then let the fearless fantasists and artists take over for the grand finale.

He was putting together the world and a historical version of it in his own way, and that made more sense than what the grown-up world proposed, still snagged by the choking effects of the war and other shattering wars that followed, and an inability to set new things in motion. His spirited curiosity was contagious, a revelation the way his transfixing, freakishly modern *Top of the Pops* appearances – surely flashed back from the future – steamed-up pop singles and future-fancying albums lustily recommended an experimental mentality. He helped create in my own mind a need to discover ways of making sense of the universe and the self by seeking out the different, the difficult and the daring.

The moment of understanding that there was a creature on the planet called David Bowie will be weighted towards 1972 because that was the period Bowie charged into his fame like he was being chased by something diabolical. All the dots he'd set up over the preceding years were joined up. He came out of nowhere with such a bang and such a series of flashes, because he had not come out of nowhere, it had been a long time coming, he had been building and building, inventing, discovering and sorting out the foundations and preparing the blueprints. His new fans throughout the nation, not knowing how many others existed, had no idea about any of this. The beauty of it was how sudden and fantastic it seemed.

He seemed invincible. I don't know if it was the relief, the sheer enjoyment, that he had finally made it, but it gave him a rock-hard certainty even in those few months before it actually took off. It had all come true, that thing he had thought about and planned since he was a teenager, a boy. There was a kind of laughter written all over his arrival in the charts and *Top of the Pops* in 1972, even when he was pulling a serious face and acting just for the hell of it like a holy prince of enigma taking charge of his surroundings.

It was as though he had been proved right in why he had wanted this fame, because it made him feel as though he had super powers, and all eyes were on him as he made his next move, which even though it was a song or a television appearance was greeted with such excitement it was as though he had flown through the sky and into the clouds or saved a city from a sudden typhoon. He had the look, focused in a pair of eyes that had definitely seen things, even if he'd made most of it up. Nothing was going to stop him, and the last thing on anyone's mind, most of all his, as he rode this incredible wave, and gathered new followers by the second, was death. Even when his songs were about death, and there were all sorts of words floating through his music that made it clear that death was something often on his mind, it was all about life. Look at me. Look at me looking at you. Look at how amazing this is. I am never, ever going to die.

1

SOLEMN PERVERSE SERENITY

I found out that David Bowie had died the way I now find myself finding out how all celebrities have died. Someone I don't know tells me. In 1977, when Elvis Presley died – and Bowie's close friend and equally energetic ex-mod rival Marc Bolan – it was my anxious mother waking me up at eight in the morning and bluntly telling me the news wearing a taut expression of tragedy inches away from my bleary unbelieving face.

Presley was forty-two – a little older than my father was when he died a few months earlier, committing a suicide that was very much not a rock and roll one – and Marc was a week away from turning thirty. I'd got to know Bolan as a young rock writer for the *New Musical Express* who was a fan who'd fallen for him hard, crushed by his charisma, in 1970, also as if the first moment I came across him was the first moment he existed. He was the first pop star I ever interviewed. (Bolan died in a car crash, my father sealing himself in a car to suffocate himself. I would never learn to drive.)

By 1977, no one else at the paper at the time was much in favour of this apparently fallen star, his time at the top over for two or three years, back then a long time; by 1977, his reputation not yet repaired, he was considered more spoiled puffed-up figure of fun than cult hero or rock legend. His ego as mind-blowing as Bowie's, both driven since early teens by a feeling of inalienable right to attention, he obviously loved the fact I loved him.

As a soft-centred teenage someone who noticed that Bowie and Bolan really seemed to know things, I watched them very closely. I wanted to know things too. It was a great time to come across the pair, because they were going through rapid changes that were like a mirror of the ones you go through in adolescence; you slip and slide into adulthood, sometimes kicking and screaming, your skin bursting open, sometimes keeping all the chaotic confusion to yourself, during days of intense, keep-out-of-the-bedroom silence punctuated with the playing of loud music and the repetition of the same song.

Your body changes, you need new sets of clothes regularly as you grow, and you achieve unprecedented levels of excruciating self-consciousness that make you want to change your body. Pop stars turned the brutal rupture of adolescence into a fantasy that helped you deal with the unstoppable often cruel adventure. They make it clear there is no need to feel any shame because suddenly you have changed into a new shape, your voice has deepened, and you develop a strange new way to satisfy some new, unspecified physical cravings that you become addicted to, which result in an endless series of mini-explosions.

I loved all the garments Bowie and Bolan wore that made me think of some sort of paradise, the make-up they wore that compelled me to think unashamedly about the very nature of being, and I loved the songs that helped me experience where and who I was on so many different levels. I was thrilled by the breathless progression of the one-thing-after-another as amazing single followed amazing single, and the way they turned the world into a theatre, and the song into a science-fiction dream.

Bolan and Bowie demonstrated through pop music brimming with clues that the mind was infinitely subtle, and that the world was sensationally visible. I couldn't put those things into words at the time, it was all just a teenage scramble of confused, unprecedented feelings, of genuine surprise and delight, a little fear and sadness even, but from a very early stage I wanted to know how to put what I was feeling into words. It was why I wanted to be a writer, and a writer about pop music.

Nearly forty years after my mum revealed that Marc Bolan had died, known mostly as a rock critic because of the seven or so years I spent at the *NME* after joining in 1976, at nineteen, as always until now ten years younger than Bowie, I find myself being called by various radio stations and television channels around Britain when there is any news, sordid, celebratory or sad, regarding a pop or rock celebrity, from Cliff Richard to Phil Spector, Rolf Harris to Whitney Houston, James Last to B. B. King.

This news often means the sudden death of a rock star or music personality, so I often first hear the sorry details from a panicky under-pressure researcher, apparently as anxious as my early morning newly widowed mother, working on some live news breakfast programme who is desperately searching for an apparent authority to give an instant, sympathetic, expert response, hopefully in five minutes' time, count down commencing now.

I have been told that on an internal system at the BBC, a computerised equivalent of the old Rolodex, my name is included on a list of those writers and journalists who should be called for their view when a pop star has been officially charged with something seedy, or has died, or has been newly streamed on Spotify. Next to my name, for some reason, it has been specifically marked up that I could be relied upon to talk knowledgeably about anything and anyone connected to any form of post-war popular music.

This recommendation of my cultural wisdom has been added, with a big cheerful asterisk next to my name, possibly as a joke, some sort of punishment for acting like a know-all about Kraftwerk or New Order, or because I did once impress some naive young production assistant with my, to them, uncanny knowledge about the Pointer Sisters or Kevin Ayers.

The calls keep coming, increasingly so now that pop and rock music is essentially part of the establishment. The dull routine commercial decisions of a processed pop group like One

Direction make the news as though they are surprising, important events the equal of the latest reports from Syria, and necessary and comforting to know in a dangerously unpredictable world. I have asked a couple of times for this indicator to be removed, but apparently it stays, institutionally impossible to remove once it has been set in British Broadcasting Corporation stone.

I mostly don't answer the phone now, letting all suspicious-looking calls go to message, just in case, because I get frustrated hearing suddenly that so and so has died and could I say something quick – frustrated if I don't know much about or like the musician, even more frustrated if I did know and like the musician, and being expected to flick a switch and give some glib comment in usually time-limited circumstances to an interviewer who is passing through the death on the way to some other pressing news item. Or even only the weather. Cultural commentators, celebrity journalists and so-called entertainment experts are expected to fertilise their increasingly threatened occupation with a new line in professional mourning. The death of the celebrity, the pop star, is one way the mainstream media is managing to keep going, through a constant supply of death leading to a constant production of souvenir products. Looking back at this period in history it will truly seem like the death of something, an era, a way of life.

At about eight in the morning of Monday 10 January 2016 my mobile rang. It was set to sound as I needed to have the alarm on. I had been up until five writing a radio script I was due to read out at a BBC studio at midday. This was the sort of thing I ended up doing because of the influence of David Bowie, who helped give me the self-belief for better or worse to think for myself as a teenager, and begin to write, and eventually, despite a shyness that could paralyse me in social settings, start broadcasting on radio and television.

The documentary I was presenting was about my experience over forty-five years of visiting art galleries, and how that has influenced my mind and pushed me down endless trails of new learning, and there was a line in there that mentioned David Bowie – and I had been playing some Bowie songs while I wrote the piece in the early hours. Some lyrics from his nutty, high-minded, blend of popcorn Nietzsche, nausea, Gnosticism and melodramatic proto-metal 'The Supermen' were curling through my mind as I fell asleep. It used a shimmering, bloodcurdling riff gifted to him by Led Zeppelin's Jimmy Page, and it sounds as though it is breathing the poisoned atmosphere of technological backfire. Humanity set on a loveless isle, in solemn perverse serenity, the lyrics sung with 23-year-old Bowie's classic rakish, cosmic cockney mix of weird, wired and impossible to know, evoking derangement with such knifelike clarity.

I'd written for the radio documentary: *The grey, morose Stockport War Memorial Art Gallery opposite the doomed-looking domed town hall and the Beckettian coroner's office didn't look particularly promising to fan of glam rock, science fiction and Alan Garner, but something was pulling me in, if only the word Art, which I knew in my Bowie- and Bolan-loving bones was never going to be an easy thing to track down but which would mean everything once I got there.* Most things I write about my early teenage period – and most other things I write about any form of personal discovery from clothing to poetry – will contain at least one mention of Bowie. All the books I have written mention Bowie. Everything I have written comes out of hearing Bowie meticulously deliver the words '*solemn perverse serenity*' when I was a teenager half-crazy for knowledge, a sucker for a cascade of mystification.

There is something about a phone ringing early in the morning that instantly suggests bad news, and in particular the worst sort of bad news. Death: that time of the morning when the night is holding onto you is when you usually discover someone close to you has died. For whom the bell tolls ... I was knocked out of sleep by the shrill, synthetic ring and the desultory, morbid vibration that accompanied it ... abruptly pulled from a misty mountain magic dream state where everything was permitted ... a gloriously strange world inspired by Bowie's suavely delirious 'Supermen' climax to his 1970 *The Man Who Sold the World* album.

Barely awake, gloomy-browed super gods dying and sad-eyed mermen tossed in slumbers still wafting through my mind, I played the message a morosely flashing blue light informed me was waiting. A young man politely told me, briefly apologising in case I did not know the news (beat) that David Bowie had died. Could I call him back immediately, so that I could comment on BBC Radio 4's *Today* show that morning; as a matter of urgency? That was it. A simple, neutral transaction, softly informing me via robotic answer machine that there had been a considerable change in circumstances. *Press 3* to delete. During the next few hours, I thought, David Bowie's name would be said thousands, millions, of times on the radio and television, a mantra helping him safely adopt his next form. *Press 4* to express your shock.

I did not call the *Today* programme back. I didn't think I would be able to instantly muster the correctly seasoned blend of succinct overview and suppressed lamentation. I needed time to process this sudden information, that over the past few years at times seemed to be close enough to have expected such an eventuality, but which then seemed delayed, certainly enough that someone who seemed close to death in his mid-sixties – songs were sung wondering if he was dying or even dead, alarm bells rang, mental preparations were made, obituaries organised – now surely might make it into his seventies. After that sense of emergency, it seemed as though Bowie had more completely returned to the land of the living, a near resurrection suggesting he might even make it into his eighties, if not his nineties.

The past few weeks had presented the cheering on-going life of David Bowie as we thought of him in the form of the release of his latest album, *Blackstar*, or simply ★, his twenty-seventh solo studio album if you include his Tin Machine albums, establishing continuity with all his others, stretching back from 2016 to 1967, and implying this chain was not yet broken.

It seemed, going by the succulent, uncanny and wounded but alert sound of it, gorgeously formed from formlessness, from fragments, music effortlessly following its own logic, that the link had never been stronger. *Blackstar* seemed like a follow-up to the illusionless *Low* and his savage and honest 1982 EP *Baal* in the way that Bowie often seemed to work out his own idiosyncratic musical chronology, following up the style and sensibility of albums in a different order to how they were originally released, sometimes even following up an album he had yet to make.

The album link was a lot weaker during the tricky, erratic 1980s, and then, more to do with a decline in the number of releases, the 1990s, leading to his heart attack in 2004. The conditions now felt right to produce a series of records that were the late-life equivalent of the vivid, gleaming sequence in the 1970s that few other musicians come close to.

In the years following his publicised illness there was enough of an apparent withdrawal from activity to suggest that he was in a protective form of self-enacted exile, a radiant exhaustion, nurturing his myth through enforced silence and a particularly discreet form of the manipulative cunning learnt quickly during the late 1960s, as he worked and plotted to get attention, and then refined during his peak commercial years.

Even the detractors questioning his artistic powers would admit he had a genius for publicity. As a sophisticated marketing man almost painfully aware of his own brand, he noted that by the first and second decade of the twenty-first century it was actually more astute to appear to disappear, in a world increasingly made up of the mere fuzzy energy of publicity, crammed with exposed celebrities, would-be celebrities, reality TV stars, social media show-offs, fame seekers, self-glorifiers, glam hunters and dolled-up pop stars following one way or another in his footsteps. He felt no desire to compete with inferiors.

As David Bowie, based on having been David Bowie for decades, by leaving a space, a vacuum, it would lead to an amplification of all the original mystery that came about because of his appearance, and the correct songs to go with that appearance. To join in with the palaver of Internet-generated fame would mean being drowned by it, dragged down to its increasingly over-exposed level, becoming nothing special. His job in the end, whatever you think about such an occupation, was to be something special, and in doing so point out everyone's specialness. Both sides of Bowie, the lover of experiment and difference and the believer in the special forces of theatre, could resist appearing for the sake of it at this stage of his life. By resisting appearance, he could be more visible.

The artist would prefer a minimalist withdrawal, a sorting through of his work, and the performer would prefer to be in control of the physical movement into old age, and what comes next. He had never joined in with what the rest were doing, even when he appeared to be. He would not do that now. He would complete the trajectory of what he had started decades before, in his own way, following his own decisions and beliefs. He would stay in charge.

Being different was now about not clamouring for space, it was about inserting yourself into truly mysterious and molten inner space, inside the mind, where the universe really spilled, not pretending you were from corny outer space. If you withdrew from making comments or statements, if you even seemed to stop producing anything new, there were plenty of others ready to fill in the gaps, make up stories, create the important data and spread the word. David Bowie had always been a collaborative process between the artist and the audience, much of what he was having been created by the response of his fans, and enemies. After the communications revolution, this collaboration would be intensified. Online versions of Bowie were creating his image, the very on-going being of Bowie, as much as anything he had done.

He kept his distance, refusing to be interviewed, refusing to engage in modern forms of constant sales talk and idle gossip, avoiding the sharing, multitasking and desperate need to stay visible of the modern celebrity, inspired by stars like him, but lacking the troubling, captivating and truly mysterious artistic dimension.

He was invisible, in current orthodox terms, but everywhere, proving that his skill at inventing himself as an idea, a product, as a coercive creative force, as futurist merchant, and then prominently positioning himself in our collective imaginations, after a two- or three-decade dip in momentum as deliberately arranged as it was enforced, was as brilliant as ever.

The build-up and release of *Blackstar* followed the announcement and performance during 2015 of 'Lazarus', his modified translation of the Walter Tevis novel *The Man Who Fell to Earth*; Nic Roeg directed the film in 1975 and Bowie starred in it at the age of twenty-eight. The musical he had always dreamt of making was not a benign jukebox musical compiling his greatest hits based around a flimsy story about a starman. He chose one of the fictional characters he had played to revisit his songs and rewrite his story; making himself more by building up the hidden desires and obsessions of Thomas Jerome Newton, the actual man who fell to earth in the book and film, playing around with the unreliability of memory and the difficulty of biography, feeling it said more about who he was and how he thought by creating more distance, and using another, unreal but vivid life, than to conceive a standard, emotional celebration.

An abstract musical play that pulsated with burnt-out gloom and disquiet, but perhaps no more than *The Man Who Sold the World*, written in relative youth, 'Lazarus' was also immersed in his own songs, giving them the feel of a pragmatic, but somehow optimistic afterglow. It still contained, for all the foreboding and depleted appetite, enough cutting traces of a particularly grave but arousing Bowie glamour to not make it seem some mournful, painful end-of-life elegy to self. Cutting, because it was Bowie after all, but as fragile as glass.

It seemed another example of how Bowie the music-maker in later years was actually bursting into life. He was finding new ways to articulate sensation, fear, the pleasure of discovery, the realities of mortality, the miracle of memory, and a whole new form of existential transition, all those themes he had managed to smuggle into commercial pop. It wasn't as though he had made a comeback. The audience had.

Bowie's new, unexpected work in his late sixties was recognised as a continuation of a very familiar idea of 'David Bowie' the mask-wearing, attention-grabbing, identity-splitting, mind-boggling, widely adored, strange-eyed, turned-on, unfathomable starman. It was about coming to life, and seeing the way forward even as you slipped back and forward through the corridors of time and pieced together your life in a new way. This activity distracted onlookers, fans, media and modern content generators into believing the man himself, wherever he was, deep inside a scrupulously constructed private space, remained as alive as the work.

The post-contemporary forms of chatter and attention had not particularly considered therefore that he was in any way close to dying. They had been filled with matter-of-fact if excited advance news and information and the eventual release of an album, now a mere follow-up to 2013's *The Next Day*, released out of the blue at a time when all that seemed to be coming from a quiet Bowie was a retrospective world touring exhibition that began at the Victoria and Albert Museum in London. Around that time, and certainly in the years before, there was more an understanding that he was very frail, and rumoured to be extremely close to death. *Vice* magazine was asking people in their sickly jolly way what they would think when Bowie died, as if he already had.

Few had seen 'Where Are We Now?', the first single from *The Next Day* coming, not even close colleagues and collaborators, and not those working on the V&A exhibition, including me (who was involved as an artistic adviser). There was no warning, no advanced publicity, no standard commercial giving the game away for the sake of it. There was no nostalgic echoing of the old ways of releasing a single, because you were not now releasing an object, but a signal, that could travel through space and time in an instant. It wasn't a single any more, not like such a thing had been in the twentieth century.

Freed of being an object, a thing you had to go to a shop and buy, it could resemble a dream, and be in the shape of the dream that all great songs can resemble. If the world was moving too fast for Bowie to take charge of it in the way he once had, he slowed everything down to a different sort of pace, a pace that suited him.

'Where Are We Now?' moved from one place to another as abruptly and strangely as his character Agent Phillip Jeffries did in the David Lynch follow-up to *Twin Peaks*, *Fire Walk With Me*. Jeffries materialised in Philadelphia having the second before been in Buenos Aires, transporting from one dreamworld to another. Bowie did a similar thing. He levitated above a pop scene crowded out with performers copying poses, riffs, rhythms and references from the past without adding much of their own imagination. Another way of avoiding competing in the way that everyone else was.

The song, a kind of homesickness for a home that never really existed, viewing the past as a strange paradise, summoned up in both ghostly and antic fashion the most alluring elements of Bowie's finest twentieth-century music and his compelling mental agility, so that there was a riveting blend of the obvious and the cryptic, of rock's classically comforting emotional power and its wilder, more disturbing qualities.

The title of the sudden album that followed, *The Next Day*, suggested that for all the looking back, for all his own rampant borrowing and raiding of the past, and now his own past and a series of selves that filled it, he was always very much about the now, and the to-be-filled-in space of what comes next. In the early twenty-first century, the now, and what comes next, was becoming as lethally tricky and dangerous as troubled, self-conscious futurists like Bowie predicted it would be, even anticipating how real damage would be caused within the entertainment world, but even as the 'make it new' modernist mantra got chewed up and scrambled in the pseudo-democratic, oddly cautious and fearful, babbling Internet era, Bowie maintained a loyalty to the purist idea of progress, and the importance of distinctive, disobedient imaginative action.

He had set up the idea of an exhibition as a promotional campaign for an album he alone knew was coming. Or, he had updated the soundtrack to the exhibition he encouraged to happen so that it didn't seem a preliminary obituary, a sentimental summing up where everything he had been was frozen inside a museum. He wrote his own obituary, without appearing to be involved, and then subverted the whole idea.

With *The Next Day* he established a fabulous, counter-intuitive absence, using the album's artwork – a severe white-squared blanking out of the beloved cover for *"Heroes"* – and associated propaganda campaign, designed with long-time art director Jonathan Barnbrook, to propose that even as the exhibition went out of its way reveal him, he was covering up his tracks, and resisting the dreary modern tendency for repetitive overexposure and a banal reduction. He had already slipped through a side door, into a side street full of smoke, and was somewhere else, even as he was about to be so available. Another shadow self had been generated.

He retreated from the very sort of diminishing hype and hoopla he helped invent, and yet with just the raising of an eyebrow, the issuing of a suggestion, the hint of a comment in the guise of a no-comment, a firm striking-out of his own past to promote an exhibition of his past, he generated immense publicity – created, selected, and processed by others, but all based on him, and his appearance, and disappearance, his songs, and most of all, his voluptuous imagination.

In the last few years of his life, he slipped more and more behind the imagination, and the work, behind symbols, clues and images he knew would provoke continual intrigue, retreated into a home in New York where he could live a family life, and count the days in all sorts of unassuming ways. He let himself slip away, knowing that as he did so the work of the imagination, what he had been up to all these years, would get stronger. A large part of that was an exhibition that could be a component in how he let his work take over from him, knowing eventually he would slip away completely.

Thoughts of obituaries, sorrow and final summaries that had been put on hold for a few years were completely ignored as reviewers examined *Blackstar* and decided that it was pretty weird, and desolate, a peculiar mix of components, as if that could possibly be a surprise considering the songs he had written forty years before, the books he had read, the drugs taken, the collaborations pursued, the travels he'd been on artistically and personally, the secrets he must have compiled at his stage of life, the years that had passed, the changes in environment, the feelings he must have looking back on his life, which was now stacked up behind him and all around him and which was clearly now something of a marvel even to him.

Just in terms of having done all that, been responsible for those faces, rumours, choruses, myths, obsessions, surprises, refinements would mean it was not the oddest thing on the planet that there was a jazz element to the new record. Even though Bowie had composed and performed music that in many ways was closer to the late *Quartets* of Beethoven or the last few records by drummer Paul Motian than the latest album by Elton John or Coldplay, he was still being reviewed as a rock act making even more rock product.

The first music he was exposed to that was to his own taste was as much jazz legend Charles Mingus as Little Richard, and the ambitious structure and restlessness of much of his music was rooted in a jazz mentality, if not a jazz sound, as much as pop music, French chanson, modern classical music and old-fashioned rock and roll. Rock had claimed him, for obvious reasons, but it was a mere component in his work. For someone who played being a rock star with such élan, he never thought like a rock star, except to work out how to play one and then sabotage the role.

Whatever *Blackstar* was, an anomaly or actually the absolute shifting essence of a Bowie formula, still alert to the music and image-making around him, the attitude as the release approached was that he was only just beginning. Death was not growing around him after all; he was still contemplating the riddle of identity, even if it was now beginning to mingle with the meditations of someone at the end of their life. But someone who had made a record as full of life, wit and defiance as *Blackstar* was surely himself full of life, even as it examined the unreliability of reality, even as he contemplated what it was like to leave the earth.

In some ways it didn't seem so much his last album but his design of what the last-ever rock album should sound like, now that the idea was more or less over. There was so much anniversary culture and sentimental rehashing connected to rock that it wasn't easy to discern that the album era, in the spirit of the vinyl album, as a novel creative act, was long over. Streaming sites were committed to keeping the album alive even as they finally killed it off.

Music could be any length now – pop songs could and should be about forty seconds now, not the three minutes they remain as though they still belonged on the seven-inch single that has long gone – and albums could grow and change over time, remixed and rethought into other states and statements. They don't need to pretend to stay stuck as the conventionally sized collection of songs. Bowie had helped more than most to establish the two-sided drama of the vinyl album that contained a specific or abstract concept; with *Blackstar* he was gracefully bringing the era to an official end. Bowie acting as a witness to a world on the verge of disappearing; he was there at the beginning, he was there at the end.

The format is continually being transplanted into a new adjustable form because of the Internet and streaming, and to make an album-shaped album, the sort he mastered so definitively in the 1970s, was increasingly an old-fashioned and outmoded operation. He was bringing an incredible more or less sixty-year-old history to a deliberate, moving conclusion. He was saying, time for something else, perhaps. Times have changed and the world is changing; time for a change. He was mourning the album as much as his own life, and wondering what the next thing might be.

But *Blackstar* was, as far as things ever are these days, on sale, out now, really not titled, just a ★, but that was mere playful marketing, surely, further investigative dabbling of a vaporising world, where time was turning a corner, an appreciation of how the world is now so commercially loaded with the kind of metaphysics once the domain of the artist, or adventurous pop singer. It wasn't a blatant sign, along with the unique lack of a photograph of him on the cover, that this was the last stage before he disappeared. The black star was not the final sighting of the man who in the most recent photos, despite a stylish but suspicious hat and a boniness that reached White Duke extremes, was larking about and laughing. That it could be taken as another Bowie album meant that everything was fine. In fact, the more I thought about it, he was in fact placing an asterisk at the end of a run of albums you could say were in alphabetical order:

The twenty-seventh was *Blackstar,* or simply ★ – a suggestion that the A to Z was over, but there was more to come, beyond the known alphabet, beyond ordinary language; a second set of letters, of communications, a rebirth. Inside the A to Z, and all the possible combinations of songs, styles, secrets, themes, discoveries, redirections, emotional climaxes, sheer drama, tension, relief, beauty, there was all you needed to know in order to construct and understand the language of Bowie.

a. *David Bowie*
b. *David Bowie/Space Oddity*
c. *The Man Who Sold the World*
d. *Hunky Dory*
e. *The Rise and Fall of Ziggy Stardust and the Spiders from Mars*
f. *Aladdin Sane*
g. *Pin Ups*
h. *Diamond Dogs*
i. *Young Americans*
j. *Station to Station*
k. *Low*
l. *"Heroes"*
m. *Lodger*
n. *Scary Monsters (And Super Creeps)*
o. *Let's Dance*
p. *Tonight*
q. *Never Let Me Down*
r. *Tin Machine*
s. *Tin Machine II*
t. *Black Tie White Noise*
u. *1. Outside*
v. *Earthling*
w. *Hours*
x. *Heathen*

y. *Reality*
z. *The Next Day*

He was not dying after all.

And then within two days of an official release for *Blackstar* he died. Those playful, at ease photos were taken very close to what turned out to be the end, another part of the illusion. A final bow, and one of those smiles that all along seemed to be as much a mask as any of his masks, that never quite seemed to make it into his ageless eyes, which were always elsewhere, slightly ahead, or already moving into another dream.

The secret, known to very few in those last months, that he was dying, soon, had held, remarkably in a world that intrudes as though on our behalf into the deepest, darkest, best-defended celebrity recesses. Friends and collaborators were emailing him until days before, even sending him birthday cards and wondering why there wasn't, as there usually was, a quick, good-natured response. Recent rumours of the cancer that did kill him had not reached the same level of intensity evident a few years before; the force field around him had grown even stronger since those scares. He had even managed to rehearse his own death, and repel the death watch that existed before *The Next Day*.

It wasn't clear how much he knew as he prepared the music that it might be his last album, and ended up being titled, designed and made to be emphatically an ending, or whether the imagery and sound was intended all along, on the way to perhaps something else, another collection, another production, the beginning of another A to Z. Up to the last few weeks he was still thinking about what was musically beyond *Blackstar*. He was even beginning to imagine a return to performance, in small venues, a small, even acoustic ensemble, nothing fancy.

Blackstar ended up being what would be taken once he died

as a goodbye, and he must have considered it was a serious possibility. The pulse of the music is as scattered as sand. He kept himself going up to the release, and then the actual act of release seemed enough. There was completion. It took his last bit of life with him. And then finally he was ready.

He would have known that if the extent of the terminal illness had leaked, it would dominate what was the most important thing to him – the work, him as his work. He did not want his final moments to be a world feeling sorry for him, or not knowing what to say under the circumstances. He did not want his life to be crushed under the avalanche and build-up to his death, and his private thoughts interrupted by a world preoccupied with his tragic final days. A world, terribly, feeling sorry for him, and already picking through his private affairs.

The final moments must be on stage, the stage of his choosing and design, dramatically lit for adventure, and he's asking you to focus on . . .

Because it was released so close to his death, this black star falling to earth as the man who made it went somewhere else altogether, and because even before he was nowhere to be seen, he managed to make death seem beautiful. The man who as a mutant symbol of possibility expressing a very modern kind of sensitivity had definitely taught a generation or two how to live and how exciting it could be was now offering clues about how to die, about how to generate a continuum between life and its conclusion.

Rock music has increasingly become a matter of death as its leading exponents and pioneers reach an age where what lies ahead for a few years is a constant stream of rock stars dying. The rock era in a very real sense is coming to an end in a series of tragic moments. The music that began as an articulation of youth and a making up of the future is entering a definite twilight zone made up mostly of memory that is taking some getting used to.

Bowie confronted the fact that death and facing up to it is now a considerable part of the structure of rock music. Not the idea of the early, random, self-destructive rock death that confirms, even celebrates, the once-upon-a-time romantic risk-taking myth, but the death that comes at the strange, lingering end as a body and a mind break down and life is about a different set of realities, a different form of out-of-body experience, and the accumulating weight of uncertainty.

He managed to present the departure of David Bowie as an incredibly elegant event, taking seriously the idea that rock music had become a new kind of religion, a true faith, but he also understood as a public figure and someone who was so adept at working on his image that this sort of a pop culture death is increasingly a matter of public relations. If publicity has created who you are, and made you visible, that doesn't stop when you die; Bowie managed to keep control of the campaign and the performance all the way to the very end. Now that he has died we can see that he began planning for this end a long time ago. When the assumption was that he was not as creative as he once was, or he had retired, he was meticulously maintaining the vibrant energy of his creation – himself – and planning for a future where his future would be over.

What the secret man behind the performer, the intensely private David Jones, felt about the ultimate deadline racing towards him, the sudden thinning out of hope, how afraid, terrified, hurt, broken, angry, hysterical, vulnerable, lonely, or not, how much pain he was in, how much dignity lost, if he was ready, how much he was protecting the actual experience behind the veils of his new work, we will really never know, as it should be.

We were given a searing deathbed scene in Johan Renck's video for 'Lazarus' where an entire life and a consciousness that hadn't seemed to have changed between eight and sixty-eight were compressed from end to beginning. There's a new Bowie persona, Button Eyes, crawling out of a child's nightmare, from the most infested corners of the imagination. The video was shot after Bowie had been told he was in remission; by the closing months of 2015 the cancer would return with a vengeance, mercilessly invading all parts of his body.

The veiled, guileful rock star, a rare animal, a faded beauty, an anguished soul, explored the origins of suffering, shaking like he was always going to be moving somewhere else, performed a public penance as though for crimes of immorality, the seductive darkness in his eye now nothing other than the darkness of the universe, and this was all astonishing. Bowie reminding people of their great potential as living, sentient beings; and compelling them to face the inescapable certainty of their own mortality.

As always the performer and the performance kept brute, sickened reality at bay, stepping out of nowhere for a while to present more clues about an ongoing mystery that had been weighing on his mind for a while, before disappearing once more. He would materialise somewhere else at some other time. He always did.

This was a metaphor for how for all the coverage and investigation into his life, schedules, love affairs, methods, performances, songs and travels, we know a lot about the theatrical movement and manners of David Bowie, but very, very little about the nature of David Jones, the hidden man. All we really know is that he invented the artist David Bowie who told us more about a life than most writers and artists ever do, a life that became more than a life. We also know that David Jones created an artwork that was the privacy of his own life. He was the soul of discretion. We knew he had a wife, we knew he had a son and a daughter, we even knew where he lived. Nosier types would know a little more, try to penetrate the force field, and make up a lot based on that little more, but in general, there was never anything solid to know behind the art, and artist.

The artist was brave, and put a little star at the end of his life, meaning, in some way, there is much more to come, and what form of me is alive now has only just begun.

At the end of life, a secret.

He had performed a last fantastic illusion that had the kind of kick only a true card-burning surrealist and someone in love with the illusion of theatre could organise. His final record – or shadowy, malleable version of the kinds of records he used to make – wasn't a perfunctory greatest hits album, or the sound of an ageing rocker demonstrating how much he had lost touch, or vainly, clumsily trying to stay in touch. He hadn't stopped wandering, or wondering, and at the end of his exploring he had arrived where he started. He was moulding the simple darkness of life with a love of life.

He was still urging something to happen. Still measuring the imagination. Still figuring things out. Still manipulating fans to think the very best of him, and have their own feelings and thoughts about Bowie reflected right back at them. Everyone would be receiving something different based on their own version of David Bowie.

He was reporting on his life and its final moments with one of those 'what if's that always motivated him to find the new, the what if you put this sort of music with this sort of rhythm and this sort of story and this set of costumes and this kind of thinking and this set of puzzles. What if you changed your mind at the last moment? What if you couldn't change your mind at the last moment?

This particular 'what if' wondered what if you imagined the kind of album Shirley Bassey – or Elvis Presley – might have made at their end of their life if they were summoning the real and virtual ghosts of a life and had developed an interest in Sun Ra, Kurt Weill, Christian Fennesz, Morton Feldman, Aphex Twin, Gil Evans and Toru Takemitsu. Or what if you imagined the kind of album David Bowie might have made if he thought what if I make exactly the sort of album I should make at the end of my life that would mix David Bowie with David Bowie in a cloud of unknowing and conclude in all sorts of ways that this is enough.

•   •   •

The phone kept ringing on the morning the world heard he had died, and more abrupt (beat) messages telling me the news in case I didn't know were left from all manner of TV and radio programmes asking me to appear on their shows, in the next hour or so, and deliver what they were looking for – someone to put Bowie into the exact nutshell I, being a long-term Bowieist in case you hadn't yet guessed, totally loathe.

They would be looking for a pleasant, accessible, straightforwardly moving summary that would somehow introduce Bowie to people who didn't really know who he was, even though it must have been decided he was important enough to feature on mainstream news and therefore surely everyone knows of him, whether they like him or not, or consider him important or just another overrated rock star from the old days.

I had quickly decided that there was something unseemly about going on live radio or television to engage in what ultimately becomes a recycling of platitudes, and threatens to enter that weeping zone that properly began with the death and coverage of Diana Spencer. The death of the princess was the start of a new form of communal mourning for the media and entertainment age, and it can often seem when interested parties, with the best of intentions, offer their condolences and impressions of the life that has just ended that they are doing it for themselves more than the recently deceased and their family.

That might be unavoidable, it might not necessarily be a bad thing, but it wasn't something I was interested in doing. I was thinking far too much and had far too much to say, about his existence and non-existence, to go on a live news programme within hours of the death being announced and distil all of this into a simple paragraph, a concise summary.

If I did make an appearance on one of those programmes, where would I begin, and if I did begin, where would it all end? I left the house and headed for central London to read my radio script at Broadcasting House, to do something entirely different than talk about David Bowie.

As I approached the BBC headquarters, shaped like a ship as though it is powering through the choppy waters of confusion, I saw the disc jockey Paul Gambaccini being interviewed outside by a camera crew. It was clearly a mourning moment. They looked like they might be interested in interviewing anyone who passed that had a view on Bowie, even if they didn't know the person they were asking had an 'expert asterisk alert' next to their name on some internal BBC system. My mobile ran again: I didn't answer. A text came marked *very urgent* telling me, in case I didn't know, that David Bowie had died. I ignored it, not daring to answer back in case I got pulled in against my better nature.

I waited in the reception area of the old Broadcasting House for my producer to come and get me. On the internal BBC speaker system, Radio 2 was playing 'Space Oddity'. It was immediately a very different proposition now that Bowie was dead. Bigger, more profound even, a little sadder sounding, and it always sounded sad, once the novelty casing had been rejected, its fate-facing poignancy and bewitching otherworldliness now blooming in a brand-new way – there's nothing I can do – definitely signalling a shift in eras. Bowie had now had those final seconds of life he was writing about in 'Space Oddity'. The final moments of calm as eternity wrapped itself around him, and showed him this other way to be, which might contain its own benefits.

It was also exactly the same, the greatest novelty song ever written – although all great pop songs are ultimately novelty songs, an insidious, possibly accidental combination of the illusory, showy and the transcendent. The real trick is writing a novelty hit more than once or twice.

As always it sounded like it was something I was hearing for the first time, as fresh as oxygen, not sounding weary and stale after its millions of plays and battering commercial uses, and even though I had heard it only a couple of days before. I thought:

it's funny that he sang it barely into his twenties but it sounds as though he could have sung that last week, like it was the very last thing he did, a sublime termination, saved until the very end, a report direct from the end, as he drifted into the darkness, and one last time turned to face the strange.

He was seeing things very clearly, so sure of himself, adrift timelessly not only inside the rapturous space of a great song, unlike any other written before or since, but also inside a vivid concept strong and enterprising enough to last for ages. The song ended, the disc jockey said his name, and marvelled in just the way John Peel never would, 'Just how brilliant is that!'

Upstairs as I prepared to read my documentary script, after a new message from Channel 5 urgently needing me, or someone like me, on their midday news, I turned my phone off. I spent an hour or so narrating my script, with the word Bowie, as I read it, sounding different but the same just as 'Space Oddity' had downstairs. I was saying the word 'Bowie' in a room not very far from the room where John Peel would have sat when he said the name that was for me the first time I had ever heard it. It could even be the same studio, in a part of the old Broadcasting House that contains eighty years of radio ghosts.

For a split second, as I travelled through time and the name, still caught after all these years wondering whether it was oh or ow, or even ooh, remembering in the subconscious nick of time the first part of his surname rhymed with Bolan, I thought of all the things I would want to say if I did agree to appear on one of those programmes, many of them being made in the actual building I was now in.

That was part of the problem – too much to say, too much music to cover, too many favourite songs, favourite albums, too many favourite years, too many Bowies to believe in, or, perhaps, not, too many myths and facts and anecdotes and personal moments and critical thoughts and contrary views and new suggestions, too much overall, overwhelming Bowie to sum him up in a minute, or even five minutes, or ten ... all that I've written about above, and all I might be writing below, how I might describe how he offered the broadest insight into the age he lived through, dwelling on his end and how he finally distilled the cultivated sensual melancholy that made all his music so special however over the top and lurid, it all flashed through my mind in an explosion of memory and reflection, and I knew in that instant that what those people calling me really wanted was a cogent statement something along the lines of:

David Bowie was the most charismatic popular musician of his generation, a cultural polymath and style icon whose artistic breadth also took in theatre, film, video, fashion, mime, fine art criticism and prose writing. Though massively admired by vast numbers of fans throughout the world, he was never comfortable with mainstream recognition and throughout his long career made a habit of reacting to popularity by experimenting with genres of music and artistic ventures unlikely to find commercial acceptance. By refusing to rest on his laurels and – apart from a misstep in the eighties when he embraced the mass market to excess – recording a series of classic albums at various times in his life, he maintained a consistent level of critical acclaim enjoyed by very few of his contemporaries. He is an enormous loss, and millions will miss his incredible talent and vision.

... when – being the steadfast Bowieist encouraged to think to the best of your ability what few others are thinking, for better or worse, succeeding or not, with an instinct to avoid reducing everything to a bland paste of praise, and a relish for energy that deliberately defies easy summary, what I really wanted to say was more along the lines of:

For a while, for a few years, with a unique form of conviction, knowing exactly what he wanted to say, and how, he was never at a loss, for words, or poses. Look at him, at all the evidence there now is, the radiant traces he left behind, and sent into the future, of the man who continually changed his shape because he could, as if he knew exactly what to do with his hands, and genitals, and lips, somehow understanding that we would recognise ourselves through the way he parodied, and adored, life, and living, through some kind of shattered distorted mirror.

What was the fastidious, doubly sensitive and weirdly alluring David Bowie thinking during the decade, which at the time didn't seem to as such have a name but is now generally known as the Seventies? He was all over the shop, treating the Seventies – which was where the twentieth century truly went POP!, after the Sixties had gone mad preparing the way for what was to come, which would get madder – like a planet, a place to explore, a place to visit, and leave, a place to discover, and lose yourself, a place to make up your mind about what it is you wanted to do. Bowie made it seem at the time like what he was doing was calculating exactly how amazing the future could be, a future that was always on the verge of happening, but always just out of reach. He proposed an alternative reality, a number of alternative realities, getting to the very essence of what we want from our pop stars, who should, essentially, be at the dazzling forefront of the militant young using art as a cover for more direct action.

More than any other sort of pop artist, Bowie shows the way forward, maps, possible routes, with his imaginative logic, his tart tongue, his zoomorphic spirit, his love of dazzling with contrasts, his camp intensity, his scintillating nonchalance, his flighty defiance, his celebration of Pleasure, his slippery skill at locating, absorbing and transforming the idea of being different, and his controlling, self-conscious ability to make connections between the strangest things – between Jayne County and Anthony Newley, lipstick and Japan, tenderness and a revolutionary instinct, before and after, clowning and mimicry, jazz and dream, Kurt Weill and the Who, Brecht and Bassey, beauty and beast, sensuousness and nobility, magic and loss, person and reality.

What makes you great, he was suggesting, is not necessarily your individual works, but your very existence and personality. I came to the conclusion very early on even if I was just making it up that he thought the most astounding things, sometimes very calmly, sometimes in a deep frenzy, about what it was to think at all, how comic, deeply tragic and astounding it was to move from thought to thought and use these thoughts to make yourself up, to invent who you were going to be from moment to moment. He was thinking about what it was really like to be a performer, a man, a woman, a star, a singer, a writer, an entertainer, a traveller, ambitious, lover, haunted, disguised, photographed, lonely, individual, tycoon, addict, sexual, spectator, spaceman, something, before it was too late, always hoping it would never be too late.

Anyone who loves pushing things to bizarre conclusions, and who relishes improvising their way through life, who sees life as a risk, but there's no need to panic, and who is encouraged by a lonely compulsion to stretch and extend themselves, will feed off Bowie's roaming, boastful and magnificently un-linear energy. For those who cannot bear the idea of not being loved, then look to how Bowie played with his public image, and committed himself to the cultic power of art and artificiality, the magic power of evasion. He added to Charles Baudelaire's table of modern heroes – the poet, the flâneur, the dandy, the gambler, the worker, the ragpicker and the prostitute – with his version of the cosmopolitan, and his dream of a star.

Or I might on the spur of the moment take the opportunity to actually reason that I had decided once and for all what my favourite Bowie album was, something I have never been able to settle on since about the time of *Diamond Dogs*. Or maybe work out a system that was an equivalent to astrology in how you could understand an individual's personality by knowing what their favourite Bowie albums were, a way of working out what kind of person they were, or thought they were – what sign were you Bowie-born

under, were you *Low* with *The Next Day* rising, *Hunky Dory* with
Lodger rising, *Let's Dance* with *Space Oddity* rising, *"Heroes"*
with *Blackstar* rising, *The Man Who Sold the World* with *Heathen*
rising, *Scary Monsters (And Super Creeps)* with *Black Tie White
Noise* rising, *The Rise and Fall of Ziggy Stardust* with *Aladdin
Sane* rising, *Young Americans* with *Let's Dance* rising, *Station to
Station* with *Diamond Dogs* rising, *Lodger* with *Santa Monica '72*
rising, *Changesonebowie* with *Changestwobowie* rising. If pushed,
I would confess to being *Low* with rising *Ziggy* under a *Blackstar*.
I would finish by wondering what Bowie-sign Bowie himself would
be? I decided this was exactly why it was best I didn't go on the
midday BBC *News*. This would not be the expected eulogy delivered
in a state of mediated shock.

As serious as I was being, still looking for ways to accurately
reflect the true, or truer, truest, spirit of Bowie, the artist always
in disguise, not the inflexible received wisdom, it might look as
though I were being flippant. It would seem I was not properly
accepting my role as professional mourner aiding Bowie's moving
journey to his long home.

As I left the BBC recording studio, Paul, a radio producer friend
and colleague, was waiting for me. Knowing I was not going to
answer my phone, he had found out I was in the building and so he
came to find me. He was working with John Wilson, the presenter
of the BBC Radio 4 nightly arts programme *Front Row*, and they
were very keen that I appear on the show live later that night to
take part in a discussion about David Bowie. The whole forty-five
minutes of the programme was going to be dedicated to Bowie.

I find it hard to say no to my friend's face, and John from *Front
Row* calls me, and promises there will be plenty of time to deliver
more than just a brief cursory summary. My mind starts racing,
already trying to think of a way that I won't merely repeat what
everyone else is saying. I can't help it. I blame Bowie. He made
me think this way. He made me write this way.

For a while I consider delivering a section of something I wrote as part of my contribution to the *David Bowie is* exhibition that started its life at the Victoria and Albert Museum in 2013 before setting out on a world tour via Chicago, Paris, Bologna, Melbourne, Tokyo and scheduled to end in 2018, but which may yet travel for longer. *David Bowie is* was a conceptual kit/concrete poem/manifesto I wrote as an abstract summary of Bowie that could be used in both the exhibition and marketing.

It could be split into component parts and lines and used as a series of slogans, notes, clues, cut-ups, catchphrases, quotes, lines, paragraphs, lists, anecdotes, facts, lyrics, theories, interruptions, subtitles, headings, strategies, instructions and facts, an attempt to produce a form of less sterile text to the standard pieces that get used in exhibitions to describe the exhibits. There is a lot of the real in the exhibition, but also a lot of the surreal, of the thinking it is very difficult to fix in place, and reason with, and so it felt right to include the possibility of occasional sightings of another kind of less formal text. For all the cataloguing and combining of information, it was always good to keep things open, as open as the work was always meant to be.

It was also a way of moving between and connecting all the Bowies there were – glam Bowie, tabloid Bowie, experimental Bowie, mad Bowie, mod Bowie, lurid Bowie, lost Bowie, rock star Bowie, occult Bowie, collaborative Bowie, Australian Bowie, drag Bowie, secret Bowie, Berlin Bowie, interview Bowie, film Bowie, scandal Bowie, sex Bowie, Brecht Bowie, art Bowie, young Bowie, Jones Bowie, old Bowie, your Bowie, my Bowie, and amidst all these fragmented Bowies, fragmented Bowie. There is a lot of ground to cover when considering the life and work of Bowie, and this was a way to cover a bit more of that ground, through a random combination of fact, allusion and impression.

There could be a similar effect in the exhibition to how one of Bowie's lyrics would dart somewhere else through a sudden edit, a jump cut, a putting of one world with another, a move into another part of the dream, of his history, allowing a layering of one time or place over another, which for me suited the way I thought of Bowie and therefore how I imagined he thought of his own work.

It needed a title so that it didn't merely become David Bowie: the exhibition. I'd called it *David Bowie is* because for all the 'was' the exhibition contained, all that gathered past and accumulated memory, it became in the arrangement and style a new work, and a new kind of work. A work that was meant to communicate the sense that David Bowie *is*. Who is he? What is he? He just is. And also:

David Bowie is dancing at the edge of the world

David Bowie is a standing cinema

David Bowie is a white boy from Brixton ending up on a black TV show

David Bowie is the space invader

David Bowie is telling the same story repeatedly altering the story either slightly or profoundly at each retelling

David Bowie is calling his next album *The Best Damned Haircut I Ever Had*

David Bowie is a pop of the cherry

David Bowie is William Blake singing Danny Kaye

David Bowie is inside his own head

David Bowie is yearning for a future that will never come to pass

David Bowie is living on a mad planet

David Bowie is never doing anything out of the blue

David Bowie is cultivating the power to charm

David Bowie is developing an apocalyptic imagination

David Bowie is swaying through the crowd to an empty space

David Bowie is Man Ray singing Billy Fury

David Bowie is every sight and sound to me

David Bowie is feeling hunted

David Bowie is saying thank God for books

David Bowie is saying to be totally alone hurts worse than a knife

David Bowie is thinking a really convincing theatrical death is best left unseen

David Bowie is never at a loss for words, or poses

David Bowie is seeing two lovers sit on a bench by the Berlin Wall

David Bowie is addicted

David Bowie is an avant-garde lunatic

David Bowie is reading before it was even written that we are

living in a world where there is more and more information but
less and less meaning

David Bowie is Lewis Carroll singing Jacques Brel

David Bowie is saying that he has got so many shells he has
forgotten what the pea looks like

David Bowie is dada dandy

David Bowie is scanning life through the picture window

David Bowie is overlapping his own agonies and the agonies of
the time into his most powerful work

David Bowie is thinking of ways for us to become what we
should have been but never were

David Bowie is who knows

David Bowie is thinking that every so often our bodies are
completely fresh material

David Bowie is a confirmed futurist, basing pop music on
his belief that a true artist dreams ahead, he anticipates a
breakdown in music industry and media certainties, and
prepares himself for the science-fiction future he always craved.
A future where his twentieth-century music will still exist, and
still sound contemporary, and in a Borgesian sense, *otherwise*

David Bowie is strung out on razors and slash-back blazers

David Bowie is knowing that the acceptance of the accidental
is a mark of artistic confidence

David Bowie is placing himself here, there and everywhere, making himself at home, and then moving somewhere else

David Bowie is turning us all into voyeurs

David Bowie is falling asleep at night as a rock and roll star

David Bowie is a palpable presence and he's all these crazy images rushing past these bizarre imaginings enclosing his fans in his embrace he's real and unreal private and illusion all flickering and blurring

David Bowie is William Burroughs singing Anthony Newley

David Bowie is overrated

David Bowie is the 1950s in the 1970s in 2001 in the 1930s in the 1890s in the 2040s in 1984 in 2016

David Bowie is wearing yellow shoes with a little strap across them like girls' shoes and shoe man Andy Warhol adored them

David Bowie is feeling temporary about himself

David Bowie is wanting Friedrich Nietzsche to sing I'm not a prophet or a Stone Age man just a mortal with the potential to be a superman

David Bowie is not explaining himself .

David Bowie is reading the words: My grand theme – who is human and who only appears (masquerades) as human? Unless we can individually and collectively be certain of the answer to this question, we face what is, in my view, the most serious problem possible. Without answering it adequately, we cannot even be certain of our own selves. I cannot even know myself, let alone you. So I keep working on this theme; to me nothing is as important a question. And the answer comes very hard

David Bowie is not just himself, but all the objects he creates and surrounds himself with

David Bowie is predicting soon there will be nothing left of him

David Bowie is just the ghost of a story

There actually was a real poet on the David Bowie *Front Row* programme, Lavinia Greenlaw, who reads out something she is reluctant to call a poem, because she has not had the time to process the news and do the work over time that a poem often requires. There is no time for that in an information-stricken world where the news never stops, as though it is the glue holding everything together, or the opposite, an energy pulling everything apart.

What she reads is certainly a series of images and very personal responses to Bowie that would not have been heard anywhere else. This seems to me to be in the correct spirit; to find some new knowledge by finding a new way of putting together Bowie with your own life, of introducing the fresh blood the myth of Bowie always requires. My 'poem' would now seem more like a form of sales talk – although that wouldn't necessarily be inappropriate.

The other guest was Jonathan Barnbrook, who has worked closely with Bowie on his artwork since *Heathen*, after first working on the design for Bowie's wife Iman's autobiography, and had just finished collaborating with him on the cover for *Blackstar*. A move on from the defacing of *"Heroes"*, one way of representing physical change as you age, it now seemed as though this had been a deliberate decision, to reflect the ultimate withdrawal of the singer, and replace him with an abstract symbol. Jonathan said, no, there were other reasons why the black star; there had been no conversation about it being the end, a conclusion. No melancholy connotations. It wasn't necessarily a way of symbolising this was Bowie's last character, a descendant of Ziggy that didn't need Bowie to exist. The star stood for glamour, and how Bowie loved to share the power of glamour and his idea of glamour with the rest of the world.

With the three of us talking, plus an interview John had done with David Bowie a few years before, and responses from musicians Bowie had worked with, there was in the end very little time for any of us to say anything at length. In John's interview, Bowie is playing the role he could slip into effortlessly of likeable English comedy actor who happened to be a rich intellectual rock musician, a sort of warped, self-deprecating English Renaissance eccentric with a few anecdotes carefully stored away he could always rely on. Nothing to scare the children.

Bowie as comedian more than rock star who could collaborate with Ricky Gervais and SpongeBob SquarePants as coolly as he could with Brian Eno, Pat Metheny or Martin Scorsese; I think of telling the story he told at his Berklee College of Music address about when he was playing a show back in the early 1970s in some run-down working-men's club in the north of England. In full Tokyo space-boy costume, sky high on high heels so he is tottering not walking, he is also in full, narcissistic pop star mode, possessing the glittery hard-on of unabashed aloofness. He asks the venue manager where the toilet is, and he is told to use the cracked and stained sink on a wall at the end of a corridor. 'My good man,' he says, 'I'm not taking a piss in the sink.'

'Listen, son, if it's good enough for Shirley Bassey,' he drily replies, 'it's good enough for you.'

It did occur to me when John asked how much he would be missed that in a way what we think of as David Bowie had not in fact gone anywhere. We cannot miss David Bowie, because as a creation, a creation who created, he is still with us, and probably more so now he has died. This is why the transference from one stage to another with *Blackstar* was so evocative; we could actually see in action the release of a new sort of life force. Something new had taken on a life of its own, fanned into being by the web, which even though it is now not called the World Wide Web, is still worldwide.

There was a widespread display of grief from a vast range of people emotionally and intellectually captivated by the things he had done, there was a genuine cathartic experience, but there was also something else going on. I didn't exactly feel I was going to miss him because the Bowie that exists in my imagination had not gone; that would mean the wiping out of all traces of his existence, a true collapse into an abyss of all his songs, ideas, characters and performances, a plucking from the Internet of everything he had ever done. A sudden, terrible silence, which would also require a sinister wiping of everyone's memory. That would be a hellish loss; the Bowie I knew still lived. I could still communicate with him, and he could still communicate with me. That Bowie could still grow.

We can perhaps miss what next he might have done as a musician and an artist, but how much more could we really expect? The work is the life, is the life of David Bowie, and the work still exists. The work is also the afterlife, and it perversely receives a considerable boost of energy now that Bowie has died.

He had already passed so much of himself into his work that you could learn more about him there than you could from the man himself. There is a sort of immortality when such powerful work is created, even if the person who created the work does not know they have become immortal. That's the curse; you live forever, or as long as there is time, but you don't know it.

Bowie's songs, his videos, the photographs, the characters he invented, the printed myths and stories were all created, and they have a life and have the potential to live for a very long time and continue to communicate with people long after he has died. People will react to them like they are alive.

The songs will continue to cause an effect. Bowie's death, and the strange combination of there being so much of him left to embrace that seemed to have its own considerable dynamic, made me think there is something in the idea that art can be a living substance. Something very real survives after the death of someone who is responsible for the creation of certain works of art. It is more than a symbolic immortality. There is a reaction to the songs as though they themselves contain the actual life of Bowie, a complicated, evolving dynamic that carries on as a power you experience as though it is a living thing. The greater the artists, the more of their life they put into their work, the more it has the qualities of life itself.

After the broadcast, frustrated that I didn't manage to articulate what I was feeling, I realised the only way I could begin to say what I wanted to say about David Bowie was to write a book. This would be my response, as a writer who started writing because of musicians like David Bowie. This would be how I could work out who and what David Bowie is. There are plenty of books about David Bowie. 'Thirty seven!' I remember Bowie exclaiming in wonder or despair in an interview. That still didn't put me off.

Not enough, I thought. There are so many Bowies, multiplying all the time, and there can easily be more books. There needs to be more to try to keep up with what he was doing and how he did it. Different versions of the same thing that all combine to help create 'David Bowie', where everyone who has a thought, an opinion, a fascination, a memory is contributing to the finished product. Even David Bowie himself was only a contributor. The main one, but he needed the attention of others to complete the concept, the overall effect.

I suppose writing a book is my way of still searching for the flaming dove, 'that bluebird', of following to the bitter-sweet end where the solemn perverse serenity is going to take me. Only through Bowie perhaps will I find out. I can't help myself. It's his fault, I have to see what happens. I have to find out what Bowie means to me, and what history he now tells. And once I start, I have to finish, whatever happens.

Everyone has their own Bowie, based on their own biases, age and taste, where they live, what they do, and everyone can now construct their own biography of Bowie using material available online. Anyone can know anything and everything they want to know about him by doing a few searches, and following the links. There are a cloud of witnesses.

So why the need for a biography? Because the biography can still locate, invent, imagine the kind of connections that keep the myth turning and returning in a way all the facts and opinions online cannot do, because every Internet entry about Bowie is separate, and separated from a wider context, buried among details about the rest of the world but somehow not belonging in that world. The book moves out into the world, through the world, becoming part of it – the world where he operated, and lived, the world that made him what he was. It becomes part of that world.

The facts and statistics are piled up, but they exist in their own vacuum. Despite all the chat rooms discussing Bowie now literally to death, paradoxically this pins him down like a butterfly under glass; the biography keeps him moving, setting him somewhere else, even if it can only go over the same ground. The same old ground will always be different to whoever is looking at it, and describing it. The same old ground can always become new ground when the subject is David Bowie.

A biography is what I could do to keep collaborating with the idea of David Bowie, to ensure that life force still grows. I think it is worth it. He should stay with us as much as the great writers and artists do, and that means we keep telling the stories, playing the music, inventing the theories, imagining the 'what if's.

Everyone has their own Bowie, and this will be mine. How I think of him becoming himself in the 1960s, the way in the 1970s he seemed to become so many different versions of himself and constantly replaced himself with another, and another, until he almost wiped himself out. How he recovered in the 1980s, and then almost disappeared again in a different way, matching the excitements of the 1970s that exaggerated him with a kind of blankness that almost turned him invisible. How he spent the 1990s looking forward to a world that was to come where there would be no record business, and the Internet would begin to replace reality with a madder copy of itself, and there would be opportunities for everyone to invent their own image, rename themselves, change their identity, their sex, their location, become a creation of their own making, share their lives with millions of others, generate their own brand of fame, stretch reality around them. How he showed how much he had designed his life – in the way everyone can now do – when very few could do, or even think of doing, such a thing. And then he showed us another way ahead by designing his death. The death that rearranged his whole life; as though he had been a city that was abruptly reassembled into a whole new geography as soon as he was gone.

Everyone has their own Bowie. This is mine, and it goes exactly in this order. Sometimes it goes in chronological order, sometimes it collapses into itself, and after all it was Bowie that said 'the straightforward narrative should be relegated to the past', so sometimes inevitably that will happen.

This is my Bowie. It is not true, it is not false. It is not right, it is not wrong. Some things he did are more interesting to me than others. The 1970s surrounded me, all those departures in style, so there will be a lot of that, but there are the years before, the years after, then the twenty-first-century aftermath, and what comes next, as his life becomes something else again and again, and is remembered in constantly surprising and inventive ways.

Each era I think needs to be written in a different way, to reflect where he was, how obscure, famous, inspired or broken, and what was happening around him.

In the biography I write, which by its very nature is exactly the one I want to see, I would want to know:

a. where has he come from and was there one point where the chain effect began – literally a leap of the imagination – that led from Brixton and Bromley all the way via Berlin to *Blackstar*.

b. what is the nature of the collaboration he has had with other musicians, artists and writers, with others that don't particularly fit into a category, since the early 1960s?

c. what does it all mean to me and how does that connect with what it means to other people, the religious warriors who obsess about him online, the fans who have been there for long years at a time, the casual fans who move in and out of the story, the fans that have only just arrived and will arrive, the new clients hearing his name for the first time after he has died. (The question being: who wants to know?)

d. what is the relationship between his life and his work, following on the Susan Sontag proposal that you can know a life from the work, but you can never know the work from the life? So the work for me is the life of David Bowie and the construction of a response to that work over the years by writers and fans is David Bowie. So will this be a biography as much about that as a life, and in the end that construct is the life he wanted to be the one we thought of when we thought of David Bowie. A volatile mixing and merging of fact and fiction, with if anything an emphasis towards the fiction as much as a lot of it appears to be the facts.

e. will it be a book ultimately about magic?

f. or smoke and mirrors?

g. will I attempt to do the impossible, and summarise him in one sentence; *all you had to do was ask him a question, and he turned on.*

h. can I write it in ten weeks, as if I have given myself the equivalent conditions that Bowie would have had when he made an album in the crowded, fluctuating 1970s, but without what became for a time his preferred diet, the essence of his life, the four packs a day of titanically strong Gitanes, the cocaine, the red peppers and indeed the milk straight from the carton?

2

A DANCING STAR

David Bowie is not here

David Bowie is where we start from

David Bowie is arriving and departing at the same time

David Bowie is halfway between what it means and what you'd like it to mean

David Bowie is one thing or another

David Bowie is alert to the distorting and falsifying potential of images

David Bowie is convinced there is not action without the imagination

David Bowie is saying something to someone about something

David Bowie is suggesting you cannot explain the flower by the fertiliser

David Bowie is not yet

David Bowie is aware that he is dreaming and yet continues to dream

David Bowie is a face drawn in sand at the end of the sea

David Bowie is a medley of narratives in which the author's own is just one

David Bowie is entering a secret London

David Bowie is wanting to be noticed

David Bowie is cultivating the power to charm

David Bowie is making himself up

David Bowie is moving from the place where he was born

David Bowie is doing the work he was born for

David Bowie is roaming for years and years

David Bowie is wanting to live

David Bowie is on the prowl

David Bowie is finding a place where he can live intensely

David Bowie is amusing himself in Soho

David Bowie is escaping into Soho

David Bowie is in search of the new world

David Bowie is moving from street to street

David Bowie is rejecting the confines of his bedroom

David Bowie is groping through the London fog

David Bowie is gathering himself

David Bowie is crossing the border between suburbia and bohemia

David Bowie is a face in the crowd

David Bowie is making a scene

David Bowie is dancing a furious boredom

David Bowie is a flash in the pan

David Bowie is a brilliant mimic

David Bowie is introducing himself

David Bowie is not talking

David Bowie is needing to be something more than human

David Bowie is thinking he is David Bowie

David Bowie is not David Jones

David Bowie is giving birth to himself over and over again

David Bowie is a Capricorn – ambitious and determined,

extremely dedicated to their goals almost to the point of stubbornness but patient and happy to wait for their ship to come in

David Bowie is owning every day between his birth and his death

David Bowie is born as David Robert Jones, on Wednesday, 8 January 1947. Another addition to a world that has been added to hour after hour for thousands and thousands of years. Here was simply another baby born during a particularly cold, snowy English winter not destined to help much in dealing with the lingering dispiriting effects of the war, to an anonymous working family riddled with mental illness trapped on plain cramped streets at the dismal margins of a broken city. There was still food rationing, a general, pervading sense of limited possibilities, any luxury and break from routine was a distant fantasy, and the wider world was being secretively cut up, shoved about and reorganised in ways that didn't necessarily promise peace and prosperity. Having children after a nasty stunning war was a way of introducing some fresh innocent life, and positive, hopeful light, into this miserable, oppressive national darkness, in a form the poorest, battered and most powerless could control and instigate, desperately craving a creative togetherness that created its own temporarily liberating free pleasure.

David Jones shared the same birthday with the first Dr Who, William Hartnell, with Graham Chapman of *Monty Python*, with Gypsy Rose Lee, Shirley Bassey and Elvis Presley. There are various suggestions about what time he was born, as though this might make a difference, in terms of the moment he entered the world, on planet earth, the exact accidental time amidst the vast flat-out unfathomable swirl of billions of years that he made his very first spectacular appearance. This is when he decided to turn up, or when it was decided for him.

I like the idea he was born at 11.50 p.m., a mere ten minutes before midnight and 9 January, another day, and another life, altogether. A last-minute gasp. Manipulating his circumstances already, he fought to be born the same day as Elvis – and Shirley.

3

MADNESS AND BEAUTY

If for the beginning of a biography of David Bowie, we do indeed go back to a beginning, where would we locate that? Is the beginning of the man we are interested in actually the birth and early years of David Jones, or do we take the beginning to be the moment he changed his name and became David Bowie?

If the man of interest is Bowie, then that particular change, when he assumes the name everyone knows him by, is really the beginning. It's an artificial beginning, but then everything that comes because of Bowie is as artificial in a way, and is all rooted in that initial decision, when he slips into another role, another persona. All decisions that are made in the service of creating something are artificial, in that they don't exist in nature, they are not of the world. They come from the mind, they are made up, they are a solution to a problem, or the imagining of a direction to take, but they are in their own way artificial, a production, however honest and pure the intention.

He's encouraged to change his Davie Jones name because there is already another entertainer called Davy Jones at the time he is making his first professional moves into music, and that Davy Jones is becoming at that time one of the biggest pop stars in the world, the lead singer of the Monkees. There are other, more obscure David Joneses in music as well. For someone who is so determined to be different, it is not necessarily a problem. To be himself he must become someone else. It would have been nice to do it under his own name, but this doesn't bother him, because to achieve the sort of success he is interested in, he must continually become someone else.

It can also be seen as a positive sign: that someone with his name turned into such a teenybop idol. The fates didn't quite align to mean that he was the Davie Jones that succeeded, but they must have come pretty close. After all, the Davy Jones of the Monkees was English, and like Davie spoke with the sort of accent that belonged to no actual recognisable district or area in England except one made up mixing something apparently posh and well-modulated with something vaguely fashionably young and cool to confirm to an international audience he was very definitely English. In some ways Davie had done well at the audition. His turn would surely come soon, as long as he changed his name. For a while, he's obscure enough for Davie Jones to be enough of a distance from the Monkees' TV-driven hysteria. As awareness of him heats up a little, he needs more of a difference. The Davie has to change. The Jones has to change.

Once freshly named and newly qualified, he would then pursue a life in entertainment that involved so many additional changes as he confronted and then skipped outside the short attention spans then deeply embedded into the pop system. Things were moving fast as a new breed of young, driven musicians discovering their own secrets descended on this emergent form of music that gave so many chances for self-expression. To stay ahead, for longer than a year or two, or even three, was quite a task and required considerable speed of thought.

The interest of the new pop musicians in the early 1960s came from the theatrical side or the art side, or indeed from both at the same time, now very much a possibility – the fact that you could combine the techniques of show business with the craft and tactics of art was one of the central elements that made the sudden British contribution to rock so unique and vital, so that it didn't end up an insular All American activity. The British vaudevillian tradition, the music-hall approach, which in itself had its own ingredients of anarchy and subversion, a contagious, slippery comic energy, was mixed with some of the more serious experimental principles of modern art and design thinking to create a whole new hybrid and suggest a multitude of different ways to combine arresting, novel performance and exuberant appearance with the deeper purpose of art. Popular music got a conceptual kick, extending it beyond being mere entertainment, and in that sense a mere imitation of forms that had come before, and that opened up everything.

The two sides could be endlessly played around with once they came together; the music hall side exaggerated and deformed, given a deviant form of style and contemporary exuberance, by being connected with the procedures and intentions of modern visual art, and modern art was given an exciting charge by being associated with the mischievous tongue-in-cheek antics of British music hall.

There was another combination of elements to add into this novel synthesis. The particular brand of show business that rock and roll was producing in America, with its own distortions and glamorous perversions of various performance traditions, and its own essential articulation of a new kind of liberating optimism, was where the early British pop and rock musicians looked for their early cues and clues about how to play and perform. Extrovert, neatly wild American rock and roll, where the rejected outside was suddenly given, at least in a fantasy setting, wonderful new privileges, was filtered through a very particular distinct British sensibility, which could be equally as introvert as extrovert, and a different kind of twist was given to this growing music, accelerating the rebounding changes.

There were so many suddenly available permutations and possible directions in how to blend and bind these new energies. One area would quickly influence another. Fashions consequently came and went as new sounds were found and exploited, and quickly changed as yet another new set of sounds were discovered.

Bowie was quick to realise that to avoid being locked in to one fashion moment it is best to already look and sound as though you are somewhere else, preferably in the area of what it can be estimated is about to come next. He was aware from an early stage that he was to treat himself as product, however grandiose, moving and authentic he might want that product to appear. He started thinking about what a rock star was before certain parameters had been set in place. His learning and curiosity about art and its evolving, corrupted close cousin advertising made him think about the idea of being a pop personality in a more sophisticated manner than a mere musician would.

This self-consciousness and willingness to be so protean when it came to his style and sound would be the act of a devious opportunist on the make, but also of a sharp, hungry, unstoppably skittish mind. It can sometimes seem as though one of the motivations to be so fluid and volatile was to make it almost impossible for a biographer to ever be able to pin him down, or follow one specific trajectory that is any more revealing than another.

He wanted to be the only one who really knew how he worked, and how it worked, and what he was doing, and why. It was going to be his secret, to the end, and if along the way he was very polite to those who asked questions, as if there was any kind of literal, revealing truth in his answers, or he appeared to be losing his mind, and his body, in pursuit of a self-consciously artistic derangement of the senses, then this was all part of the construction. It all then fed back into the construction, keeping the edges, and the centre, blurred enough for his greater purpose.

This gave him the kind of inner strength required to maintain the illusion. He didn't want to create anything that could ever be so fixed it could easily be summed up inside a book, or article, or review. He didn't want to be explained. What excited him was what couldn't be explained. What would keep him interested in himself, ultimately the most important thing, in terms of sustaining his appetite and internal powers, was that he could not be easily explained.

If his life as David Bowie was to be a work of art, about being an artist, singer, star and mystery, symbolising the extraordinary changes in modern life at the end of the twentieth century, then it was always going to be an abstract, conceptual piece, highly open to interpretation. To take only the artist, and develop theories from there would only tell a part of the story, missing out so much. To take the musician and singer seriously as the central basis of David Bowie is to report on some endlessly fascinating moments. The composing and making of the songs and records, the time in the studio, the relationships with musicians and producers, with the media, then the relationship with fans, can be and is in many different places discussed and pored over at considerable length.

The soundtrack to his mercurial activity and ultimately constant fame appeared to supply endless evidence about who he was and what he was thinking and feeling, as much as it seemed to create a more opaque mask, a stronger defence and deeper protection. The songs, as tremendous as they regularly were, existed because pop music during the time he was alive was how you achieved the type of elusive self-expressive presence Bowie was hungry to establish. It took you straight to the heart of everything in one go, in the way not even a film, or book, or work of art, or brand name at the time could.

A book that only concentrates on his stardom and its consequences will be a fabulous, racy read, but at its best as an accumulation of gossip and speculation will tip over into fiction, although however extreme will probably still be as close to any truth as a book that scrupulously compiles details of what was happening at any given time. A biography that takes on the mystery might well be my favourite sort, but it will still have to pay attention to the ordinary facts and the spinning fiction, because the mystery existed in one part as a method and result of building the idea of David Bowie. Bowie built the idea of Bowie so that eventually others would be responsible for what that idea was, because their contribution would shape and refine the product once he had taken it as far as he could. He would then objectively enjoy the results, witness the adaptation of his original idea into something else altogether because of the accumulation of reactions to the image and history of David Bowie.

The mystery approach will have to take account of the tabloid star, the wilful artist, the emotional, and emotionally defunct, personality, and the overactive musician/performer, how he exploited both his limitations and his found and given talents, and how the mystery emerged and evolved because of Bowie's endlessly changing relationship with the world around him and the response of people to what it is he does, and appears to be doing. Bowie's adaptability and his ability to transfer that spirit into his work, and his songs, was a major contribution.

And whatever the take, however abstract the response to the abstraction, however orthodox the attempt to summarise such a story, it still has to deal, or not, with those years before David Bowie actually became Bowie. When he was officially someone else, and, to an extent, the time, the only period really, when he could be considered an average person, in an average setting, which is itself intriguing.

The details of that averageness become thinner and thinner as we move back in time through the 1950s to the year of his birth. Perhaps amidst that averageness there might be the one sign of a moment when we recognise the David Bowie he was to become, the very beginning of a chain reaction that never stopped firing for sixty years, but by the very nature of it being pre-Bowie the circumstances lack the resonating complex tensions and a more visible relationship with an outside world that came later and helped generate the mystery. This pre-Bowie, mostly pre-performance time, is a different sort of mystery, it's a far less public time, and even then the details that have been established have been dressed and distressed as a pure sort of information by being dragged into the story of Bowie. Sources and details are sparse, and they have been overused in terms of suggesting how he became David Bowie. The details might be what we would be expecting to find when we construct the early story of someone whose entire public image is a series of illusions, performances, digressions, experiments, false trails and inventions.

When the ambitions and cravings were forming and warming up, on the way to becoming burning, if we take those early years at face value, he was just another English teenager with dreams of making it, of being special, eyeing up the new rock and roll, film and TV stars as surely the perfect way to live a life. There were a lot of these teenagers about.

Maybe he stood out in his classes at school for being different, for wearing his hair in an unusual, slightly daring way, for having a certain, immersed strength no one wanted to challenge explicitly, for trying out different sorts of clothing and being the first to discover certain forms of rare, imported music. There were plenty of those around the country as well, though, and very little guarantee that those different from others in an average school in an average part of the world would end up being actually different from the rest of the world. Ultimately, there was no one else who did the kind of things he did in the way he did them, in so many genres and at so many different times. Where did that begin? Was there a particular moment? Were there many, and none of them meant much, or can ever be known to be real, until they all combined at the moment he changed his name?

The hunt is on to uncover the reasons why he wanted to appear different from the others around him, as if this will explain perhaps his continuing need and fascination with being different, to be set apart from everyone else, and yet the object of their attention. Not only did he want to appear different, but from early on he had clear ideas how he wanted to enact that. Where does that come from? Why him, and not those other average young English dreamers waking up to rock and roll and everything that followed?

Where did he come from? Was his first thought, a beating in his heart, a flash of stunning colour in his mind, a sudden visceral, almost terrifying realisation – that he was so small, and he knew nothing? He was so small, and far away from guidance. He had no sense of direction. He needed to know things to become bigger. He wanted to be big, because he was afraid of being small. Later, when he knew many more words, he would be able to say what perhaps his first instinct was, as he first got his bearings, realising after the boxed-in black of the womb striving to be fed that this was now the reality, a human reality, which was going to take some getting used to, and some dealing with. 'I always had a repulsive need to be something more than human. I felt very puny as a human. I thought, "Fuck that. I want to be a superhuman."' Before he had the words, before he could think and dream, he had a kind of skull-busting ambition that would mean he was going in a certain direction already. After all the palaver of being born, after all that, his first instinct was, I must change. A self that goes on changing is a self that goes on living. What drove him to create his very own environment?

Is it possible to take David Bowie back into David Jones, heading back into a more ordinary world, into family, school, home, London Englishness, and find a word, a sound, a sighting, a classic Proustian smell, a detail in a dream, a pattern, an argument, that began the chain reaction, the opening up of a mind that allowed so much in, and in a way, to a point, allowed so many people in?

There are some details that have become a near fixed part of the story. He never really helped open those years up. In interviews, when asked, he was always polite, and offered a few glimpses and memories, but they were so generic they could belong to anyone of that age living through that time, as though he had snatched the details from a film or a book, possessed the life of someone else and grafted them onto his own. There has been an invention of the details before he became Bowie, and before the press started to follow him and his collaborators, and leave behind real solid traces, not these dream traces, and spectral images of an invented 1950s life that tends to have the quality of something Philip K. Dick would write, about a fabricated life worn as a convenient disguise by someone with ulterior motives who has spent as much time manipulating his past as preparing his present and organising his future.

During the time he was exploring how he could make his presence felt on the Internet in 1998, Bowie unexpectedly considered those dimly lit, barely flickering, early years, writing – blogging, really – about them with a real sincerity, like they had actually happened after all. He still distanced himself through the use of an arch little pun for the title of his provisional entry into memoir. He called his recollections 'The Early Ears', and they were much more confessional than his usual informative posts, which had a neutrality that suggested another hand as much as his own.

They were written for subscribers to his website, so they were penned away from the outside world, written for the eyes of fanatics only, and in 1998 websites were still in their early days. The mainstream world hadn't yet fully appreciated what a difference the Internet was going to make to reality, and how we would connect to each other. Bowie had, and was already, too early really, working out how he could use it for his ends. The tabloid chasers of dirt and scandal weren't looking, and at the time Bowie wasn't what he had been twenty years before.

Feeling protected enough to try some personal musings, he remembered, memories of memories, some early moments, and they featured a strong appearance by his mother, Peggy Burns Jones, with whom his relationship had traditionally been troubled. This raw material was gratefully received by those 1970s chat-show hosts in Britain and America who fancied themselves as part entertainers part therapists:

Sundays were the nearest to a non-stressful period that I can remember in our house. The aroma of food hit the spot and the radio soothed with its own diet of strangely britlove sounds. 'Oh, I love this one,' my mother would say as Ernest Luft stroked the clouds with 'Oh for the Wings of a Dove'.

Her voice would soar in ambitious unison, effortlessly matching Ernest note for note as she delivered the gravy boat to the table. 'All our family could sing,' she'd inform my father and me. 'We couldn't do much else but we all loved music. It was thought I'd have a career in music at one time … But I didn't have the chance did I, I had to work for a living. Then you came along and put paid to any plans I might have had in that direction.'

At first when this slow-burning accusation began its build, my dad would try and defuse the situation with a joke or a sympathetic rejoinder, but not wanting her platform taken, my mother would whirl her unwelcome bitterness at life's unfairness around her head and around the room.

By the age of ten, I knew these pronouncements of my mother's backwards, and I'd intone them under my breath along with her, counting down the seconds to when she'd be finished so I could listen to the Little Richard song on the radio properly, compassionately forgiving myself the ignoble act of being born with the fast-growing realisation that if I were Little Richard I wouldn't have to live here any more. And she'd be free to go and sing, too. And dad would have the house to himself without her berating him for some injustice or other that life had delivered her.

These kinds of personal confessions didn't last long, as Bowie soon left behind that very bloggy notion that just because you can say something with no filter you should. Even Bowie, obviously not publicity shy, but averse to directly revealing himself, fell for this new temptation before correcting himself, and reverting to the neutral, the chatty, the not really real.

We see Bowie having his version, or reporting it that way, of what others would have with him later – the sighting of something so extraordinary and so distant from your usual experience that it does make you wonder if these visions have arrived in your, in this case very English, very confined world, dominated by a cross, thin-skinned parent, as a flaming, precisely targeted sign of a way out. 'I could be like that . . . I don't have to be what my mum and dad are, I don't have to live where they live, and how they live.' Little Richard in this instance is the David Bowie for David Jones. Before Little Richard, it had been Acker Bilk, a smooth jazz clarinettist who could still make the pop charts after rock and roll arrived, first as a part of the late 1950s trad-jazz boom in Britain, and then in the early 1960s, because of the melody more than any jazz all but drained from the dream-lapping 'Stranger on the Shore'.

As soon as anyone heard Little Richard exclaim 'Awop bop aloo bop awop bamboom' it was obvious things were moving on from ballroom. For Davie, Little Richard shot into his life like a religious revelation – he remembered later, or it became part of the invented myth, that it was like 'I had heard God' – and here was a living, screaming solution to the reality that young people in the 1950s were not allowed to confront vocally or even consider. The idea that your parents, one or both, and family, and surroundings and traditions, could be the problem, and that the next stage of how your life was being organised for you, school, was also a problem of emotional and indeed intellectual confinement. To be a child was to be a slave, and to some extent that would never change even as you became an adult.

The immediate world around him at this time had been invented for him, or at least prepared for him, by his mother Peggy and his father Haywood Stenton Jones, who became known as John. David's religious background was a hybrid of Anglican, Catholic and Jewish, guaranteed to leave a few tangles in the mind.

Haywood's parents had died when he was very young, so he was raised by an aunt and in foster homes and children's homes, and he was thirty-five when David was born, not yet married to Peggy. That would come eight months after David arrived, because he was still in the process of divorcing the woman he had married in the 1930s, Hilda Sullivan. The course of love for many during those pre-war, war and post-war years was rough and chaotic, messed up and incoherent to mirror the unstable external world which was offering no template for order. Haywood had a child with his mistress during the war, Annette, but Haywood and Hilda took custody while their marriage was repaired. When Haywood left Hilda for Peggy, Annette stayed behind with Hilda who was unable to have her own children.

Peggy had two children before David – a son, Terry, born ten years before David, just before the Second World War in 1937, who spent his childhood being erratically and frustratingly handed around family members, and a daughter, Myra Ann, who was adopted outside the family. Terry was always a mystery to Davie. The word used at that time to describe someone like Terry was 'mental'. 'I was never quite sure what real position Terry had in my life, whether Terry was a real person or whether I was actually referring to another part of me.'

Bowie was born into a cracked, unsettled family, a mother and father meeting after a series of broken relationships, an older half-brother with aggressive mind-breaking problems not particularly embraced by his stepfather, an occasionally seen half-sister who lived with his father's ex-wife, and a half-sister who was nowhere to be seen, and who disappeared into another life. There were other barely mentioned members of the family being claimed in the middle distance by various institutions, an aunt on his mother's side rumoured to be lobotomised, one found aimlessly wandering the streets after being missing for some time, these unspecified problems deeply buried in confusion and denial at the time, problems with what were called 'bad nerves' being reduced to being whispered about or completely ignored. If it wasn't talked about, it didn't exist. There was so much darkness in and around; the search was on to find some light. Was there a curse on his mother's side, of madness and beauty that he was inheriting?

Both parents were smokers, at a time when smoke was everywhere inside the home and outside, as if it was the norm, and smoke was a natural part of being human and social. The house would have been filled with smoke, and Mum and Dad would drift into their own dimension made up of smoke and their own thoughts. It was inevitable that Davie would inherit the love of the cigarette, an easy way to lose yourself, and deflect attention, dragging deep on this convenient life-giving essence. It created a certain regularity and structure to the day that otherwise might lack any coherence. It was an instant, cheap, shop-bought disguise you could slip into anytime and anywhere. Once it is in a house, it invades the space, it creeps into the curtains and sets up camp, where it never leaves. Davie would take the smoke with him for most of the rest of his life, whatever other changes there were. The first cigarette he has is a menthol one on top of the 410 bus going to school; it was, he said, a rite of passage into adulthood.

Bowie's dislocated family was made up by halfs, steps, illusions, the unreliable, the insecure, outcasts, ciphers, refugees, the mad and the missing. Do those spaces, dissolves, handovers, erasures, degraded rituals, insinuations and vagrant, transient connections contribute to a certain psyche, one that adapts easily to roaming, that expects – even needs – situations to change, to slip somewhere else, become something else, leaving behind rumours, ghosts and hints of other worlds that never fully materialise that you can still cultivate and explore in your imagination?

Was there something in this particular, irregular family environment, a series of absences as much as stubborn conflicts, that produced an effect that first sparked something in his imagination? From a struggle to deal with tension, laid over standard 1950s routine and habit, and that inflexible formality of the times, and from an escape, a release, into the one space where he could control things around him, and create characters that were out of reach, all his very own?

David Jones's father seemed both absent and present, close but distant. 'He tries so hard to understand me,' Bowie will say in a 1968 interview about a newly observed 'Restless Generation', a 'classless pop free-for-all', with a 'heroes of our time' subtitle. He despairingly articulates generational differences in a way that would be expected in the late 1960s: 'His upbringing was so different we can't communicate. He and all his friends were in the army during the war – an experience I can't imagine – and he takes naturally to iron discipline. Discussing religion embarrasses him, and to get emotional about something, well that's only fit for the servants' quarters, like mental illness.'

Thin, compact, tidy, he was there, in the house, but very much in his own space, someone who seems so much a man of his English time, the reserved, troubled middle-aged man – this was pre-pop culture, when middle age seemed planted firmly in your late thirties and early forties – who had no method of expressing his internal workings, apparently no desire to, and certainly never did, definitely not in front of the children. Expression of his desires, lusts, appetites, reckless energy was obvious in his behaviours and his relationships, but day to day, he would be the classic quiet man, withdrawn to the point of vagueness, but with a definite edge sharpening the atmosphere at home, perceiving it as some sort of weakness to talk to his son about anything deep and emotional.

He is accepting his role, and in this story, his role, along with his wife and her dull, dulled mind, which would come to haunt and embarrass her son, is to be a parent of David Bowie. All of the rest of his life disappears behind that one thing. Apart from his position as the father of David Bowie he is barely perceptible, a closed book.

He realises that he has been given a character that can never particularly break out of the background, never explain his dreams, and so he plays the role accordingly, appearing when he does without giving anything away about his deeper personality. There is no point. He is background detail, lost in thought, drifting through the smoke of his life, spied as little more than a frown and a fixture, preoccupied with what remains unknown. He is given very few lines.

David Bowie would mention in one of those interviews where he added a little pointed detail to those dimly lit early times that he could never, ever talk to his father, as much as he loved him. Being emotional together was simply not going to happen. Bowie describes a world that many teenagers in that period that extended from the Fifties right through the Sixties and Seventies would recognise – the sanctuary that their bedroom became, the limits of their very own world, with the outside world beyond beginning as soon as they left behind the safety and personal contents of their room. 'It really was my entire world. I had my books up there, my music up there, my record player. Going from my world upstairs onto the street, I had to pass through this no-man's-land of the living room, you know, and out the front hall.'

David Jones would be one of those teenagers building a complete world in their bedroom, connected closely to a swiftly blossoming imagination, which they would eventually transfer into the outside would. It was as though the intention was to turn the outside world into a vast, active version of the music, books, magazines, pictures, dreams and ambitions that filled the precious bedroom.

Men like Haywood in that limbo time after the war and before the loosening of ties that came later considered it to be a failure as a man to allow their children to see any vulnerability, spontaneity or even particularly enthusiasm. They were taking their responsibilities seriously, or at least making sure it seemed that way. Even the taking of a holiday, the pursuit of family pleasure, was treated as though parenting was effectively a strict job. You set an example by displaying almost a resigned acceptance of your fate, resigned to being not fully alive, softened by regular holiday time attempts to add a little enforced colour and excitement.

This dampened, inherited idea of how a father should behave, rooted in discipline and natural hierarchy, a basic British notion of knowing your place even in the privacy of your own home, meant that men like Haywood were strangers to their children, even as they lived with them and were more or less the closest human being to them. David's proximity to this person he loved most who was also so inscrutable and secretive, a mystifying, unknown and unknowable alien in a humdrum human body, must also have mingled with his bedroom existence and become an influence on his imagination. His father couldn't help but loom large, however cut off, preoccupied, elsewhere, and become a big part of those early influences that recommended which way to go, and which way not to go.

The strong implication was that as a person Haywood was more than he seemed to be, that he was hiding his real self, essentially playing a character. He had other things on his mind at all times, but would never let on what those things were. Was he solving some deep mystery, possibly what had happened to his life, his missing relatives, with the appearance of a clipped, unflappable metaphysical detective being played, ironically, by a very sensible and inconspicuous seeming but actually obscurely apocalyptic Bing Crosby?

Like his mother his father once flirted with the notion of becoming a singer. As an idol, in the way your parents can be early on, and in a world where rock and roll heroes had not yet quite arrived into your teens, Haywood would have been subconsciously analysed by David for clues about how to behave and how to fit into the world. This awkward, repressed, apart English presence would have been something either to follow, or contradict, or both. He would try to shake it off, but also accept it was part of him. Very quickly as well, once rock and roll arrived, bringing with it new feelings of freedom, that subdued, serious 1950s Englishness would look out of this world, and Bowie with this 1950s sensibility lingering in his character could look as out of this world when he was stripped of all performance paraphernalia as when he was in full dress-up mode. His very being, coming from this intermediary zone, when modernism was almost quaintly in place, had an alienated, courtly otherness, and that accent, even when it was apparently his own, seemed like someone using a disguise.

Other flickering, fictional-seeming details emerge of the street outside young David's bedroom and first house in Brixton, made up of mostly recently arrived Jamaicans, with some Irish interlopers. Dad Haywood doesn't have a particular job for a while, and seems on the edges of near show business, owning 'a sort of club for wrestlers' until drink nearly ruins him, and he takes a steady job in public relations at the Dr Barnado's Homes children's charity. (This mix of working in promotions for a famous children's organisation that historically cared for abandoned children and orphans is an intriguing mix of a Victorian atmosphere – Fagin's gang – and the modern media.) He worked in Stepney Causeway, the East End area where Thomas John Barnardo opened his first home in 1866 for destitute young boys sleeping on the streets he would scour the local slums to find. His father would occasionally take David to work, and he would play with kids at the home, where he slipped into another state, easily imagining he could be one of these children, entirely on his own.

There wasn't much money, Bowie recalled. Mum also worked to make ends meet, as an usherette in a local cinema. It wasn't an easy life, in terms of money, or the ruptures inside the family. The family moved when David was six from eclectic Brixton, filled with department stores, theatres, cinemas, the lively markets increasingly serving black immigrant customers, but battered after the war having been substantially bombed. The Jones family left a few years before Brixton became a pre-eminent centre of Afro-Caribbean identity and culture in Britain, and made a would-be aspirational move to what Bowie would refer to as the 'crummy' part of Bromley but which was certainly separated from the unprecedented social changes erupting in Brixton. He changed schools, from a local infant's school in Brixton to an infant's school in Bromley. At school in Bromley, academic talents and a certain six-year-old determination to master things are noted, and a reputation as a bit of a scrapper standing up for his rights. There are attempts that fail to correct his left-handedness, because it suggested the sort of difference that wasn't allowed.

Brixton, for all its hard times and its thriving new community, noisy night life, close links to central London, could feel like it was at the centre of something. Bromley, also devastated during the war, birthplace of H. G. Wells, was further to the south-east, nine miles and half an hour by train from central London, and with much more of a feeling of being at the boring, featureless far edge of things, stuffed with genteel, uniform homes all seeming to be hiding something behind very English mostly closed curtains. That Englishness was a curdled combination of the nondescript and the intense.

Photos of Bromley in the 1950s, inevitably in black and white, have the quality of reflecting a town that was only staging reality; there was not enough going on for it to appear a convincing reality, and no sign that anything in particular was going to happen, apart from more of the same. It was one of those locations at the far reaches of a big city where you will always be trying to work out where you are. You could easily feel marooned.

All that amassed evasion and the post-war concussion, the attempts through controlled homeliness to create comfort after the catastrophe, makes the Bromley where David Jones heads towards his teens a classic example of a culturally weightless place where everyone seems to be doing the same thing, eating the same food, watching the same programmes on television and listening to the same music. Perversely, it would have seemed an alien world crammed with the trivial, perfect for his adored but alien father trying to keep out of trouble, but there would have been a motivation for young David to find shelter, a personal space, that was as far removed as possible from this insignificant in-between town. The question of course was not really was there life on Mars, but was there life in places like Bromley, so distant from the centre of things it might as well be millions of miles in outer space. The blandness forces the imagination into new areas.

The family moved two more times to places they could afford inside Bromley in the next four years, ended up in a house in Plaistow Grove that Davie lived in for ten years until 1965. As they moved, nothing really changed other than a deepening of their domesticity, as though his father, the existential nowhere man par excellence, was interested only in escaping scrutiny from outside forces. He was craving invisibility and illegibility, concealing himself inside an unremarkable nowhere in order to avoid anyone or thing getting inside his inner being. Wherever you went in Bromley, you were not coming across a new sort of meaning, and any independence you found was minimal and ultimately temporary. The moves his family made were the pre-Bowie beginnings of his travels; a getting used to the idea of being on the margins, but on the move, looking for something just around the corner.

A rock and roll song, a book, a film, a comedian, flashy clothes, the thought of doing something like that for himself, a basic, elemental relieving of boredom, was how meaning would be created in his empty, actually creepy world, how this repetitive, placid nowhere was ultimately humanised through an incorporation of outside glamour. He was lost in this place that was both uncertain and made up of assumed certainties where beliefs and enthusiasms seemed suspended, during those years just before when popular culture became where more and more people would find their attachments and get their bearings in an increasingly complex world. He would become a pioneer in the interpretation and exploitation of popular culture not least because he was at the right age to grow up with it as it spread around the world.

His mind was becoming vividly impressionable in response to an urge he felt for his life to be made to mean something. There is no official sign or sighting, apparently no confession anywhere, that suggests where this urge came from, which means for any sense of those origins we are looking to his withdrawn father, his difficult, disturbed, but quick-witted half-brother more than implying that madness is the only true freedom, and the suspiciously quiet, uneventful streets of Bromley, coexisting with nowhere in particular.

The nowhere place settled into his mind as an everywhere place; all his songs were more or less set in a nowhere filled with characters adrift in a meaningless but potentially dangerous media landscape where nothing can be known for sure, a territory that he began exploring and defining for himself in Bromley. You would have to believe in something else.

To David Jones, the simmering normality and the unknowable, downtrodden inhabitants of Bromley submerged in the everyday would have been really weird; what those occupants would have considered weird was to David his necessary establishment of the normal. He started to work out what his normal was, based on the clues that were making their way into places like Bromley on the radio and television and in newspapers, reacting to how his father was, how his mother behaved, the intermittent sightings of his half-brother.

The forced creation of a home didn't make a home for David; he found his home in the imagination, where there were no limits, and certainly nothing that resembled all the identical nothing that surrounded him in Bromley. His imagination could turn the plain local shops into something poetic, because they had a suppressed difference, a sense they contained something else, from the outside.

He was free to speculate in an area so neutral it could abruptly mutate into something else; it was not fixed, it was adaptable, it was waiting for something to happen, and even though those that lived there were not interested in sudden change, after a war that changed everything, there was a sense you could make up your next move, a change in your circumstances, in a place that was so fluid and so open because it was so blank. Bromley would not have turned the young Davie Jones on but something struck him about how the place, because time had apparently stood still and space was so unfixed, could adapt itself to different circumstances. Surely there was so much that needed to be filled in, and surely so much would soon arrive to fill in the blanks.

The blanks of who David Bowie is before he was David Bowie begin to get filled in more with details that blur between fiction and the known facts, and more details that become fact the more he mixes with other boys on their own journey away from their isolation inside Brixton and Bromley. At three, he's caught by his mother seeing what happens to his face when he uses some of her make-up. She tells him he looks like a clown. This sounds fantastic to a three-year-old.

He's four. We know something, a fantasy, the truth, a bit of both, about Davie Jones at four, because in 1968, during his most innocent of periods, when the would-be rock star dabbling in Buddhism and being taught mime by an acquaintance of Marcel Marceau had all but given up on the seedy obviousness of fame and retreated into a sort of childlike hippie family life, he wrote a song called 'When I'm Five'. It's the Beatles' 'When I'm Sixty-Four' in reverse. He sings it like a child pretending to be an adult pretending to be a child, which is as creepy or as charming as that sounds. He's clearly thinking about his boyhood home when he writes it, plaintively, or just because it suits the Beatles-inspired childhood refracted through the prism of the Summer of Love, happy-go-lucky mood he's in, or plausibly acting out, at the time.

He's four and wanting so much to be five, which at four seems a lifetime away. How will he ever get there? It's his most immediate ambition, a way that he can change who he is, and become someone else, almost an adult, someone who can deal more successfully with a chaotic, confusing world around him, where grown-ups walk too fast. He's in a hurry to grow up. He's had a bad day, because Raymond kicked his shin. He gets headaches in the morning. He fell and cut his knee. Daddy shouted loud at Mummy and he dropped his toast. But Bonzo licked his face and made it tickle.

When he's five he can wash his face and hands all by himself. He can chew tobacco and spit it out like his Grandfather Jones. He can read the magazines in his mother's drawer. He can go to school in August, if he's good. He will eat a butterfly and it won't make him sick. He will jump in puddles and laugh in church and marry his mum and let his daddy do the washing-up. He sees a photo of Jesus and asks him if he will make him five. Please make me five, Jesus. Only Jesus at the time seemed to have the power required. He wants so much to change, to become this incredible other person, five, for things to change, and make sense.

He's falling over a lot, and scraping the skin off his knees. His body seems out of his control sometimes. He cracks a mirror, and sees himself fragmented into hundreds and thousands. He's singing carols on the streets of Bromley at the age of six or seven raising two guineas – two pounds and two shillings – for the Bromley Blind Club. Some people paid money to hear David sing for the first time.

He discovers the power of illusion watching his older brother doing coin tricks, making them disappear. He did it for Davie on his own, but then he would do it for others, and Davie couldn't believe their faces. Terry was tricky, and he'd tricked them. It gave him a kind of power inside the erratic static of his madness.

Davie loses a tooth, and puts it under his pillow. The next morning, the tooth has gone, and there is a shiny sixpence there instead. The tooth fairy has visited. The world is truly full of magic. Life is a bag of tricks you carry with you.

He's playing the recorder at school with a little ability, singing anonymously in the Burnt Ash Junior School choir, inspiring his teacher in a dance class at the school to remark, as if seeing years ahead, on his unusual, artistic movements and astonishing poise. Some rock and roll singles were delivered into the house by his dad, American singles lifted from a jukebox once their use was apparently over with no centre, just a hole an inch or so wide in the middle of the label. Asked to select a few he wanted, he found himself listening to the Platters, Fats Domino and his most dramatic of saviours, Little Richard. In a world where these sorts of sounds and groups were few and far between, their appearance inside a small house pressed inside an ordinary street in Bromley would have been momentous.

Terry returns from doing service in the RAF when Davie is about ten, and he is miserable, crying for no reason. He slumps into an almost vegetable state. He begins having psychiatric help, and then eventually he disappears, into the home he would stay in for the next few years. No one can get through to him. Davie is still not sure he even exists outside his head. He disappears for years, and then turns up out of the blue, distressing his mum – she would think he'd died, a long, long time ago.

Davie's thirteen, and collecting obsessions, stretching out to wherever an outside world materialises. His dad buys a short-wave radio primarily for listening to music. The radio makes international communication possible and, eager for information and new cultures, David tunes the dial, scanning for unusual signs of life. Suddenly, China and Australia are within reach, signals bouncing off the atmosphere and returning to earth on the other side of the planet. You can hear people thinking. It's as though he is at the controls of his own research and development centre. There's the scientific quality to the equipment, knobs, wires and dials standing out in a very non-gadget-era house, and also an art to tuning it in.

He finds the US Armed Forces in Germany transmitting broadcasts of American football games, gets hooked on the hypnotic nature of how the results sound and the photos he finds of the glamorous team uniforms, with their over-sized shoulder pads that seem to a Bromley boy designed in almost atomic age proportions. It was a far-fetched passion at the time, but American football has a coded bizarreness that excites his curiosity, particularly intensified through the magical qualities of the short-wave radio.

He develops a late-night habit of listening to every game he can. This is only the beginning of his campaign. He studiously writes to anyone he thinks might be able to help him get more information – the US Embassy and the US Naval Forces in Europe building in Grosvenor Square, Mayfair – and the polite, earnest enthusiasm in his letter gets him the magazines he requested but also an invitation to the embassy with his dad; it's a little bit of jaunty pro-American propaganda at a time of deepening Cold War tension between the US and Russia.

He's given a tutorial in the very un-English rules of American football, distantly related to rugby, which he explains he plays at school, as a scrum half, an equivalent of a quarterback. To his delight he is given some equipment donated by a local air force base, including those fetching shoulder pads which David possibly likes as much for how they excitingly extend his body as for their actual function. A photo makes the local *Bromley & Kentish Times* in November 1960 of a serious-looking but very composed David Jones in school uniform and tie wearing the pads and holding a football helmet. They look like some steampunk version of an astronaut's spacesuit. In his first piece of press coverage David is described as leading a revolution, even if it is a 'sports revolution'.

This is at about the time Elvis is in Germany serving in the 3rd Armored Division, drafted in 1958 at twenty-two and chosen as the ultimate symbol of the newly transformed teenager to help remake the image of the military and become an ambassador of American culture. It tamed him, made him respectable, but pushed him into the centre of American popular culture. American culture is getting to young British people and galvanising them in all sorts of ways, as though American design and sound supplies the answers to what seems so humdrum at home.

A few years before, David sees a cousin get up and dance to 'Hound Dog' by Elvis Presley, and what occurs to him more than anything is not necessarily the song, or the sound, or the voice, as astonishing as they all are, but the fact that his cousin was uncharacteristically being moved by something, and being moved to move. At eight or nine he's considering it a genuine possibility he could move people in the same way, or at least an anecdote was created decades later that generated such a perfect little memory of a cocky little schoolboy setting his sights on something out of this world. 'I'll be the greatest rock star in England. I just made up my mind.' This might, though, have been the average thought that an average young boy was having at that moment, and not necessarily a sign he was actually going to try and become that.

It's not all America. Elvis and Little Richard get tangled up in a potent European dream. He's fourteen and he is watching Robert Wiene's silent classic *The Cabinet of Dr. Caligari*, one of the founding creations of German expressionist film, influenced by German expressionist painting and itself an influence on the whole genre of horror, all the way to Davids Cronenberg and Lynch.

Filled with distorted sets, crooked buildings and twisted land-scapes lacking any right angles, expressing the distorted mind of the narrator where even daylight is darkened, most of the film was a flashback, which then includes flashbacks within the flash-back. The story in the flashback was created by an inmate in an insane asylum. Davie will see in this movie the world as a mad person might see it, warped, confused and unbalanced, and there is no definitive ending, nothing is as it seems right to the very end. It's not entirely clear where sanity ends and the madness begins.

He is getting a peek as though through a peephole into Terry's mind, and he's horrified and fascinated. He will never forget Dr. Caligari, the mysterious, menacing carnival man, the drunkenly askew streets and buildings, the make-up on the sleepwalking fortune teller, the unnerving predictions of death. Perhaps he saw it too young, perhaps he saw it at exactly the right time, when he was looking for answers to questions about madness, and how you spot the signs. He will never escape its shadows, and the light it threw on the darkness of the mind on the way from turning from boy into man, as he went through the change.

We now know, though, or can imagine, that there was a difference about this boy. He wasn't going to be average for long. The world was moving too slowly for him; his mind was so fast, like it was from the future, where things moved faster, and stimulation and simulation happened all the time from all directions. More than just another kid dreaming of becoming the south London version of the trailblazing American rock and roll stars flinging flashy entertainment explosions over into British life, he actually wanted the world to go faster. The older he got, the faster he wanted it to go. He didn't care for a while how fast it went and how dangerous that became, just as long as it was faster than it had been around Bromley. He's looking for the part of his education he never got.

He starts buying records, which will lead to the biggest expansion of the context of his life, a rapid intensifying of the sparking contact between his isolated imagination and the imaginations of others. Fortunately, Bromley of all places has a great record shop, almost planted there for his own use, where he can make his detours into other worlds, and in 2003 he would look back in wonder. Listing his then current favourite twenty-five albums for *Vanity Fair*'s November edition, which ranged from Linton Kwesi Johnson to Igor Stravinsky, he goes back to Bromley via Charles Mingus, and the place where he started to find wonderfully different music:

In the early Sixties, Medhurst's was the biggest department store in Bromley. In terms of style, they were to be pulverised by their competitors down the road, who stocked up early on the new, 'G-Plan' Scandinavian-style furniture. But Medhurst's did have, unaccountably, a fantastic record department, run by a wonderful 'married' couple, Jimmy and Charles. There wasn't an American release they didn't have or couldn't get. Quite as hip as any London supplier. I would have had a very dry musical run were it not for this place. Jane Greene, their counter assistant, took a liking to me, and whenever I would pop in, which was most afternoons after school, she would let me play records in the 'sound booth' to my heart's content till the store closed at 5.30 p.m. Jane would often join me, and we would smooch big-time to the sounds of Ray Charles or Eddie Cochran. This was very exciting, as I was around thirteen or fourteen and she would be a womanly seventeen at that time. My first older woman. Charles let me buy at a huge discount, enabling me to build up a fab collection over the two or three years that I frequented this store. Happy days. Jimmy, the younger partner, recommended this Mingus album one day around 1961. I lost my original Medhurst copy, but have continued to re-buy the print through the years, as it was re-released time and time again. It has on it the rather giveaway track 'Wham Bam Thank You Ma'am'. It was also my introduction to Roland Kirk.

He finds new things that he can love, and imitate and fantasise about, and increases knowledge of things he starts to find exciting. He is hungry for information as though he perceives that this is a kind of protection. He finds more and more things in this emptied landscape that appeal directly to his mood. These finds are not the property of everyone else around him; it's not anything of interest to the strange elders that offer few clues about the future, only their constant version of a spiritless present.

David Bowie in later interviews refers to David Jones, in this weird conflation of how it was, how it has been decided, and how it has been replayed many times, as passing his eleven-plus examination, and not attending the more traditionally minded, academically orientated Beckenham Grammar School but the Bromley Technical High School for Boys. Here is a fork in the path mentioned many times, as though taking the grammar school path and a more conventional reflection of budding intelligence would not have yielded a David Bowie.

The Technical School was still a regimented, scholarly school requiring a uniform and organising internal competition between various houses, teaching pupils in what would seem archaic and mechanical ways to someone already tuned in to rock and roll, cinema, radio and television. The school was still in what Davie would call the posh part of town, always clinging to the 'credible for a working-class pop musician' notion that he didn't belong to posh.

By the third year, the school split the boys into various streams; languages, technical engineering and, even though it was deemed to be for the 'losers', art, with coverage remaining in maths and physics. This emphasis on art was perfect for someone with a mind growing like Davie's. His courteous and inspirational art teacher, smartly turned out and partial to neat brown suede shoes, Owen Frampton, in his early forties, known by his loyal pupils as Ossie but not to his face, and the incongruous, tolerant department he helped run was also perfect for Davie. Frampton helped widen his interests beyond art and drawing to graphic design and typography, further enriching his imagination. He was getting a thorough, modern arts school education in his mid-teens, years ahead of most others his age.

Right after the war, where he had served as a gunner in North Africa and Italy, Frampton taught lithography, painting, ceramics, design and printing at Beckenham Technical School while in the evenings studying himself at Beckenham School of Art. His post-war appetites were committed to the idea of educating the next generation in challenging pursuits that were more or less the exact opposite of going to war. The skills required to master them would be considerably more romantic and constructive. Education could be about joy, and change. It could move things forward by looking forward when so much about formal education is dominated by repeating information and systems from the past.

Frampton stimulated a passion for design in his students by getting them to work on things they would be interested in – book covers, record sleeves, posters, TV titles, film credits, packaging, and fabric. The selling of product, sometimes even the selling of mundane, everyday items, was being transformed into a flamboyant, exciting dream, instant, accessible works of art that were far more relevant and powerful than what was in the galleries and museums, and Frampton spotted this and encouraged his students to observe and exploit it. It didn't matter if for a while the traditional was treated with contempt; the traditional would disappear if there wasn't the creation of something new that gave the past something to connect to. The war had demolished thoughts of the future; there was inevitably going to be an incredible desire to recapture a sense of purpose, which would take shape as a desire for progress, for the new.

The one thing that is leading to another and then another in an increasingly pulsating imagination as David Jones moves into the brightening, broadening 1960s is particularly accelerated while learning under Frampton, whose mind moved quickly and covered a lot of ground across art and design. For someone needing to find a new framework to make sense of the modern world, even if he didn't know it, a teacher like Frampton was perfect, a life-changer, even a lifesaver. Even someone quickly affecting a cool demeanour like Davie was in constant need of influential older figures in his life.

Davie was a couple of years older than his art teacher's son, Peter Frampton, who asked him once when Davie was about fourteen what he was listening to. This was just before the arrival of the Beatles. 'Buddy Holly,' he replied. He taught Peter some Buddy Holly songs. Along with his school friend George Underwood, the three of them would sit around on the steps at school sharing two guitars playing Eddie Cochran and Buddy Holly, nerdy chums on the verge of discovering other wilder needs. Peter Frampton would later become a pop star, and then a rock star selling millions of albums in America, as if it was that easy to walk out of colourless Bromley and into rock history.

Bowie's confident enough in his own abilities to take a ukulele to skiffle sessions with his friends, to slap a tea-chest bass knocked together at home out of an old wooden broom and tea chest and slowly pick out unorthodox chords at a piano, already developing his love for strange chords. This group of Bromley teenagers quickly copy early British skiffle acts like Lonnie Donegan, the Vipers and the City Ramblers, which were the first to respond to the over-there-coming-over-here sound of rock and roll, creating the first commercially significant pop music genre in the country. The no-nonsense, happy-go-lucky Englishness of this relieved response to rock and roll, rooted in high-spirited British folk and the lively trad-jazz boom more than the mystifying blues, made it a more accessible route into covering this irresistible new music. It would be described as the punk music of its time in the way it encouraged a lively, rough-and-ready do-it-yourself quality that achieved the ultimate aim of inspiring youngsters to think for themselves and organise into new gangs of curious creative musicians capable of composing their own music.

Hordes of teenagers found a way into making music having never previously thought of it as a serious occupation, blocked by formalities, institutions and limited access to the concept of music as a real, intimate pleasure directly relevant to their lives. Another detail that has the quality of something planted back in time by some ghostly force because it seems exactly the type of detail that is required at this point in the story was when Davie was about eleven. A report exists of a skiffle show he performed with George around the campfire at his local Scout camp visit to the Isle of Wight and in this review he is described as 'mesmerising ... like someone from another planet'. This early review contains suspicious hints of most other reviews he would receive in his life once he was truly up and spinning as David Bowie.

He dreamed of owning a saxophone, an unusual instrument for a twelve-year-old to choose, but a raging early ambition was to be a horn player in Little Richard's backing band. Brother Terry, a fluctuating, fractured mind flickering in and out of the plot, in and out of the smoke, had also introduced him to modern jazz by Charlie Mingus and John Coltrane. For a tender, jumpy mind, such music could seem soothing, make sense in how it circles and chases and sometimes catches up with the crazy meaning of things.

After much pleading, his willing dad bought him a particularly flash-looking creamy-white Bakelite Selmer with glamorous gold keys on hire purchase for a few shillings a week. Davie paid him back delivering meat for the local butchers. Later, rearranging his past into the correct order, or another order altogether, searching for the best story to tell about his malleable past, he claimed he bought the sax after reading Jack Kerouac's *On the Road*, as if he could easily wander into the same world just by playing jazz. 'I wanted to be like Sal Paradise and Dean Moriarty, and I succeeded as much as anyone could in a dump like Bromley.' The saxophone is the wide open spaces of America, symbolising trips into its vastness made up on the spur of the moment, jazz music as the spontaneous creation of a map of a better America. For David the horn was something he could put in his mouth, close his eyes, and drift into another place.

Eight lessons came with the sax paid for by his parents, and he stuck at it. He was taught in nearby Orpington by Ronnie Ross, one of his favourite jazz saxophonists whose number he claimed he found in the phone book and simply called up. A fan of Johnny Hodges and a hard-working professional tenor sax turned baritone player who had appeared at the Newport Jazz Festival in

1958, Ross had worked in the Ted Heath Big Band, backed Cleo Laine, formed a quintet called the Jazz Makers who released a 1959 album called *The Swingin' Sounds of the Jazz Makers*, and would guest on a tour with the Modern Jazz Quartet. There is a rare record from 1958 where he played with John Lewis of the MJQ and the Stuttgart Symphony Orchestra. One critic once said if it wasn't for Gerry Mulligan, Ronnie would have been the best baritone sax player in the world.

Ross got Davie to play when they met up, and told him 'that was bloody awful. Let's start working on you'. The very keen David Jones was impressed by this first contact with a versatile, stylish and professional musician, and it is one of the first sightings of where he would work with someone who helped him and he would use them again as part of an ongoing, constantly evolving collage of collaborators and sidekicks. Ronnie turned up later – after a fleeting cameo on 'Savoy Truffle' from the Beatles' *White Album* – playing the beautiful baritone sax solo at the end Lou Reed's 'Walk on the Wild Side' that David Bowie produced. The sound materialises on this evocative, deadpan tribute to temperamental New York bohemianism like a wispy ghost from another time and place altogether, like a lesson that David Jones once had in a cramped front room behind listless lace curtains in motionless Kent. It's the oblique signature of Bowie. Ronnie finds it hard to believe that the Davie Jones he taught is now David Bowie.

Early sightings of Davie photographed in quickly formed, quickly disbanded groups a few years later show him knowing the right way to handle a saxophone so it looked like he knew what he was doing, and already knew how to turn a pose. Few others would have thought to study how a sax player threw shapes while they played, but he needed to know, he needed to look the part as well as being able to blow.

The listening to records and learning to play – and casually hold – the saxophone is where a mark can be established that anticipates the beginning of an interest in an energy that would lead to the end of Davie Jones. The offbeat, unusual energy captured on records heading into his bedroom from unknown places a little more riveting than basic Bromley, gives him a clear view of who he could and must be. Learning an instrument, and not necessarily what everyone else is learning, becomes a part of the process, of finding and mastering his tools.

Old worlds are being safely destroyed by these new sounds and words that are preparing the way for a radical new environment. The old categories of thought that were dominant in 1950s England, crystallised for Bowie in Bromley, where the world so far had been flat, would be an encumbrance. Instinct drives Davie towards an appreciation of the details and potentials of this new environment that seems to be running in parallel with his own entrance into teenage years; he becomes a teenager in 1960, so a whole new decade, the light of the '6' replacing the gloom of the '5', ushers in unstoppable change.

There is a sense of how certain schoolboys around the nation in the years after National Service finally stopped calling up new recruits in 1960 – helping those Sixties to rapidly change as seventeen-year-old lads were no longer required to give compulsory service and had plenty of time on their hands – and those not either part of the upper classes or trapped in poverty were having very similar school experiences. At least, the stories of secondary and grammar school boys visiting their careers masters and telling stories of woe as their wilder but often deadly serious ambitions were instantly winnowed down, misunderstood or just plain ignored are very common.

Many born in the years after the end of National Service will recognise David Jones's story. He is asked by the careers adviser what he is planning to do after he leaves school. By now, his head has expanded, his fanciful imagination developing an egotistical crust, and he replies that he wants to be a saxophonist in a modern jazz quartet. Having had some lessons with world-travelling Ronnie Ross, listening to New York jazz with his mercurial but supportive half-brother, this wasn't as far-fetched an ambition as it might seem in a dull Bromley classroom. The careers teacher strips back all the details that make it improbable and in his experience totally impossible, and breaks this down to a desire to have a career in music, which would therefore mean in some selling or factory work. The suggestion he made was to become an apprentice in a local factory making harps.

Owen Frampton enjoyed teaching David Jones. He remembered in an unpublished memoir that 'whatever the necessary ingredients are to produce vintage school years, they must have been mixed in exactly the right proportion in the years 1960–66'. He recalls – 'of course' – David Jones and his friend George Underwood. Suddenly, a fixed moment of a near real-life character vibrating between David Jones the schoolboy and the David Bowie he was heading towards, the young boy beginning his rehearsals for later incarnations. Frampton describes his already unusual pupil, clearly one of his favourites, as being unpredictable, and beyond the understanding of his less flexible teaching colleagues at the school. He remembers Bowie even at fourteen as acting as though he was some kind of dominating cult figure. In the fast-changing 1960s, Frampton was already used to seeing the emergence of individualistic schoolboys, and unsurprised by the new ways they were finding to express themselves. He wasn't surprised, he concludes, when later Bowie dyed his hair and shaved his eyebrows. He could see it coming – here was a boy he realised had plenty of personality, and was craving for new ways to project it.

He had the tutor for the musical instrument, the school mates he could form skiffle groups and play records with, the mentor in the art of design and the marvels of collage, a half-brother to take him to the splintering edges of things, a father to issue enigmatic warnings about the threats of inner tension. He then found a teacher in style and the wearing of clothes that the Beatles, the Who, the Kinks, Small Faces and the Stones would fully distribute into a wider world three years later from a local mod called Leslie he travelled into London with on the train from Sundridge Park on Plaistow Lane, Bromley. (Oddly enough, my father's name was Leslie. You can imagine if this is an imaginary Philip K. Dick biography of David Bowie, *The Man of Many*, each person reads the name of their father when Bowie is calling up this particularly significant mentoring father figure.)

Davie had been originally intrigued but not convinced by the sight of some stray suburban Teddy boys displaying the working-class mid-Fifties high fashion of long drape jackets, tight drainpipe trousers, waistcoast and suede brothel creepers, with luminous green or pink socks and a Brylcreemed quiff. There was a local Ted in Bromley called Eric, a bit of a nutter, bright ginger hair, razor blades sewn into his lapels to repel potential attackers. He used to stand around on his own on street corners swinging a metal chain like a bear driven mad being caged in a run-down zoo.

By the late 1950s, certain adaptations of the look had led to the shortening of the jacket to bum-freezer length and the replacement of the creepers with sharply pointed winkle-pickers. The Teddy boy look was mutating into the modernist look as a reaction to what was becoming hackneyed, the greasy quiffs and winkle-pickers.

Leslie was one of those embryonic individualists emerging from working-class south and east London, most born at the end of or just after the war, belonging to no known or named group, who would then be called modernist, which would be shortened to 'mod' in 1962, and planted deep in the mainstream by 1964, the European existential element long discarded. Leslie's taste suited David more than the hammy, ageing Teds.

David Jones's mentor would put together clothes like a collage – the short tight Italian jackets with white linen trousers and bright pink socks with eye shadow to match and heeled Chelsea boots – and the highly absorbent David Jones saw no contradiction in setting out to copy this highly solo look, as much as he could on limited pocket money. The key was to stand out, not to disappear into the nowhere of Bromley, and possibly get trapped or turned invisible. If you stood out, then surely you always would.

Leslie also backcombed his short, soft hair a little into a bouffant and parted it in the middle, a little poncey, but David noticed that he was not actually effeminate. In fact, he was quite tough and looked like he was quite capable of looking after himself in any skirmish. Pastel eyeshadow, but hard. David loved the pirate 'jaggedness' of the two things being fastened together, the clear, fearless statement that Leslie was not one thing or another. He was both, and neither, unrealistic and totally realistic, and something else, something new. The modernists were dedicated to the idea of making a big entrance at their local clubs, displaying their dressed-up-to-the-nines aspirational arrogance through the sharpest, least duplicated aggregate of short tailored jackets, narrow trousers and chisel-toed shoes. They matched their affinity for dressing well with an intellectual hunger; a leaning towards the fashionably existential, a world where writers and philosophers were glamorously connected to movie stars and jazz musicians. There was an ego-driven desire to match the physical style with inquisitive mental smartness. A sharpness all round; in appearance, in the mind. Suits from Italy, reading from Paris.

Baggy, comic and creased British demob suits were rejected in favour of tight Italian tailoring coupled with a Hollywood zest. Confidence was being represented through clothing that had never belonged to any local war-torn adult. It was an exaggeration and alteration of conventional cut and drape, a flamboyant parody of formal adult clothes, a self-assured, pushy commandeering of a brand-new territory.

That early Sixties English world was as grey and lacking colour as is traditionally reported, and any new colours tended to be muted brutalist concrete merely complementing the existing dour brick, damp grey pavements and depressing slate roofs, gaudy signs of consumerism not yet running rampant on billboards and television. The colours there actually were, splashed over these new clothing daredevils, would have seemed even more vivid and enlivening. Here were brave beacons dressing on the edge of ridicule showing the way through the gloom into a bright beyond.

Davie Jones is right there in the early receptive part of his teens when one of the first youth tribe styles is forming. The dramatic, conspicuous strands of what became the pure pre-1964 mod look, feeding into all pop silhouettes that follow and regenerate, are coalescing around him as he falls in love with the promise of fashion. He has a front-row seat. He witnesses the changes and adjustments that are made quickly by those in the know to ensure they are always ahead, not part of the herd. As soon as they are caught and copied, they make a move into newness.

He takes an interest in girls, and not so much, it seems, boys, although he likes looking at what they wear, and isn't averse to issuing boasts to friends for the sake of an already developing character he fancies being that he is bisexual. Girls are more his thing though in the real world, and at fourteen he and best friend George are eyeing up the same pretty girl, Carol Goldsmith. George gets there first, and arranges to meet her at a local dance hall. Competitive David is not happy when he hears this, and manages to persuade George that she is not interested in him, far prefers David, accepted because she felt sorry for him, and is not going to turn up.

George finds out that she does turn up and waits for him for nearly an hour before giving up. The next day George hears underhand David gloat that he has stolen Carol from George and that she is now his. Furious, wanting to have it out with David who won't take the bait, confronting his self-serving tactics, a frustrated George abruptly and uncharacteristically punches David hard in the face. His knuckle lands in Davie's left eye damaging the iris sphincter muscles. The school is shocked, Owen in particular.

David is rushed to hospital, the eye is saved after weeks of treatment, but the injury leads to anisocoria, a relatively common condition that causes the pupils in each eye to be different sizes. In this case the pupil in David's left eye would not close after the trauma and a series of operations. In most people who have the condition, it is not as noticeable, just a slight difference in size. With David Bowie, the difference in size is pronounced, the left eye blotted out by darkness, giving the illusion that one eye is watery blue and the other dove grey, and for the boy who wanted to be different from anyone else, it became an internalised, physical manifestation of his imaginative vagrancy, an ethereal scar, a subtle but categorical distinction, something that set him apart as someone apart whenever he needed to look as though he was from somewhere else not of this ruined world.

George was mortified, but over the years David shrugged the incident off, the pair remaining friends, saying that George in fact did him a favour. He would joke that after it happened, he could sing better.

He is officially no longer average. He has a permanent romantic wound which also interferes with his depth perception, giving reality a cubist kick. He can safely feel different and anyone only has to look at him to see the evidence.

It embedded an indelible thread of fugitive originality in his appearance, giving him something he couldn't have got from anywhere else however hard he foraged. It worked as part of the overall effect when he was dressed up in fully costumed display, playing cold fish, secret agent of change or peripheral being, and it was still there when he was withdrawn, modest and undecorated. In fact it was almost more eerie when he was more or less off glam/alien duty. Even at his most ordinary-looking there was a tell-tale trace of the bizarre, the seductively off-centre, the unbalanced pupils explicitly the entrance and the exit of his fantastic imagination.

• • •

There was nothing left for Davie but to become part of a pop group, get to know what that means, precedents already being set around the country by restless school friends rapidly learning new chords, acquiring new instruments and techniques and moving on from the very limited – almost parodic – skiffle. Their groups had names intended to communicate something sharp, modern, stylish, tainted with American-ness, a bit Western outlaw, a bit beat, a bit Space Age, very much influenced by Buddy Holly's backing group and how the Crickets becomes an instant gang brand – there were the Searchers, the Echoes, the Viscounts, the Tornados, the Tremeloes, the Pacemakers, the Animals, there was instant English mischief – Dave Dee, Dozy, Beaky, Mick & Tich – and of course the sharp-suited Shadows and the early quick-witted signs of the Beatles, and first hints of a more abstract, poetic style with the Zombies and the Hollies.

In 1962, Davie Jones joined his first group, the Kon-rads, all sixteen and seventeen, formed by his close school pal George Underwood and Alan Dodds the year before. The name came from a pun on clean-cut singer and actor Jess Conrad, who played a dreamboat pop singer in a play, *Rock-A-Bye Barney*, and a TV series, *The Human Jungle*, and is then groomed by television producer and pop impresario Jack Good to actually be one for a couple of pre-Beatle years. Good was inspired by the scandal caused by Bill Haley's 'Rock Around the Clock' to start the first rock-and-roll shows on British television; he thought some of this new energy was perfect for TV. Good's dynamic new shows had helped launch the first English rock stars Marty Wilde, Billy Fury and Cliff Richard, but Jess made the soft-centred sweet English Elvis Cliff seem like piano-smashing rip-roaring Jerry Lee Lewis. His chart life is all over by 1962, not least because for all his good looks he had next to no voice. An early hint to Davie: get as much voice as you can, even though it might be too much for some.

Davie pestered George for months to let him into the Kon-rads.

George leaves, and he finally becomes the group's saxophonist and a backing singer after answering an advertisement in a local paper, possibly the only one who did. It was never Davie's group, and his attempts to jazz things up with distinctive Wild West outfits and sundry gimmicks including a fine kinky quiff, and an early name change for him to Dave Jay, were a little too ambitious for the rest of the group. Davie went for Jay in tribute to the sax-heavy instrumental beat group Peter Jay and the Jaywalkers, never much more than a cult outfit despite being produced by north London Phil Spector, Joe Meek, and supporting the Beatles. They were definitely on Davie's radar, and an obvious template for Kon-rad group photos.

A year of solid, low-key semi-pro activity in church, village and school halls performing largely covers of the Shadows, the Beatles, Dave Clark and Chris Montez and a limited sense of adventure was increasingly frustrating Davie, already hungry to experiment. He was looking to the hipper, more urgent Chicago blues sources that the Yardbirds and Rolling Stones were freely appropriating. The Konrads, finally losing the irritating hyphen, lacked his determination and resourcefulness, and, they were quick to admit, his definite canny charisma – certainly he had more than their main lead singer, and the kind of gifts that made girls pay attention even in the smallest venues. The rest of the group just wanted to play music, have a laugh, get girls, and he was constantly inundating them with ideas, designs, logos, possible musical directions and plenty of new images.

Davie started writing songs with guitarist Neville Wills so they didn't have to cover songs like Cliff's 'The Young Ones' but they mostly stuck to covering pop hits of the day. Davie would sing Joe Brown and the Bruvvers' recent hit 'A Picture of You' – and a favourite of John Lennon's at the time, due to some cracking haywire harmonica, American rockabilly singer Bruce Channel's 'Hey! Baby'.

Record labels desperate for new young talent led to an

audition at the Decca studios in West Hampstead in north-west London. The local Bromley paper was breathless with anticipation, but Bromley's pride and joy the Konrads with a lacklustre demo version of their own 'I Never Dream' failed to join the Jaywalkers – and the Rolling Stones and Tommy Steele – on Decca Records. But then the Beatles had also failed their audition for Decca at the same studio twenty months before – because guitar groups, according to Decca, were on the way out.

Davie didn't sing lead, but if he had done maybe the recording wouldn't have been wiped and we would have got to hear him singing at sixteen earnest pop words written by the group's guitarist, Alan Dodds, about never dreaming he would fall in love with someone whose eyes are, naturally, so blue. On his first ever recording, the first time he's in the recording studio, where most of the work we think of when we think of David Bowie is done, he's in the background, and then lost. Soon, by the end of the year, he's no longer in the Konrads.

He keeps moving through a pre-history period so classic even in its messiness it can seem scripted, a patchwork of false starts, half-hearted detours, close shaves, significant meetings, near misses, lost chances, and obscure collaborations. It's all very random, most of the details are mysterious, but you can see it in the photos he appears in at the time – the only true, unbendable facts, his off-centre eye damage setting him outside the obviousness of everything else – the confidence that demonstrates that he's making his way through it all like he is fully aware that some incredible end result is predestined. It's like he knows so much is in store for him, as though a ghostly part of his future has spun backwards and instilled in him some abstract knowledge. He knows somehow that he is gaining all the time. He just has to be patient or, perhaps, keep being completely impatient.

One thing for sure is that whatever this sixteen-year-old is up to as he becomes seventeen, and all around him pop music is making the world go faster and further in the minds of the young than it has ever done before, to the point of collective freak out, is that he is pulling himself out of Bromley, and moving further and further away from his parents and the incoherent family set-up they've landed him with. Day by day, discovery by discovery, catching up, wanting to keep up, opening up a new place to inhabit, of his own design, one that fits into the new pop-land, where he is finding art as much as entertainment, coming across instant concepts of love and sex, all of it taking place beyond the streets around him that lead nowhere but other places just like them.

The Hooker Brothers were Davie – possibly still calling himself Dave Jay – singing and playing some sax along with his old school pal George on guitar and vocals. They last only a few weeks, playing a summer season at the Bromel Club in the Bromley Court Hotel in Bromley Hill. They take in more blues, acknowledging John Lee Hooker by taking his name, and reach 'The House of the Rising Sun' the interesting long way via Bob Dylan who'd got there himself stealing a fair amount and dreaming it into another state of mind. They add drums to it, approving of their own genius, and then the Animals release their version, with drums, which makes the group, and Davie learns again he is not the only one on the prowl for difference and newness, and that it's not going to be a case of simply adding drums to achieve lift-off, and separation.

Sometimes they try to get other gigs as Dave's Reds and Blues, more giggling puns, and a little hint of mischief, taking in the blues they're studying and the colour of barbiturate pills. While he's part Hooker, part Konrad, part Jones, part Jay, part stray, he leaves school at sixteen with no qualifications except an O level in art courtesy of the nurturing Owen Frampton, who would also, as part of his caring for his boys beyond the call of duty, arrange interviews with a variety of contacts he had in London advertising agencies and art studios. When Davie told his mum his intention was to now become a pop star, she promptly responded by arranging a job as a down-to-earth electrician's mate.

Courtesy of Frampton, David Jones landed a job perhaps more suited in July 1963, as a trainee commercial artist/visualiser with Nevin D. Hirst Advertising agency in New Bond Street, London. His job was to prepare sketches and work on conceptual ideas for possible ad campaigns. The few months he spends doing this, never feeling comfortable at how his imagined, freewheeling artistic talents were being squandered in such a restrictive, commercial setting, also take on the aura of something set into the script because it would be great in this particular story if this is what happened. Years later, embedding this period further into the story, he mentions his boss Ian, 'a groovy modernist with Gerry Mulligan short-crop haircut and Chelsea boots, who was very encouraging about my love of music. He would send me on errands to Dobell's Jazz record shop on Charing Cross Road knowing I'd be there for most of the morning till well after lunch break.'

It is too perfect that the man who was to be defined by his ability to generate conceptual ideas and create campaigns intended to promote himself as pop star would spend time in an advertising agency. He would stick together images and bits of type and sketch out ways to sell product by placing one colour, shape and piece of text with another, and rehearse all sorts of ways of selling all kinds of product, coming to an understanding that everything and everyone is ultimately product, and that a pop singer and a pop group need an image, a presentation, a persuasive, alluring conceptual basis just like anything else that is bought and sold, to change the mind of a consumer and influence behaviour.

That there are no signs of any campaigns he might have contributed to or doodles of ideas suggests he probably made a lot of tea, did a lot of running about fetching and carrying and filing away hundreds of photographs for his superiors. He saw enough to pick up enough about how to structure a campaign and realise a concept, and enough to know that regular hours and office orderliness was not the life for him. But he gets a precious, practical inside look at the time advertising has become the aesthetic experience cultural theorists instantly diagnosed it as, and gets further education in how to make a name for yourself in a world changing because of mass culture.

After a few months of being somewhere else in the background, working out the coolest brand of cigarette to smoke, he is gone. Another shift in emphasis, another potential route dissolving like it was always meant to, and when the story is told always does.

The next group he is part of now takes priority. Rootlessness rather than the fixture of full-time work. He's back with George in the King Bees, and they take the name for this group from the debut 1957 single of a swamp blues singer from Los Angeles, Slim Harpo, which the Rolling Stones would cover in 1964 on their debut album and the pre-Pink Floyd the Tea Set record later that year. The insistent rhythm was triggered by country bluesman Lil Son Jackson's 1951 'Rockin' and a Rollin'', which in turn by asking to be rocked, all night long, raided decades of blues songs that were settling around the words 'rock' and 'roll' as a way of putting certain tremendous, inexplicable urges and energies into new streams of thought.

Slim could put on a lively show, and was commercially adept at blending rock and roll and country into his harmonica-stressed blues, and was a part of the stew of influences reaching not just the Stones but the Yardbirds, Van Morrison's Them and the Kinks. This was where Davie's instinctive trend-spotting mind was at the time, feeling that the blues, how it had splintered into rock and roll, and the spirited English transformation actually hitting the charts, was his best chance of finding a sound and landing a record deal.

Bowie still believed in writing letters as a way of getting things done. Asking for some investment in his group, he wrote to swashbuckling entrepreneur John Bloom, then making a controversial name for himself taking advantage of a law that regulated prices on British high street stores. Until 1964, and a new law motivated by his actions, all shops had to charge the same. 'In Russia,' he once said, 'the prices are set by the state. Here they are set by the establishment.'

A former door-to-door salesman and academic failure selling paraffin and kitchen goods, he used aggressive advertising to sell cheap twin-tub washing machines he had imported from a Dutch manufacturer called Klean direct to the public, to avoid the price regulations. He discovered the world of direct selling and heavy discounts, and changed the nature of shopping in the UK. It was the household convenience of the American Dream, taking drudgery out of the kitchen, making it to everyday Britain where in the early 1960s luxury items like fridges and vacuum cleaners were beyond the means of the average household.

Something in the idiosyncratic and inventive approach of Bloom, and his accidental invention of a modern, revolutionary way of selling, must have struck Davie. Maybe it was the new-fangled washing machine working wonders in their house thanks to Bloom. He told Bloom he could be the King Bees version of Brian Epstein 'and make another million'. He asked for a few hundred pounds for some new equipment to help 'one of the most talented up and coming new groups on the pop scene'.

Bloom failed to respond with any cash, but didn't totally ignore the cheeky approach, no doubt recognising a like-minded, rule-breaking opportunist. He hired the King Bees for his next wedding anniversary party – the group flopped, playing raucous, pretty tuneless post-Stones R & B to unimpressed, dressed-up dinner party guests. More usefully, he sent a telegram to Davie's home with the number of a friend, Leslie Conn, a talent scout for the Dick James Organisation, who published the Beatles.

At a time when nothing had yet settled down in British pop and no rules were established, responding as much to Davie's enterprise as anything, Conn made a quick, expedient decision that south London's King Bees were as likely to follow the Stones' take on the blues into the charts as anyone else. He started working with them, and his contacts were strong enough to get them the traditional West Hampstead Decca audition, and then actually a single deal.

It's obvious their debut record 'Lil Liza Jane' was recorded, A- and B-side, inside seven hours. It's described in a press release sent out at the time as a 'beaty, action packed disc which features the direct, no-holds barred Davie Jones vocal delivery'. Consider the Kinks were about to produce 'You Really Got Me' and the Animals 'The House of the Rising Sun', and the Beatles were already up to 'A Hard Day's Night', it sounds fairly roughshod with drums that need a good kicking, outside of the definite enthusiasm, rough charm and actual sheer delight that they are making a record. It sounds like seventeen-year-old pop fanatic Davie is thinking more of the Pretty Things than the Stones, but wraps his mouth around the word 'Jane' with full stylised Jagger force, a sort of fey fury. On the B-side, he's still in Hamburg, chasing John Lennon's shadow. These are the voices, faces and influences hemming him in at the time, the obvious copying of something that is itself an obvious if spunky copy. It's right that we hear Davie at this stage, to acknowledge how far back David Bowie actually goes into the history of British pop; he's in there as it is all coming together, but it's more interesting that he's present, watching, listening, preparing, than what he is actually doing.

Conn takes composing credit in time-honoured controlling management tradition, and superficially it's a crude, plain white English pillage of a blues song, but the song is an arrangement of something that contains its own murky, idiosyncratic history of popular music rooted in pre-Civil War minstrel shows where music was a means of channelling unruliness into a controlled spectacle. It is slave spiritual, folk song, dance game, evolving into a jazz standard, and a country blues, and eventually reaching Nina Simone. She absorbed and refracted all of this history in a 1960 version that was most likely to have inspired the King Bees, although they manage to not make it sound as fascinating as its long undulating journey through time and genre. They chucked it all into a throwaway garage version.

Davie as copywriter and self-mythologising cheerleader is designing himself with more flair in a press release sent out with the record, and showing a discrimination and self-assuredness, and wit, not appearing on the actual record. Bits of the collage he is making out of himself are already in place; to some extent he has still got to catch up with his roaming instincts. 'David's favourite vocalists are Little Richard, Bob Dylan and John Lee Hooker. He dislikes Adam's Apples, and lists his interests as Baseball, American Football and collecting boots. A handsome six footer with a warm and engaging personality, Davie Jones has all it takes to get to the show business heights including ... talent.'

The record disappears on or not long after its 5 June 1964 release, and so does this particular Davie Jones, quickly bored with following a quickly growing queue of British blues bands a little too solemnly acting like they're from the American Deep South, mocking up outrageous swagger and rubbing electric riffs into their skin as if this will make it darker. It's all too fake for him, and yet not fake enough. It doesn't allow enough for his mind to stretch as far as he believes it can, so far out that he doesn't just look like one of the crowd. He needs to find someone else to play, and others to play with.

He's so restless that a few weeks after he joins his next group on the recommendation of Leslie Conn, the Manish Boys, he is ready to move on again. An unwieldy, scruffy collection of average musicians from Maidstone in deepest ordinary Kent, the town's image indelibly stained by its infamous prison, Davie moves out for a while to rehearse and get to know them. Hard working above anything else, they embark on a thankless tour backing the American singer Britain took to its heart, Gene Pitney, and a small northern package tour in early December with Gerry and the Pacemakers, Marianne Faithfull and the Kinks that sets them outside their well-trodden backstreet south-east territory of hotels, youth clubs, halls and Soho clubs, up to theatres in Wigan, Hull, Newcastle and Edinburgh, finishing in the Futurist Theatre in Scarborough. These are areas and venues where David Bowie will later mount his final assault on heights of fame. For now, that's as far off as these broken cities up north seem from his southern home.

They're making no money, not least because there are seven of them, and are yet another south of England R & B gaggle eyeing the motivational impact of the Rolling Stones. There were close to a hundred new young blues groups in Greater London poring over imported records on the Atlantic, Chess and Sun label, which were used as tutorials in how and what to play. Most of them took their names from a blues song as though this sealed their authenticity; like the Rolling Stones, the Manish Boys took their name from a Muddy Waters song.

Davie initially assumed the Manish Boys must need their Mick Jagger, if not their Brian Jones, but his current obsession, apart from the emerging sound of the Who, was the appearance, and committed, proto-heavy metal voice, of Keith Relf, the lead singer of the Yardbirds, who would feature in quick succession a holy trinity of virtuoso English guitarists, Eric Clapton, Jeff Beck and Jimmy Page. The Yardbirds were moving and changing as fast as a restless fan like Bowie wanted, already pushing the derivative white blues towards psychedelic pop and a heavier, feedback-laden, power-chord-driven rock in ways that were tugging the Stones into new places.

Rock at the time was being beamed in from unchecked pirate radio stations working around closed-shop airplay restrictions on the BBC and Radio Luxembourg, and satisfying the lust for pop, soul and R & B that new fans could hear any time they wanted to, increasing a sense of underground urgency. In the mainstream, rock is being marketed mainly through the 45 rpm single, and the idea of the top 40 hit, and associated teen mer-chandising, in the final years before the album emerged as the central, more thoughtful form of a growing, more blatantly sub-versive counterculture. The cultural and media bias at the time is towards treating rock whatever its enterprise, inventive power, even pretension, as potential fodder for teen fans.

For all his serious musical ambitions and more cerebral atti-tude, Keith is noticed by female fans, and Davie, for his hair, a thick dirty-blond mop spinning to the shoulders with full fringe falling dreamily over the forehead framing soulful-looking eyes that made him look very vulnerable and pretty, and a close rela-tion of cute but doomed Brian Jones. (Both Relf and Jones were destined for early, extremely unromantic rock and roll deaths.) Davie would adopt this floppy, lost puppy look almost hair for hair. The rest of the band would mill around him, preferring a more down-and-out look, and were not so keen on the idea of an actual hairstyle and what that might mean.

Just before the Manish Boys set off on their pop package tour of the north, Davie Jones, bored with the grinding touring rou-tine, with what he called later as 'just surviving', takes on a less musical almost Dadaist role that leads to his first appearance on television. It's the first sighting of Davie inventing someone else in order to get some publicity, and in this instance, he was not publicising his music or the group, who would be used merely as his props. He was not even promoting himself as such, although he was planting his image into the history so that our one sight-ing of the very good-natured, slightly impish seventeen-year-old from Bromley gently plays with our mind and encourages us to explain this anomaly as the very first, sweet gesture of a master manipulator.

His Keith Relf-inspired pop-singer hair now thick and luscious and his occasional success writing attention-grabbing letters inspires him to make up a mock society initially called the International League for the Preservation of Animal Filament. It makes a feature in the *London Evening News* written by reporter Leslie Thomas, an old Barnardo's orphan boy who would soon write a novel about National Service in the 1950s, *The Virgin Soldiers*, adapted into a 1969 film starring John Lennon. (David Bowie auditioned for this film, and ironically had to cut his hair to army length for a role he didn't get, although he can be briefly spotted as an extra.)

The Thomas feature was an unusual profile of a pop singer, more a comic turn delivered in deadpan style, the kind of thing usually printed on April Fool's Day. The title of the piece 'For Those Beyond the Fringe', referring to the irreverent, satirical British comedy revue formed by fiendishly clever comics Peter Cook, Dudley Moore, Alan Bennett and Jonathan Miller in 1961, made it plain to those paying attention that all was not as it seemed.

Davie explained he wanted to protect 'courageous' long-haired male pop singers who had to 'go through hell' wearing their hair down to their shoulders. David of Plaistow Grove, Bromley, Thomas explained, was in the process of enrolling members, and hoping for P. J. Proby and, of course, the Stones and the Beatles – Davie nimbly putting his name in the same paragraph as the leading pop stars of the moment, and using the word 'indignities', not bad for a mostly unqualified working-class teenager. 'Everybody makes jokes about you on a bus and if you walk past navvies digging the road, it's murder.'

Thomas's piece concluded that the society would give long-haired men a sense of belonging and support them when too many people are poking fun. Davie's PR instincts were right, and the piece led to an invitation to appear on the 12 November edition of BBC2's popular topical news magazine show *Tonight*, anchored by the well-loved and highly skilled broadcaster Cliff Michelmore.

The show deftly mixed the serious and the light-hearted, the bespectacled, balding Michelmore was affable, but with just a hint of the stern schoolmaster, which played well against the limply articulate, well-bred but quietly indignant character Davie Jones adopted, mop hair freshly washed, holding his own well against the smooth, experienced host, both of them grazing against camp in their own way.

Davie had changed the name of his society to the more informative 'Society for the Prevention of Cruelty to Long Haired Men', and spent a minute or so putting his case surrounded by the silent Manish Boys sheepishly playing members of the society, obedient bumpkins, not really buying into the scheme, and probably wondering how this was going to help promote the Manish Boys. Especially when Davie was implying that by wearing their hair long, and being called 'darling' and mocked about handbags, they should really be called the Girlish Boys. They're being used, and it's plain to see as Davie stands out, that his brain is wired in ways theirs never will be, already with an unsentimental, mercenary take on cultural currents, and he can almost be seen dismissing his merely musical helpers.

The society that never really was dissolved as soon as the programme was over, and David Jones as the founder and chair of this absurd campaign appears like a mirage in the history of David Bowie, as if to say, at this point in time, I know the music isn't up to much, and I haven't found my voice, but I do know what I am doing. I know how to make my point, even though I don't know yet what my point is, so for now, it's just nonsense, it's simply that I exist. Watch me now.

It's the most coherent, original thing he does in this period, acting out almost a set piece on live television, standing out for a moment, an advance phantom of the living work of art he would be described as later, and then leaving it behind, drifting back into the average, the hard slog.

The group worked non-stop from May 1964 to March 1965, becoming Davie Jones and the Manish Boys after a few weeks, making little impact, but his association with where pop music is at the time, even though he can't make it anywhere near the centre, is given a boost. He gets more invaluable experience in how easy it is among all these hundreds of semi-pro groups faithfully copying records to make no impression at all however much you care and think that what you do is worthwhile, but comes in contact with those who are moving forward, fast, including other teenagers actively and radically processing a cyclone of cultural and musical information.

The Manish Boys got to make their particular single, a poignant souvenir of their time never finding an audience. Leslie Conn's contacts include the Chicago-raised producer Shel Talmy, who'd landed a job as house producer at Decca by claiming he'd produced the Beach Boys. He was always looking for young rock and roll bands in England, sensing different kinds of opportunities, working on many of the determined, dynamic new groups at the time including the Who, Manfred Mann and the Kinks. He worked hard to take more primitive British equipment and create a definite, original home-grown sound that could stand next to the American originals, using the eighteen-year-old Jimmy Page to play rhythm guitar on those early Kinks singles and then adopting him as his favourite session player.

Eighteen-year-old Davie's oddball charm worked on Talmy, who admitted he didn't think the songs Davie was writing 'had a snowball's chance in hell of making it, but I thought, he's original and brash, let's take a flier. I thought he was incredibly talented, bright, he impressed me as knowing exactly where he was going.'

The A-side of the Manish Boys single was a respectably simmering cover of a 1961 song by Bobby Bland, 'I Pity the Fool', Davie's vain boyish attempt to sound worldly wise and coolly immersed in the moment lifted up a little by the Page guitar, clearly on a different sonic and psychic level. Page showed Davie a few things on the guitar while they were hanging out in the studio, including some handy chords Davie would use later in a different incarnation, even, he would joke later, ones used in

'Space Oddity'. Not enough of a telepathic spark for a firm new collaboration to take hold, but enough to set off some subterranean energy. Bowie's interest in the occult was originally rooted in a simple competitive need to be cooler than Page, who he knew was fascinated with 'wickedest man in the world' Aleister Crowley. He decided he would try and do enough to even scare Jimmy.

The B-side is the first recorded Davie Jones song, 'Take My Tip', with Page on fuzzed-up guitar, then a brand-new technique, and what Talmy called Davie's 'weird' music that turned out to be in his view six or seven years ahead. It was the rushed, packed sound of an ambitious, hyperactive pop fan with a fondness for unusual, dramatic chords plucked from jazz and a fondness for wordplay and Mose Allison-style storytelling who is beginning to understand that a great song must also haunt your dreams and engage your emotions as much as make you dance and psych you up.

He manages to rhyme please with tease and act plausibly like a pop singer singing about attracting a special girl, but is also mentioning inside two and a quarter minutes sharks and tigers who possess the sky, making like a shark in a pool of fish so as to be free, being scared, having something bad on your mind, and in reflecting what's clearly on his aspirational mod-like mind he issues a manifesto: you got to act tall, think big, if you wanna make a mark ... gotta get ahead, get a car, get fancy clothes. He was finding words all over the place, in books, in shops, in advertising, in films, in conversation with people who didn't realise they were being mined for material, from the mouths of the plodding public on the buses he rode on – where for a while he found a place to do a lot of his thinking – discovering that the world in all sorts of ways is a treasure house.

The poor Manish Boys get their television show to promote their single, appearing in the first week of March on BBC2's short-lived early evening pop show *Gadzooks! It's All*

Happening, wiped from existence, and most memories, but which featured acts such as the Who, the Animals, Marianne Faithfull, Tom Jones and the Rockin' Berries in its seventeen-week run, attempting to anticipate trends rather than follow them, like the relentless *Top of the Pops*. The BBC, God bless them, were constantly trying to work out what to do with this new music for and by the young that was clearly taking over. How did they portray rock music? As just another branch of show business, a temporary aberration, a limited new branch of variety and music hall, or an important modern contribution to the culture of the nation? To be treated like a youthful contemporary art form, or a merely energetic entertainment that could be as silly as it could be challenging?

The producer who booked the Manish Boys admitted in the *Radio Times* that he was not booking very far ahead because 'the scene changes so fast'. So there will be surprises, wrote the *Radio Times*, like the Manish Boys, little known outside the London clubs. They were described as coming up with another new sound, 'sax pop', which was hardly as propulsive as Georgie Fame, Brian Auger or Graham Bond's cooked-up jazz rock, and as a genre didn't even last as long as the show it was briefly showcased on. The programme gets engulfed by the fast-changing scene, and so do the Manish Boys.

Davie looks for a smaller group with a little more clout. He's skinnier than ever after months of performing, long fair hair getting scraggy and dirty at the roots, lips dried out from dehydration, washed out, undernourished teenage skin needing some love, goofy teeth as crooked and chipped as an ancient stone circle. He's making plans and hustling people from inside public phone boxes, pressing dirty coins into the slot with the single-minded purpose of a Vegas gambler believing the next drop of the coin will lead to the jackpot.

He is still auditioning for unknown bands, alongside other hungry, broke and savvy singers like scraggy mod beauty Steve

Marriott, who soon joins mod central the Small Faces and lends a little local colour to Davie's evolving vocals. In May 1965 Davie gets invited ahead of Marriott – the saxophone playing and singing his own songs could have clinched it – to join another Kent group, a trio loud enough to rival the Who, the Lower Third, who formed in 1963.

He's soon spending time in the group's converted 1950s ambulance bought for £170 which they treat as workshop and hotel. They play the usual shoddy venues around the south, occasionally making a dash into the dark north. He fails to convince the rest of the group to wear make-up to get an audience response – drummer Phil Lancaster assumed he means clown make-up at first, which he thinks would be a laugh – and heads into another intense period sharing time with another grubby, unhygienic gang of boys earning a few pounds a week each. Very slowly, they build up a tiny following as a regular opening act at the Marquee Club in London, but not creating any real momentum, and during the summer, bookings are falling.

He's still being limited in these groups to rock, blues and soul, even though his interests are clearly wider, to the outer reaches of music, and way beyond music. It's not an easy alliance between him and this group he gets grafted onto, which for a week or two seemed like a good idea. He's not put off; he must know something, putting up with the gruelling conditions, building up a store of knowledge he knows one day will be useful. He's playing an observer, he's biding his time, getting to mingle in his obscurity among those in the know who are creating and recreating the scene and the next scene, picking up tips and techniques.

The leaders, the big brands led by Jagger, Lennon, Townshend, Davies and co., two or three years older, were, he knew, doing things better than he could, generating better slogans, choruses and riffs, more accurately catching moods, mastering the current vortex of change, causing a lot of it, reacting to Vietnam, revolution, decolonisation, LSD, free love, miniskirts, student unrest, and he waits for the right sort of space to open up that he could fill. When the time came, he would be ready. This was the study period, as if not being sucked in and permanently locked in to this pop period was his intention. Here was another place in the front row that he landed, as the world went pop!, so that it would eventually take over the world, completely altering how ideas can pass from one generation to the next and the nature and impact of fame.

With the Lower Third he makes the obligatory debut single, writing both sides. A press handout for the first release on Parlophone of 'You've Got a Habit of Leaving' reveals for the teen audience apparently desperate for intimate, even medical details the height and weight of the group. The character Davie is now playing is five feet eleven and weighs nine stone. He likes painting and dislikes 'in crowds'. He doesn't say he likes sounding like the Who, but then the single makes that clear, like it's been torn from the very fibres of the chart-conquering mod men complete with careering mid-song eruption – it's produced again by Shel Talmy who retains his talent-spotting faith in Davie and his hyperactive songwriting even though it seems to be going nowhere, and even though Pete Townshend of the Who, coming across the group valiantly opening the show bottom of the bill at a Who show on the south coast and chatting with Davie, drily noting he's trying to write like him, musters up only enough enthusiasm to say, well, there are a lot of groups that sound like you.

Davie has a hand again in an optimistic press release announcing another single, at ease with the pretence in making things seem better and healthier than they were, buoyantly announcing that all was well and that Davie Jones and the Lower Third were the group to watch that year. The *Tonight* television appearance is described as 'The Legendary Banned Hair tale'. Gaze on, he says, using a word he clearly favours, as their next seven-inch record 'Born of the Night' rushes up the chart. Stand astounded at the brilliant backings for Davie: Tea-Cup on lead, Death on bass, Les on drums. In the end, there was no gazing, and no standing astounded; the record was never released.

In 2000, David Bowie would return to 'You've Got a Habit of Leaving's' B-side, 'Baby Loves That Way', a barrage of non-Who and non-Yardbird influences that means it ends up like a garage version of the Band paying tribute to the Swinging Blue Jeans. It shows how much Davie Jones is shedding his skin, his averageness, to the extent you can see a new creature materialise, still wet and raw and difficult to make out, but definitely there. It's the first sign of a David Bowie we might recognise, so many influences and different registers jammed together it trembles on the edge of being something unique, and the one thing he needs to reach a next stage, a voice that doesn't sound like it wants to sing 'I Can't Explain' or 'All Day and All of the Night', a Brit singing like an American trying to sing like a Brit, is also starting to expose itself.

Another sighting of this strangely seasoned new character blearily crawling out into the open was the het-up heavy blues version of 'Chim Chim Cher-ee' from 1964's hyperreal fantasy of a London that never was, *Mary Poppins*, that the group tried out on stage. In a rock world increasingly anxious about perceived street credibility this fascination with Disney whimsy would have seemed jarring, but in the jazz world these enriched, enterprising Disney showtunes with their over-bright melodies were regularly used as the basis for advanced improvisation, and more magnetic mapmaking.

Davie knew his jazz and his saxophonists, and in March of 1965 an interpretation of 'Chim Chim Cher-ee' was the opening track on John Coltrane's follow-up album to *A Love Supreme*, *The John Coltrane Quartet Plays*. The Lower Third aggressively played it at audition for a BBC television show along with a proto-funk James Brown song 'Out of Sight', but the uncomfortable reaction of the producers was that they sounded like they were out of tune. They were probably more out of time.

It's a rum hybrid, this materialising new voice and personality made out of perky pop, rebel rock and miscellaneous borrowed otherness from swing to Disney, a true ugly duckling, and it would take a long time for it to settle down and mature, but there's a tone, timing and emotion that shows one day it will take flight. He would wipe away the traces of a lot of the music in these years of observing, prospecting and preparation, but in 2000 as the B-side to the single 'Everyone Says "Hi"' he returns to 'Baby Loves That Way', written when he was a pop music baby, and treats it with the kind of ravaged tenderness that would emerge more distinctly in the last music of his life, as though he was allowing the once lost, layered past to haunt him, and taking it as a new kind of inspiration, accepting and honouring his combative youthful attempts to become someone.

The sometimes impetuous, sometimes considered decisions he was making at sixteen, seventeen and eighteen about his music were laying the foundations for the later performer. That pale, gangly, spiky Bromley boy was responsible for David Bowie, as a great natural mimic with a desire to become a character in the songs he was singing and possessing a fast-forming original mind, stubbornly forcing his way into a packed, highly compet-itive pop music scene rapidly evolving from a singles scene to an album universe.

The *Kentish Messenger* proudly predict a top-thirty position for local boys Davie and the Lower Third's debut single, which they inevitably call 'catchy', but there is no such surprise. Conn's contract comes to an anticlimactic end, and Ralph Horton, an ex-road manager for the Moody Blues, takes over, concentrating on Davie rather than the group, knowing enough to spot where the real opportunity was. David and Ralph become more an item than Davie and the group. He travels less and less in the group ambulance, preferring Ralph's Jaguar, and stops helping with the carrying of equipment. There's a certain aloofness that develops as he takes more seriously the idea that the arrangement is very much him and a backing band, as if such arrogance was a necessary factor in equalling the ferocity and popularity of the Who.

Ralph's got some ideas, or he has agreed with some ideas that Davie has. Change the name of the group. The guys need to look sharper on stage. Change the name of the singer, because Davie isn't enough of a difference from Davy, and in most mainstream publications that give him a mention it is being misspelled as Davy anyway. Ralph had been in conversation with Manfred Mann manager Kenneth Pitt, who he had asked to help with the management of Davie, and even though Pitt didn't feel it was something he wanted to do at the time, he also recommended a name change as well.

During a busy September, where the group have four weekly shows at both the Marquee and the 100 Club, Davie announces at a rehearsal that he is changing his name. The new name could have come from someone who worked at the Barnardo's charity with David's father, a name he would hear and liked the sound of. It's also mod-sharp, like the large Spanish-style knife notorious and highly mythologised knife fighter, frontiersman and Louisiana folk hero Jim Bowie used before he died at the Battle of the Alamo.

Davie would have seen Jim Bowie portrayed by Richard Widmark in John Wayne's 1960's *The Alamo*, and Jim Bowie was featured in the final episode of a 1950s *Walt Disney's Wonderful World of Color* TV series, *Davy Crockett at the Alamo*, played by red-headed Kenneth Tobey, known throughout the 1950s for appearing in science-fiction films like *The Thing from Another World*, *The Beast from 20,000 Fathoms*, *It Came from Beneath the Sea* and *The Vampire*. Jim Bowie was also played with a certain brooding Presley panache by the English actor Scott Forbes in a long-running TV series *The Adventures of Jim Bowie*.

Maybe one Bowie led to another, which then led to another. He goes with the name, because, he rationalises later, it's a name used to cut through all the bullshit of life. David Bowie is born in a drab, peeling rehearsal room in the middle of nowhere on 16 September 1965. Ralph writes to Ken the day after to say that he has made the change. The new character makes his first stage appearance, as if everything that came before can be erased, with the Lower Third still grimly hanging on, at the Marquee Club on 8 October 1965 supporting Gary Farr and the T-Bones, regular Marquee headliners that year along with the Graham Bond Organisation, Jimmy James and the Vagabonds and the Spencer Davis Group. In the Christmas Eve edition of *Melody Maker* there is small advert towards the back among other classified ads. It simply says: BOWIE.

He is now David Bowie, and nothing changes.

The next powerful producer with big hit credentials challenging himself to see if he could make head or tail of what on earth Bowie was thinking and turn it into the hit his initiative and flair seemed to merit was Tony Hatch. He'd started making records in the late 1950s for the first wave of English pop stars Adam Faith and Bert Weedon, and was a versatile, cocky, utility version of ruthless but dignified Beatles producer George Martin – and as fond of the new stereo potential – and the film composer John Barry. He had a mind as packed with pop reference points as the young Bowie, if not as much sense of mystery, and was adept at novelty songs, comedy records, theme tunes, crooners, orchestral lounge, folk, beat groups, with a particular speciality at flamboyantly framing the new wave of female pop singers pop was introducing, including his wife and co-writer Jackie Trent and a long-standing professional relationship with Petula Clark. The year before he'd written the immaculate pop song 'Downtown' for Petula, and produced and arranged it, making good on the claim they were the British equivalent of Burt Bacharach and Dionne Warwick. Hatch was based at the Pye label, unglamorous, industrious home of Lonnie Donegan, the Searchers and the Kinks, and that's where Bowie went next.

Hatch certainly knew how to deliver the best sound and

structure for a big-selling storytelling song, and seemed a smart if straight choice for Bowie. He was beginning to work out how to mix the details of a reporter and historian with the images of a poet and a self-referential presence. Maybe songs were how he was going to make things happen; write about something, about what you want and where you want it to be, and see it come true. The next few songs he wrote show him making the move between the grafting, needy Davie Jones of kitchen-sink Bromley and the David Bowie of a fantasy of his own making via a London he seemed to be making the subject of a musical more Sondheim than Rodgers and Hammerstein.

It seems too good to be true that David Bowie and the Lower Third's first single for Pye released a few days after his nineteenth birthday was called 'Can't Help Thinking About Me', something else planted back in time to create the perfect title for the first David Bowie record. The great 'you' of pop music, to include the listener, the 'You Really Got Me', the 'You've Lost That Lovin' Feelin'', replaced with a more challenging and troubled and even paranoid 'me'.

Even extreme musical dramatist Hatch can't do anything commercially with a song that packs the detail into the verse and then flattens out during the chorus, where nothing uplifting or charged can happen in a song that's really about leaving home and confronting the unknown. Bowie can't yet transfer his ego and dash into a pop chorus, so he is always straining, falling short, and the atmosphere he captures is all about cold railway platforms, ashamed mothers, a blackened family name, fear of school the next day, insecurity, rattled nostalgia, being blamed for some emotional crime, and the constant, and always on his mind because it's right at the centre of his mind, me me me. The basic message to be taken away is, he's on his own, he's got a long way to go, and 'I hope I make it on my own.' On the B-side there is more me, 'And I Say to Myself', because Davie Jones is now playing David Bowie as both a cold fish and an exhibitionist and trying on this new me, and it sounds as though he is thinking aloud about how to write a song, or at least a B-side, and how do you end a song?

The single does not sell and only makes an unofficial chart that can be influenced with some money, in the *Melody Maker* music paper. He's on his own at the end of the month, walking away from the Lower Third after one last show at the Marquee and then a miserable finale and an abortive cancelled show in his hometown of Bromley where the group crumble without even a handshake let alone a hug. He had to break up the band.

David and Ralph drive off in the Jaguar, Lower Third have nothing left but their ambulance and a future of not making it into a history David Bowie had taken control of, even at this obscure stage. A first interview with *Melody Maker*, the one place he has had a hit, introduces the David Bowie who will use the music press to advance his case, construct his characters, display his multi-talents, and propose various twists he's thinking of.

In this short piece he's already pouring out information; he's helping Tony Hatch work on a musical, designing clothes for a Carnaby Street boutique, intending to become an actor, envying Tibetan monks, planning a trip to see the monasteries of the Himalayas, is a student of astrology, a believer in reincarnation, claiming that the whole of Western life is wrong, that people in London especially don't know what real life is, and excuses his lack of success by concluding he's taking too many musical risks for the audience to understand him ... yet. 'But I'm sure it makes their musical life more interesting.' He was a great talker, and great at talking himself up. He has quickly learnt, this candidate to be the quickest learner in a pop world seething with fast learners, but not necessarily the best of listeners, that over-statements, hard-core confidence, grand claims and whatever you can get away with land him the publicity he instinctively knew is the most important thing about pop music, always was and always will be.

They're called pop stars, but really they have always been hype stars. The ones that make the most PR noise obviously get the most attention; making the best-sounding, coolest pop of the time is part of the publicity campaign, not particularly the sole key to getting the attention. The pop system was set up from the very beginning based on the idea that you can get plenty of attention without making great music, but you cannot get attention by merely producing fantastic sound. That was part of the whole point, if there ever was a central point.

Bowie, then very much the creation of Davie Jones, is fabricating a rich inner life, and this is what he is selling, more than his music. It's still too early for him to break into the holy hit parade, and the troubled church of *Top of the Pops*, despite having the ingenious musical brains behind 'Downtown' on his side. They cancel each other out. Hatch can't find the heart of the song that is the next single, 'Do Anything You Say', and is frustrated having to use the musicians in Bowie's new group, given a name that ends up meaning the exact opposite of what it should, the Buzz. All of Bowie's ideas go missing when it comes to naming his new group, and producers making top pop songs always prefer to use their favoured session musicians when it comes to getting their sound on a record, even when they're using a group.

Hatch and Bowie keep trying and for the next single it's out of sad, disengaged Bromley and into the centre of the city, 'feeding the lions in Trafalgar Square' for the next instalment in his unofficial musical about London, and back to a 'me', a character feeling and looking just like him at his age with his lack of money and roots, wandering the Soho streets at dawn after a night on the town, coming down from some induced high, seeing beauty and possibility where others might see dreary and ordinary, living a drifting life, dreaming with friends, making the best of nothing much going on, but always on the edge of adventure, because he's never going to be boxed in, however low. For Hatch, who admired Bowie's vision and facility with language, what was tripping him up was that he saw a place in his pop songs for 'dustbins', but Bowie knew that litter and rubbish, what everyone else was throwing out, was where you could find some of your best material. For a while he lives out of the dustbins on the backstreets around Carnaby Street.

He's made it, but only out of Bromley, not into his imagined future; he can't make that up, yet, and he puts a melancholy gloss on actually how far removed he is from the centre of things, hoping the 'I dig everything' feelings might get him close to the 'Downtown' mood. Towards the end he lets some sunshine in, to throw some light on that side of London, 1966, that was seen to be swinging.

Hatch has more to work with, gives Bowie his best, most ear-catching pop sound yet, not least because it is the most artificial and made up, a vivid studio concoction not trying to recreate and thus sonically exaggerate a perfect live sound. It's still not a David Bowie that anyone wants. The truth of a fabulous pop sound is that it is a lie, it is processed, however authentic-seeming the source material. Because it is made in a recording studio requiring the correctly balanced blend of equipment, wires, amplification, acoustics and emotions, of technological precision and human estimation, it is always the sound of machines dreaming as much as, if not more than, technical proficiency and musical knowledge.

Bowie's pushing to realise a pop that bends his numerous influences out of shape and combines the actual and the surreal, fascinated by how what a pop song is actually doing is melting together words and images to produce a new kind of commodity, and few can hear it. He's making up a self out of his own disguises, and no one cares.

A pop hack like Hatch, however excellent he is in his world, even as he has his own levels of genius, cannot envisage the conceptual dimension necessary to locate the music Bowie needs, with his warped and warping coalition of the experimental and theoretical and the middle of road and ornate, bubbling on the frontiers of perception. He possesses a voice and a style that loves to take the stage and sensationally soar over the show-business top, a Judy Garland using song to create shelter from harm, but he wants to resist classification, sing about the wayward ideas moving through his mind, and see things before anyone else, a Jacques Brel singing the changes, having the dreams, and night-mares, of a J. G. Ballard. He wants to create his own world but be adored by millions. The only route forward is to ensure that the world he creates includes a character closely resembling him who is adored by millions.

Bowie's out of synch with time even as he's in the middle of it and sharing the same access to imagery and mood as his near peers. Ray Davies is only a few hundred yards away over the river with his London elegy a few months later, 'Waterloo Sunset', a dream within a dream of London released in a 1967 where pop has reached a sophisticated, high-minded state far removed from even three years ago.

Bowie has kept up, but in his own singular, separate, deviating way, working hard, getting deals, making records, with the cor-rect seeming and enthusiastic producers, but constantly missing the boat, and the point, succeeding only in setting up the ragged history of someone who would actually one day be the star he believes he will be, constantly circling around the heart of his own story. Life continues to be elsewhere.

When he gets close, he seems to get even further away, as if his past is going to repeat itself forever. It's amazing he gets another chance after Hatch and Pye fail to solve the puzzle, but he does. It's meant to be. It's in the stars. It's in his eyes. He can persuade anyone to let him have another try. He's still a kid, more or less. He refuses to sink underneath this maelstrom of pop action and reaction and be lost forever. Detach from it, or be drowned by it.

Eventually he will be the right person in the right place. What is driving him on despite all the disappointments and flops that could cause a hypersensitive teenager to give up and enter a monstrous sulk? Sheer bloody-mindedness? Unbreakable self-belief in his own talents? 'I've been a bleedin' big head for as long as I can remember . . .'

He is developing a near religious certainty that reality was merely an extension of his mind, all his to manipulate and direct. He desperately needs to locate psychic safety faced with the disjointedness of his family and the equivalent disruptiveness affecting the modern world. He needs to make peace with who through no fault of his own he found himself to be. He was embarrassed that he'd swanned out of school, Bromley, Mum and Dad, friends, bands, ad agency, and couldn't bear having to go back, tail between legs, not cool, just arrogant and naive, a pitiful example of the completely crestfallen, just another average teenager after all. He doesn't know what else to do. He has found a way to take control of the script, to test his inner reserves in order to build a new world of the senses. He is beginning to create a parallel world which comments on our own and which shares many of its characteristics.

This attitude would be more useful as the forward-moving 1960s, once they fully cracked open the grey 1950s, spilled over into the fragmented, apprehensive 1970s.

Was he ensuring his character was living out the mantra 'what does not kill me makes me stronger', forging himself in the crucible of pop culture, record business and media events, allowing himself to be burnt and pummelled so that he would emerge stronger and more fired up? If that was the case, it was time to introduce some unexpected new catalysts and make some new connections. After all, he was approaching twenty. His teenage years were over.

4

JUST WATCH ME

David Bowie is accepting if there is no struggle there is no progress

David Bowie is reading 'artists should take the meaning of revelation into their own hands'

David Bowie is refusing to be thought of as mediocre – there's no point in doing anything unless it astounds

David Bowie is still getting educated

David Bowie is suggesting to whoever will listen or read or need to find out in neither music nor art have I a real style, craft or technique. I just plummet through, on either a wave of euphoria or mind-splintering dejection. This can often all be held together by a bloody-minded determination to create something that was not there before. It probably comes from the need to have seen it all

David Bowie is trying to connect

David Bowie is avoiding the real world

David Bowie is beginning to haunt you

David Bowie is realising pop stars are meant to be weird

David Bowie is telling you what you want to hear

David Bowie is stealing himself

David Bowie is making connections between the strangest things

David Bowie is getting things done

David Bowie is digging beneath the surface

David Bowie is taking advantage of what the moment offers

David Bowie is putting two and two together and making the lips part like silence set for alarm

David Bowie is killing time

David Bowie is seeing that everything around him is alive

David Bowie is getting himself out of the way

David Bowie is wondering who he is today

David Bowie is hiding behind others

David Bowie is having an identity crisis

David Bowie is impatient with people who are impatient with the speed of change

David Bowie is dreaming up the world

David Bowie is gonna have to be a different man

David Bowie is knowing it takes a lot to become someone else

5

AND I WANT TO BELIEVE

New arrivals believing that David Bowie had a future helped overcome the perception that even by nineteen he had failed too many times to be considered exciting new talent worth investing in. Incoming representation made it seem as though he was always beginning again. Just when Bowie needed new impetus, it would arrive.

Ralph Horton decided he needed a partner in management and at the end of 1965 asked shrewd industry veteran and would-be pop Svengali Kenneth Pitt to help out. For a while, being cautious, he didn't commit one way or another, hovering enigmatically in the background while he made up his mind. When he finally saw Bowie during the Lower Third Marquee residency, he felt the same strange inexplicable tingle as Talmy and Hatch, and he was of the persuasion to be taken by Bowie's demonstrative, off-kilter presence, how he used his body, and his singing of Judy Garland rather than any sweaty re-treads of the blues and botched attempts to be as flash mod as the Who. He agreed to assist Horton, but stay in the background. The plan was that Horton would look after the art and Pitt would take care of business.

Pitt's experience included being part of publicity teams promoting British tours by Mel Tormé, Frank Sinatra and Duke Ellington in the 1950s, Dylan's 1966 electric tour, and helping organise Manfred Mann and push them into the charts. Pitt's varied record, his association – however tenuous – with legends, his proven ability to break not necessarily obvious acts, and his fresh faith in Bowie's potential was more than enough to lure Bowie away from Ralph's jag. In Bowie's eyes Pitt had definite if rather formal show-business flair. Pitt in turn relished that side of Bowie that was as much brassy Bassey and showy as nerdily musical and as struck by the Who and the Yardbirds as the next plain, spotty teenager.

He could see an old-fashioned showman but one that knew how the showman can be as deviant and dark as the experimental extremist, someone who could locate a connection between Sammy Davis Jr. and Samuel Beckett. Rock was beginning to take itself seriously as part of its inevitable growth spurt, and what elsewhere might be viewed as tasteless kitsch was for Bowie merely part of his pursuit of an escape from drudgery. It's part of a construction of a different sort of identity that, once the ego kicks in, as it must if you totally believe in yourself, can flip over into delusions of grandeur, and expectations of transforming yourself into a visionary. Which are actually great qualifications to sing songs at the very top of your emotions. To rearrange yourself as part of this process requires a close study of the self in all sorts of ways; seeking out the soul, inspecting it, testing it, learning what it is, so it's then part of your world, and your music.

Listening to the great torch singers, the fabulous standard-bearing balladeers, the extravagantly sentimental easy-listening comforters, the comedic storytellers honing an erratic but satisfying artistic timing is just as much a part of this craving for dramatic originality, because they too, without making noise, smashing rules and creating an obvious rebellious, subversive fuss, are in their own way flexing existential muscles. Bowie could find the next in the unlikeliest, most inappropriate of places.

Whatever the reasons, Pitt didn't just see another Jagger or

Relf, another scrawny white kid singing the knocked-off blues in a grim jobbing rock band. He saw the basis of a new thing, and with his experience in film and theatre as well as music he fancied himself as being the person who could make it happen. By April 1967, Pitt had taken sole charge of Bowie. Ralph was roughly ejected. Pitt was part of a tradition of gay pop managers orchestrating British pop from inside even as they existed in the margins, from Brian Epstein with the Beatles, to Kit Lambert with the Who and Simon Napier-Bell with the Yardbirds; seeing the world in a new, different way, needing careful negotiating skills, tending to have a more sophisticated aesthetic than their young bands, refining and directing the rough, unformed intelligence of their charges. Their influence became part of the 1960s pop sensibility, catalysts not just in the business, but in the application of image and content as well.

Pitt was absolutely charmed by Bowie, and Bowie stayed with Kenneth in his flat on Manchester Street in smart Marylebone, London W1, very near to the Wallace Collection, a palatial townhouse Bowie would wander into containing a vast collection of miscellaneous fine arts from the fifteenth to nineteenth century including Rembrandts, Van Dycks and Titians.

A happy lodger, David would dance naked around the sitting room, revealing an almost totally hairless pasty skin-and-bone body and a large, unruly penis, demonstrating his trust in Pitt and perhaps also teasing a little this undemonstrative and relatively hidden gay man. This was a time when homosexuality was still illegal in Britain, fraught with a certain sense of danger, and unostentatious gay men like Pitt stepped very discreetly through the danger, prejudice and rampant ridicule. Through the Sexual Offences Act of 1967, homosexuality would be decriminalised in July for private acts between two men who were both over twenty-one, but the tensions remained.

(It was the policies of the genial-looking Labour Home Secretary between 1965 and 1967 – at forty-five the youngest since Churchill – the progressive moderate, mild radical and social moderniser Roy Jenkins that led to a liberalisation on the laws of divorce, abortion, homosexuality, the abolition of capital punishment and the outlawing of racial discrimination. There was also a significant relaxation in censorship of literature, theatre and film. This rush of change in the laws had been set in motion by the passage in 1959 of Jenkins's Obscene Publications Act, itself a result of his attitude that the existing taboos were intolerably inhibiting. He was a big believer that the state should not limit or obstruct personal freedom. In his personal manifesto for the importance of a Labour win in the 1959 election after eight years of Conservative rule, 'The Labour Case', he stood for a society in which everyone will have the opportunity for a full and satisfying life. It would be another four years before the Labour Party won power – helped, some witnesses commented, only half-joking, by the arrival of the clearly un-Tory Beatles – which they held for the rest of the 1960s.

All of this rapid and wide-ranging legal revising of restrictive regulations was running in parallel to the compelling expansion of popular culture, which both encouraged the new liberalisation but was also stimulated by it, and given more space to operate. It was the swinging Sixties manifested as steadying political reform. They needed to coexist, for those settled on this side of an actual revolution, so that society wasn't changing in a lop-sided way – personal laws and public laws were being adjusted and updated in close alliance. When Jenkins used the phrase 'the permissive society', he meant a civilised society, to the disgust of his opponents who felt it led to a degeneration of society and an irresponsible, hedonistic selfishness, and who would get their revenge as soon as they could.)

Pitt, a cultured figure from a wealthy family, was more than any other early management figure the next stage on from stepbrother Terry, Ronnie Ross and Owen Frampton, as much a teacher and guide as a music industry operator with his own range of contacts and hit and miss techniques for pushing talent into the charts. Like many managers in the British music business, Ken had a reserved, calm manner, like an affable dentist promising there will be no pain. He dressed neatly and anonymously, and had a certain measured aura, a practised, solicitous method of giving nothing away without seeming rude that Bowie would fold into his own developing persona. Bowie liked having this kind of grown-up, mature man about town with assured manners who'd met some of his heroes looking after his interests.

For a while, he was Bowie's main protector and adviser. It seemed the most secure of his professional relationships so far. Bowie sheds those around him at some speed not necessarily out of coldness or cruelty but out of a survivor's instincts; once he has used up the energy and cultural intelligence of someone, they are of little use to him any more. Bowie is shed and unceremoniously dropped in return by those who have gone as far as they can with him, or move on to others as a natural part of what they do, so he learns not to take this personally, and doesn't imagine anyone he spurns or leaves behind will either. There is too much at stake, he believes, to spare any feelings for anyone he leaves behind. It's every man for herself.

Bowie needed a constant flow of new knowledge because that was how his mind worked, how the one crucial, enlightening thing leading to another that began somewhere deep in the midst of a Bromley boyhood continued, and kept his all-important, life-making imagination expanding. He will take from those close to him for as long as they can supply him new recommendations and suggestions for anything he can use and get pleasure from and add it to his own vital stock of reference points. The more unexpected and out of the ordinary, the more obscurely outsider, the better. In a world speeding up and increasingly fast-filled with new stimulations and aesthetic inventiveness, now with the choice so severely lacking in the 1950s, he requires people he can rely on who act like antennae, to supplement his own constant scanning and screening of what's happening – and what has happened that he might have missed – what's out there to use, borrow, adapt. Once he's taken it and it becomes part of his imagination it belongs to him.

Pitt showed Bowie a new world, and Bowie was keen to see it. Ken took him to the theatre, one of his passions, in a year when in London's West End there was Joe Orton's aggressively saucy *Loot* and Barbra Streisand starring in her Broadway smash hit *Funny Girl*. Orton had an inexhaustible appetite for reading, a desire to demolish respectability, he loved blending the macabre with the commonplace and became a hero of the new sexually fluid counterculture generation. Streisand plays Fanny Brice doing whatever she needs to in order to get a break in show business knowing she is not a typical beauty. Midway between the two you can find a David Bowie.

There were other interesting productions showing in the West End that year. Famous drag artist Danny La Rue in *Come Spy With Me* appearing as an Irish nurse, diplomat's escort, cabaret stripper and a whole host of other female characters, and the great Ron Moody, born the same day as David, recently Fagin in the musical *Oliver!*, playing the legendary early nineteenth-century garishly costumed and warpainted pantomime clown Joseph Grimaldi in *Joey Joey*. Listening to the music Bowie was about to make – and the video for 'Ashes to Ashes' featuring a Grimaldi-like spectre – you can believe Bowie saw some of those productions.

Like some modern Professor Higgins educating a rough-around-the-edges wide-eyed working-class vagrant, Ken brought news from New York that Andy Warhol and the Velvet Underground were chronicling a coverless test-pressing of their first album including 'I'm Waiting for the Man'. Bowie leaps on it like something by Edith Piaf that came from Ginsberg, Coltrane and Dylan. At the final Buzz show in unlikely Shrewsbury in December 1966, he's giving perhaps the very first public hearing in Britain of the Velvet Underground's 'I'm Waiting for the Man'.

Pitt encouraged Bowie's reading, suggesting books by Oscar Wilde, a master of deception and an influence on Orton. Bowie was an eager reader, and rushed to look at Ken's bookshelves when he first went round to his flat, the erstwhile modernist complimenting him on his collection, especially André Gide and Albert Camus. Ken pushed the side of Bowie interested in more direct theatrical entertainment, but Bowie was happy to go that way having got nowhere trying the orthodox rock star approach. Ken had been weaned in the square, buttoned-up 1950s, but the principles of promoting talent were still fundamentally the same, and they required a consistency of message. And when it was time to change image, it was time to change image.

The mod style was too clichéd now, the all-conquering likely lads were adopting new counterculture clothing as mod flowered into bohemian, middle-class hippie, or stripped right down into working-class skinhead; an all-round entertainer with a fashionable, slightly deviant hippie-ish twist appeared the correct new formula to Pitt, a Tommy Steele with psychedelic flowers on. When I interview Pitt in 1985 around the time his book *The Pitt Report* was published, he said it was a mistake that people thought he wanted to turn Bowie into a new Tommy Steele. He said he was interested in getting Bowie the status, the fame, of Tommy Steele, which didn't mean much even in 1966 when Bob Dylan was threading a blazing stream of consciousness through pop songs. There's no doubt there was a square-ness about Ken's approach, rooted in the simpler 1950s, when show business was not tangled up with spiralling anti-establishment alternative energies. He said:

David when he first came to me said that he wanted to go into theatre and into musicals. This is rather interesting because this is what I wanted. I wasn't looking for a singer who would become nothing else but a pop singer, struggling very hard to make a hit record and then doing nothing and struggling again to make another hit record and finally when you stop making hit records, your career is over. That's not what I wanted. I wanted someone who could go into a wider field. This is what David liked, I explained it to him and it's what he wanted, and it's what we set out to do.

(I had ignored for many months the fact that on YouTube there was (so it said) an interview between me and Ken Pitt, as I assumed it was a parody, as that kind of thing does happen – although why anyone would have wanted to mock up an interview between me and Pitt I wasn't sure. I had no memory of conducting it; I had clearly lost 1985, when I was fighting and losing a pop battle of my own in trying to maintain the 1984 success of Frankie Goes to Hollywood, which I was involved with. When I did listen to it, I still didn't remember it, and it seemed as though it was a remarkable reconstruction of something that had never happened, although, again, I couldn't work out why anyone would go to such trouble. Eventually I had to accept that it really was me interviewing Ken Pitt on a radio programme.)

I don't seem to like his book and, ironically, I asked him who would be interested in reading about David Bowie's struggle? Because those kind of struggles with the details of getting a contract and a radio play seem to ruin some of the mystery that makes David Bowie so remarkable.

The book was intended to be a report first of all. I had no intention of writing a book per se. I just wanted to write down everything that happened day by day and the book has been criticised because it has so much minute detail. But I think that the detail was very essential to Bowie fans and for people to get a proper understanding of what was happening in those days. And I think that the fans should know that David had a very, very hard struggle because out of that struggle obviously grows some kind of determination and David did have this great determination to eventually succeed and he overcame all those difficulties.

You can tell that Bowie picked up some of Pitt's imperturbable graciousness for his own eventual, carefully put together interview persona.

There were already many ways to read Bowie, then just one of many characters Davie Jones had unveiled on the way to working out who he was, and Pitt's particular reading at a time before genres and styles had settled down and everything was up for grabs was that Bowie was more than anything a dashing, slightly arty song and dance man. There weren't many of them around. For all anyone knew at the time that might be the gap in the market he could fill.

Pitt, still in partnership with Horton at the end of 1966, approached the Deram label, a subsidiary of the first record label to release record albums, Decca. Deram was a marketing reaction by Decca to the emergence of the rock album. The big mainstream companies were beginning to create in-house underground labels with different, possibly cooler names to try to keep up with a world that was splitting into singles artists and album artists. Decca with Deram, and EMI with Harvest and Phonogram with Vertigo, were trying to stem the flow of these new underground artists wanting to sign to labels designed more in their own image, like Island and Track.

At the major recording studios in central London a shift system would often develop where pop records designed to be played on daytime radio made by such shrewd manipulators of the popular imagination as Mickie Most were recorded during the day, and in the evening, at night, the experimental, darker music would be made. For a while, there was a crossover between one and the other; Mickie Most would use the endlessly imaginative Jimmy Page and John Paul Jones's bass and arrangement on his pop hits, and then they became Led Zeppelin, many dark moves on from daytime pop, in fact, with their policy of eschewing singles, the actual, neo-devilish embodiment of anti-pop.

A new style of rock group was experimenting with where they could take their music beyond the blues and their lyrics beyond love, taking the jamming into a free-form area creating a sound as much space jam as blues jam, with words more hallucinogenic than romantic. Albums were becoming a new art form, no longer an arbitrary collection of singles, covers and fillers. They were how newer, bolder acts expressed themselves, reflecting the unique madness of the times, and any fame they suddenly had, and found room to explore. It allowed them to stretch beyond the singles format, make bigger, more nuanced statements, edgier sounds, and step beyond the trivialising teen market.

In 1965, Bob Dylan released *Highway 61 Revisited* and *Bringing It All Back Home*, the Beatles released *Rubber Soul* and *Help!*, and outside of pop, John Fahey, the Sonics, Jacques Brel, and Jackson C. Frank were creating coherent pieces of work given descriptive titles like books or films that were still more the territory of jazz. Albums by the Rolling Stones, Them, the Who and the Beach Boys were still jumbled collections mostly remaining star struck by their idols, with no discernible internal rigour, harmony or conceptual flourish.

The Kinks with *The Kink Kontroversy* were beginning the move from one state to another, moving on from revamping R & B with English nerve, dropping the covers, and starting to confess their state of mind and an urgent need to reflect their own self-discovery and frustrations with the world in their music, and do it in a more British way, a north London way; 'will this depression last for long', and, sharing a feeling that Bowie had about the future, 'I wanna know just what's in store for me.'

By 1966 the Beatles were packing a *Revolver*, the Beach Boys were making *Pet Sounds*, Bob Dylan kept control with *Blonde on Blonde*, the Byrds were in the *Fifth Dimension*, the Mothers of Invention were issuing the instruction to *Freak Out!* It was already a different planet from the year before; the titles of the albums were less likely to be cute and snappy and thought up by marketing departments. The Kinks were now *Face to Face*, not just their first great album but their first real album, in the way we now understand them, the Stones were in an *Aftermath*, beginning to leave behind the blues, writing their own songs, trying out sophisticated arrangements, using different, more worldly and non-American instruments, getting personal, and finding like their immediate peers that lacing their treasured blues and American rock and roll with an English eccentricity, lustful cockiness and libido generates an uncanny new hybrid, quickly called psychedelia.

Pitt came to the conclusion that Bowie had failed previously because he was too complex and contemporary to be a mere singles act targeted at teens. There might be a whimsy about him, but his humour, sensitivity and teeming ideas meant he needed a whole album to contain it all. Hearing some new post-mod tracks Bowie has worked on, including 'Rubber Band' and another instalment in his intermittent London opus, 'The London Boys', Deram agreed that there was something different enough to give him an album deal.

Bowie admitted 'The London Boys' was a rare piece of open, undisguised autobiographical writing, a light he couldn't stop shining into his inner life, and where he actually is and was, a glimpse past the disguises to his actual lonely reality, while others, and him elsewhere, imagine and read things into what was going on at the time and invent scenarios for the sake of furthering a convenient theory.

'The London Boys' is closer to the idea that at the time he was living out of a van in a Soho side street, not quite the Merry Prankster, living in fear of failure, of losing face. He's found some friends who care about him, but they'll quickly drop him if he doesn't keep up, and wear the right kind of clothes, which have turned out to be a uniform after all. He's left home, given up his job, but it might be a mistake. He got what he wanted, but it means he's on his own. There's a sense the scene has moved on, out of Soho, into other, less fixed, more underground spaces, where a hurdy-gurdy revolutionary spirit hovers in the air, and he has to muster up a new kind of courage to find out where to go next. He's got nothing, he's on the run. He's replaced one nowhere with another nowhere, and a different cast of people he can never really get to know.

In the wider story, the one a biographer wants to construct, where there is a certain logic to how things are flowing, he's creating a fantasy, and making all the right moves to fit it together how he wants to, even as he doesn't seem to be getting anywhere – except we all know he will – but here is a message in his music, an actual memory, an isolated sense of doubt from someone exposed, not hiding behind an illusion. The one thing that carries forward from this song into the future Bowie is the infusion of melancholy, and at the edges, doubts about his sanity, which would often haunt him for real, for unreal, and the conceptual and media spaces in between.

At the end of 1966 Deram released the demos produced by Bowie that Pitt had played them, 'Rubber Band' as the A-side, with a repetitive, careering brass sound that seems as much an influence on Michael Nyman's baroque minimalism as a failed attempt to recreate Brel in a Beatly, new British setting.

There was a fascination with traditional symbols of British national identity and a trend for placing them in new, more playful contexts – the fashions for military uniforms and marching bands reflecting a different, increasingly open-minded Britain that created a hybrid of the new and old without the old taking over. There was also a desire to reframe the influences of a postwar childhood in the mind-bending new context of psychedelia, to develop a radiant mental agility that had begun in a less free era but which still stood for freedom; what if the Goons, *Alice in Wonderland*, *The Wind in the Willows*, C. S. Lewis, Charles

Dickens coexisted with experimental pop music? This was what started to separate British psychedelia from its American counterpart: the intense, snug craziness of living on a small island with a ludicrous, overreaching history, its own regional accents and slang which made things more disorientating if you used them in rock and roll songs, and a constant disruptive tension between discipline and disorder.

'Rubber Band' was released with the usual Bowie-directed, over-optimistic press release, again in a way the best thing about the single. Faced with the usual at best nonplussed, at worst completely indifferent, outside reaction to their new hopeful, Deram were quickly wishing they hadn't signed him to make a whole album, which he more or less completed before they could stop him. Some at the label also noticed on hearing 'Rubber Band' for the first time that they hadn't signed a new Ray Davies or, you never know, a new Scott Walker, but what sounded to them like a second-rate Anthony Newley, at the time about as far removed from hip as you could get.

Pitt had worked a little with Tony Newley, which impressed Bowie and may have convinced him to work with him. To amuse Ken, or just because he's mastered the impression and thinks it will suit his jaunty, theatrical new material more than trying Jagger or Relf, he unashamedly comes out as a Newley fan on his latest songs.

Pitt tends to be blamed for ushering Bowie too much into what is seen as cabaret, thinking of the Newley who talked to the animals with Rex Harrison in *Doctor Dolittle*. Bowie, though, didn't put up much of a fight, and was actually more likely influenced by the side of Anthony Newley that could be closer to Bertolt Brecht than Batley Variety Club, who appeared in a spot-on spoof Elvis film *Idol on Parade*, the one who wrote the words to Shirley's 'Goldfinger', and Nina's 'Feeling Good', whose early 1960s albums included classics like 'Love is a Now and Then Thing' and 'In My Solitude', the one who once played the devil on stage in full horns and tail and peeled an apple using the tip of his tail.

When Bowie said he was influenced at the time by Anthony Newley and the 'space mysticism' of Syd Barrett's Pink Floyd, anyone who had come across Newley's truly absurdist and surreal 1960 series *The Strange World of Gurney Slade*, as Bowie had, would conclude that of the two, Newley was actually the more psychedelic. In fact, the spirit of Gurney Slade was a link in the chain that went from Lewis Carroll via the Goons to the mind of Syd, and the infectious, documentary zaniness of the Beatles' *A Hard Day's Night* and beyond that to *Monty Python*. As a fan it meant Bowie had, as he said in an interview in 1971, 'a depth of understanding on the satirical level that the other kids hadn't achieved at the age of thirteen' – or he was a fan because he already felt like that.

Bowie, the consummate mimic, expertly caught Newley's voice, the cockney kicks, showman kinks and jerky, self-conscious idiosyncrasies, but he was as much an influence on Bowie for his eclecticism, the constant turnover of vainglorious semi-autobiographical characters, his constant striving for the next big thing at a time – the late 1950s and 1960s – when it was next to impossible to introduce anything experimental into the mainstream.

Newley had been a child star, and was deemed respectable enough in the late 1950s to be allowed to produce a sitcom, which ITV imagined might be a commercial version of Tony Hancock's very funny pompous buffoon, the epitome of the barmy, baffled side of Britain that needed a little gentle ribbing, and hopefully ultimately replacing.

They did not expect what they got, which was an agitated comedy about displacement and disorientation in the early media age that came out of Kafka as much as Jacques Tati. It was as though *The Dick Van Dyke Show* was being written by Philip K. Dick. Nothing bent reality like this on television until

Twin Peaks. This was where music hall mutated into metaphysical farce. He'd been the Artful Dodger in David Lean's *Oliver Twist*, and here he was cutting up logic like a madcap William Burroughs fearing for his sanity. This was a reality where the lead performer by necessity was commenting on where he found himself in a story he was both in control of, and at the mercy of.

The ultimate aim of Newley's deformed comedy was to resist the predictable and lacerate an audience's complacency. One episode featured a skit on the power of advertising and the construction of images for the purpose of selling, commenting on media manipulation as though Newley were a student of Marshall McLuhan, but knew his Max Miller, and described a world where the individual was continually fighting a battle against mass conformity. Is technology my tool, or am I a tool of technology?

When it was shown, television had only recently joined print, radio and film as a principal method of communication and entertainment. Newley's lost masterpiece slipped through the cracks; no one saw it coming, few realised you could use television as a canvas for any kind of art, like cinema, so the unfiltered thoughts of a stranded, apprehensive mind were channelled straight into unprepared living rooms, landing in the open minds of any children that happened to be on the lookout for forbidden thrills. Not long after no such thing would come near to being allowed; not until there was Chris Morris and Armando Iannucci in the 1990s was there anything as abrasively, deliriously topsy-turvy.

For thirteen-year-old Bowie stuck in his drained suburban wasteland watching this vivid, wonky deconstruction of suburban atmosphere, a television show that was a TV show within a TV show refracted through the consciousness of a hypersensitive light entertainer trapped inside his own fantastic illusions, it would have been like taking LSD. It would have prepared him for *Dr. Caligari*.

Flashbacks would occur for the rest of his life: Gurney Slade was Major Tom, Halloween Jack, Ziggy, Aladdin Sane, the cracked actor, Thin White Duke, Button Eyes, the invention of a self-contained character that headed out into a reality beyond reality in order to make sense of the world. Once those sorts of anxieties and excitements are awakened they are difficult to ever quieten.

It was this aesthetic take on the potential of entertainment to subvert expectation and a need to keep doing different things, even if some of those things were lightweight and silly that was the influence on Bowie more than the voice. It ultimately gives him a far greater range and ambition than if his influences only came from inside music, from rock and roll and the blues, or within a specific alternative political framework. There was no particular message, as with Dylan, even when he seemed to be issuing commands, recommendations and warnings. As Nabokov said, the writer should not have to deliver messages, because he is not a postman.

It makes sense that Bowie's first full album would reflect this obsession with the unconventional, renaissance mind of Newley in the way the Stones' first was steeped in the blues and early Dylan was wearing the clothes of Woody Guthrie. The all-round, cheeky chappy entertainer Bowie was inspired by had an underestimated range that extended from the quaint middle of the road to so far off the beaten track it bordered on the outer limits of reason. This zipping together of easy listening and an uneasy mental state was at the heart of Bowie's intentions for his first record, rather than an attempt to contrive a family friendly audience-winning cabaret pop. It was the skeletal version of a formula he always stuck with.

For the sake of a peaceful life he would eventually go along with the general, inhibited rock history view that he didn't really know where his head was at the time, and didn't know whether he was Max Miller or Elvis Presley, but it's the perfect debut, in this biography, with its convoluted mania, for the overlit, overworked, overthought, youthful beginning of his recording life, which also ended perfectly, on the dark side of life, a past remembered vaguely, like the light of a dying candle. In between, everything else between light and dark and back again, dedicated to introducing people to different worlds, torn between fantastic, fraught fame and wanting to renounce the world like a monk.

His producer this time was Decca's in-house producer, una-bashed, unvarnished blues freak Mike Vernon, a specialist in recording groups out of the British blues boom from Chicken Shack to Fleetwood Mac. He had just made what is considered the greatest, purest of British blues albums, John Mayall & the Bluesbreakers' *Blues Breakers with Eric Clapton*, not least by generating a carefully achieved live sound that was not going to suit the intricately arranged and orchestrated songs Bowie had in mind. Vernon didn't like the idea of a pop Newley, whether it was the mannered, non-rock and therefore inauthentic voice, or anything philosophically, and suspiciously, deeper. He thought making the album would broaden his horizons; how much it did so, or didn't, can be seen from the fact he never worked on anything quite like it again. He was too sensible to add the necessary, luxuriant otherworldly dimension to Bowie's intense, often rousing little fantasies.

Another way of seeing this record was that Bowie, adapting to his circumstances as he often did, the man who never wanted to fit in also being the man who wanted to fit in, tailored his approach to the germinating sound of his new label, which was only a few months old. The label's second release by Cat Stevens 'I Love My Dog' had been a top 30 hit, and for all where Cat Stevens would head once he signed later for Island Records as a more elegant introspective singer-songwriter, this single had novelty written all the way through. It was labelled Baroque Pop, which would also be used for Bowie's debut Deram material. Bowie would later remark, if it was a battle between him and Stevens, 'Cat won.'

Another early Deram release was by Barry Mason, who had written big mainstream hits like 'Delilah', 'The Last Waltz' and 'Love Grows (Where My Rosemary Goes)', and his 'Over the Hills and Far Away', not in the same instant class, was more production impressionist than song, an attempt using phasing and effects to make something middle of the road seem gently, psychedelically modern.

All of Bowie's thinking, second-guessing, mimicking and cross-referencing, plus the tension with an unconvinced Vernon and the mildly mutant house style of his new label, the fact that the recording was mostly packed inside a week, meant *David Bowie* takes its place in pop history as one of the oddest of pop albums, a start so askew it could easily have been a finish.

The singles taken from it while Deram waited to release the album were Bowie trying so hard to get a hit he didn't care how poppy, novelty and cod-cabaret he went, or trying hard to sabotage any hit potential by crashing into parody, or a sly, far too quick-witted satirical examination of where English pop music was at the time, itself in a weird, warped, carnivalesque location where time was shifting between dreamy nostalgia for some imagined pre-war idyll and a futurist, drug-inspired mind expansion. Recorded music, with all the new multi-channelled technological trickery newly available to create effects, could create comforting and yet disorientating aural flashbacks from a past that never was.

'Love You till Tuesday' goes out of its way to be the very sonic definition of the word 'groovy', but doesn't lift off, with Bowie keeping his chilly distance from the idea of a love song while singing a love song. In terms of hitting the heady moment, it came a frail, distant third to Pink Floyd's 'Arnold Lane' and Soft Machine's 'Love Makes Sweet Music', released a few weeks before. 'The Laughing Gnome' takes too literally a certain, playful childishness, a new innocence that was in the air as bell-bottomed hippies shed their inhibitions, painted their faces, dressed up in oversized, mismatched clothes made for lounging around and hung flowers from their hair. About an antic creature related to the Smurfs and Puck, it goes out of its way to be the very sonic definition of silly, and does lift off, into its own jokey farce, with Bowie testing all sorts of tolerances to their absolute limit. If you have the courage to do this, you have the courage to do anything.

Bowie had the courage to go even further, and at the same time as his pop career is turning into a children's song, he's also moon-lighting in perhaps the most unfortunate rock group of all time, a group whose story is buried in a 1960s that never swung, that was just stuck. It's as though he is determined to walk off into nowhere before he could reanimate himself. Anything you regret, sooner or later there is an opportunity that arises out of it for growth. You have to get in trouble. You have to make mistakes.

In March 1967, after three months playing no shows while working on his album, Bowie joined in with the Riot Squad, who'd been dutifully slogging for years, performing small, grubby venues almost daily, regularly releasing records that went nowhere, clinging on to the hope that one day something would somehow click. Pop music is happening all around them, and they pass right through it without sticking.

Until recently they had been managed by pioneering record producer Joe Meek, but on Friday 3 February, Meek shot his landlady and then himself at his Holloway Road studio-home. They split after this incident, but half the group decided to carry on because they still had some shows booked. A month later, they asked Bowie if he would help out.

It was an odd alliance of artists becoming known for not having what it takes, despite the right contacts, and the constant support of record labels and producers. The tragic death of Joe Meek to say the least also did not seem a particularly good omen.

Bowie agreed to join in an unofficial capacity, deciding not to tell Pitt in case it interfered with his Deram contract. Being

Bowie, immediately responding as a fan to hearing their debut album and making instant changes to his own style, he insisted they let him determine the set list and they let him bring his Velvet Underground prize 'I'm Waiting for the Man' into the group, and songs by the Mothers of Invention and the Fugs as well as some of his own, including a song quickly reacting to the Velvets called 'Little Toy Soldier' that became his pseudonym in the group. His influences were already ahead of where they had been with the recording for the David Bowie album; perhaps he was using this exercise as a shield from the release of 'The Laughing Gnome'.

The first Bowie Riot Squad show was as support to Cream. The group, in awe of their new frontman, who in person had a kind of self-confidence and surefooted cool they had never come across before, let him use them as a chance to try some of his wilder ideas out in a way his last few groups hadn't. He finally gets to wear some make-up on stage, and try out some flower-power props and gaudy costumes. During his brief run with the group, he experiments with clumsy mime and some scrawled self-applied make-up techniques that look more like soldiers doing a pantomime in a prison camp than any early sign of glam rock. They look Bonzo Dog Doo-Dah Band loopy rather than Velvet Underground pop art explosion. It's dressing up to find a new identity, but not done with enough panache to make it anything other than a drunken-seeming stunt. Bowie the toy soldier departs a few weeks before his debut album is released, as if the enterprise had been a sketchy rehearsal for another life.

A scatter-brained first sighting of eventual full-blown esoteric Bowie themes, universes, eccentrics, cupboards, fears, wanderers, confessions, shadows, observations, charades, clues, screens, mirrors, tricksters, manners, fancies, his first album conceals his ferocious ambition and raging intellectual pretensions behind faintly unsettling near-suicidal cuteness. This is perhaps because many of the ideas were first worked out when Bowie was working with Tony Hatch and they brainstormed about writing together a musical called *Kids on the Roof*, openly inspired by Lionel Bart's *Oliver!*

Some songs from it appeared on *The World of David Bowie*, the second Bowie album I bought after *Hunky Dory*, and in early 1972 these songs from just a few years before seemed ancient and crumbling, written by a distant, disturbed relation of the David Bowie of *Hunky Dory*. Now that his death, and the Internet, have changed the time around him, edging him closer to the timelessness he was always considering, they seem closer, and more a part of his overall strategy. He had to start somewhere, and he kept starting, and this was one more place to start.

If it had been the only thing he ever did, it would now be a cherished lost gem by a kinky, enigmatic twenty-year-old king of exceptional experimental novelty, a debonair, playful and squandered suggestion of a non-existent, fascinating, longer career that could have changed absolutely everything.

Classic, enduring albums released in 1967, ones with the adventure, impact and conceptual coherence he would aspire to equal, as a voracious listener and processor of other music, included *The Who Sell Out* by the Who, *The Piper at the Gates of Dawn* by Pink Floyd, *The Velvet Underground & Nico*, *Sgt. Pepper's Lonely Hearts Club Band* by the Beatles, *Cold Sweat* by James Brown, *Are You Experienced* by Jimi Hendrix, *Procul Harum* by Procul Harum, *Something Else* by the Kinks, *The Serpent Power* by the Serpent Power, *Forever Changes* by Love, *Easter Everywhere* by the 13th Floor Elevators, *John Wesley Harding* by Bob Dylan, *Mellow Yellow* by Donovan, *Surrealistic Pillow* by Jefferson Airplane, *King & Queen* by Otis Redding and Carla Thomas, *Evolution* by the Hollies and *Scott* by Scott Walker.

Such records would make him think about what he was doing as a singer a little more intently – there was no real audience for the music on his debut, because he was making pop for a reality that never happened outside his head, so he went looking for one. This didn't mean completely abandoning the reality that only happened inside his head, where he would remain the best actor in the world.

If you chose a single of the year from the number 1s, you have 'I'm a Believer', 'Puppet on a String', 'A Whiter Shade of Pale', 'All You Need Is Love' and 'The Last Waltz' to choose from. If you roam wider, there's 'Waterloo Sunset', 'See Emily Play', 'White Rabbit', 'Let's Spend the Night Together', 'Purple Haze', 'The Wind Cries Mary', 'Light My Fire', 'I Can See for Miles', 'Happy Together', 'Respect', 'Ain't No Mountain High Enough', 'Itchycoo Park'. Bowie was on the outside of that, very aware of how much, with 'The Laughing Gnome' and 'Love You till Tuesday'. He knew, as much a critic as a performer, of other music and his own, that there was some work to do.

Only the resolved mod sweetheart photo on the cover and the album's artwork and lettering give you a direct clue it is the 1967 of *Sgt. Pepper* – the whole pop world, and the beginning of the world beyond, looking that way while Bowie's debut is left to more or less pay attention to itself. Truly a tribute to the misshapen Englishness of Anthony Newley, who few knew was a lost genius smothered by circumstances, an erased Mr Versatile. Another death, but Bowie was already sure this was going to lead, again, to a new life, another somewhere else, some more tourism, another story to throw people off the scent, other places for them to visit, a further exaggeration of his presence, even as he remained obscure.

Deram immediately lost faith with someone possibly actually mad who had delivered an album almost designed to appear in lists of twenty all-time terrible debut albums. Pitt didn't. He knew, from the inside, from close up, how much space there still was for Bowie to visit, to move through, and to create.

The debut album actually did finish with what even the

detractors should agree was a perverse flash of genius, with a London foggy ghost story, the light black comedy of 'Please, Mr. Gravedigger'. A near recited poem set to music and sundry sound effects from scraping spades to falling rain, Bowie packing the Newley into a John Betjeman influenced by Ivor Cutler and Edgar Allan Poe, it featured a rare recorded pop music sneeze and a general, sniffly mood of vengeance and gloom. Every Bowie album from this apparently anomalous beginning features the presence of death in some form – and his first hit would as well – and even on his first, stuffed with a procession of gnomes and oddballs, whimsical feints, deliberate confusions and twee excursions into the known, he can be found, contaminated by the conditions of the world, believing he can think like an artist, staring into the abyss.

And then there was, relatively speaking, silence. If people had developed an allergic reaction to his voice, which they seemed to have done, then what else but to keep silent. Turn to mime. No words, and no voice. Use the body, gesture, expression to get across what he had to get across.

David Bowie came across Lindsay Kemp in 1967. Kemp was another elusive, eclectic and roguish personality with plenty of heroes from Fellini to Chaplin and Ida Rubinstein, constantly moving through a life embedded in potent family myths who was making his story up as he went along, creating more myths, and possible and impossible lives, for himself ... Dancing on the kitchen table almost from birth, seeing his first ballet with David Hockney, sharing a flat with a yet to be discovered Steven Berkoff, time as a female impersonator in raucous northern working-men's clubs stuck between the comic and the stripper, sacked from the Ballet Rambert, from a teaching position at Goldsmiths College. There was also an appearance in the powerfully strange occult British film *The Wicker Man* as the shifty father of seductress Willow, played by the five years younger Britt Ekland.

Kemp briefly studied with the modern mime master Marcel Marceau, learning how the body speaks and how to tap into your physical and psychological energy. A specialist in a mysterious theatrical form of expression where ballet, mime, pantomime, spoken word, music and theatre coil around each other, for someone like Bowie, on the hunt for free-spirited mentors that can escort him over dangerous borders into virgin territory, Kemp was the perfect guide. In performance, silent, able to be anything he wanted to be, the clouds, a bird, the sky, a super being, a puff of smoke, a mirror. Offstage, telling endless stories, mostly about himself, weaving himself into his own legend.

Kemp was using Bowie's 'When I Live My Dream' as the curtain-rise music to his show *Clowns*. Pitt and Bowie had been hoping this song would be the next single, but Deram were hesitating. They had learnt what others had learnt before them: for all his appeal in person and mighty, contagious self-belief, for all his attempts to be sweet and light, Bowie might as well be singing in Chinese considering how commercial he was.

Kemp's choice of song to open his *Clowns* show was the earnest last track on side one of his debut album, slick with wimpy strings, where Bowie's slaying dragons and banishing giants, letting dreams cascade around him, thinking a pop song needs some love, confessing to being a dreamy kind of guy even if people were laughing at him, and nicely cracking the choked-up ballad croak of Newley. If you know the performer who later would do '"Heroes"', it sounds unfocused and naive, but if you didn't, and in 1967 songs all didn't exist in the same space and time and had to appear one by one, separate from each other, then it would have suggested some kind of magic, even if only of what would come next, once the dreamy dreaminess stopped.

Bowie came to see the final night's performance and was enthralled by what he saw, glimpses of a whole new other world. He went backstage to say hello. Kemp was instantly struck: 'It was love at first sight. He stood before me like the archangel

Gabriel. He expressed his desire to learn from me and so I invited him to my flat the following day. We had a lot to talk about.'

Bowie dived head-on into the chaotic and splendid life of Kemp, where you could live, and dress, how you wanted, not by following staid elders or limited fashion freaks, but by following your own instinct. Bowie was introduced to a very free world. Kemp's everyday life was theatre. He noted how Kemp dressed in extravagant clothes, but not like the pop groups of the day were dressing. Get attention through flamboyance was Kemp's motto. Be free and become yourself. Be an artist in order to lift spirits. This cosmic self-help advice appealed to Bowie, not sure who he was, what the ultimate purpose of performing was, but knowing if there was no real answer it was always useful to think about those questions, and change because of it on the way to finding the truth or the best sort of lies.

If Kemp was a clown, and in performance he would often appear to look like one, then he was a postmodern clown, toppling the sanctioned and the sacred, the formal and the fixed, and reviving them in a new fashion, creating a sense of renewal and change. Bowie instantly tuned in to this facet of Kemp, and had no problems – he was the laughing gnome, after all, on the road to Ziggy and Jareth – incorporating some of the methods, and madness, of the clown, as corny as that might seem to some. As he said about his time with Kemp, 'I joined the circus.'

Dressing as a woman, too, or wearing make-up was no problem – not like it would be for prosaic, one-track-minded drummers and bassists worried about girls getting the wrong idea. Mixing up the sexes led to the new forms of freedom Bowie craved, by challenging deadly routine in the most fundamental way and interfering with the entrenched logic of the one thing we appear to be given for sure, our gender.

Drag is supercharged theatricality, and Bowie would use a version of it to cut free of the restrictions that held him back at the beginning. Kemp opened the gates in terms of him understanding the importance of movement as the very essence of life. Movement is life. This thought would actually change the way Bowie made and then performed rock music.

Bowie was a quick learner, always receptive to new hybrids, devouring these new ideas, an avant-garde complement to the more mainstream education in the arts that Pitt was giving him. Kemp in turn found himself learning things from his new protégé, their tastes coinciding at performers like Jacques Brel. Kemp loved Bowie's songs, saw through the confused production and jumbled influences to the spirit coalescing deep within, as though he could sense what was to come, responding to Bowie's early moves like a fellow artist not a pop critic. He felt Bowie was doing with his voice what he was doing with his body.

Kemp taught Bowie to dance, or at least to move in a fluid way. It was never dance, but it was something that enabled Bowie to mesmerise his audience, to draw them in through movement, a glance, a killer gesture. His costumed arm casually draped around the shoulder of his guitarist Mick Ronson during his debut *Top of the Pops* performance of 'Starman' that has penetrated pop legend was a form of dance, a transfixing moment where actual rules of existence were challenged and rerouted, a move into the past and the future at the same time, a transfer of power in a way from the old world to a very new world.

Bowie communicated in a split second that he understood how the female element of his personality was part of his masculinity. Everyone whatever their sexual persuasion who was alive to the moment felt a definite sense of sexual arousal, and in essence it was a dance movement, the art of gesture, filled with distilled truth, something Bowie learnt from Kemp. When he looked direct into the camera, into your home, into your very soul, and announced he had picked on you-*ooh-ooh*, he was singing only to you and only for you, and inviting you to the free world he belonged to. He was doing it using the techniques of a clown.

Bowie flits from Pitt to Kemp and back again through the

precarious, racy neon-lit Soho streets, although how much that meant from body to body is never clear. Kemp claims they were lovers, but Bowie, in this version of the biography, prefers to keep that thought hanging in the air. He might as well be with both at the same time in different rooms, and dreaming something else somewhere else at the same time. There is enough of him to go round, or he leaves it all to the imagination. He spends a lot of time with Kemp, and they feast on fish and chips, and the flesh of their imaginations, and the energy that sparks between them spills into their performances.

Months pass after his short, hare-brained stint with Riot Squad, and he plays no rock shows after the release of his album. He is truly keeping mum, stunned into silence by the reaction to his misunderstood gnome and other ridiculed songs. He's working on his mime, and his make-up after his abortive, sloppy attempts in Riot Squad. The silent months also have David with his impressionable mind contemplating slipping into another state of being altogether.

Relishing the idea of being on the road like a Kent Kerouac and encountering random experiences and unexpected notable humans, having left his parents behind, he was falling in love willy-nilly with exotic people and concepts, and he was ripe to fall for the apparent consolations and revelations of an unorthodox religion, one that promised to cleanse you of nasty Western prejudices. The new rock and roll openness was so open it was letting all sorts of interlopers, opportunists, heroes and villains inside, to see what was in it for them.

Bowie was on the verge of shaving his head and taking vows, making a move many of the hippie flower children and susceptible rock and roll newcomers were toying with, thinking better of themselves by thinking of themselves as spiritual seekers. He was tempted by Tibetan Buddhism, what he called 'the dark side of Buddhism', a religion in exile, with its own wanderers. He fell under the spell of an unconventional, controversial guru,

Chogyam Trungpa, who had distinct style and a reputation for all his wisdom as 'the bad boy of Buddhism' with a known alcohol problem and a reputation for an open and active sex life with his students. In 1969, Trungpa denounced his monastic vows, beginning to live the normal life he craved that contradicted the vows of a lama, but continued his mission to bring Tibetan teachings to the wider world.

Trungpa was credited with bringing Tibetan Buddhism to the West in the first place, one of the last to be schooled in Tibet when the Chinese occupation began. Moving to Oxford, and then Scotland, would have been like landing on another planet. He attracted rock musicians, poets and artists which then became, deliberately or not, part of a recruiting process to find fresh devotees, to turn their new distant patches of Western land where they'd been forced into 'little Tibets' and keep the colonised land alive elsewhere.

Fans following rock stars a little too slavishly would follow what they followed. Trungpa felt that metaphysically inclined artists and musicians were 'fellow warriors against delusion'. He moved to the west coast of America in the early 1970s, and Joni Mitchell visited a few times, considering him one of her greatest teachers, and wrote a song about him, 'Refuge of the Road', where she meets a friend of the spirit, who drank and womanised, and she sat before his sanity.

Later, Steve Jobs of Apple, with guru leanings of his own, would become in his own way a follower, noting how sharp and clear Trungpa seemed to him, and struck by some of his slogans . . . First thought, best thought. Magic is the total appreciation of chance. Things are symbols of themselves. My mind is open to itself. What I call normal you call insanity. And vice versa. Jobs was also interested in attracting followers to a new kind of religion and in showing them his distilled, dubious version of salvation.

Trungpa's Samye Ling Monastery and teaching centre in

a former hunting lodge on the Scottish borders was the first Tibetan Buddhist monastery in the West, increasingly a destination for those attracted to the promise of suddenly fashionable spiritual liberation and a peaceful, mindful community amid a dangerously chaotic world. The hippie period brought a fresh wave of confused, susceptible and sexually liberated youngsters looking for love and support into the arms of lamas, brought up in a Tibet marooned in a sixteenth-century state suddenly transported into the twentieth century, who sometimes had a very loose view of how bliss was to be attained.

Bowie was ready to enter this Tibet transported to Scotland to study and retreat from a world he was increasingly seeing as damaged and damned, and in effect become another character, with another name and identity, or just back to plain, freshly ego-less David Jones.

On the other hand, it looked good and hip in the publicity handouts, and there is a version of Bowie that actually spent that summer, and autumn, of 1967 lazing around, feeling a little sorry for himself, going to the pub, chasing more down-to-earth bliss, and licking his wounds, or having them licked. Becoming a monk was a mere passing fancy. This is according to Pitt, who later claimed he didn't even think Bowie had ever been to Scotland, but that was because Bowie was extremely good at separating parts of his life, and keeping things from Pitt that he would disapprove of. Spending time at Samye Ling, the alert, more street-wary creature would certainly have spotted that the whole thing had elements of a cult, even a sham. Whether a good thing or a bad thing, a treat for the mind or a delusion, those centres of teaching and the absolute commitment they require can lead to participants, without directly being coerced, becoming almost hostages.

The principles of Buddhism definitely interested Bowie – non-violence, the emphasis on wisdom, the meditational practices, and the intellectual glamour involved in the rituals and isolation of a monastery – but like Joni he got all he needed from the 'crazy wisdom' of Trungpa after a few meetings. There were others he could learn such things from, like Bob Dylan – the purpose of art is to stop time – Jack Kerouac – dreaming ties all mankind together – Allen Ginsberg – observe what's vivid – and Lindsay Kemp, who, loving putting himself at the heart of the story, and boosting his own legend, would claim it was him that stopped Bowie jumping from his circus to Trungpa's possibly sinister sanctuary. Gesture is mute poetry and poetry is dance which speaks. He didn't say that. He mimed it.

At the end of 1967, Bowie became an official part of Lindsay Kemp's touring mime troupe, and participated in a new production Kemp had choreographed to Bowie music, *Pierrot in Turquoise, or the Looking Glass Murders*. Kemp felt that with Bowie, their talents were doubled. For Bowie, this was a more exciting group to be in than the tired, hopeless rock bands he was used to.

Bowie featured as Cloud, interpreting the action from a ladder, with Kemp as Pierrot. Other characters included Harlequin and Columbine. There is the Piano Player playing the piano, but naturally there is no sound of a piano. There is love, jealousy, revenge and murder, and Bowie singing mostly new songs that are already resembling the ethereal, prog folk, cocktail acid jazz, avant-cabaret and gilded pop experiments that will soon form the sounds of his second album. He is passing through Cloud, looking down from above and commenting on weird, wonderful action below, so that he will become Colonel Tom, Ziggy, Aladdin Sane, Thomas Newton, Thin White Duke, Jareth, and eventually Blackstar, back in the Cloud.

Working with Kemp was a crash course in the very idea of theatre, and where it had come from, what the original sources were. This was his equivalent of further education, a follow on from Frampton's more materialistic, plastic media teachings. He learnt about a process that began with a need to communicate with the gods through movement in religious rituals, seeking protection, a successful harvest, a victory in battle. As the gestures and movements are set free from religious needs, still deeply symbolic and imaginative, with facial expressions and hand gestures, and compelling signs of intelligence, theatre emerges. From ancient ceremonies, and the desire to disguise oneself in order to take part in ritual dances, the actor appears.

As weird and grotesque as Kemp and Bowie's Pierrot show seemed to those with a distaste for the exaggeration and gurning daftness of mime, even a little fear of the nightmarish, inhuman mute elasticity of it all, for Bowie it was a revelation. He could see what he had got so wrong with the Riot Squad, which ended up as laddish slapstick closer to the Marx Brothers than Ionesco and Genet. Theatre was rooted in a form of communication that developed before the use of language, and for the sake of his own education, he needed to understand and experience that, learn about the relationship between movement and the voice, how the voice depends on movement, before he could further his ideas for mixing pop music with drama and performance. If he really did think of himself as a kind of teacher, then he had to have things to teach.

There were twenty-five performances, mostly at the Mercury Theatre on Ladbroke Grove in London's Notting Hill, the first home of the National Ballet, and by the 1960s a workshop mostly used by the Ballet Rambert for rehearsal and classes. A Mercury Theatre performance of *Swan Lake* starring Moira Shearer features in the Powell/Pressburger ballet classic *The Red Shoes*. It was one of the locations featured in the July 1968 Don McCullin publicity photo session for the Beatles during the recording for the *White Album* called The Mad Day Out.

For a few weeks, Bowie went solo as a mime artist, poor enough in what his real life had become to take some part-time work at a print shop and audition to appear in television commercials. On 19 May he appeared at Covent Garden's Middle Earth club,

which began in a cellar as a centre for a growing hippie underground music scene. Whatever was 'right now' at the time would
first happen here, and where the star of the show would often be
the club's light projection, alive to the point of seeming to have
a conscience with shape-shifting, three-dimensional-seeming
colour mimicking random flights of a fertile imagination, aiding
and abetting whatever altered state those inside were in.

John Peel was a resident Saturday night DJ, and other regulars
in this fertile lysergic atmosphere of experimentation included
Soft Machine and Tyrannosaurus Rex, the group formed by an
old mod acquaintance of Bowie's, Marc Bolan, which played
a form of ornate, arcadian acoustic rock and roll as though it
had first emerged in the Middle Ages in Middle Earth produced
by Hans Christian Andersen. It was hobbit rockabilly, where
the Incredible String Band's fancy knotting of Celtic folk and
Middle-Eastern atmosphere was attached to half-remembered
dreams of Eddie Cochran, and Bolan's music was as separated
in its incensed innocence tumbling over to childishness from the
rest of the pop universe as Bowie's debut, but more mysteriously
beautiful.

Marc Bolan was Mark Feld, and so was also adopting identities, trying different styles, slipping between doomed pop groups,
and had arrived at his surname by taking the first two letters and
the last three letters of Bob Dylan. He originally used an acoustic
guitar and his sidekick Steve Took used bongos, toy flutes and
bells because they couldn't afford electric instruments. All his
BBC radio support came from John Peel, who would also host
some of their shows and read out poems about moles as if it were
the most natural thing in the world.

At the time, Marc was ahead, playing theatres and bigger
halls, and by 1969 about to release his third album, *Unicorn*, an
enchanted, deeply odd masterpiece where hazy echoes of rock
and roll rhythms were filtered through a sitar-like drone. The
songs about chariots, crocodiles, gypsies, sea beasts, wizard

hats, grotesque creatures and misty coasts were produced by the young American producer Tony Visconti playing a medieval Phil Spector based in a mythological Persia.

Ex-session and nightclub guitarist Visconti had moved to London from New York at the end of the 1960s, coming over at the invitation of another American, Denny Cordell, who he had worked with in New York. Visconti assisted Cordell as he worked on 'A Whiter Shade of Pale' by Procul Harum, and by 1968 was working with Bolan and Tyrannosaurus Rex. He was close to both Bolan and Bowie, but ended up working mostly with Bolan in the late 1960s because, he said, Bolan loved making records and worked hard, whereas Bowie was lazy and didn't have the same commitment. This would change later, when Bowie could see how much difference Visconti made to Bolan's music, making contagiously real and distinctive the provisional impressions in Marc's head.

Bowie appeared in June 1968 at the Royal Festival Hall performing a mime piece as support to Tyrannosaurus Rex, 'Jetsun and the Eagle', solemnly fusing his interest in mime with his fascination with the history of Tibetan Buddhism. Neither Marc nor David had yet worked out how to climb out of the underground, but seemed happily locked in to the ideals of the hippies. Their minds were racing, though, towards something that in hindsight we can see was an inevitable combination of mod self-consciousness, androgynous hippie dress and turned on, almost parodic rock and roll style that would be called glam.

As the last year of the 1960s began, they were touring the country as acoustic gypsies, David Bowie as one of the 'Friends' on a bill described as Tyrannosaurus Rex and Friends. Their audience were gentle, bongo-banging, bell-shaking, star-watching, sweet-seeming, nicely stoned hippies. This is how Marc and David ended the 1960s, friends again after separate mid-decade shenanigans, having begun the 1960s as shiny-booted and snappy-suited aspirational mods looking to build their own down-to-earth empires of cool. Originally they were

driven by the idea that youthful fortunes could be made quickly
with the right idea, the right song, and the right costume.

Now, having stepped from one scene to another, always just
making it to the next stepping stone, keeping up with all the
changes like shrewd, quick-witted opportunists or impressionable cool hunters, they were cute pied pipers in velvet and lace,
boy princes of the creative interbred underground, wearing the
curly hair and kohl eyeliner they'd both taken from Syd Barrett
of Pink Floyd who'd blown his molten mind on an acid trip in
the Welsh Mountains.

He'd been forced to abdicate from his reign as psychedelic
sultan, leaving Bolan and Bowie to lead an idealistic raggle-taggle
of hippies disillusioned with the middle-class life most of them
came from, who believed more than ever that love and togetherness would change the world, with no idea that the sincere
peace and love vibe could ever crash to the floor and lead to their
beloved acoustic minstrels betraying their adoration by turning
to electric guitars and posing like sexed-up sell-outs on the make.
They became products, at home being displayed on *Top of the
Pops*; exactly what the hippies hated. For a few months, Marc
and David lived the dream, but behind the gentle vibes they
hadn't lost the idea that with the right idea at the right time in
the right place ... they could become monsters.

David Bowie met the actress Hermione Farthingale during the
summer of 1968 on the set of a BBC drama called *The Pistol
Shot* based on an Alexander Pushkin short story. Produced
for an anthology series called *Theatre 625*, it featured a dance
scene choreographed by Lindsay Kemp, who naturally involved
Bowie. After the recording, he strolled down with her from
BBC Television Centre in west London to Shepherd's Bush tube
station. She was a Kent girl, the serious, thoughtful nineteen-
year-old daughter of a Home Counties solicitor, and a classical
ballet student with ambitions to be an actress who had recently

appeared as an uncredited chorus girl in Richard Attenborough's *Oh! What a Lovely War.*

It's about time a girlfriend enters the story, and that Bowie should fall in love, with a tall, gentle and very smart and mysterious hippie girl with streaming centre-parted red hair in flowing flower gowns who inspires him to enter a settled down creative period that pulls him out of his songwriting lull.

He leaves central London and moves with her to a flat near the Brompton Road in South Kensington, where they become a couple wrapped up in each other. They work, play, dance, chant and sing together. The first name of a group they decide to form is Turquoise, after the Kemp production, which itself was named following Bowie's suggestion because it best represents the light blue that Buddhists meditate on, referring to the limitless heights of ascension, the blue of the sea and the sky, and which promises a safe journey and long life and has the ability to absorb sin.

He puts an ad in the *International Times* for a third member of what he calls a mixed media trio asking for an acoustic guitarist speaking/singing for exciting project – 'must be alive'. John Hutchinson, who had been part of the short-lived Buzz, joins up with Bowie again as the guitarist, but for him it was a little 'arty farty'.

Turquoise soon becomes Feathers, acoustic like Tyrannosaurus Rex, Bowie sat cross-legged as Bolan always did, flamboyantly strumming an acoustic guitar, featuring mime and poetry, as if it were truly a happening. David, Hermione and John make up the trio in a promotional film the still loyal Ken Pitt got made at the end of 1968, investing his own money. It featured Feathers, but it was all about Bowie, featuring the range of his repertoire that a mime would explain by one second laughing and slapping his thighs and the next second by rubbing tears from his eyes and pulling a sad, sad face.

Pitt was still convinced Bowie was destined to be a star, believing that the failures were because no one was ready for him, and that would surely change. He was patiently putting up with all the flighty changes in mood and appearance, his occasional strops, taking it as a good sign that Bowie was now in a relationship and focusing on one project. The problem for Pitt was that Bowie would get excited about a project for a while, put everything into it, and then lose interest, and turn to some other new obsession.

Hermione would find out Bowie had the same problems with a steady relationship. He was totally infatuated, loved being with her, plunged into her aura, gave her all his attention, but there was still room for roaming, and as he grimly reported later, 'I couldn't keep it zipped up.' He behaves wonderfully badly, still only twenty-one, with an abiding and continual interest in sex without any sense of shame or guilt, separate from any binding relationship, a part of his experimentation with sensation and identity. Each fleeting meeting is with a shadow that, as with his half-brother Terry, Bowie can barely believe actually exists.

Hermione realises before most that you can have a little David Bowie, you can even have a lot of David Bowie, but no one can ever have all of him. There is always going to be something he keeps to himself for himself. He has, perhaps, a sterile heart, outside of his work. Struggling with the idea and sheer commitment of falling in love, which occupies so much of his precious mind, he is inept in a relationship, rather than intrinsically a bad person.

When he strays, he becomes someone else, and when he returns to his relationship, he snaps back and continues as though nothing has happened, and has no conception that one thing affects the other. He hates the hurt he causes, but cannot curtail this need to cruise, to take quick, inconsequential detours. He also had that tendency a lot of the males in this new, apparently liberated world shared of still expecting their women to do the sewing, the cooking and the cleaning, as if they were no different from suburban housewives. Even the geniuses like Joni were still pressed into girlfriend roles with their music reduced to craft status.

Not particularly impressed by David the prototype pop star, and definitely not impressed with his sloppiness, and moral slipperiness, how he had these other, blurred lives he would abruptly disappear into, and then return as though nothing had happened, Hermione left him after a few months for one of her own, another dancer, and for the chance to further her career, which she saw as just as important as David's. She got a part, still only as 'dancer', in a forty-song high-camp film version of *Song of Norway*, an operetta based on Norwegian composer Edvard Grieg's attempts to create a Norwegian national music that featured Edward G. Robinson as a piano salesman and Florence Henderson who went on to be the mum in *The Brady Bunch*. It did not as the producers hoped become another *Sound of Music* or *Paint Your Wagon*.

In the Pitt-financed film, which was given the name *Love You till Tuesday*, made up of a series of minimally staged songs, what in a decade or so would be called pop videos, Feathers resemble vaguely sinister, too cheerful, too wide awake, but yet too knowing children's television entertainers. They reflected how the first set of hippies taking advantage of a new permissive society were retreating into a slightly giddy childhood. It was as though they wanted everything to begin again so that this time there would be no corruption and nastiness.

The trio wear nice clothes with cheerful patterns, the boys have clean white shoes, and the girl naturally is barefooted. The boys lightly teased, carefully brushed hair covers their ears but isn't end-of-the-world, druggy long. Lovely Hermione pronounces the words of the songs too crisply, like someone who thinks pop music is beneath her, John is visibly embarrassed by not playing in a group more like Pentangle or Jethro Tull. The only thing missing is some puppets.

David is clearly the star trying to not stand out too much, like it's an early version of his late 1980s group Tin Machine, where the man who became someone by being like no one else now wants to be just a member of a group, someone who has done extraordinary things finding it now more extraordinary to be ordinary.

There is no clue where the music is going when Feathers are playing some of Bowie's perkiest, more bitter-sweet songs riding the swings and roundabouts of the 1960s. There's a complete lack of any trace of his new favourites the Fugs and the Velvets, or even any of his old, weirder favourites, or where he's been with Kemp, the information he's been gathering from peers, contemporaries, entertainment America, beat, jazz, his dreams, his covert adventures.

Any musical clues there are about where he is going, if not music in general, come in a song about an astronaut in space that Bowie wrote feeling frustrated that the coverage of the space missions dehumanised the astronauts and turned them into 'automatons'.

'Space Oddity' in this early demo form still had the sing-song, play-acting qualities of being a children's song for child-like adults, but there was something more accurately menacing and desolate in the lyrics, Bowie genuinely upset and concerned, wanting to express his feelings about a coming event that was on a lot of people's minds. It was as though all of the 1960s had been heading like a rocket to this one achievement; and, down on earth, there had been a procession towards the idea that music was about freedom and it should be free, and there should be a massive free festival that symbolised this change in mood.

It was while working on the half-hour film that it was decided they were a song short. Bowie had a number of sketches and works in progress he would bring to Feathers' rehearsals; this one was taken a little further with some help from Hutchinson. Originally, once Hermione had left Bowie feeling crushed, and the remaining pair were deciding to become a duo in the style of Simon and Garfunkel, it was a duet. Bowie as Major Tom. Hutchinson as Ground Control.

Bowie sang it in a cheap theatrical silver-suit mock-up of a spaceman bought at Dandie Fashions on the King's Road in Chelsea, west London, an epicentre of the Sixties scene where nouveau rock peacocks like Jimi Hendrix and Brian Jones would find their silk frills and plum crushed velvets, dressing as the new aristocracy on a nostalgia trip distorted by acid. To see Bowie not dressed like he was trying too hard to fit in, or not fit in, in futurist non-hippie, non-mod, almost austere silver made a placeless sense of anything he had tried before of his imperfect, estranged, slightly nervy appearance with one pupil almost obliterating his iris, because he might not be from around here. Space had helped him find his own space.

The other sign of where Bowie was going was generated by a few minutes of solo mime, *The Mask*, given a friendly narration from Bowie in a make-believe cut-glass English accent he borrowed from the other Davy Jones, in case people couldn't quite follow the gestures and expressions. This could have been simply another character, a small link, but a link nevertheless, in the chain between the unformed, enthusiastic teenage trier and the world-famous rock god deftly organising his astonishing farewell shivering at the thoughts of what's under the bed; or, as has sometimes been proposed, the mime might be the central performer that Bowie ultimately is, the mimic, the clown, the mute storyteller freed from the dilemmas of truth and falsehood, stripped of the convoluted language and imagery he drapes himself in when he sings. At heart, he is this pure, unrobed theatrical being – and he merely plays at everything else, the pop star, the rock and roll shaman, the conceptual master, the storytelling dreamer, the entertainment swindler, the self-confident icon. He is not to be trusted even as he is to be loved.

In *The Mask* he's wearing buttock-clinging white tights and loose-fitting frilly white shirt, and his face is plaster white as if to remove anything human. As part of a memoir to be pieced together from his own words – or silences – this helps us with the section devoted not only to where he was at the time, more a skilled mime artist than a jobbing musician, but also with what was going to happen next. He gives us a glimpse through a twilight zone filter of the phantom script he is following.

He's walking home 'sort of endlessly' and he looks in a junk shop window, and there it was . . . the mask! He goes inside and tries it on. It's a perfect fit. It's made for him – he was born to wear it. When he gets home he tries it on for 'me mum and dad'. They laugh at his antics, and he's pleased with himself, and takes off the mask. Then he tries it for his mates at the office, and they think he is such a card, they laugh, and he takes off the mask. At the pub in the evening, it gives everyone a big laugh. Oh bravo! 'It soon gets around' that he has become a fantastic performer. At a local concert he is given loud applause. Autographs, film, TV, it all happens, wearing the mask that he can then take off. 'It has a strange effect on me,' he admits and it goes to his head. He still manages a triumphant performance at the London Palladium, the very top of the show-business world. He bows and receives a standing ovation and accepts the cheers when, much to his horror, the mask sticks to his face. He cannot get it off. It smothers him. 'The papers all made a big thing of it. How I was strangled on stage and suffocated. The funny thing is, they didn't mention anything about a mask.'

Bruised by the loss of Hermione, never quite mustering up the necessary adult response to keep her, he moves to Beckenham, north of Bromley, to stay with Mary Finnigan, a journalist a few years older who was living on her own with two children. He's an unconventional lodger, but that's how Mary likes it, and her children adore him, because in many ways he's more child than adult.

Another relationship mixing the work, play, love and Bowie's restlessness starts after a piece of theatrical late-night seduction Mary describes as 'a work of art'. This time the collaboration reflecting the idealistic underground interests of Mary and Bowie's new acoustic inclinations, and a need for both of them to make some extra money, led to them running a Sunday folk club at the Three Tuns, which soon became the Beckenham Arts Lab. It was called 'Growth' because that was the sincere belief, in the idea of progress, self-expression and activism.

For three shillings a week, 15p, you could see David Bowie as he transformed into sensitive, earnest troubadour developing a more complicated, allegorical approach to songwriting, indelibly infected by an obsession with the mysteries of consciousness. He was still the storyteller, but he was now reflecting intensely on his own presence and role in the circumstances and consequences of those songs, and looking out to where Terry might or might not be, where he was housed and in what circumstances.

The original Arts Lab was an alternative arts centre founded on Drury Lane in Covent Garden in 1967, a combination of cinema, cafe, theatre and gallery space encouraging the cross-disciplinary openness of the new spirit of the times, a place where the unclassifiable could easily take place, where exhibition, poetry reading, light show, film, dance or any combination could happen. It's part of the new alternative dream of a 'free city', part of a diverse cultural revolt against discredited values and systems. It's where John and Yoko could appear to fashion their post-*Pepper* avant-garde take on how and why the Beatles were over, and why another sort of momentum and language was needed. Writer William Burroughs lurked in the shadows, drawn by the wayward experimental energy.

Bowie would rehearse and perform his mime act at this original location, developing his own personal take on what he's learnt from Kemp, and part of the Arts Lab manifesto was to encourage other locations to create their own independent centres run along similar lines, blending a desire for anarchic freedom with a consciousness of the community where they lived. By early 1969 there were over fifty Arts Lab centres around the country, and Bowie was taken with the idea of having a venue where if nothing else he would be able to play.

There was a split in the counterculture between those who believed that the imagination was a magic wand, that it was enough to change the world from inside the mind, by making things happen through dreams, partying, sharing, letting progress happen naturally as the result of artistic endeavour. The other side believed the only way to create change was through a more physical, real-world combination of conflict and engaged ambition. Bowie was very much of the former camp, and his setting up of an Arts Lab reflected a belief in the hippie dream of 'come the revolution' that for a while verged on the fanatical. Even eventual disillusionment with the hippie ideal would not shatter his belief that wonder could make a real difference, and that artists be an explicit example of change, accepting Bertolt Brecht's insistence that all art served political purpose, whether implicitly or explicitly. For a while he considers helping to run the Arts Lab his main occupation.

Mary and Bowie threw a fundraising event for their Arts Lab that would help them find permanent premises so they could develop their idea, which at the beginning was limited by being in the back room of a pub rather than a multilayered multimedia house ideal for happenings, a total environment, even with the incense, candles and primitive home-made version of the Middle Earth light show.

People started to attend regularly, and brought their own poems, paintings, sculptures and stories, and contributed to a weekly newsletter. There were encouraging signs of imaginative interior life blossoming in quiet unexceptional Beckenham, showing how ideas that were originally the preserve of the avant-garde were beginning to reach into the static suburbs, and affecting the spirit of previously listless-seeming spaces.

In 1969 the outdoor pop festival, rooted in the jazz festival, established itself as a way of tapping into the communal, spiritual and nomadic elements of the hippie movement; temporary settlements where the utopian principles could be smuggled into the cities and the countryside, and begin infiltrating the wider world. Festivity, but with a radical intention to replace the old with the new.

Blind Faith and the Rolling Stones at the free festivals being held in Hyde Park and Bob Dylan, Jimi Hendrix, the Who and Joni Mitchell at the Isle of Wight sealed the music festival as the ultimate manifestation of a rock world that had changed so much in just five or so years. Even though a small number of people relatively speaking directly engaged with the inner belief system of those radicalised hippies who were new warriors, dreamers, troublemakers, misfits and agents of change, the highly charged and intoxicating soundtrack to the revolutionary zeal was extremely popular.

On the same August weekend as the Woodstock Festival becomes the setting for the historical centre of the hippie dream, where peace, love and understanding can become real and save the world – and turns the Who into superstars – the Beckenham Arts Lab have their own free festival. Woodstock, originally conceived to fund a recording studio and artist retreat in Woodstock, is held at Max Yasgur's 600-acre dairy farm in the town of Bethel, outside White Lake, in upstate New York. Organised for an audience at best of around 50,000, 200,000 tickets were sold, the estimate of the final audience is close to 500,000, and it is described as the biggest music event in history. David and the Beckenham Arts Lab throw their festival at Croydon Road recreation ground, and 3,000 people attend.

In its own small way, with the big names failing to respond to Bowie's sincere request for help, it also sets a precedent. Despite the lack of famous names turning up, the sun shines, John Peel favourite Bridget St. John and singer-songwriter Keith Christmas appear, there's a slightly deranged puppet show, and a distracted, solo Bowie manages to sing some songs from what will be his second album. He's got other things on his mind.

His father died on 5 August, and is buried five days before the festival, and Bowie's rattled and not in the most communicative of states, wandering through events in a daze and keeping his distance. He's in a filthy mood, a black presence with a ghastly pallor among all the colourful fun of the hippie fair. The Woodstock Festival, forced into being free, ended in serious debt of over $1 million and seventy different lawsuits. The Beckenham Free Festival makes an £800 profit from various stalls selling food, drink, souvenirs, jewellery and candyfloss. Bowie appears to prefer the idea that no money was made, as though the notion of a profit completely contradicts the not-for-profit spirit of the enterprise, even though it is meant to be raising money.

He makes another move, allowing himself another change of mind, having passed through the sweet, alluring hippie smoke, into yet another, more analytical, state, saying in his own way an un-fond goodbye to the spirit and illusions of the Sixties. The entire enchantment seemed suddenly foreign to him, especially now there is no Hermione, to soften his jumpiness, soothe his doubts and keep him in one place.

He's making his mind up about the unreality of believing in the pure hippie way that the world can a better place, before that attitude becomes more general and widespread, before the Rolling Stones get snagged by the violent anti-Woodstock of Altamont, where Mick Jagger had to come out of character before he got killed, and never quite made it back to his old, defiantly swaggering self except in parody form, where the free world as symbolised by the free festival turns out to be a false dawn. The dream of freedom without responsibility leads to darkness as much as light.

Even as his friends, fans, colleagues, lovers old and new and a grateful local community are happily revelling in the positive summery south London vibes, he is seeing it all as too naive, too

provincial and too small-minded. He didn't seem to be pretending to think the philosophy of a new civilisation as represented
by the Arts Lab model was the way forward.

He'd talked to Mary in the weeks leading up to the festival
for a thoughtful interview in the *International Times*, and he
appeared committed for life – to the extent that he defensively
suggests the only reason he had released a single as commercial as
'Space Oddity', which was released a month before the local free
festival to coincide with the Moon Landing, was to promote the
Arts Lab venture. He wanted to make as many different people
as possible, from heads to skinheads, aware of the mission of
Arts Labs, to liberate the personalities and spirits of people who
never considered they were in any way artistic.

He believes his role as a pop artist is to use entertainment to
draw attention to the injustices and inequalities of the world. A
hit single would spread his ideas around. He plays the role of
unofficial, abstract spokesman for a new way of changing minds
so well it is hard to believe he was putting on a front – or maybe
at this stage of the story, this is where he needed to be, modifying
his thinking even at the moment he is speaking, on the way to
becoming who he was destined to become.

> I'm not into educating people to think my way. I don't go out
> of my way to turn people on to how I think. If they agree with
> me that's great and if they don't they don't. What might be of
> interest to people is the energy in my songs, even above the
> words. I'm playing energy games. That's how I see it. I do think
> that Bob Dylan and others have sped up changes. Without the
> communication levels they have created the things that have
> happened would still be ten years in the future. The revolutions
> in Prague and Paris, the underground scenes in London, they
> wouldn't have happened without the Beatles and Dylan. The
> reports in the paper about the war in Vietnam would have
> just been reports in the paper without the pop people giving

it greater meaning. Pacifism has found a voice, and that is something I believe in.

He is thinking so fast about his role that even as his support is clarified for the Beckenham Arts Lab community spirit, which he claims would withstand the attractions of a number 1 single, he has moved on. He leaves behind those like Mary who believe this was his future, that he had dedicated himself to a cause, deeply misunderstanding that really he was so elsewhere in his mind and his needs, he was never going to join in with such a doomed mission.

He sheds another skin, faces another way, and on the day, as the free festival is happening, jolted into a darker presence of mind by the death of his father, the embarrassment of none of his famous contacts turning up, and his essential fragility taking over, he witnesses at close quarters what he sees as the death of innocence, the final fading away of the Sixties dream.

He's become disillusioned with the Arts Lab, and he sees the participatory element diminishing, so that it is just becoming a venue where people come to be passively entertained, not be part of a progressive, provocative thinking process. The revolution of individuality and diversity had become a group movement, and ended up with imitators rather than participants. It is not attracting a new sort of public. The Arts Lab becomes merely a part of Beckenham, somewhere to go – the only place to go – rather than a way to imagine a world beyond Beckenham, the all-important extraterrestrial 'out-there' where things really take shape. Therefore, it becomes absorbed back into Beckenham, nothing more than a small, unambitious local venue, and fades away.

He's diagnosing the impending apocalyptic gloom just around the corner in the middle of hippie rapture, as if he prefers to look out of place than be part of a crowd. He can't hide his disgust at the frivolous, trusting, balloon-blowing antics of those at the free festival and within days he's channelling his transformed new self into a song, because he has learnt that is where he can process his fretful, restive responses to the real, and unreal, world around him.

His friends think his strange, irritable mood on the day of the festival is purely because of the impact of his dad's death, but they soon discover he is thinking deeply about other deaths as well. The feelings of loss for his father, for the once-buoyant hippie spirit, for old ways of connecting, with the holding of hands and the sharing of dreams, for a pastoral England that fed into psychedelia, and a natural humanity his father seemed a curious, repressed remnant of, and essentially for the loss of his youth, are mingled together in a new song that is written quick enough to appear in a few weeks on his second album.

He's moving so fast beyond where he was just a few days before that he is already naming the song after something that has just passed, 'Memory of a Free Festival'. This is a song he could have planted back in time from some distance, like those early memories he seems to have created and refined, to suit what the history should be. He is sensitive enough to see that what has only just peaked is already over, and it would quickly seem a remote historical period, and sensitive enough not to be completely cynical, but remember the moment as something that was lovely, and special, but an illusion, sweet, but sadly empty.

He could be remembering Woodstock as much as Croydon, the hippie children, dropouts and crazies having their hash cake and eating it, but he is rewriting his own history as he goes, building up the fantasy, and at the same time shaking his head sadly, turning a corner and heading off somewhere else, down a road that hasn't yet been built.

Another label was, after some deliberation, prepared to try to crack the difficult commercial case of David Bowie, and another album was released in November on Mercury Records, in the last few weeks of a decade that for Bowie turns into quite a combination of climax and anticlimax, prefacing other menacing counter-forces that Bowie sensed or imagined being marshalled. (When he signs to Mercury, they have very few other acts; one they did have was outsider moon-loving hillbilly on acid the Legendary Stardust Cowboy, somewhere between primitivist genius and novelty act, and among a stack of Mercury records, he's given his first three singles. Bowie doesn't quite know what to make of his label mate, not sure if it's Tiny Tim or Harry Partch, but admits he likes the 'idea' of him, and one part of his name.)

Bowie knew what was coming, either because he really did know what was coming, had some insider information, or because he had such an influence on what was to come – the shifting of values, the collapse of reason, a powerful shift in consciousness – that his prophecies or more accurately the warning of a hypersensitive mind in the new, post-hippie songs on his second album have the quality of being remembered rather than written.

He changed things around from his first album so much that what at the time seemed too far out and oblique would eventually take on an almost documentary quality. He was announcing a new kind of species; he was diagnosing a new set of circumstances that would change what it means to be human in these new songs, some of which had the bouncy, Lionel Bart theatrical at their edges, but some of which appear domestic and brief, others of which appear to take on the universe itself and accept that we are accelerating into the unknown.

Free festivals that were already losing their higher meaning, walking on the moon was just going round in circles, the loss of a loved one, the loss of love, and innocence was all on his mind; Bowie felt that something was ending which meant something was about to begin. He was developing an apocalyptic mindset, in the original sense of the word as a prophetic revelation or disclosure, and his disillusionment becomes an opportunity to reveal things previously hidden.

The second album was re-released in 1972 as *Space Oddity* when everything had changed and he was the star, just three years after its initial relatively neglected release as another *David Bowie*, another earnest introduction to his range and compulsions as though he was going to keep releasing a debut album until one of them was a hit. Selling himself in America in the early 1970s, rewriting his past as much as he could, he refers to the second *David Bowie* album as his first album.

Parts of it sounded like it was made in 1967, and he's still having trouble turning his mental intensity and jazz-wired melodic agility into a suitably magnetic chorus, but this time the *David Bowie* album, as his own miscellaneous combination of folk, psychedelia, pop and upgraded showtune, predicted where the music of David Bowie would actually head over the next few years. Parts of it sounded like the Bowie that made *Hunky Dory* and *Diamond Dogs*, not least because musicians and collaborators are now arriving who will stay with him into his new lives and adding their dynamic interpretation of Bowie's being.

His own new sort of thinking was now beginning to get a more appropriate musical setting, where he was not forced to try to compete with what was happening around him, or made to squeeze his odd thinking into possibly palatable but ultimately askew shapes. He had musicians now who could move with him and around him and who he could move with and around; a spontaneous collaborative jazz spirit taken into pop and rock.

Visconti didn't produce 'Space Oddity', unlike the rest of the album. He feared that Bowie, desperate for success, had contrived a cynical slice of exploitation to cash in on the Apollo 11 expedition to the Moon. He didn't think it fitted with the other songs, where Bowie was uncompromisingly exposing a consciousness trembling on the edge between hippie hope and a certain, animated despair.

Visconti's assistant Gus Dudgeon was handed the task of producing 'Space Oddity', the first record he completely produced on the way to early Elton John. It took a newcomer to help crack the Bowie problem: someone who had not yet established their own techniques, who could invent a fresh style based around the song itself and what it was about, which, if it is not about a tragedy in space, or an allegory about drug use, or a romantic break-up, is an eloquent parable of loneliness capable of multiple interpretations. Dudgeon, from nerves or discernment, went so discreetly over the top, he turned it into a compressed brilliantly dust-free space opera, full of synthetic space and spinning detail, with an exquisite, yearning sound reflecting the song's gravity-free sadness that for the first time created a distinctive recorded music stage for Bowie to occupy.

He could throw his arms wide and sing to the back of the theatre, and lean forward and whisper in your ear, and the opulent soundscape, oscillating between a primitive lo-tech Stylophone and poignant semi-orchestral strings, could take it without Bowie seeming madly needy. Many have taken credit for the use of the Stylophone – Marc Bolan claims he gave the toy synthesiser to Bowie, or session man Rick Wakeman, playing Mellotron on the track, bought it at a shop near the studio for seven shillings (35p.). The Stylophone made the song sound fragile and nostalgic, out of control, representing a flimsy rocket about to disintegrate; the strings, arranged by Paul Buckmaster, made the song sound perversely futuristic and grand, representing the rocket as a beautiful streamlined miracle of technology that could take humans to an impossible new place. At the time, Bowie trusted the opinion of Bolan as much as anyone. He took it round to Marc's home, and played it to him. He was thrilled when Marc announced, 'It's gonna be a hit, Davie.'

Visconti had his plans for presenting the elastic, travelling mind and jazz-weaned free-form melodic presence of Bowie, and it wasn't far off where Dudgeon went, going with the idiosyncratic flow and nebulous structures rather than strapping him down, but without sacrificing glamour and modern edge.

Visconti's vision was of a prog-pop south London Bob Dylan set in a shoreless place we can now see anticipated cyberspace but which at the time seemed druggy, because everyone must get stoned, and it was still destined to keep Bowie in an alternative, distant dimension.

'Space Oddity' rode the space wave, after a little initial nervousness from the BBC about the exact nature of those 'protein pills'. The BBC had finally made their response a couple of years earlier to the distracting impact of unlicensed pirate radio, and conceived a pop-orientated Radio station, Radio 1, which was their cautious but confident version of the more underground pirate stations. They took some of the pirate disc jockeys, and pretended as best they could that they were as hip and happening as the pirate stations had been, but they couldn't shake off the prim BBC attitude that they must care for the welfare of the nation.

Any hint of sex and drugs in songs, a touch of the revolutionary, had to be filtered out, and any reference to the actual grown-up urges and sensations at the source of pop and rock had to be increasingly symbolic and discreetly implied to slip past the rigorous censoring rules and regulations. The BBC could not be seen to be encouraging any interest in values that contradicted assumed moral decency and its official role in protecting the nation's mental health.

Those 'pills' might actually mean that the song really was about what some people imagined, an allegory for drug-taking, for being ushered into painless, glorious bliss, for intentionally slipping away from the limited everyday into an eternity more comforting than worldly reality. Ultimately, the convenient idea it could be played as a song about an astronaut to accompany the moon-landing mood of the nation overcame any doubts that Bowie was singing about something else. At worst, he was being a little bit mystical and spiritual, but absolutely not advocating hard drugs.

As Bowie and Mary were throwing their Free Festival, 'Space

Oddity' began to climb the charts. It reached number 5 before its fuel ran out. His dad didn't quite get to see him in the charts; the death of the man who helped Bowie fall to earth laced Bowie's first success, with a pop song about suicide and a whole planet suffering the blues, with down-to-earth melancholy. Haywood Jones's part in the story had come to an end. He takes some parts of Davie Jones with him.

The perfect script, perhaps, has it that 'Space Oddity' was number 1 the July week that Neil Armstrong walked on the moon, but it wasn't yet in the charts even by that Woodstock/ Croydon weekend, and it didn't enter the *Billboard* top 100 – it would be another four years, when Bowie was Bowie, a certified rock and roll starman, for that to happen. The American number 1 the week of man walking on the moon was Zager and Evans' 'In the Year 2525 (Exordium & Terminus)' – a God-fearing warning about technology developing without any spiritual development or moral responsibility – and the British number 1 was Thunderclap Newman's 'Something in the Air'. Both made their own sense reflecting the lunar and hippie mood distracting people from more earthly tensions.

As a hit, it didn't bring Bowie with it. As he said at the time, 'Space Oddity' was an artistic entity all of its own, and it was bigger, as a space age souvenir of the successful Apollo mission, than the singer. The song was a success because it seemed in the general Apollo climate that Major Tom was a heartbreaking hero, not because it was an extraordinary compression of the final seconds of a life into a beautiful song, as solitary in its structure and sound as the experience it was describing.

Bowie himself as a performing artist was not the reason for its success; that would come later, when the song was re-released and became his first number 1, when he was not a mere side act in the bigger circus, when he was becoming the circus, and communicating with the rest of the planet from a distance generated by the sort of fame that was making him seem alien.

He had a journalist's sense of where the story was, but also a poet's skill to see further, and take the idea further, and give people a series of puzzles to work out, based on their own view of their world, and their personal take on the story. The deeper stillness and fear that the lonely, disengaging, completely calm singer was reporting from inside all of that empty, endless space as he voluntarily drifts into darkness and lost-ness, leaving behind a blue planet, blue as in melancholy, was not the reason it was a hit. Only years later would it become apparent that it was a more complex, anxious response to the Space Race, and earthly isolation, and then it would lose its reputation as being a novelty song and the real drama emerge.

Bowie was also taken with how Stanley Kubrick and Arthur C. Clarke had created a very pertinent version of post-contemporary religious myth in their construction of the 1968 film *2001: A Space Odyssey*, incorporating in their expedition to the stars, intentionally or not, a myriad of mythical elements. The lack of passionate dialogue was also appealing, imagining a future world where language is in decline, as if this also symbolised the mind-numbing and de-personalising threat of too much technology.

The film got produced as a part of a temporary Hollywood reaction to the changing times and audiences, when for a brief time they encouraged more experimental approaches and the artistic expression of philosophical, perfectionist but ultimately still commercial directors like Kubrick. A rare cultural epiphany perfectly in synch with the historical moment, when frontiers were still spoken of, the cryptic mythical symbolism and esoteric imagery packed into the film generated powerful responses from audience and critics. It was an unfamiliar representation of a very different reality, but audiences were drawn in by this unknowability, because it was so ingeniously rendered. You didn't know where you were, but you went along with it because the illusion was so seductive.

Bowie identified this, and the sinister hints of a very plausible future where people are emotionally managed by corporate companies, where man and machine are naturally fused together. He recognised something highly evocative in how the film, as Clarke wrote, 'used hard technology to construct a launch pad for metaphysical speculations'.

This emotional power that could be harnessed by a work of entertainment with high-minded artistic pretensions – or a work of art with pretensions to entertain – encouraged Bowie into believing his music could and should satisfy people's needs for wonder and awe, and become a way to fill in the spiritual gap for those with increasingly godless upbringing. It became an influence not only on the obvious response of 'Space Oddity' but also on the longer, more elaborate and prescient tracks on the second album: hazy, drawn-out epics of paranoia, social and personal unravelling, and post-human divergence, the six-minute 'Unwashed and Somewhat Slightly Dazed', the nearly ten-minute 'Cygnet Committee', the seven-minute 'Memory of a Free Festival' where the sunshine is produced by a machine, the five-minute 'Wild Eyed Boy from Freecloud', unfolding like a magic carpet between the Bowie that was and the one that will be. He imagines a new generation as progenitors of a new form of humanity that will struggle to survive while they are bombarded by pseudo-realities.

The elements that tend to be labelled as 'prog rock' on tracks such as 'Cygnet Committee' were not necessarily being inspired by or sharing the inspirations of the progressive rock that was still in its early form at the time. Anything complex, long, multilayered, distorted, epic, featuring strange sayings, cosmic yearnings and pastoral dreams tends to be called prog, but there was no such word at the time. There were just young musicians using rock instruments and amplification, and the new worlds of new drugs, to play with form in ways that were as much taken from jazz and the avant-garde or romantic classical as the blues that originally prompted rock.

On 22 April 1969, Bowie was at the première of a dazzling work of experimental musical theatre depicting a representation of insanity – Peter Maxwell Davies's *Eight Songs for a Mad King* for baritone and six musicians with text by Randolph Stow. It would have been as anarchic and psychedelic as any rock show at the time, even Jimi Hendrix and Soft Machine, and would have made Black Sabbath seem pretty puny.

'Mad King George III's' disintegrating mental state is reflected through a collage of his own words and twisted memories and music he liked to hear on a mechanical organ, accompanied by agitated instrumental textures. The howling, raving king might even be another madman who is so traumatised he had assumed the identity of the king, and he can often seem aware of his own terrible predicament, adding to the disturbing, disorientating effect. The king, though, or the non-king, is not victimised or pitied for his 'madness'. It is just another state of being, and it can be terrifying, and poignant.

The themes of the drama – the study of insanity, the wild workings of the mind, the dislodging of logic – the way Maxwell Davies coherently smashed together different musical styles, the use of fragments of language and stream of consciousness singing that goes from the silly and absurd to the dangerous, the German expressionist techniques used in the production so that the musicians are effectively projections of the king's mind – all of this would have been dead centre of Bowie's area of study, musically, aesthetically and psychologically. It would have been as much an epiphany as Dr. Caligari, Little Richard, the Velvet Underground, Stanley Kubrick and Bob Dylan. It's part of his alertness, and his instant, imaginative response to something he finds interesting once he is aware of it.

'Cygnet Committee' is a shadowy odyssey surveying the demoralising debris of a failed revolution, where he buries the hippies, charts his own progress as a thinker like it's a dream and keeps half an eye on Terry. It's the most immediate sign that

Bowie inside a few months had made an extraordinary move in his understanding of what a song could be and how to master complex themes. The traces of *Eight Songs for a Mad King* are obvious; they don't take him away from pop but they make him think about how he can find something that is his own, and deal with the forces, issues and illusions he's increasingly obsessed by. He's found a way to catch up, and even get ahead. There are traces of the king that would continue through the composition, concepts and performance of his music, through the madmen of glam, the loners and play-actors, all the way to the reflections of 'Lazarus'.

Elsewhere on his second album, on what's left of the earth of the 1960s, back among the lost flower-power souls who think everything is going to be OK by just letting it happen, Bowie also sang a tormented, tearful love letter to his great lost love, the frail, gorgeous, gamine Hermione. He says goodbye to his girl, and that particular past, as if the contract he had signed was over and he was now ready or expected to play a different character, one that might even wipe his memory unless he finds a way to remember, sometime in the future he is helping to build and can't believe will ever end.

Hermione is also having to play a new character and become someone else, and if there were real feelings as they played out the romance that would take its place in the history of Bowie, then nothing can be done about that. It was only meant to be for a short time. They played their parts. They moved on, and she might be a better person because of it, and he has other things to do, other truths to manufacture, other humans to deal with, and other contracts to sign. The kind of love he had with Hermione cannot be part of that. He must be on his own, however surrounded by other people, because the place where he is most at home, where the world makes most sense, and where his work comes from, is inside his head.

Bowie never forgot Hermione, a first, tough glance at the

disruptive realities of love. Or, if he did forget about her, to move on, he would remember her again when the time came to think more clearly about the old days, because he had no choice. He wore a *Song of Norway* T-shirt in the video for 'Where Are We Now?', about how he keeps his past inside his head.

Bowie was still out of phase with where rock was in 1969, not least because he finally had his hit single, which ended up being the novelty hit his new producer Tony Visconti feared it would be when he heard the demo. A closer relation to the moony novelty of Zager and Evans than where rock was at the time, it meant Bowie was still apart, still not to be taken seriously.

If you'd bought an album in 1969, you might have chosen one of the greatest of all time – Captain Beefheart's *Trout Mask Replica* – or Nick Drake's *Five Leaves Left*, the Velvet Underground's third, Iggy and the Stooges' *The Stooges*, King Crimson's *In the Court of the Crimson King*. Or you'd have got something iconic by the Beatles (*Abbey Road*), the Who (*Tommy*), the Rolling Stones (*Let It Bleed*), Led Zep (*II*), Scott Walker (*Scott 4*), Sonny Sharrock (*Black Woman*), Johnny Cash (*At San Quentin*), MC5 (*Kick Out the Jams*), Crosby, Stills & Nash (*Crosby, Stills & Nash*), or Frank Zappa (*Hot Rats*). The Band and Neil Young were debuting, Dusty was in Memphis and Joni Mitchell was in the *Clouds*. The best you could say was that in a year of singles like 'Proud Mary' by Creedence Clearwater Revival, 'Honky Tonk Women' by the Rolling Stones, 'I Want You Back' by the Jackson 5, 'I Wanna Be Your Dog' by the Stooges, 'The Ballad of John and Yoko' by the Beatles, 'Space Oddity' was not that far off the very best. Bowie was sneaking closer to the centre, even if that was only much clearer later, not at the time.

As soon as his first hit single started to drop from the charts, Bowie tumbled with it, falling back to earth. He wasn't destined to be remembered because of 'Space Oddity', not at the time. For a while it seemed as though it would become his own tin can that he was sealed inside, drifting off into ultimate obscurity, never able to contact planet earth again in the same way.

It was given the Ivor Novello Record of the Year award along with Peter Sarstedt's 'Where Do You Go To (My Lovely)?', another one-of-a-kind song using a beguiling, aching, folk-based ballad to smuggle an existential map of the mind into the hit parade. For a few months, but those few months felt like an eternity, Bowie seemed as though he would drift away like Sarstedt into an endless 1960s, repeating his one hit over and over again whatever else he tried as it and he became tragically retro-futurist. Forced in the first place to exist out of synch in the wrong time and space, he would be stuck there forever, perpetually a few seconds from a death he has come to accept but never quite floats into.

'Space Oddity' was just another character he played for a while. Because it wasn't all he was, eventually he would escape its pull. He was ready to take on more characters, and now he's been into space, transmitting the collapsing, ultimate adventurer's mind of Major Tom, everything he did next would have that aura of the space explorer. He disappeared around the other side of the moon for a while into the darkness, but he would soon reappear, returning to a changed world, heading for a hero's reception.

The characters that become part of the story are now turning up more and more, ready for action; the closer David Bowie gets to being David Bowie, the more details emerge, the more people who have their own take on what happened, and how it happened. David Bowie becomes more real as the evidence and interpretation mounts, and he supplies the right sort of details to satisfy and stimulate the increase in commentary and reaction.

David and Mary end their brief alliance, but keep working together, and by the time of the festival, he's with a new girl-friend, born in Cyprus with an American mining engineer father, as oddly put together as he is, as pale and slender, as abrasive as Hermione was gentle, but with obvious, screwy sex appeal. Bowie's happy to explain that they met while 'laying the same bloke', so the myth of their relationship gets the right, unreliable, unsentimental, and shifting foundations.

Angie Barnett and Bowie share the same sense of the fantastic and both appreciate similar more earthy appetites. As far as she can tell he's all sex and brains; he sees the same thing reflected back. She's two years younger than he is, and has an American pushiness that makes up for the diffidence and weird reticence he's inherited from his dad, which rubs up against his clear desire to be noticed and treasured. She's thick-skinned whereas he's so thin-skinned you can almost see right through him into the pulsating recesses of his mind. Sometimes he doesn't seem to have skin at all.

She also compensates for the nonchalant-seeming English reserve of Ken Pitt, and brings to the company of Bowie, which it is now becoming, a necessarily aggressive missionary edge, and a love for the freakier Bowie that soon helps reduce Pitt's more tastefully quirky, family friendly model to history. She took Bowie on as 'her job'. At the Free Festival, she's cooking and selling burgers, doing what it takes, to keep her new prize and help him sell whatever the dream is he's concentrating on at that time. When he flies to the next stage, pulls on another character, she moves with him, unabashed as an insatiable self-dramatising changeling herself by his constant self-revision.

More prepared for the nebulous challenge than Hermione, she leniently excuses his continual need for scattered, dispassionate sexual adventure as another intrinsic part of his irregular artistic process, which turned her on in the first place. In the beginning at least his roving desires are part of the excitement she feels at being with someone with such a voracious life force. She under-stands why he might like the idea of a love triangle; so there is always an escape route for one of them, if need be. An exit. She can cope with that, confident he'll never need to use the exit. Their smartness locks them together; it will also mean they're prone to lock horns.

In October, he spends a few weeks with his grieving mother, as a lodger in his old home dense with disconcerting memories and a time that has stood still reminding him of what he is fleeing from. He moves with Angie to a large, crumbling detached Victorian house with turrets in Beckenham carved into seven flats that looks from the outside like a gothic mansion transplanted from Transylvania.

Their flat is four big rooms, a large dining room, and an upper gallery, and later a small recording studio built into an old wine cellar under the stairs. His workspace is a big, empty room with a chaise longue, a cheap art nouveau screen, a tall overflowing ashtray on a stand and a grand piano where he'll madly work on tales of madness. This is perhaps more practically an authentic Arts Lab, where Bowie and Angie set up camp for three years, where they live when they get married, and where their son begins his life. Born on 30 May, he's given the name Zowie, like he's just another part of his parent's performance, some sort of accessory, which shows where his parent's head was at the time, high in the skies. It will take some time for him to become first of all Joey and then eventually Duncan. He grows up inside what must seem like a film, and he becomes a film director, partial to making the kind of science fiction his dad encouraged him to discover.

The inside becomes clearly influenced by his time in flighty bohemian Lindsay Kemp's home, dark green walls, stained-glass windows, silver-foil ceilings, purple velvet pillows covering the floor. Haddon Hall gets the reputation of being the scariest house along otherwise pedestrian Southend Road, before Bowie the home to a couple of professors and two cats. For those who know that the local hero, and local weirdo, lives there it takes some nerve to approach. As he does his shopping around Beckenham, catching a bus to Lewisham for his shoes and shirts, daydreaming words and melodies for songs that would become world famous, apart from anything else about him that stood out, he was the first man to be seen around those parts who carried a bag.

Inside Haddon Hall on the way to achieving a dream life: parties, playing records, Sly and the Family Stone and Lou Reed's debut, highs, walls filled with photos of film stars and fantasies, the perfumed smoke of dreams, the plainer life-giving smoke from a packet, late-night talks and supper until dawn, the vivacious Bowies, sundry free spirits, waifs and strays, random visits from brother Terry, visiting musicians and collaborators, Visconti scared to go to sleep because the house might be haunted, a different kind of family circle, planning campaigns, dreaming up mad schemes, designing costumes, celebrating the freak of being, working on songs that for a while belong only inside these walls, before they take on a greater life in another time and place, the whole, hyped-up sex, drugs and rock and roll parade, exaggerated – or underplayed – into tabloid rock history.

Angie as hitman, hustler and browbeater, stylist, geisha and number one fan, as well as wild, indulgent wife and zany mother, Bowie haunting his own story as exactly what he needed to be at the time, following the script that only he had access to, a kinky, cavalier, cosmic-minded, post-hippie lord of the manor, still the charming, hard-working, sweet-talking, sardonic, ambitious, randy, permanently broke Bromley boy twenty minutes south of central London, surely the most thwarted pop musician alive, still looking for guidance, a wreckage of spent friendships and doomed romances behind him, a patron saint of rejects, yet to visit America, with ancient teeth, future eyes, a wizardly posture and a searchlight mind who loves meeting new people and adopting new mental positions, who remains preoccupied with his appearance, as a new decade turns up, which will send him, and us, spinning through time, in a world where there is no centre, only decentrings.

Before 1970 begins, officially a new decade with the rebirth that promises, he walks along Beckenham high street, opposite the bank, stops outside a junk shop, and sees a mask in the shop window. It's perfect, he thinks. It's what he's always wanted. He goes inside, and puts it over his own face. Anyone looking on would swear for a moment he completely disappeared.

6

PUSHING THROUGH
THE MARKET SQUARE

David Bowie is noting that suddenly his songs don't look out of place

David Bowie is leaving hundreds of clues, not least about the miraculous structure of the human body

David Bowie is wondering who he is today

David Bowie is a case of mistaken identity

David Bowie is endlessly staging himself

David Bowie is on the brink

David Bowie is marking the pages of all of his books

David Bowie is showing us where time goes

David Bowie is glad to be moving on to something better

David Bowie is thinking about a world to come

David Bowie is moving like a tiger on Vaseline

David Bowie is so wiped out with things as they are

David Bowie is in possession of all of the facts

David Bowie is seeing no point in exploring ideas that have already been explored

David Bowie is what he believes in

David Bowie is wondering who we are in times such as these

David Bowie is ahead of himself

David Bowie is who knows what

David Bowie is immersing himself in the threatening possibilities offered by modern science and technology, and trying to find a way out

David Bowie is quite aware of what he's going through

David Bowie is always looking left and right

David Bowie is torn between the light and dark

David Bowie is warning you

David Bowie is a picture of the future

7

JUST FOR ONE DAY

The 1970s took their shape from any number of events, trage-
dies, trivialities, crises, obsessions, conflicts, characters, fashions,
inventions, resignations, processes and social and cultural situations. It was a decade of cults, terrorists, protests, scandals,
strikes, recessions, environmental panic and a sense of constant
crisis. It was also the decade of Bowie. He always had a dispassionate documentary maker's interest in what was happening
around him, so he thrived on the constant tensions and tran-
sitions, and channelled it into his music which became both a
distorted, dramatic representation of the times, revelling in the
unravelling and feeding off its energy, and a way of decoding it,
dealing with it, and finding escape routes.

His songs started to become a dismantling, an analysis, a prog-
nostic of social forces and currents that were only just beginning
to knock on the door, enacting what Percy Bysshe Shelley claimed
as the visionary powers of would-be poets to become the 'mirrors
of the gigantic shadows which futurity casts upon the present'.
He did this as a pop star having hit singles and chart-topping
albums inside a structured but chaotic business motivated by
profit, and by persuading a whole swathe of aimless, searching
teenagers to look and dress like him; this was quite a move on
from the Beatles and the Stones, but logical, and an essential part
of the onward and outward surge of popular culture, towards the
day it would become the establishment, and when everyone for

better or worse felt it within their constantly photographed and communicated power to act as though they were if not famous then at the centre of not just their own universe but the universe itself.

A star of the 1970s was going to be very different from the stars of the 1960s, and as the ambition of pop and its presence in lives grew, and discriminations and snobberies developed, the best sort of pop star was one who didn't just entertain and more or less play themselves but one who had greater, stranger pretensions to rearrange, and make better, or at least more tolerable, reality.

What was remarkable about Bowie in the 1970s as he finally became a pop star – initially by writing a piece of musical theatre about becoming a pop star, and then following that particular script, even as others started to take over the writing and bend him out of shape – was that he could feature in the teen pop magazines, alongside David Cassidy and the Bay City Rollers, and alongside Mud and Slade, as if he were another anodyne sweetheart pin-up built for easily dazzled teenyboppers. But in his songs and music, and in how he turned these into mobile, multilayered theatrical productions with their own distinct visual identity, he was doing something powerful and subversive. He sang about dismay and despair, love as a problem, a complication, sex as a changeable system, but it sounded at first as though he was spreading light and delight. He told us in the most drawn-out, riveting detail that we only had five years left. We didn't really think he was telling the truth, but then again it was within the realms of possibility, and he sang it like he meant it. If that was the case, he was suggesting, it was necessary to feel things more deeply.

As a writer, who almost couldn't help but develop and become more sophisticated as he was exposed to new stimuli, new artists and new feelings, he created these expressionist X-rays or photographic negatives of the deeper wellsprings of social and psychological reality. His songs, ostensibly catchy, elegantly arranged variations on standards, torch ballads and smart, loud rock and roll, were tracing and abstracting reality and attempting to portray the deeper motivations that surge below the surface of life. He could deal with a sense of dread that was hanging in the air, a constant sense of apprehension at the edges of our lives, by turning it into something exciting, that both diffused tension and examined it. This difference he had as a pop star could be sensed and felt as a teenager even if not explicitly noticed or understood.

He was tackling truths that could not be represented directly, mapping a rapidly evolving set of new social spaces not yet classified, and creating a series of blueprints that the listener and viewer needed to complete through an application of the blueprint to their own reality.

Like any visionary, he was infinitely interpretable. So everyone had a very different Bowie; for some, a Donny Osmond with added strange, for some a glam-rock idol with added spikiness, for some a primal rock star flying high by using great guitar riffs and determined, fixated rhythms who crashed into a wall when he was twenty-seven and then went off the boil a bit, for some a hypersensitive light entertainer who was amazingly also a socio-historical antenna, for some not their cold, bitter cup of tea at all, and for some a glorious, almost saintly, way of defining their difficult, lonely outsider-ness, tackling their despair at not knowing where they fitted, and resisting the claustrophobic entrapment of a grey, inflexible society.

For that latter group, which would increase in size and scope in the forty years after he first established himself, not least because of the cultural currents he stimulated, Bowie located and, using something as familiar and pleasurable as a melodic pop song, directed people towards an inner space where meaning and values are not pre-given by the norms of society. He was a knight in shining armour – all those plastic costumes, glittering gowns and figure-hugging jumpsuits – protecting the vulnerably different 'other' from aggressive incursions into their space by a faceless and remorselessly indifferent society.

He becomes a vivid, active symbol for how the restrictive values of society are not eternal truths but built on a foundation of sand that does and will shift over time. The shakiness of this foundation can be observed – through gaudy entertainment! – and this becomes a provocation to those who rely on an acceptance that the foundations of society are rock solid and correct, and can lead to ways the opposition, whoever and wherever they are, try to nullify the effect. He is searching for identities, for ways of coping with the shifting sands of modern times. He proposed how you can break outside the buzzing monotony and the great impersonal movement of the society you have been pressed into, and this makes you an activist, even if your work is a commercial articulation of the attractions of escapism. Any political comment is instinctive more than deliberate.

None of that might actually be going on, but because of the way Bowie worked and presented himself it could feel as if something like that was happening, making the pop music and the attached imagery even more alluring to the fan. It was easy to make up a Bowie where that was happening; I am doing it now, and I was doing it without knowing it as soon as I became a fan. This could be done because he was so obviously not a Gary Glitter, and there must be reasons why that was the case, reasons he was daring you to come and uncover special information – dropping those names, Warhol, Burroughs, Artaud, Nietzsche, Baudelaire. Maybe he just wanted to make it clear that Alvin Stardust was not his brother.

He might be none of those things, or not intending to be any of those things, but he kept himself open enough for him to become anything that fans and critics wanted him to be, reflecting their own wants and needs. He could be read in so many different ways, because he was so hypersensitive to his own singular reality it took him beyond the particular to a near universal view of his time.

He looked and felt and probably smelt like a pop star, but he displayed the thinking, however opulently, ridiculously and sometimes carelessly, of a writer and artist. This was because he had found, and made up, a direction for himself, in terms of how he dealt with the crisis with himself, and made an escape route from his existence as a Jones of the disturbed, cornered Jones family. To be a star – the ultimate example of getting ahead in the modern world, of making your way in the world, not least because of the material and money it would give him – and to be an artist, a philosophical storyteller making sense of the world around him through the making of myth and the preparation of drama.

It was as though he was an artist who realised that he was not going to make enough money to live the way he wanted to – i.e. not like his parents – and his day job was not working in an insurance office or an advertising agency but as a pop star. Sometimes being a pop star would become the equivalent of a dull office routine where he had to follow office hours, sometimes it would be the way he could be himself, and float free of conventional social pressures. (He knew long before anyone else how being a pop star was just another day job, with its own fixed points, constant meetings, basic uniforms and endless routines, as it became more fully in the twenty-first century, a viable career option alongside the idea of being a self-preserving, self-made celebrity. He was still searching up until his very last hours for ways to make it something else.)

Bowie was always there in this fast-moving Seventies decade, intensely present in his own madly productive prodigal presence. In the next few years, which mostly sit inside the 1970s, there become so many Bowies to follow, interpret, wonder about, spurn or embrace, because the more people have a view on who and what he is, the more records he releases, the more concerts he plays, the more interviews, profiles and reviews, the more coverage and conversation, the more blueprints he issues, the more Bowies appear. Sometimes they have different names, different faces, different soundtracks, different memories, sometimes seem even to be skin around very different skeletons, sometimes they're relatively anonymous or misleading, but they are always based around Bowie and the dissolving Jones.

It's an exaggeration of the provisional 1960s David Bowie, a version made bigger and louder by all the fame and attention, by various cultural shifts, as he moves quickly from idea to idea, sound to sound, and keeps changing his appearance and his mind. In this decade, there are an increasing number of people watching, judging and adoring, and the transformations he makes, the visual identities he slips in and out of, the publicity stunts surrounding him, the risks and dares he takes, are multiplied by how many fans fall for him and how much his style, confidence and mystery influences others.

Once the spark catches, once the prepared, courageous combination of camp, melody, enigma, fantasy, paranoia, electric guitars, shock, male make-up and flirtation took hold, and he found himself at last in the right place at the right time, nothing can stop the momentum from growing. Repressed fantasies, forbidden pleasures, rule-breaking spirit and highly suggestive erotic discrepancies are released with tremendous force into the mainstream. They make it there mostly through Bowie's insatiable mind and body, which has adopted the perfect disguise of an ambiguously sexy, deadly smart and attractively damaged pop star. He'll find that particular disguise difficult to replace.

At the beginning of the decade, he was in a group of one, looking at himself in the mirror – the mirrors, so he becomes many – still in dingy south London, getting high on making plans and thinking 'what if'; at the end of the decade he might sing that he was still alone with his tendencies and issues, but by then he had power, for better or worse, beyond his wildest dreams, to enter and manipulate people's minds, and he was all over the world, either through his own songs and characters, or through the music and pop style he had directly inspired.

If he played at playing a character who is the leader of some sort of cultural revolution, and sang about the imminence of a revolution in how people dressed, loved, posed, acted, communicated, consumed, expressed themselves, he soon had to deal with the reality that something approximating that had actually happened. There had to be someone who became the spiritual controller of a vast change in the nature and appetites of the teenager and the shape and content of popular culture, and he happened to be the one – The One – and it was a case of be careful what you wish for.

He became the chosen one, the ultimate dreamcatcher for a new generation, but the pressure and chaos of it actually being real sometimes threatened to rip the script, and the control, from his hands. He was being watched, from his point of view at times by the whole world, who wanted to destroy him. And by the end of the decade, so much was expected of him, he was handed the levels of responsibility he was always wanting to avoid. The techniques he develops to stay aloof from this onslaught of expectation, the human and artistic protection he organises as circumstances slam him to the ground, only just see him through to the other side.

By the end of the decade, he learnt how to shield himself from the corrupting, life-threatening realities of the superstardom he'd dreamt of since first sight of Elvis Presley, and the secret was in creating a character for yourself that didn't take over in the public's imagination, and ultimately in your own.

He was thought of as Ziggy and his various jagged, demented vaudeville offshoots; to some extent he still is to this day, and for a while he was himself possessed, creating the opposite effect of what he was hoping for, that they were characters he was playing and would then shed, moving on before anyone saw the next move coming, sustaining his mental energies and renewing his work. He didn't want to get stuck in his own success, be expected to repeat himself to satisfy fans expecting the same thing, and then be dismissed for having no new ideas. In pop and rock, once you were dismissed, there was very little chance of coming back, except as a revival act, almost officially forbidden from being allowed to have new ideas. The thought of having no new ideas was appalling; ideas were all he had, were what fuelled his existence, and he had to protect his ability to keep having ideas, which was his way of creating order from the chaos of existence.

He had to return to himself, or as near as he could make it, stripped of the theatrics that proved too successful and addictive, before he could slip back into other, less demanding and less dressed-up alter-egos. He needed to recover the ability to chop and change, to maintain his precious privacy by keeping his distance and giving nothing away about himself other than what he chose through art, and associated decoys and deceptions. He didn't want to return to the obscurity of the 1960s, though, he still wanted that unusual, very twentieth-century luxury combination of art and stardom.

There's a little lull before the storm in 1970, while some corrections and additions are made to his company, his theatre troupe. The curtains are closed, the audience not yet in their seats. As an actor getting ready for the role of a lifetime, he needs the best representation, the best backup, the best hair, make-up and costume, the best lighting, the best set designers, the best photography, the best choreography, the best sound, the best assistants, and the most understanding lovers – and a family that keeps out of the way, or is kept out of the way, allowing him the show-business space to concentrate on nothing but himself and the furious, adaptive tenderness of his mind.

He ends the 1960s as a solo singer with an acoustic guitar, easily classified as a folk singer. For someone with such an ego, he still feels the need to be part of a group. For someone with such an ego, at the beginning of the 1970s there was nothing better than being the out-front lead singer in a rock group. He loves being on his own but he loves being in a gang, a clique, an artistic commune. He's the complete individualist needing to have the last word who also realises he needs a whole host of helpers in order to express his thinking properly. One thing he's learnt is that he needs the best musicians.

He still doesn't know how to name a group, though, as the one he forms around him, with Tony Visconti on bass, Mick Ronson on guitar and a friend from the Arts Lab, John Cambridge, is called the Hype. They use pseudonyms and wear superhero costumes, and don't last long, suffering an embarrassing show at the Roundhouse where they are treated like idiots, which means another rethink.

He still has Gentleman Ken Pitt as his manager, and there needs to be an injection of new, more vicious energy. Pitt with his classy manners and lack of aggression finds himself no longer wanted. His contract is up, he has no more lines in the script, and he doesn't fit into the new era where intense Angie is a considerable influence on Bowie's choices and decisions. Pitt is discarded.

Bowie needs a manager who buys more urgently into his belief system, and he finds, or is found by, Tony Defries, a notoriously bruising fashion industry agent representing photographers, models and designers. He plays the role of tough, intimidating and even dangerous rock and roll manager to such an extent he ends up almost becoming the artist more than the artists he is representing. For a while, though, he's what Bowie needs, his own cunning, conniving, and bold to the point of reckless Colonel Tom Parker, to sell him to a record industry that has concluded, perhaps, that David Bowie has had his hit, his one, peculiar moment, and there was nothing else left.

When hiring his PR people the question Defries wants to know is, do you have any problems telling journalists to 'fuck off'? There will be a lot of telling journalists to fuck off, for the sake of protecting and enhancing the image of Bowie. He also likes the idea of giving Bowie some security guards even before he really needs them. His obsession is with the properties of light, because without the light focusing attention on the artist there is no star, and he is prepared to spend big, ultimately too big, on the Bowie light shows.

With his own self-conscious theatrical nature, ability to adopt identities, and an insider knowledge of the importance of image and style, Defries believes in Bowie even more than Bowie does, or at least believes in the money he thinks he can make – won over as is always the case by the dynamic ambition, his delicious, softening charm, and the ability to keep producing new ideas, and lovely new songs. He has his Elvis, someone to treat as a phenomenon rather than a mere pop star, and he even gets to sign him to Elvis's label, RCA. The stars are aligning.

Bowie begins to travel. Not only outside London or the Home Counties, to the pop north, or Scotland where he finds a little bit of Tibet. He begins a wider wandering, which never really stopped until he stopped, not even after he settled down in his last home, in New York, a city in the spirit of the Arts Lab where a new form of wandering could take over – the wandering through time and space that the Internet allowed him, the contact with new locations and connections that he could now do without having to move, which would yield him the necessary conditions to allow him to follow his chosen path as a songwriter and performer, and complete his journey in some style.

He has a longing for free space and distant lands, which had never been satisfied in the 1960s, but which at one point had led to the flirtation with disappearing into a monastery, like a troubled genius who can only find relief by tending a garden and an escape from the banality of existence not through physical departure but deep into himself. It was another reason why the life of a pop star would be good for him; it was a way to travel, keep moving, discover those distant lands and hear about others he could previously only dream about, or watch on the silver screen.

He started to move further out in the 1970s, and the first stop was America, which made his mind more active, and more paranoid, more delighted, and more disgusted. It made it go even faster, for reasons that were natural and artificial, so fast it seemed as though he would career off the planet. To be American is to always believe there can be a new start.

He travels, often by train, at night, under the endless stars, across multiple state borders, through America the land of the free, the Promised Land that never seems to have an end. It's a great theatre that challenges you to put on your very best performances, a land where the greatest assortment of people come to meet each other, loaded with hopefuls searching for a better life, fighting for more. A vast continent of open horizons and thousands of puzzling, populated towns and cities.

It was all he expected, as a dream, and it was also in the end a nightmare. How could it not be? All that optimism and hope, and art and show business, would inevitably have a dark, rotten underside. The land of his heroes, from Garland to Coltrane, Presley to Reed, Dylan to Sinatra, where Jack Kerouac started his rolling journey, his random encounters, his escape into beat, in the 1940s that would lead all the way in more than name to the Beatles, soon became an Amerika – 'the problem is not that of being free but of finding a way out'.

The collaborations that there were within a hard-core centre of people, evolving and adapting, that helped make 'David Bowie' as a construct, a piece of theatre, constantly staging and revising new productions, became the collaborations that there were with his fans and the media completing the constant blueprints he was giving them.

This collaboration is what produced the finished product, a series of David Bowies coming and going, appearing and disappearing, that exist in many ways and places all through the 1970s, and which we can only glimpse, however hard we look, the other side of the records, the hype, the rock and roll adventures, the interrogations, the running commentary he and others supply, as he travels, from here to there and somewhere else, being trailed, becoming new, becoming scared, becoming another and another, pulling others with him, pushing others away.

The biographer enters through one door out of many. There are hundreds of ways into Bowie of the 1970s, and each way in leads immediately to hundreds of new directions, which themselves spiral off into a new set of directions. He becomes the moving target, putting people off the track as much as making it obvious what he was doing, leaving all sorts of traces, but editing as he goes along, becoming an intermittent feature in his own packed life.

I have set myself a challenge, and must follow the route I first choose, roll the dice and follow where it tells me to go. I cannot change direction. The moments I come across, that I remember, become the ingredients out of which I make a montage. It is impossible to tell in detail what happens in a day, let alone a decade, or a lifetime, and the 1970s that follow could be told, and read, in a day. It is Bowie of the 1970s in a day. A life in a day of David Bowie. There were thousands of days in the 1970s, and every day he's up to something, and making moves, disappearing into his own story, turning his back on having it properly explained.

David Bowie's 1970s in 140 scenes featuring
certain deletions, omissions and oversights

1970

*'I don't know where I'm going from here
but I know it won't be boring.'*

1.

He is spotted first of all wearing a dress, even if for a while you couldn't actually find him doing so. For a while the album went missing and was impossible to find, but the thought of Bowie on the cover wearing a dress, hair tumbling to his waist, playing with some cards, and apparently himself, was too much to bear.

The rumour that he was wearing a dress on the cover of his latest album, *The Man Who Sold the World*, which stayed unreleased for months, created more excitement than can be imagined in the early twenty-first century, where everything gets turned into material to briefly digest and bicker about. It might have turned out he wasn't wearing a dress at all, but the thought he had worn one created the equivalent impact of the hit single he – again – wasn't having after the random success of 'Space Oddity'. It didn't put him on *Top of the Pops*, but it created a hunger for a man wearing a dress to one day appear on the show.

Mick Jagger had already worn a sort of dress, at the Rolling Stones Free Concert in Hyde Park on 5 July 1969, but the truth was it was more a fancy tunic than a dress, almost a long frilly shirt. He could have been wearing pyjamas, a symbol of how the modern pop star was as much introducing the idea of highly informal relaxation into the modern world as anything particularly incendiary. Rock's revolution was as much about changing the way people dressed as the way they thought; ultimately, it might be its main impact, creating a new dress code rather than inspiring a variety of ways to test the limits of reality and challenge the status quo.

Jagger's 'dress' had been designed by Michael Fish, a young tailor who had started making inventive variations on the idea of the man's shirt for various bespoke Savile Row shirt-makers. He changed the cut, making them looser, and extended the collar, making the points larger and wider spread, pushing the whole silhouette somewhere else, adding wider ties with wilder prints in vivid colours. The ties spread wide enough to be called 'kipper ties', one of the most recognisable shapes of the set-in-stone groovy swinging Sixties. If the papers wanted to know which shirts you wore, it was because of designers like Fish.

His Mr. Fish boutique in Mayfair opening in 1966 catered for the rich and famous or those wanting to be rich and famous, and for those pop and film stars needing to stand out and reflect their apparent flamboyance even if they were still wearing suits with shirts and ties. The label of his own designs would say 'Peculiar to Mr. Fish'.

He made clothes to be noticed in. Those looking for a new approach from previous generations even if they weren't gay were drawn to dressing in new, defiantly exaggerated and softer ways, in velvets, silks, ruffles and frills. Men didn't have to disappear behind and into their dour, replicated clothes any more, marching altogether in the same way to the same miserable end. Fish would say that his clothes weren't about taste, or a desire to be necessarily chic. He said, 'Actually, I think I'm rather vulgar. Revolutionaries have to be.'

Bowie was wearing Fish on the cover of *The Man Who Sold the World*. Bowie called it a man dress, cut for man's body. It could, in relationship to Mick's pyjamas, be a dressing gown, giving us an insight into how rock stars could bring the off-duty, aristocratic comfortable into the everyday, except the way Bowie wore it, provocatively lounging in a mysteriously decorated room clearly designed for pleasure, with long, straight hair more insidious in-doors femme fatale than fresh-air hippie, made it very clear he was saying something other than this is how I relax. Actually, he was very relaxed about appearing as much female as male, or perhaps, neither one nor the other, something else altogether, that was beyond the immediate concerns of gender, and was simply a prophetic human energy that required a different form of attire.

It didn't particularly suit the grandly mental music but then none of the album covers designed for *The Man Who Sold the World* did. For a few months, to those of us who were new Bowie fans, *The Man Who Sold the World* was a mystery album, one that had gone missing and apparently deleted almost as soon as it had been released. It had appeared in America at the end of 1970 with a cartoon cover featuring a blank speech balloon where a line referencing records, guns and drugs was reckoned too provocative. The cover would now look at odds with the overall range of Bowie covers, not least because it would be the only one apart from his final album with no image of Bowie, but also because despite being commissioned and briefed by Bowie and linked to the forbidding mental asylum at Cane Hill where his half-brother spent considerable time as an in-patient, it seems removed from the record's careering sound and crazed, charged mood. A cartoon closer to the cartoon eeriness of Dr. Caligari might have been better. Bowie took against it, preferring an alternative cover idea eventually used for the British release in early 1971.

The opening song 'The Width of a Circle' was a seething, ceremonial report on some devastating sexual encounter with a godforsaken mix of man, beast and god in some godforsaken mix of heaven, hell and the damp, dark local park. It's one way of remembering the violence of adolescence, the brutal rapture as you leave childhood behind and innocence crashes all around you.

This was one hell of a way to begin the decade, to begin an album, to introduce a new self as the curtains rise, with an electrifying saga mixing rape and rapture and a coiled, spine-tingling guitar riff replicating a ravishing penetration of the unknown, his knees are shaking, his cheeks aflame. He's bursting out of masturbatory solitude.

Here we are, in the year of the first pro-gay rally march through London, 2,000 strong, being taken into what for many was the most mysterious of places: where man and man and many horned and tailed forces merged inside one unnamed, unexplained and uncharted cavern. Lurking there in passages that wind back on themselves, both hiding and revealing, an intestinal darkness, was a combination of emotional carnage, mysterious passions and shared bliss. And a monster, his tongue swollen with devil's love, facing into a burning pit of fear. Breathe, breathe, breathe deeply, Bowie implores, and that's just what you do as a listener, and even among the snake venom and angry gods, the most charged, threatening line somehow is 'he ... showed me the leather belt round his hips'.

What Bowie was dressed in on the cover is probably what you would wear after, if not before, such an occasion, recovering in carefully arranged style, the only thing missing one of his necessary, reality-enhancing cigarettes and a dense sensual curl of temporarily intoxicating, but ultimately unsatisfying, smoke.

The Man Who Sold the World was where Tony Visconti and David Bowie worked out how to collaborate in ways that brought the best out of each other. Visconti would say that on the *David Bowie* album he produced most of that 'we had no idea what we were doing', with Bowie turning up at the studio with sketches, scraps of ideas, fragments of musical passages. On this album, initially as a theory, and then with the practical help of guitarist Mick Ronson, they discovered how to set up the concept, the plot, and then piece it together.

Each album they would work on could change in sound and

style, reflect and mix a range of genres, experiments and forms, but always be faithful to the central premise, what story Bowie was telling, reflecting his latest travels, the latest manifestation of his obsessions, and where his mind was. The sound might not be necessarily consistent, but the artistic impulses would be. Few other pop artists could achieve this however hard they tried, knowing because of Bowie how fantastic this made them look: to have the ability to move across sound and style, to change identity, to alight in a different place, and always be the same artist. It was not an approach you could copy, it had to be an integral part of your entire reasoning. Only in the twenty-first century, when the shape-shifting aesthetic was easier to replicate, would a similar principle emerge, in a music that might be pop, or hip hop, but needed a new name to describe its altered post-vinyl process.

Bowie as a recording artist began most coherently with *The Man Who Sold the World* not in the sound that was found for this particular stage, which would then just become a part of the storage area Bowie could parody and re-appraise in other places, but in the way it became apparent that each production would require its own sound and design. It shouldn't dart around the way Bowie's mind did, jumping from style to style within the same record. The words and sentiments would take care of that. The sound of the record became the location he was inhabiting.

The *MWSTW* sound was now part of Bowie, and because it became a template, because of Ronson, for the Spiders from Mars, its heat would make it through to Ziggy, *Aladdin Sane* and in a diminished, haunting form to *Diamond Dogs*, and intermittently beyond. Conceptually, it existed in a world of its own, and no other Bowie record sounded like it, because no other Bowie record covered the same subject or was set in the same place.

Bowie was creating the equivalent of plays or films, and each one required its own location, cinematography, sound, cast, structure, even language. A Kubrick or a Fellini film is always a Kubrick or Fellini film, but it is always somewhere else, in another time or place, another country, with its own landscape, weather and emotions. Each Bowie album would be in a different country, be a different country, and where he'd been once might turn up later on another album, but always as a memory, a dream, of that place, never that exact place again. He was moving, and he moved through music that was about that movement, and captured that movement of the mind as well as the body, until he stopped moving.

It was a jazz approach if anything; a rock version of the differences between the different periods of Miles Davis and Ornette Coleman. Same mind, different times, different music. Bowie used musicians and a combination of overlapping collaborators and distinct rhythm sections from album to album period to period much like Miles did, as a mobile, shape-shifting orchestra of many different forms and sizes that could represent where his thinking was, so that the music was always fluid and evolving, keeping the same spirit, repeating themes, but always materialising somewhere else. The self that keeps on changing is a life that keeps on changing. Miles travels from sidekick in the bebop revolution, to post-blues hard bop, to modal invention, to free-form intensity, to spaced-out rock-jazz, a relentless drive to be original again and again and invent new ways to play, to be.

The similar spirit where Bowie is a bandleader as much as singer can be seen on the guitarists that Bowie would use after the initial breakthrough with Mick Ronson; different sorts of players for different situations, used as a part of the experimenting to locate a new sound: Earl Slick, Carlos Alomar, Robert Fripp, Adrian Belew, Reeves Gabrels. He goes through guitarists, and rhythm sections, and sundry makers of texture and atmosphere, to help construct his new sonic districts like Miles goes through keyboardists, bassists, drummers and instrumental stylists.

Even when Visconti did not produce Bowie, as happened immediately after they'd cracked the problem with *The Man*

Who Sold the World, because Visconti at that point was helping to create Marc Bolan's developing fantasy of fame, the principle would hold. Bowie was the director, in total charge, and he assembled the best team possible to achieve the sound and vision of a project. He would never have one sound, but you would always know it was him even before you heard him sing.

As an escape from being the delicately featured solo trouba-dour elegantly strumming acoustic guitar and treading on the sweet toes – or paws – of Donovan and Cat Stevens, Bowie was looking for the relief of a blazing rock sound on his next album, the kind of soul-shaking Who/Kinks/Yardbirds hard, arty anglo-rock sound representing a vivid change in cultural circumstances, the splicing of English energy and an appropriated Americana that he had never managed to achieve throughout the 1960s. Here was a chance to rewrite that history in the way he had rewritten the history of his debut – something he would continue to do, re-imagining what his debut album would sound like if he began at different times in pop history, all the way to his final album.

2.

He is a romantically irrational, already acutely self-reflexive 23-year-old, loftily rehearsing creative genius, as horny as Lucifer, a gawky manic eclectic obsessed with the provocative joys of juxtaposition, naturally attracted to excess and outrage, anxious he might be accused of some mental infirmity, blatantly relishing the alleged thin line between mental illness and artistic creativity, between mere eccentricity and absolute delirium, understanding the instabilities of the categories of male and female, preoccupied with his own physical sensations and the tortured history of his own soul, helplessly infatuated with the highfalutin, keen on acknowledging and addressing a strange world that is not exactly reassuring, intensely fascinated by the apocalyptic, mortality and religious ecstasy, dazzled by the mongrel interconnection

between human destinies, crazily ambitious to rise above mediocrity, sincerely believing that art can transform the world,
beginning to follow the voice of his nature and impulses which
wildly oppose prevailing laws, rules and conventions, struggling
to work out how to sonically represent constantly coalescing
internal perceptions and his belief, using pop music, that time is
a living thing only made sense of by death.

For *The Man Who Sold the World*, an album as much about
the tortured mind of the artist as the tortured mind of his half-
brother, he wanted the sound he wished he had possessed in the
mid-1960s, a proto-heavy metal that actually emerged before
Cream, Hendrix, Jeff Beck and Jimmy Page came up with the
correctly charged, wound-up blend of riff, rhythm, volume, speed
and power yet still with its ancestry in the structures and mys-
tique of blues and folk. This was the power trio plus voice that
would become the central classic form of rock – its symphonic
centre, even though sonically it was related more to the string
quartet, the combination of volatile space and intuitive interplay,
and the constant search for a new dynamic within a very rigid
set of sonic rules.

Bowie's metal madness was a fantasy heavy rock, a grim,
disjointed hint of glam to come, which is why some rock critics
had trouble with it; there was something not quite right. It wasn't
nostalgic, or futuristic, it wasn't clumsy or underpowered, but it
didn't sound like it was in the middle of the present it was obviously referencing.

To the expert, it seemed over-staged, strangely too emotionally passionate, and therefore contrived. Maybe it wasn't manly
enough, or it was too womanly, certainly containing a more complicated, more ecstatic quality, the interchange between energies
usually set in opposition to each other, in a music usually using
purely clichéd male concepts of pounding and trouser-bulging
exhibitionism.

Bowie wasn't necessarily making a fuss about this. It came

naturally. 'Male and female. Let's just call the whole thing off.' For him androgyny was a mental thing as much as a physical one, an expansion of perception, which is where his more literal followers and copyists often missed the point, assuming it was simply about appearance, girl as boy, boy as girl. In Bowie's mind, 'as different as the sexes are, they intermix', and this makes his heavy metal – and any other genre he appropriates and manipulates, from funk to folk, rock to soul, pop to jazz – a very altered proposition. The music and words are always refracted through an androgynous mind.

He also knew more than he should have. His musical knowledge meant he was almost overqualified to make a straightforward heavy metal, loud in volume, limited in concept. Among his reference points were Henry Flynt, there was Peter Maxwell Davies, and there was *Pithecanthropus Erectus*, Charlie Mingus's 1956 masterpiece prefiguring free jazz, anticipating collective discoveries to come, and a beginning point for the conceptual idea of the album. It opens with an immense ten-minute four-movement tone poem charting the rise and fall of man from first standing up, through ruling the word and preaching his superiority, to hubris, slavery, and extinction. With just five players, two sax, bass, drums and piano, the sound is monumental and unyielding.

Mingus was preoccupied with the future of the species, was ambitious enough to want to take huge themes and turn them into music, and his influence made Bowie no stranger to the structurally uncompromising ten-minute epically moody album track tracking the rise and fall of civilisation, the highs and lows of the mind. The twists and turns of 'The Width of a Circle' rise out of the imagination of someone who had savoured the flamboyantly ambitious genius of Mingus.

His heavy metal brilliantly resembled the music it was clearly imitating or celebrating – because Ronson was as an enthusiast and technician as convulsive and precise a player as Beck,

Clapton and Page, and Visconti was adept enough to copy the merciless, free motion of Cream's bassist Jack Bruce – but it was somehow out of synch. It was heavy, in sound and texture, but somehow lighter. It was a bit Broadway, really, but with the fury of something that had artistic integrity. Bowie had replaced the tart Englishness of Newley and the arch whimsy of Barrett with a more expressive power – he was still play-acting, though, often to the point of a melodrama that seemed out of place in rock where a gritty authenticity was the prime element.

It was a theatrical production in the end, not the definitive sound of Bowie, but an intellectual projection that suited this particular collection of science-fiction stories about madness, death, genetic engineering, mysterious controlling forces, primitive Stone Age semi-humans, the tension between good and evil, man and machine, possibly set inside an insane asylum or a blasted landscape, all that's left of the real world, which are interchangeable, and where we are all surrounded by others and completely on our own. There were no hit singles on this album.

But if you hear it at the right time in the right place in the right frame of open mind with the right kind of lust for life and the right hormonal balance and a pure innocent need to understand the dynamic of life and experience the astonishing fantasy of language – so essentially, you believe in Bowie as a two-hearted time-travelling philosophical magician with a bulging brain, inviting you to climb inside his skin, his finger on a dazzling cultural pulse that has yet to start beating – it is entirely exhilarating, showing off in a way you can relate to the possibility of looking anywhere, not just where you are told to.

Somehow he was heartening the anxious by cajoling them into self-expression, just as he had been by his heroes and influences. There was this feverish acceptance of the shape of life as it is, this agreement to be bound by an unknown fate, music connecting with the energy of the turbulent flow of life – producer Tony Visconti's implacable bass guitar mixed up high, menacing the very foundations of the earth – delightfully projecting a sense of the magnificence of life, the joy of life, but addressing the need to be reconciled with the transience and fragility of human life, the arbitrariness of catastrophe, the impossibility of distancing oneself from imminent danger in an age of enveloping media, the terror of . . .

3.

He is as close as ever to Marc Bolan in 1970, and before Mick Ronson becomes his guitarist of choice, before he climbs inside the early membrane of the Spiders from Mars, Bolan is playing his self-taught, abstracted rock and roll guitar – how to play Chuck Berry on a spider web – on 'The Prettiest Star', the delicately down-to-earth follow-up to 'Space Oddity'. It's produced in January 1970 by Visconti, so there is a dreamlike glimpse of what T. Rex would sound like with Bowie singing, or what the Spiders from Mars would be with Bolan as the guitarist.

In an interview in *ZigZag*, Bolan wishes to clarify that even though mentally they are very close, 'to make love wouldn't be repulsive to me. It would just be a bit of a bore with bums, and it'd hurt.'

The prettiest star might be Bolan in the final few months before one of them at least finally makes the switch between wanting attention so much and then getting it – one day it might as well some day be you and I will rise up all the way. It might be about Bowie's new wife, Angie, who he marries in 1970, and who he nicknames Star.

On the B-side, 'Conversation Piece', Bowie the failed, starving and broken-hearted artist, finding out now Hermione has long gone where the end of the world is – a flat above a local corner shop – who has never been more alone, his only friend the Austrian owner of the grocers downstairs. It's a last sighting of the average world and the averageness he is about to leave behind, a last moan of self-deprecating, set-up self-pity, where he's invisible and dumb. He's taking a walk to sort himself out, worrying that you'd never know he'd had 'all this education', he can't think of a word to say, he can't see the roads and the bridges for the rain in his eyes, and he can't see the river for the tears in his eyes.

•   •   •

In 1970, if you fancied something by a male singer-songwriter, you'd be tracking down Neil Young's *After the Goldrush*, Van Morrison's *Moondance*, Elton John's *Tumbleweed Connection*, George Harrison's *All Things Must Pass*, Harry Nilsson's *Nilsson Sings Newman*, James Taylor's *Sweet Baby James*, Bowie's *The Man Who Sold the World*, Kris Kristofferson's *Kristofferson*, Syd Barrett's *The Madcap Laughs* and Tim Buckley's *Starsailor*. For something else, Nico's *Desertshore*, Captain Beefheart's *Lick My Decals Off, Baby*, Can's *Soundtracks*, Fotheringay's one and only self-titled album. Black Sabbath and Iggy and the Stooges were in some kind of fight. The Velvet Underground were *Loaded*. Led Zeppelin were at number *III*, the Who were *Live at Leeds*, Deep Purple were *In Rock*, Jimi Hendrix had a *Band of Gypsys*, but *The Man Who Sold the World* still seemed heavier. The Kinks were selling *Lola Versus Powerman and the Moneygoround (Part One)* but Bowie's still seemed more conceptual. For 1970s top pop single, 'Your Song' and 'My Sweet Lord' were in the semi-final having beaten 'Alright Now' and 'Black Night' with 'Tears of a Clown' and 'Lola', which beat 'You Can Get It If You Really Want' and 'Voodoo Chile'. The year ended with five great number ones, 'Tears of a Clown', 'Band of Gold', 'Woodstock', 'Voodoo Chile' and 'I Hear You Knocking'. Bowie's 'The Prettiest Star' with Marc Bolan on guitar and 'Memory of a Free Festival' sold in the hundreds.

1971

*'You make up little stories about how you feel.
It's as simple as that.'*

4.

He is changing sex on a whim as if it can be done that easily and
painlessly, perhaps after a long sleep, as if it is a personal choice
and within his control, a straightforward way of renewing his
energy and history. He has the strength of a man and a woman's
grace, and vice versa. He is a woman, for now, and at some point,
he would become a man once more. The change of sex did not
alter his identity. He was the same, but allowing one of the many
selves, the many parts, he realised were inside him – there could
be hundreds – to appear in public.

5.

He is wearing a dress, a flowing and picturesque garment, on a
local Granada TV show recorded in Manchester singing 'Holy
Holy', a song that wasn't on *The Man Who Sold the World* – the
record company decided there were no singles on it – and released
as a single. No one seems to notice the dress, or the song. Some
reviewers now hear him as a second-rate Marc Bolan, who has
taken his curls and kohl and bewitching fairy-tale boogie into the
lurid everyday reality of *Top of the Pops*, which means millions
are now paying attention, and he's being treated like a prince.
Bowie is noting this with some interest and envy.

Bolan, of all people, had cracked it, with what seemed to be a
simple case of turning up the volume of his music, exaggerating

the swagger, shrinking the name of his group, intensifying his self-belief, and the adding of a little sexually ambiguous glitter under the eyes to his feminine tumbling curls and free-flowing hippie clothes of silk, satin, velour and velvet. Maybe riding the swan he was singing about seemed somehow connected to the promise of sex. Petit, pouting Bolan in flimsy vest, a pair of tight loons and feet encased in satin ballet shoes, plus the sparkle around his eyes, was where glam began for many.

In the underground clubs and open-air rock festivals, a little playful glitter on a man wearing an orange velvet smock featuring an embroidery of a dragon could easily pass without much notice. On *Top of the Pops*, thrust into the orderly homes of the nation, many vainly clinging on to those increasingly discredited post-war formalities, it was a mind-bending mini-revolution. Bowie would take the drizzle of glitter on the cheeks of Bolan, the wearing of clothing that could be borrowed from a girlfriend or borrowed from a surrealist manual, and turn it into a full-blooded assault on sexual conventions.

On the long drive through the night back to London he sits in the back of the car and talks about how he is going to cut his hair and make it sing – get rid of those borrowed Sixties' curls, which died with Hendrix, got lost with Syd and now belong to Bolan – and take off the dress. Not that he's going to climb into a pair of torn Levi's. He's going to come up with something so far the other side of conventional pop or film glamour it will really make people stop what they're doing and look in his direction. He's got nothing to lose. Scandal was still the best route to causing the transformation of life he believed in.

6.

He is beginning to go through the change. For a while it seems as though he doesn't want to be the one who fronts the idea of 'David Bowie'. Perhaps there can be a series of performers who front each production, who become the characters; it doesn't have to actually be him. He is not the actor, he is the writer. He is not the monster, he is Dr Frankenstein. He lets Peter Noone, once of Herman's Hermits, the ultimate example of a pop group formed to cheer up people, take one of his most melodic songs, 'Oh! You Pretty Things' and turn it into a single with the help of Mickie Most. Bowie is already noting that the surest sign of popularity is your songs becoming mobile, with a life of their own, by being covered and translated.

Mickie Most knows a certain hit melody when he hears one, and this one had been carefully crafted by Bowie the student of the Hollywood musical, knowing how seemingly frivolous and disposable songs can be about important subjects, and how they use melody and structure to provoke a sense of wonderment. He knows that in order to be remembered as a musician, your songs have to have the sort of melody that people will use to bring back the past they want to remember, and where they were when they first heard it. A great pop song is the future that already sounds like the past; a kind of instant heaven on earth. Most ignored, or didn't even notice, the central, urgent meaning of the song, which contradicted the idea of heaven.

Bowie writes in high-spirited, happy-go-lucky disguise about the developing battle of the generations, about post-industrial youth with the new luxury of endless leisure hours to occupy, turning it into a fantasy where a new race who seem to resemble angels are about to use a mysterious new energy to fuel their advanced civilisation. (At the time the mysterious new energy was emitted by a pop song or a rock star; forty years later it would be coming from a screen, a piece of technology, a celebrity brand, a communications device or system.)

Mankind as we know it may well be destroyed in the process. Peter sang it as the jolliest, toothiest version of the jolliest, toothiest Bowie – on *Top of the Pops*, temporary light of the nation, with its own internal issues between the positive dancing surface and more sinister depths – as though it remained his contracted duty to comfort the nation. It becomes Bowie's indirect chart follow-up to 'Space Oddity', told in the body of someone else, without him having to actually get in character.

It's another song much starker and darker than the sparkling surface suggests that plants a few early warning markers about how he wants to warn us – for real, or for show-business real – about a dangerous, untrustworthy world creeping towards self-destruction while appearing to make life seem brighter and livelier. He will use the basic entertainment form of crowd control that pop music is becoming to comment on insidious forms of crowd control that are leading the human race to their catastrophic end. Songs that work out how to survive the oncoming chaos themselves become part of the way to survive.

Another rehearsal for future ventures comes in the form of Arnold Corns – yet another awful group name – where Bowie, under contract to Mercury, hides himself still further, in a mock rock group fronted by another substitute, this one representing the theatrical, cross-dressing Bowie, dress designer Freddie Burretti, one of the new team being formed by Bowie and Angie to turn the conscious-raising south London folkie into an intersexual creature of the space age night. Freddie had been raised in Hackney, moving to Bletchley at fourteen, before racing back to London when he was eighteen, with an approach to dress that was the equivalent of Syd Barrett's approach to songwriting.

Bowie met nineteen-year-old Freddie at El Sombrero (later Yours or Mine) underneath the Sombrero restaurant on Kensington High Street, one of those underground London gay clubs with feverish libidinal energy where hundreds of carefree dance-hungry people crammed into one place could act without fear among their own making history through the night in ways they couldn't upstairs and outside. It was only recently a world where the word gay had appeared as a softer, inside signifier for homosexuals; not long before they were only known, to intimidate and threaten, as queer, puffs and fags, with less specific places to go where they could be free. The decriminalisation in 1967 hadn't changed things that much, not for a couple of decades, in terms of what happened outside the privacy of the bedroom. Freedom had to be found somewhere else, usually underground, in clubs where loud music was played, to bring bodies together, and you were able to dress and behave how you wanted, until the spell was broken.

This was a laboratory for Bowie and Angie to operate in, a place they raided for characters, ingredients, outrage and attitudes to inject into their planned creation. This was where they found the blood and thunder, scales and zest, lust and fluidity of Ziggy. A decade later, still locating new tribes like a surrealist anthropologist, he would be recruiting for his 'Ashes to Ashes' video in a similar fashion from a next generation of now post-Bowie acolytes experimenting with clothes, sexuality, gender and image at the Blitz Club; the gay clubs, comfortable with those remaking, finding, their bodies and beings with extreme new looks, would be the first to let in the early, dangerous-looking punks and then the new, no-name post-glam and punk weirdos that followed, eventually labelled in the tabloids as the new romantics.

There was a frisson of scandal and an intense, unique sociability in such places that Bowie loved; rent boys, hookers, drag queens, sugar daddies, closeted office workers, miscellaneous mystery characters, swollen shadows and Freddie Mercury when he was a second-hand clothes seller blurred among artists David Hockney and Francis Bacon, drag artist Danny La Rue and clothes designer Ossie Clark. All with an urgent need to say something and have it acknowledged.

Confident and in charge of proceedings in their own protected sealed-off location before they returned to their more veiled, coded lives, these hustlers, hedonists, transformers, loners, adventurers and translators were turning their lives on the margins into instant spectacle and works of art, taking real risks with their lives, and Bowie snatched this bold, liberated, if closed-off, approach to existence and being, imagining that Ziggy was one of them. He would be let out to play, bringing with him his experience of all that hidden, cunning, churning energy, and channelling it into the mainstream, via *Top of the Pops*, making sure it was still alive and unzipped enough not to be tamed, anticipating the boldness that was to come as gay life was more accepted.

He tried to make Freddie a star as a proto-Ziggy, but no one was interested, and the correct balance would return – David Bowie carried on trying to make himself a star, and Burretti with his eye for extreme detail, for turning tailoring into fantasy, and the delights of a far-fetched fabric, continued designing the suits and shirts for whatever Bowie was going to turn himself into.

The idea of using others to project Bowie's theatrical fantasies was not going to work, and it would make him more Lloyd Webber and Rice than Lennon and McCartney or Jagger and Richards. It would not seem real, but a weakened, unloved version of the real. The only way he could properly finish off his creations was to be both composer and actor.

7.

He is on the cover of *Hunky Dory* wearing the exotic dreamed-up face and silky blond hair of a 1930s/1940s Marlene Dietrich, of a ghost of Garbo, from an age of persuasion when the Hollywood studios knew exactly how to keep the impossible faces of their stars in the minds of the audience. He's gone back in time, to one of the great original sources of modern glamour, to prepare for the great leap forward.

8.

He is transcending the fraught categories of male and female. His Dietrich/Garbo exists in a sunken dream, looks at the camera like she's turning to face the strange, is given an artificial boost of drained but dramatic colour, is reborn each time she becomes a new character, reads Nietzsche and listens to the Velvet Underground and Bob Dylan, experiences the tangible benefits of both sexes, and has the potential to be a superman.

He is in New York trying to get up and sing in a folk club, but he was no folkie just because he had an acoustic guitar, because they'd seen him in a dress and a change of sex is against nature, just like playing an electric guitar.

9.

He is travelling to Washington, New York, Philadelphia, Chicago, Los Angeles and San Francisco on a promotional tour. Rod Stewart had just done a similar tour, not necessarily to sell records, but to introduce himself. Rod made a bigger impression, and hadn't been seen wearing a dress. Rod is soon breaking into the charts. David isn't.

10.

He is available again as a singer, no longer on Mercury Records, and Tony Defries is selling him in America. He signs to RCA at the end of 1971, a label as desperate to revamp a tired reputation as Bowie. The songs they're played from *Hunky Dory* get under their skin, and so does the encouraging, determined, slightly intimidating words of Defries, and they can't help making an offer. Tony Defries sets about establishing a new management company, Mainman, based on the old Hollywood studio model, with Bowie at the centre, hermetic and individual, like Warhol is at the centre of the Factory, surrounded by acolytes, creatives, catalysts, protectors, run on the same principles of love and tension, that makes music to make myth, and money, and fame, regardless of any rules.

He is going to see the London performance of the Andy Warhol production *Pork* – based on tape recordings from Warhol's Factory made a few years before – and the actress playing Amanda Pork was from New York, Cherry Vanilla. She becomes friends with Bowie and Angie, visiting the Sombrero, having tea at their flat. She will become part of the team, 'the magical machine' that helps look after, style and publicise Bowie. 'I was a little ray of sunshine that helps the flower grow.' Others that had been part of the cast and crew of *Pork* would become the core of the people working for his production company mainly based in New York – Wayne County, Tony Zanetta and Leee Black Childers – so that his parallel Factory is populated by actual Warhol cast-off superstars.

11.

He is the songwriter getting better and more sophisticated all the time, a singer now sounding as much like himself as anyone else, and he knows so much more than he did about the ways and woes of the world from even a year or two earlier. He's learning more about what and who he is, and what it is he does, which is something to do with the combining of image and music into one place to make something more than just sound and vision.

He's outside London, and still inside it, beginning to touch up the wider world, and still staring into inner and outer space. The sound has completely changed, from the album before, and the album before that, but there are those traces of where he's been, he couldn't be where he is now if he hadn't been there, and it's still Bowie, being Bowie, with too many thoughts to sink into, too many directions he can go in, able to rearrange his musical style to suit where his mind has taken him.

Hunky Dory was everything he then knew about himself as a 24-year-old, and his love of music, art, self-promotion, self-awareness and the vexed, vamping glamour of show business, in one forty-minute place. It was a piece of work that said, I have grown up, and this is how I have grown up, by being interested in these sorts of things, and in having the confidence to become those things myself.

Here was another version of a debut album called *David Bowie*, another imagined beginning, another set of elaborate, portable blueprints for a multifarious pop music arranged by a one man many that copied everything and was starting to sound like nothing else. Tony Visconti is occupied with more Bolan and T. Rex, so his producer is Ken Scott, from the school of George Martin, where the producer doesn't really have to know what on earth is being talked about and sold, and what the ramifications will be.

The producer has to know how to turn the songs into grand, or intimate, fantasies, made out of time itself as much as voice, musical instruments, technology and technique, where Bowie the singer glows and flows as much as his thinking. His voice doesn't sound stuck in the moment, but sounds like when you hear these songs in thirty, fifty, a hundred years, in whatever unimaginable setting, it will still seem as though he has just that human minute thought of what he is singing, and it's between you and him and what's going on there is no one else's business. This version of his 'debut' album does not sound like it is set in 1971, like the first one sounded like it wanted to be in and of 1967; if it is set in a 1971, it is a science-fiction 1971, one that is being remembered from centuries ahead, when the images and symbols strewn throughout 'Life on Mars?' are the ruins of a long-lost civilisation. It is about ideas and dreams and icons that might date, but the record itself does not date, however much we are led to believe that it was released in 1971.

Hunky Dory is another dusty but gleaming *David Bowie* junk shop, bedroom, intricate multilayered cavern of obsessions, infatuations, compulsions, children's songs, fancies, parodies, crushes, poses, roles, feints, mimes, warnings, musings and gossip, this time, as fairy tale, space opera, unplaceable and starry-eyed as it got, it seemed set inside sinister borders, still with a wary sense that we're having a party but there will come a time when the party is over. He is making more sophisticated the way he can make the ordinary into something extraordinary, and the extraordinary ordinary.

He paid tribute to Dylan, Warhol and the Velvet Underground,
setting them inside a musical he could easily write about any of
them, casually placing himself in such company, as if to say, it
takes one to know one. I can see you, now you are going to see
me. And if Hollywood musicals are all about Hollywood, whatever else they might seem to be about, Bowie musicals are all
about Bowie, a commentary on his fantasy world, his techniques
and his style. Each song from the musical holds up a mirror to
his thoughts, and expressions. He can look like the Velvets, like
Dylan, like Warhol, because he slips inside their myths in the
guise of paying tribute.

Hunky Dory was a theatrical production, each song placed on
a stage as with *The Man Who Sold the World*, about his discovery of the extent of his own playful, serious mind, and his ability
to read that mind, and tell other people all about it, and how
much it had changed, and hadn't, since he was a teenager, when
he first started to get excited about using music and borrowed
images to process and project his emotions.

12.

He is writing as the Actor some sleeve notes to *Hunky Dory*,
but leaving most of what's going on open to interpretation. He's
only giving so much away because of the fact he has written
these songs about these things; he's not going to give any more
away other than: 'Changes' is about changes, 'Oh! You Pretty
Things' is about when Angie was pregnant, 'Life on Mars?' is a
sensitive young girl's reaction to the media, 'Kooks' is about what
is going to happen to you when your mum is Angie and your
dad is Bowie, 'Quicksand' is a first sighting of America, 'Andy
Warhol' is about a man made of media, 'Song for Bob Dylan'
is about a man made of Bob Dylan, 'Queen Bitch' is the Velvet
Underground out of London, and 'The Bewlay Brothers' is the
latest in the series of David Bowie confessions.

13.

He is a father, but as he sings on 'Kooks' – a close first cousin to 'When I'm Five' – a new kind of father, about as far removed from his own father as he can get. This does not make him a better or worse father, but a very different one.

14.

He is a crooner, or a remote, fabulous singer like Frank, half tender, half tyrannical, but his 'My Way' is 'Life on Mars?' which is lush but also austere, grandiose but ominous, alienated but provincial, set in a timeless and spiritual dimension. Bowie had written some words for the French melody 'Comme d'Habitude' that became 'My Way', but they were rejected in favour of the Paul Anka ones Frank would sing. 'Life on Mars?' elaborated by a sumptuous Mick Ronson string arrangement is if not his revenge then his dream of a world where his song is how people at important climactic moments present their life and their times.

It's about the fantasy you enter when you want to forget the problems of the contemporary world in a darkened theatre, and you might have fallen asleep and be dreaming, but your dreams are cinematic, and they are all yours, and only make sense to you. We are presented only with the fragmented record of certain fantasies, and our response to them depends a good deal upon our own fantasies at the moment.

If there had been the equivalent of a Hollywood studio able to control and change what Bowie was doing, alarmed by the cross-cutting, random flashbacks and its innovation far too arty for the throwaway B-movie they were expecting, they would have asked for the storyline to be clarified. Bowie sings it as though nothing could be clearer, and you can listen to the words without really hearing them, and in the end the only thing that matters, what the song might be about, is that music washes away from the soul the dust of everyday life. He's enacting a ritual.

15.

He is playing 'Andy Warhol' to Andy Warhol when they meet in New York, and Andy wants to scream, to himself, because Bowie also tries out a little mime, wearing one of his dresses and a large floppy hat, giving Andy a kooky version of himself he thinks he will like. Andy's skin crawls. Bowie's no one at the time, just another hopeful trying to impress the great wizard of blank. To the Factory crowd, he's just an overeager English tourist with a creepy gift.

Warhol thinks Bowie might a. be mad. b. look like a clown and be mocking him or c. be able to read his mind. He's not sure if the song is flattery or criticism. The idea that he looks a scream alarms him, and he's nonplussed by the some of the lyrics. He thinks, he's thinking about me, and thinking about me taking a snooze, what a really, really boring thing to do.

Bowie has to work hard to get inside the Factory, because the security at the building is complicated, and made to spurn intruders, which he is really. Warhol had been shot, after all, and Bowie might have thought he was dressed to impress, but in the Factory zone, he's just another freak who might be a harmless groupie, but might have a real grudge.

When he finally does get inside, he thinks of Warhol as looking like the Living Dead. His wig was the wrong colour, and his skin seemed fake. Andy gives David Bowie some 'David Bowie' by photographing and filming him, but his heart's not it in and nothing really develops. They bond a little over Bowie's golden shoes, because Warhol began his career in shoes, but that ends up being a little chat about shopping. Small talk gets smaller between two characters who having nothing small to say, until there is nothing but awkward pauses.

They are not made to mix. It's like two Dr Whos meeting in the same space and time; the universe might explode, or just slowly whimper to a halt. Bowie does not enter the inner circle, or get photographed in tight, whispered insider conversation with Warhol,

Jagger and Reed at Studio 54 or Max's Kansas City. They part knowing nothing more about each other than they did before they met. They must keep their distance from each other, until it is safe for Bowie to play Warhol in a film, and actually, within reason, be Warhol for a while. Until then, he takes a little bit of Warhol with him, as part of how he works the world. Warhol doesn't think much more about him after he leaves, dress tucked between his legs.

16.

He is singing 'The Bewlay Brothers', the missing link between nonsense and a masterpiece, an insight into how his mind works, and perhaps how some minds don't work, and how much information passes through it every second needing to be deciphered and re-distributed, causing so much pleasure and pain.

It's the classic example of a Bowie blueprint that needs, that challenges, the genius of a listener to work out what is going on and who the Brothers are. David and Terry, trickster minds blown? David and Marc, leading, turning, each other on? David and Davie, weaving the episodes of their life into an incoherent plot, creating chaos from the order of existence? Lennon and McCartney, who he intends to outwit? Every line seems taken from a different place, a different song, each line another mask, or another taking off of a mask.

He's employing a way of writing songs that is very different from the more conventional storytelling songs he still uses. It's a performance, not a story with a beginning, middle or end, and it generates its own context. This is pure imaginative verbal invention, locating a place where language intermingles with deepest consciousness. He's crafting words to subdue the formless void of the world, as though he were aware of T. S. Eliot's essay 'That Poetry Is Made with Words': 'Poetry, if it is not to be a lifeless repetition of words, must be constantly exploring "the frontiers of the spirit." But these frontiers are not like the surveys of geographical explorers, conquered once and for all and settled. The frontiers of the spirit are more like the jungle which, unless continuously kept under control, is always ready to encroach and eventually obliterate the cultivated area.'

He's picking up the pieces he finds around him in the ruins of a shattered culture, and gluing them into a collage. It's a technique he would use throughout the rest of his writing life. It can seem like a random set of motifs, but there is seamless movement, it becomes an elegy unified in its diversity. It seems to wander aimlessly, but there is purpose in the wandering, and the song completes itself linearly, taking on a crystalline spatial structure that replicates a pattern of human emotion.

Bowie is just loving how certain words sound when you sing them, how heavy thoughts can be, and how light and dark, revelling in language, and the power each word has to cast a spell, a spell enhanced by being set to music. The words themselves aspire to a kind of music as though they are not going to be set to music; like music, the words exist as a self-entering, self-generating, self-complicating, self-resolving form. It relates to the outside world and straight facts with connotations, feelings, words as historical repositories.

'Frankly,' he once said, 'sometimes the interpretations I've seen of some of the songs that I've written are a lot more interesting than the input I've put in.'

It's a true test of how much you really like Bowie as thinker rather than mere entertainer, and how much you might believe he was aiming to share the speed and splendour of his mind for the good of mankind. 'Bewlay Brothers' is a rambling, pretentious pop song mocking those who even begin to entertain the notion that there is method behind the madness, who stupidly think that it is worth trying to interpret, or it expresses how much Bowie had a voice that was so original and versatile it disarmed close scrutiny as to what it was actually saying. He is technological prophet, he is show-business fraud, and he is both.

• • •

In 1971, Carole King of *Tapestry* was queen, and you'd be scoring your favourite albums by Joni Mitchell (*Blue*), the Who (*Who's Next*), T. Rex (*Electric Warrior*), Bowie (*Hunky Dory*), Alice Cooper (*Killer*), Leonard Cohen (*Songs of Love and Hate*), Deep Purple (*Fireball*), John Lennon (*Imagine*), Roy Harper (*Stormcock*), Pink Floyd (*Meddle*), Black Sabbath (*Master of Reality*), Rod Stewart (*Every Picture Tells a Story*), Sly and the Family Stone (*There's a Riot Goin' On*), John Fahey (*America*), Serge Gainsbourg (*Histoire de Melody Nelson*), Gong (*Camembert Electrique*), Marvin Gaye (*What's Going On*), Traffic (*The Low Spark of High Heeled Boys*), Funkadelic (*Maggot Brain*), the Stones (*Sticky Fingers*), Faust (*Faust*), Led Zeppelin (*IV*) Paul McCartney (*Ram*), Can (*Tago Mago*), or Cat Stevens (*Teaser and the Firecat*). Pop single of the year was between Mick's 'Brown Sugar', Rod's 'Maggie May', Marc's 'Get It On' and John's 'Imagine', but non-hit single of the year was Bowie's 'Moonage Daydream/Hang On to Yourself' as part of Arnold Corns, secretive advance notice of the change he was about to make. In September, *The Old Grey Whistle Test*, the BBC's alternative to *Top of the Pops*, is broadcast for the first time. No dancing girls, no miming, no silly jokey links delivered by day-glo DJs smiling too much to seem human. The first show featured Lesley Duncan, a quiet influence on Bowie's more reflective side, and America. Bowie will make good use of both sides of the BBC's music policy.

1972

'I'm an instant star. Just add water and stir.'

17.

He is landing amongst us like a missile.

18.

He is observing himself becoming the star he always knew he would be, making sense of the life within a life he was living, like a film within a film, which now would be filmed.

19.

He is needing a special pair of red leather boots to step into this new world, as he crosses over from the atomised counter-culture into an unclaimed zone on the brink of apocalypse he can arrange however he wants, free to launch himself as though brand new and to shape the future, one that is brighter today, because he alone seemed ready.

He is becoming Ziggy Stardust, through which he finally becomes a popular figure, a fantastic beast stitched together from astonishing new twisted cult musicians he's getting a close look at, and getting really close to, because they're more his style, and the flesh and myth of obscure old legends who lived on the far-out edge of things. Ziggy is emerging from electric fluid, the death of dreams, the blood of heroic losers, the quilted stuff of fashion pieces of material bought on a local market stall, at Liberty of London, coming to life inside sprawling, mind-warp pavilion Haddon Hall, which looks like it has been struck by lightning a few times in order to energise this new being.

20.

He is Ziggy, the chameleon culmination of everything he has done, all his research and development, and flops, false starts and failures and clumsy attempts to draw attention, and everything that has happened around him as managers, agents, publishers, acolytes, friends, journalists and lovers loyally resist the facts and figures that suggest he will never be anything other than a fascinating, peculiar sideshow.

21.

He is getting his hair cut down into spikes and coloured as red as the sky at night by Sue Fussey from the local hair salon where his mum goes, based on a photo in a fashion magazine, becoming on the Bromley streets a winsome suburban alien, a cute skinny preoccupied freak prowling the grey pavements with invention on his mind.

22.

He is appearing on stage, out of nowhere it seems to his new audience, with a flash of future perfect post-show-business Elvis, imaginary curtains rising to the meta Las Vegas sound of a bone thrilling, be bold, be an artist, be a hero, be ready for anything fanfare taken from the *Clockwork Orange* combination of Beethoven's high and mighty 'Ode to Joy' and the electronic Moog treatment of Wendy Carlos, who had once been Walter. It's an almost casual attack on the rigid distinctions between high and low culture, between so-called serious music and pop music, the past and the present, male and female, and dramatically sets up how what is to come is going to symbolise a series of hybridised identities, un-centred energies and a dislocation of categories. Those attending a Bowie concert at this time expecting the *Hunky Dory* folk stylings with light cosmic dressing will feel assaulted by the sheer naked nerve of the man, or drag queen, or mutant messenger, or whatever he now is. He is still playing *Hunky Dory*, but the act is now all about Ziggy Stardust, which means absurd costume changes, a light show and timing lifted from a musical where Little Richard plays Jesus Christ and Iggy is Judas. It cannot be taken seriously, and perhaps he isn't taking it seriously, but it is incredibly fantastic.

23.

He is now backed by the Spiders from Mars, his best name for a group yet, but then it's not really Bowie's, it belongs to Ziggy, as Bowie will for a while, and Mick Ronson is joined by Trevor Bolder on bass, with sideburns dripping off the side of his face spray-painted red and blue, and Woody Woodmansey as burlesque warrior on drums. His best group yet. They act like they are, and they are, the best trio since the instrumental nucleus of the Jeff Beck Group. The first official stage show featuring Ziggy and his Spiders is at the Toby Jug pub in Tolworth on 10 February 1972.

24.

He is using an interview in *Melody Maker* to make an announcement, one of those places he goes when he's in the mood to play, make claims, and rewrite his past and future. He is gay, he says. Always has been. The writer of the piece, trusted by his new PR team, in fact a flatmate of one of them, Michael Watts, pins him down, for now, in his new character, in the language of the times, when homosexuals were mostly spotted as frothy caricatures in strangely light-hearted entertainment, as a swishy queen, camp as a row of tents, a gorgeously effeminate boy, with his limp wrist and trolling vocabulary. He's picked up this new behaviour on his travels and can play it to a T. Watts plays along, but sees how much it's for show. 'There's a sly jollity about how

he says it, a secret smile at the corners of his mouth.' The rock
critics who at the time are the main mouthpieces for how Bowie
is grooming himself cannot take too seriously that their darling
is doing anything other than playing with the idea, for added
fun and games, the lark of it, and that he remains rock-steady
heterosexual who loves causing a cleverly worded fuss to get
attention, and no more.

25.

He is introducing Ziggy, at not-yet-filled university shows and
town and city halls, and for those not sure about the make-up
and mascaraed come-on's, the moment Bowie gets on his knees in
front of Ronson and plays at licking Mick's strings, the amplified
and illuminated punch of the music into their brain is enough to
convince them this is about power, and transcendence, about the
shattering of rigid sexual classifications presented in the guise of
furthering the cause of style.

26.

He is 1972, which becomes a common year for fans to remember
a first encounter with Bowie, not least because that first Ziggy
Stardust tour cut through the land, trailed by shock, horror
headlines in the newspapers, landing on target after target,
provincial teenagers lusting after their very own idol, their very
own entrance into otherness and other forms of expression. It
was actually a personal risk to admit to liking him, which added
to the excitement.

What can even now seem very contemporary about his music,
because it had enough mental energy to transcend the fashion it
seemed to be all about, made the impact seem all the more dramatic in the early 1970s. It really did seem as though something
out of time had burst into being in the middle of a very static,
wary age.

He materialised into a malingering post-war Britain, which

was dealing with additional problems and potential desolation. As a schoolboy turning fifteen at about the time Ziggy Stardust was becoming a sensation, I would take my copy of his records to school, which was something you did then, both to swap records with someone else for a time, and make clear where your affiliation lay in the world of pop.

Albums could become part of your clothing, a way of instantly breaking apart the uniforms we were all given to make us all look the same and keep us in our place, and you would hold them because they would be the one thing you owned that was something you had chosen, that represented who you really were. It could be dangerous as well. At the time, pinning your colours to the house of Bowie was seen by those into the apparently more grown-up world of Led Zeppelin, Deep Purple and ELP as a silly, teenybop act. There was something suspicious about Bowie, and therefore about any lad who had a soft spot, and therefore possibly a hard spot, for him. As these fans also took the musical high ground, their contempt for Bowie's lack of musical talent could challenge a fan's commitment to the limit. The amount of abuse I received for championing Bowie in those last few weeks before he actually had a hit was considerable – on 'Changes' because how could I like someone who had a stutter, Daltrey's f-f-f-f-f not counting, and on 'Starman' because the 'la la las' suggested he hadn't thought of enough lyrics and was having to pad out the words. Very definitely he was pop, and that was a light, superficial, trashy insult next to the alleged authentic roar of Led Zep, Pink Floyd and Black Sabbath. You were therefore a queer, a faggot, a puff. The blows could rain down on you as you paraded Bowie on the cover blatantly parading his own worrying fanciness.

I remember a few of us, those who braved the contempt, going to someone's house, where we all listened to the Ziggy album, with what must have been almost erotic reverence. Again and again, it was hard to stop. It was the greatest thing we had ever done, sharing this moment of entrance into a brave new world. We'd think of this moment, the biggest change imaginable short of losing our virginity, for the rest of our lives.

27.

He is playing Manchester Free Trade Hall, where I see him for the first time in concert, actually get within a few yards of him, and as excited as I was I had no idea what was about to happen. I turned up hours before, just hanging around outside the theatre along with a few others, keeping our distance from each other, hoping for a glimpse in the flesh of someone I now so intimately knew the sound of. I saw the van turn up with the equipment, which made it seem like the countdown had begun. The hairy roadies rolling the gear into the doors at the back did not look like they knew much about Mars, mostly beer and denim. They were going to build things, I guessed, build the stage in the shape of a rocket, and not actually fly it. This is how I remembered that night, a memory of a memory:

I saw David Bowie on Friday 21 April 1972, and it was one of those times when everything seemed to change. Bowie was at the time pretty much a one-hit wonder for 'Space Oddity', recently a cult album artist, just beginning to play around with his image by appearing to come out in a quickly notorious Melody Maker *interview. So to some he was, bluntly speaking, a pervert. He began the year releasing 'Changes', which didn't make the charts, at the time another one of those secretive Bowie songs, off the back of the arty-fairy December 1971-released* Hunky Dory, *and spent the rest of the year changing by the day as if profoundly offended that it wasn't a hit, that he wasn't yet a superstar, forcing everyone around him to change with him, to keep up.*

Bowie willed it to happen that year, he was pure force of tarted-up nature, and at the end of April, in Manchester, a few weeks into the Ziggy tour, he was at the absolute theatrical peak of his newly minted hyper-ambitious powers of persuasion. I was barely fifteen, making first moves out on my own doing my very own things, fresh innocent fan putty in Bowie's hot, shameless 25-year-old hands, and it was only something like my fifth live gig, and there's nothing quite like seeing a fully made-up codpiece-sporting man-thing inspired by A Clockwork Orange, Andy Warhol, the Velvet Underground, William Burroughs, Jean Cocteau, Marc Bolan *and* Iggy Pop *suddenly burst into dead, drab Manchester and set your life on fire.*

Even better, he pretended, or actually believed, that he was a skinny alien pop star called Ziggy Stardust keen on mock-fellating his silver-suited guitar player in strobe-induced slow motion as if this was how you worshipped things in his sect. This was what you wanted a pop concert to be – a dream of sex turned into loud, savage rock and roll theatre, every song a desperately outrageous story about feeling high on life even as the world was crashing to the floor around you. He may have just released Hunky Dory, *which I was only just beginning to make sense of, but he was already trashing his way through the tumultuous surreal life story of* Ziggy Stardust and the Spiders from Mars. *He was promoting an album that wasn't even out yet, so sure that these new songs, which you'd heard hints of in other contexts over the previous few months, were strong enough to bounce off their newness right into the minds of those who were already convinced.*

There were only a few hundred denim-clad scruffy-haired virginal earthlings in a theatre that could hold a couple of thousand, early fanatics inspired by fishy sightings of Bowie in orange hair and red plastic boots smooching with guitarist Mick Ronson on The Old Grey Whistle Test *whilst playing music that seemed to fuse Led Zeppelin with Liza with a Z, the Who with Dalí, Lou Reed with the Wizard of Oz. Acoustic, folk-shock* Hunky Dory *songs were the sweet, trippy aperitif for some impossibly ravishing hard-core Ziggy fantasy, domestic details and exotic*

travel reporting before an abandoned leap off the planet. I was
in the eighth row of the stalls – a 60p ticket grabbed the morn-
ing the box office opened – a couple of rows behind an adoring,
cheerleading Angie Bowie, already known as a combination of
wife, sister, adviser, adorer.

Bowie, as single-minded as any performer I've ever seen, was
some kind of demon in a tizzy acting like some kind of super-
star seeking soulmates, using the sharpest most reinforced of
rock riffs to illuminate his presence as a higher power, ignoring
the empty spaces in the hall, knowing next time he was around
they'd be filled, committing himself to turning us on, so he could
turn himself on.

28.

He is releasing 'Starman' as a single in April. To some it's clearly
the direct follow-up to 'Space Oddity', as though this is what
happened next to the man in space. A reaction to an executive
consideration at RCA that yet again he has made an album with
no obvious hit single – 'Changes' at the time seems too full of
tricky changes to be a hit, to become a beloved anthem of vital
transformation – because he still finds it difficult to distil the
jazzy, deviant fever of his mind into an instant radio-friendly
chorus.

'Starman' is a way of imagining there must be by now a formula to making a David Bowie single. It starts in outer space. It
starts with an ethereally strummed acoustic guitar. There's one
of his great opening lines that instantly place you somewhere
else, in another life. If the chorus that will pierce the fog and
send him into fame is missing, because he still finds it difficult
to bring himself to deal in the obviousness that is the soul of a
great chorus, then what would Judy Garland do? How would she
reach into the minds of an audience who only want to remember
a piece of music if it stands up for itself and claims a part of their
life? She can do this without sacrificing her power, even if she

does sacrifice a bit of her innocence, possibly even her life force. It's a risk worth taking.

29.

He is telling a story, and building up a picture. He is drawing in the listener, and establishing a memory that he wants to become a myth. He is remembering the excitement he would feel, coming across Little Richard, or the Who, or the Velvet Underground, or silent, miming Lindsay Kemp, when he was listening to the radio and hearing new worlds, watching television, going to the cinema, and bouncing into new minds and bodies. He is going overboard, but this time he is going to do it in the chorus, like Judy would when she was soaring over the rainbow, like Marc does when he makes it plain and simple that a pop single comes down to nothing but the boogie. Bolan has become a spellbinding pop star by stating very emphatically and without any irony that he was born to boogie. I love to boogie, sings Marc, crazy enough to think that people will believe him, and that was that.

Where has the boogie come from, that becomes part of the key to unlock glam stardom? It's a fourteenth-century synonym for heretic, it's a seventeenth-century description of those who commit vile acts like sodomy, it's a nickname for the devil, for hobgoblins and bogeymen in general, which leads it to be attached to nineteenth-century slaves, who took the West African word 'm'bugi', with them, meaning devilishly good. This all becomes mixed, diffused and fixed into music by being the name used for a form of 1920s jazz known as boogie-woogie, which emerged from rough music being played in honky-tonks, which itself formed out of a piano sound reflecting the new clickety-click train-sounds being made on the railway lines criss-crossing America, which had been built by slaves. This unruly, excitable music would be played at house parties, the soundtrack to the pandemonium of pleasure, and to 'boogie' comes to mean to party. Great music is about a great party that is being held some-where in the distance and which if you can find it will make a world of difference to your life and your reality. To boogie is to party, to vault into a protected place where all your troubles are vanquished and you can instantly change who you are. You will feel no shame at this party. This is no time for shame.

30.

He is saying, the starman is saying, because he looks exactly like the starman, sexy but sexless, friend but alien: let everyone lost in a world of confusion and imminent devastation have a party. It's clear looking at him, and the people he hangs out with, that anything goes. Finding the chorus, the star melody, in the shape of a graceful vocal leap high into the sky, he eventually makes it onto *Top of the Pops*, where the BBC generously, possibly acci-dentally, allows minds to be blown. He sings in this song within a song, about how he's heard of this radiant new singer who has so much power he might really scare your parents; he looks directly into the camera, a singer who's lighting up a dreary nation, and he's calling someone to pass on the secret, which happens to be you, and only you. The guitar becomes an electrifying Morse code vibrating into the psyche.

Years of experience had told him where that camera was, what was through the glass, for when the moment came, and what to do with his face as he looked at the camera. He drapes an arm around his guitarist. He takes his time. There's that fleeting smile at the corner of his mouth. The difference in the eyes. A subtle shift of physical emphasis. An imperceptible thrust. A cosmic ejaculation. He plants a seed. In just a few seconds it starts to grow.

31.

He is the starman travelling the vast unimaginable distance from the space inside the inner mind into outside reality.

32.

He is a star in that moment, his own star among the stars he will always be referring to – the prettiest stars, morning stars, stardust, superstars, shining stars, black stars. Bowie is immediately setting a new limit to where normal can go. Those previously in charge of normal were going to be replaced. The action needed the chorus, the story, the boogie, the suggestion there is a new movement you can belong to if you come this way, but is more powerful than the song.

Forty-five years later, such an action, a pose, an apparent provocation, happens all the time, everywhere you look, not about change any more but merely part of the decoration of how things are, a signalling of your own carefully sorted virtue, cool, hipness, shared identity, announced in a vacuum where there is no real danger.

This sort of thing happened then only occasionally, because there was so much space around a pop song, a television show, a singer, an event, and it took real nerve for a man to wear make-up and dye his hair bright colours. There were hardly any places where something like this could happen, especially where the action could reach millions of people in an instant, before audiences got bigger but more fragmented, and the consequences slowly spread mostly by word of mouth, almost a series of smoke signals, each telling adding more power to the legend.

Events like that were isolated, because only a few had the access, and the connections, and the skill and mettle, to attempt it, and the event was instantly over, gone, unrecorded, a memory of a dream of a memory, and it could not be repeated, and replayed, and recovered. To keep it alive you had to think about it a lot, and talk about it, exaggerate it, and check with your friends that such a thing had happened, and feed off the energy of their response.

If, as the singer, you knew what you were doing, and were wearing the right clothes, shrewdly expressing the idea that a pop star must have genuinely alien qualities, you could fill all of that free space around the event that the communication devices had not yet invaded, where only the imagination could venture, and take control of the world around you and the direction it was heading.

33.

He is freaking out like a moonage daydream, as though his whole life had led to such a freak out. The Ziggy Stardust album duly materialised in June, the shocking out-of-this-world end of the world presented as the greatest show on earth coupled with an entire idiosyncratic history of rock and roll, fronted by a flashy, sensationalist saviour. By the time he returned to a sold-out and screaming Manchester Hardrock venue in September later that year he had become the irreplaceable superstar he promised he would be. Fans were already dressing like Ziggy. Boys were wearing make-up. Girls were staring at his glowing groin. In-betweens weren't feeling so in-between any more. They'd found their shape-shifting and empowering champion. The Free Trade Hall show was the spectacular otherworldly sighting of something exceptional, wonderful and slightly sinister speeding towards its fantastic entertainment destiny.

34.

He is learning that the best way for him to be real on stage, as real as he wants to be, is to become someone else.

35.

He is not having a hit in America, because 'Starman' is released at the same time as Elton John's 'Rocket Man', produced by Gus Dudgeon of 'Space Oddity', which was lost in space in America. The industry people and radio stations know where they are with Elton, but Bowie makes no sense yet, because he doesn't seem to know where he is, chopping and changing his hair, labels and music, indulging in hyped-up hipster rock and roll slang like he's half American and made it already, who does he think he is, and what's with the ray guns. He's probably nothing more than packaged trendiness, a fad that might not even make it enough to ever have to pass.

36.

He is having to impress an indifference, a don't-believe-the-hype, a cynicism of journalists flown over from America at the urging of Defries to see Ziggy in the context of flashy new British fame, where the cosmic jive and mama-papa space invading should make more sense. It is like they are dropped into *A Clockwork Orange* that has been turned into an episode of *The Monkees* that's parodying an episode of *Star Trek* with Davy Jones in drag, Mickey Dolenz wearing red lipstick and Peter Tork as a robot being fellated by Michael Nesmith dressed as a rock and roll hoodlum set in a merrie new England built on a back lot in Hollywood where the 1970s seem closer to the 1860s than the 1960s. To make them feel at home, Donny Osmond's 'Puppy Love' is at number 1 in the UK charts.

The blasé of journalists are coached out to the north of London sticks to watch the final show on the six-week Ziggy Stardust tour which is in the juicy 'rise' part of the trajectory; Bowie in Britain is day by day becoming a star, and 'Starman', about a very different sort of 'Puppy Love', is beginning to take off. He can feel Ziggy beginning to fit him more snugly, the mask dissolving into his silvery skin, and the audience is buying in to the fantasy and starting to actually scream. The journalists have been promised by some PR mouth getting carried away that Bowie is 'the new Elvis'. At first sighting he seems like the tenth Alice Cooper. Bowie's America, too, looks as fake and over-stylised to the Americans as the London of *Mary Poppins* does to the British.

The show still appears bogus to the Americans, Bowie seems to be looking at himself being someone else, and the light show, the mock fellatio, the rock-hard precision of the Spiders, the sprayed silver blond on blond guitar hero display of Mick Ronson are seen through a distancing mist – it's built so much for a particular teenage audience that those used to seeing the Stones, the Who, Iggy and the Stooges, all that piled-up, pile-driving majesty, see something removed, see the tightly choreographed, pretty cheaply done theatrical production that it is, fronted by a very skilled actor not yet skilled enough to act – like Dylan – so well that the acting falls away and he appears in the whole realness of himself.

It would take a few more months before he absorbs Ziggy enough and attains a level of unstable aloofness the Americans can identify as unapologetically self-centred, before he begins to persuade the unmoved Americans given their first sight through the writing of journalists that he is a new sort of star, not an old-style performer dressed in forced hype, silly glitter and camp desperation.

37.

He is sat in a large, impressively ornate suite at the Dorchester Hotel on Park Lane overlooking Hyde Park, having tea with the free trip, the bad mood, the he's not even actually gay of journalists. They pause upon finding him quietly charming and shyly civil, and not out to hustle, and if that's a bluff, it's very nicely presented. He is in the glam science-fiction equivalent of his whimsically tailored Sunday best, a shiny white suit scattered with polka dots, a waist the width of a soup can, an exposed bare chest that looks made out of white chalk, the platform shoes that give him height and a kind of gawky, shaky quaintness, nervy fingers as thin as the cigarette he holds, both to put in his mouth and suck the life out of, and to use as part of how he poses when he's got nothing to say. The smoke winds around his body like it's his imagination seeping into the room.

His friends turn up to help certify his credentials and they happen to be Iggy Pop and Lou Reed. They are newly signed to Defries's new management company Mainman that Bowie thinks is a kind of Arts Lab with Factory ambitions and Defries thinks – as if this is the same opinion – is a home for the kind of weirdos and assholes that can make a lot of money.

At the time, this means Bowie the fey fake – and yet such a charmer in person – is joined in the eyes of journalists by loathsome Lou and crackpot Iggy. The Monkees sitcom dissolves into an awkward farce. Bowie just wants to be liked. Iggy just wants to be fucked. Lou just wants to hurt someone, or maybe get someone to hurt him. He's asked if he is now living in London, and this particular episode ends with Lou staring straight into the camera and growling: 'You call this living?'

38.

He is acting quickly, now he's in the spotlight. Once people were paying attention, how could he resist showing them what he's got up his sleeve on his audacious, full-of-life, cheating, opinionated mind, on a quest to write the greatest opening song to an album, the greatest closing track? He had a feeling he could do it, and then fill in the rest. Now he'd finally got 'David Bowie' out of the way, and cracked the debut album conundrum, he'd managed to turn the pop world into his own stage, and meanwhile his personal obsession with glamour, posing, carnality and the end of the world – or the end of another addiction, fascination or love affair – had become the fashion of the time, and a genre he could mock, parody and play around with even as he acted out being its greatest star/opportunist, spraying the limitless colours of pop through the tense, nervous 1970s with pessimistic glee.

39.

He is saying on the sleeve of *The Rise and Fall of Ziggy Stardust and the Spiders from Mars* that it is to be played at maximum volume.

40.

He is powerful enough this year to be in so many different places at once; if someone checked at how he was managing to save one of his favourite groups, Mott the Hoople, and also set up on a different sort of stage two of his rock heroes, Lou Reed and Iggy Pop, they would note that on some days he definitely seemed to be in two different places at the same time. *Ziggy Stardust and the Spiders from Mars* had many sources, but Mott, Iggy and Lou were part of the methodology, and in the year Ziggy arrived he extended his influence. After years of everything he touched turning to old, now he knew how to turn the power on. He turned Mott the Hoople into a hit act, put a new frame around Iggy Pop, and managed to give Lou Reed a novelty hit, his version of 'Space Oddity', 'Walk on the Wild Side'. As if his real job, behind the superhero masks, is being a kind of opinion-forming cultural philanthropist, Bowie generously, or self-servingly, publicises, promotes, saves, knows, sympathises with, advises, writes for, produces, makes over, turns on, shares the stage, and the page, and the occasional secret, with enough others for it to be easy to place him very close to the centre of the pop universe, a human Google through which you can search where pop has bounced and rebounded since the 1960s.

Lou, Mott and Iggy – or Lulu and Dana Gillespie – don't sound like *Ziggy Stardust and the Spiders from Mars*, but they are part of the same music scene, one that Bowie, with an astounding amount of surplus energy, was imagining in his head. Music from an imaginary city on an imaginary planet. The fan in him never went away.

41.

He is hearing that Mott the Hoople were about to split up, having about as much success after four albums on Island Records as he had in the 1960s, and after suggesting they record 'Suffragette City', a piece for the Ziggy project, which they don't want to do, figuring at the time he is not actually a hit machine himself, he writes 'All the Young Dudes' for them. He sets Mott the Hoople and a myth-making reporting of where pop culture was in the early 1970s according to his close reading inside a song. This was his version of the news. In the news, your big brother was stuck at home with the Beatles and the Stones. Times had changed. The new set, bounding into the future, had their T. Rex.

When their uncompromising singer Ian Hunter heard it, he was immediately impressed even though he was reluctant to be helped by Bowie, seeing it as a sign of weakness. The alternative was splitting up, but he thought that was preferable to looking as though they were the puppets of someone else. 'All the Young Dudes' changed his mind: 'I'd waited all my life to sing a song like that.'

42.

He is moving from the pubs and clubs into the theatres, and he has been consulting with the white rabbit and Lindsay Kemp, and the fusion of music and movement, mind and memory is more and more dramatic.

43.

He is afraid to fly, sure that will end in flames, troubled by a premonition of death he once had, and is sailing on 10 September 1972 on the *QE2* for the week-long journey to New York. Each day that passes puts him further and further away from the debacle at the Dorchester.

44.

He is swanning around America like he's walked on the moon arm in arm with Barbra Streisand, like a Hollywood star, staying at the swankiest hotels and zooming along the streets and highways in darkened twenty-foot limos turned into mobile nightclubs while the venues he plays are not full. Tony Defries's attitude is that if you show America that you are a star and you behave like one, they will assume you are one.

David Bowie is thirteen
years old in 1960.

David Bowie is in
the Konrads in 1962.

David Bowie is in the Buzz at the Marquee Club in London, April 1966.

David Bowie is wearing his 'Space Oddity' corkscrew hair in Hyde Park in 1969.

David Bowie is with Tony Visconti in Trident Studios in London in May 1970.

David Bowie is 'jamming good' with Weird and Gilly and the Spiders from Mars, January 1973.

David Bowie is seen off on an Inter-City train by wife Angie in 1973.

David Bowie is recording for the *1980 Floor Show* at the Marquee Club in London with Mick Ronson, a final appearance as Ziggy, October 1973.

David Bowie is Halloween Jack in 1973.

David Bowie is smoking in a yellow suit holding cut-and-paste scissors in 1974.

David Bowie is with wife Angie and son Zowie at the Amstel Hotel, Amsterdam, February 1974.

David Bowie is backstage at the Grammy's in New York, March 1975 with Yoko Ono, John Lennon and Roberta Flack.

David Bowie is a poster for Nic Roeg's 1976 film, *The Man Who Fell to Earth*.

David Bowie is in black and white on stage with Carlos Alomar and Stacey Heydon on the *Thin White Duke* tour in 1976.

David Bowie is with Robert Fripp and Brian Eno thinking of "*Heroes*" in Hansa Studios, Berlin, 1977.

David Bowie is playing keyboards for Iggy Pop in San Francisco in 1977.

David Bowie is just a gigolo in 1978.

David Bowie is attending the première of David Lynch's *The Elephant Man* on 28 September 1980.

David Bowie is a global sensation on the *Serious Moonlight* tour at the Milton Keynes Bowl in 1983.

David Bowie is Major Jack Celliers in *Merry Christmas Mr Lawrence* in 1983.

David Bowie is filming a scene for Julien Temple's *Absolute Beginners*, May 1985.

David Bowie is Jareth in *Labyrinth* in 1986, breaking the gentle hearts of many young virgins.

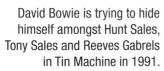

David Bowie is a star on the Hollywood Walk of Fame.

David Bowie is trying to hide himself amongst Hunt Sales, Tony Sales and Reeves Gabrels in Tin Machine in 1991.

David Bowie is close to Lou Reed after Lou receives the George Arents Pioneer Medal 'for excellence in the arts' from his alma mater, Syracuse University, at the 'W' Hotel in Union Square New York in 2007, a block from the old Max's Kansas City.

David Bowie is never happier . . . with Iman at the 'Keep a Child Alive' sixth annual ballroom, October 2006, where Bowie sang in front of an audience for the last time.

David Bowie is at the Victoria and Albert Museum, March 2013.

David Bowie R.I.P.

45.

He is becoming something else in the Amerika he loves and loathes, because it's the home of everything he believes in, and can't believe, and it's where the end of the world begins, not with a bang but an assassination. Amerika accelerates the mutation from Ziggy, not so much because he is believing he is Ziggy but because he is believing he can become something better. Ziggy plus America equals an impersonation of an impersonation.

46.

He is not hanging on to himself, he's already outgrowing the costume, or it's outgrowing him. On an album not released officially for nearly thirty years, a recording from *Live Santa Monica '72*, you can hear him, singing and chatting between songs, a monster flirting with its own strangeness, picking at his skin, which he's not as comfortable in as he was, pulling at his hair and wishing it was another colour, another shape, as though that might be all that was required for another, necessary transformation. As an album, it is tremendous, his best live album, now and then his best album, because Ziggy, in one sense just a few months old, is already going through his teenage years and he can't keep still, and he will soon be embarrassed by his younger self. For the moment, every moment is an orgasm, every ovation a love affair.

You can witness Bowie electrically, internationally, a little deliriously winning over America with pilgrim zest, weirdness and narcissistic grandiosity. He was new to the world and his new famous self, but filled with stories, sex, cataclysmic glam, and Mick Ronson's fingers, shoulders and strings, releasing freshly opened earth orbiting pop star powers, already with a better repertoire of songs and poses than anyone else in the galaxy. He can't pull the mask off, and no one can tell he's wearing one.

• • •

The Rise and Fall of Ziggy Stardust and the Spiders from Mars goes back in time, when rock and roll was assuming its first shape, and ahead in time, to what appears to be the end of the world. It begins with telling us we have five years to live, patching together Beatles post-vaudeville melodrama with the Velvets' dispassionate reverie, and ends with a suicide, tear-jerking Nana Mouskouri stabbing the heart of Elvis on his 1968 comeback special, another one of those Bowie deaths rooted in a fear of death representing a fear of not becoming what he wants to be. It was the album of the year when all this was going on . . . the Stones were in *Exile on Main St*, T. Rex were as high as they ever got with *The Slider*, *A Clockwork Orange* and *The Godfather* were soundtrack albums as well as films, Can were at *Ege Bamyasi*, Jethro Tull were *Thick as a Brick*, Matching Mole, Neu! and Roxy Music debuted, Popol Vuh made *Hosianna Mantra*, Faust made *Faust So Far*, Captain Beefheart and the Magic Band had reached a *Clear Spot*, and the best solo male albums were by Neil Young (*Harvest*), Nick Drake (*Pink Moon*), Lou Reed (*Transformer*), Stevie Wonder (*Talking Book*), Curtis Mayfield (*Superfly*) and Randy Newman (*Sail Away*). Some might say what about Elton John (*Honky Château*) and Rod Stewart (*Never a Dull Moment*) and where would you put Joni Mitchell (*For the Roses*)? Top 1972 single was a vicious fight between 'Starman', the dizzying, homoexotic 'John, I'm Only Dancing', 'Virginia Plain', 'Walk on the Wild Side', 'Telegram Sam', 'School's Out' and 'Layla' – Gilbert O'Sullivan's 'Alone Again (Naturally)' put up a good show in the early rounds, ultimately losing out to Nilsson's 'Without You'. Out of nowhere, 'The Jean Genie' snatched the crown, a sign of where Ziggy now was, deeper into the competitive scandal of it all, deeper into the androgynous smartness, deeper into the idea that the music must now change shape to keep up with how his mind and body are changing, and where he sees and hears Roxy Music are.

1973

'Put on your best clothes. We're finished!'

47.

He is in the charts in the first month of the year, 'The Jean Genie' hanging on after Christmas and failing to knock squealing Jimmy Osmond from number 1, sharing a riff plundered from Muddy Waters and the Yardbirds with hammy glam Sweet, another RCA act. They have spotted what he was doing in the dressing rooms at *Top of the Pops* over the last few months, masking his bony south London ordinariness with satin, silver and slap, which seemed like a good laugh. *Top of the Pops* is where you go to show off how you've made it, the louder and even sillier the better. As far as they're concerned, it's all music hall, in the end, with Marshall amps. They've given their whole act a gruesome panto makeover, to the extent they end up being more face-pulling pint-swigging lad drag than beautiful.

Bowie turns the stolen blues riff into the swollen, savagely insouciant 'The Jean Genie', Sweet into the classic glam pop stomper 'Block Buster!' – one telling the queer story of Iggy Pop as though he is an undead creation of Jean Genet and Aleister Crowley smiling like a reptile making underwear from dead hair, the other about a creepy pervert, Buster, who must be blocked from stealing your girl, consciously or not tapping into the as yet unknown underlying sleaze of *Top of the Pops*. There's a line 'he's more evil than anyone here ever thought' seeming in hindsight to be a direct reference to the slimy, smiley disc jockey Jimmy Savile, one of the show's smug hosts, the man who helped invent the role of disc jockey but who seemed a descendant of Aleister Crowley, and whose predatory and psychotic behaviour included herding young girls from the *Top of the Pops* audience into his various vile nests, raping under the cover of pop.

It was pervert versus pervert for number 1 in the hit parade, which says something about where pop was at the time, beyond the silly platform shoes and extreme glam costumes, which were a real distraction, a shiny cover-up for truly shocking, darker currents. Sweet's repulsive creep makes number 1; Bowie's meta-creep is number 2, but this is remarkable considering what an intense mirror of Bowie's deviant consciousness it was, a description of sleaze and vermin tucked inside a pop song.

He is bumping into one of the writers of 'Block Buster!', and to his face with the straightest of faces he called him a 'cunt' for their riff outdoing his. He then cracked one of his most charming smiles, and offered his congratulations – but the first exclamation was probably more correct. He had not yet had a number 1, even though he acted, onstage and off, as if he had.

48.

He is becoming the cover of the *Aladdin Sane* album, with photographer Brian Duffy and the make-up artist Duffy chooses, Pierre La Roche. La Roche was brought up in Algiers, and moved to London via Paris, becoming the lead make-up artist at Elizabeth Arden before going freelance to pursue a more experimentally theatrical approach to make-up, to make the face come alive in different ways.

Duffy had worked on the 1973 Pirelli calendar with controversial pop artist Allen Jones, a specialist in the controlling and neutralisation of desire, and airbrush artist and illustrator Philip Castle, who had designed sets, ad campaigns, logo and posters for ultra-perfectionist Stanley Kubrick's 1971 *A Clockwork Orange*, including the roughly hand-drawn but futurist lettering.

He had also designed the cover for Nik Cohn's classic book about pop music coalescing into a secular religion, *Awopbopaloobop Alopbamboom*, published in 1969, and a coolly androgynous poster for a camp, pop-art film version of Michael Moorcock's *The Final Programme* also known as *The Last Days of Man on Earth*. It was part of a breed of early 1970s films, *Soylent Green*, *No Blade of Grass*, *A Clockwork Orange*, *Logan's Run* and the *Planet of the Apes* sequels, almost ecstatically heralding a pessimistic future for mankind based on a trashed, distorted version of the swung-over 1960s and the aftershocks, a peculiar reaction to post-war uncertainties and contradictions, that *Ziggy*, *Aladdin Sane* and *Diamond Dogs* fitted into.

The *Aladdin Sane* cover team is in place, and Bowie, another ultra-perfectionist and specialist in dealing with the forces of desire, at his most comfortable working with the very best, allows them to work on him, and transform him. The shoot is matter-of-fact and low-key. You would not be able to tell it would make such a difference to how we think of Bowie, another one of those images that invents the concept of the album it is representing as much as if not more than the music, as sensationally standout and confident as that is. The moment the photograph is taken is a silent moment; it is done, it doesn't draw attention to itself. There is no explicit awareness that this will change the direction of things for Bowie, become one of the most vivid ways he will be remembered.

The loose idea is to present Bowie as a modernist, reptilian genie, after 'The Jean Genie', a naked creature popping out of a puff of smoke to grant your requests, representing the reanimation after Ziggy into a new form, like Dr Who going through one of his regenerations. He has walked into the studio on his own with his hair now a golden orange, standing on end of its own accord now that it is used to it. He sees the session as a physical performance, a piece of acting, very aware as always how potent and transfixing the right image can be, and how transcendent a new appearance must be in order to move on from the now very notorious and tricky Ziggy.

The costume for this photograph, causing the elevation of a performer into a dream of the future, so that he never grows old, is a lightning flash painted onto Bowie's face. A piece of Panasonic packaging lying around in the studio featuring their original, primitive 1930s logo becomes part of the brainstorming between Duffy, his assistant, Bowie and La Roche. The Panasonic logo is the chunky cartoon outline of a lightning flash – the kind now used to display battery power on a mobile phone. It represented the almost occult new age magic of electricity when it was first designed in the 1930s. La Roche uses red lipstick to fill in the outline, and the final image is softened by airbrush master Castle and mutated into the gently genderless, electronic inhuman, with dissolving flesh robed in silver mist and a dream tear spooling by his shoulder, his eyes shut, wondering, waiting. He was ready to grant your wishes.

La Roche also turns Bowie into the pop star as serene, seductive man of myth from somewhere other than the 1970s and planet earth with the simple addition of a golden astral sphere to his forehead. Ziggy is evolving into a higher being having made the world of pop different forever. He stares ahead, deep into the future, seeing things for the first time.

49.

He is on *Aladdin Sane* plunging a Jagger into the heart of Ziggy, the masked rock opera about rock and roll, and re-imagining it as the rock album the Rolling Stones would make if they were into Brecht, Brel, Burroughs and Ballard, with the hard, articulate and memorable pop songs that begin to pour out of him like molten gold. The Spiders from Mars are now playing with absolute sureness like a real band who had been on tour and developed a proper relationship, which makes it thrilling as a rock sound, less radiant as a temporary, on the edge location for Bowie's singular and signature coupling of the easy listening and the experimental. It is a pop album, but Bowie can't help but remain the member of a class where there are no other members, and write lyrics that are beautiful and batty, daydreams and documentaries, with a strange clarity of feeling even when they seem to be edging close to the maddest flower of Albion, English nonsense verse.

The disruptive, even alien force is Mike Garson, who almost sarcastically chucks random fragments of fractured, bejewelled free-form piano over the Spiders' sincere, earthbound rock and roll, especially on the title track, with the sure knowledge of someone who had heard the solo jazz piano of Cecil Taylor and Paul Bley. It's Liberace fed on the cosmic rays of Sun Ra, refracting the inner tension of America, and Garson was obediently following Bowie's orders to create some freak motion by knocking things off balance to stop things getting a little banal. The result in the oddly square world of commercial rock was officially the strangest piano many had ever heard, with a lusciously lopsided gait and pace that seemed to curve space like the musical equivalent of Einstein. Garson will say that of all the 3,000 pieces of music he has made, this is the one every week someone will want to talk about.

Aladdin Sane was still an experiment in the imagination, from a singer with a total belief that storytelling has the power to postpone if not completely cancel the apocalypse, and it still plays with the same themes as Ziggy, just a little recombined, where stardom beats death, time needs death, the end of the world is nigh, cold dark chaos is at the end of time's arrow, at the possibly post-Holocaust end of gender there is the simply human where we mutate into higher forms, 'reality' and 'truth' are forever being lied about, mostly in America, land of divisions, excess, power. 'Drive-In Saturday' was intended as the follow-up to 'All the Young Dudes' for Mott the Hoople, but singer Ian Hunter wanted to arrange it more into something he might be in control of, still scared that he might become a mere puppet of Bowie. It stayed with Bowie, and becomes one of those tantalising glimpses of a mutant genre that does not particularly get pursued, where doo-wop emerged after glam.

50.

He is travelling around the world between February and May, crossing the Atlantic by ship, touring America by bus and train, crossing the Pacific by ship to Japan, heading home on the Trans-Siberian Railway on a 6,700-mile journey via Paris and Moscow. He is in Moscow on May Day, witnessing an all-day display of Russia's artillery might. 'After what I've seen of the state of the world, I've never been so damned scared in my life. After America, Moscow, Siberia, Japan, I just want to bloody well go home to Beckenham and watch the bloody telly.'

51.

He is becoming a cat from Japan, wearing the saturated creations and Japanese theatrical finds of Kansai Yamamoto, who he's met in New York, who made clothes not meant for man or woman, but whatever came first, or whatever comes next. Clothes meant for a figment of the imagination, for a mind that refuses to be tethered, for an entertainment guru that loves to look the part. He imagines what someone with a face as unusual as Bowie would wear, and takes it from there. Even if you somehow fail to remember that face, you'll never forget what he's wearing. Each costume has its own name and probably a life of its own when it's not turning Bowie into Ziggy . . . Tokyo Pop, Space Samurai, Spring Rain, Woodland Creatures.

52.

He is announcing from the stage at the Hammersmith Odeon in west London on 3 July that 'This show will stay the longest in our memories not just because it is the end of the tour but because it is the last show we will do.' Attuned to the rhythms of show business like no other rock star, a student of marketing and the art of the stunt, he is in character as he makes a statement guaranteed to shock an audience and media now thoroughly committed to his existence. He is Ziggy saying this, but this thought is too subtle, and too bogus, to consider. It's assumed he has retired. His new fans are in shock having embraced the whole idea of Ziggy, as if he were a real part of their fragile world. There are tears, as though the fabric of existence has a tear in it.

53.

He is unsentimentally distancing himself from Ziggy by releasing the bedroom scrapbook *Pin Ups*, which sweetly scrutinised his teenage Brit-invasion pop influences from his new perspective as pop star, rewriting his past, offering thanks, featuring covers of favourite songs by favourite groups, the Pretty Things, Them, Yardbirds, Pink Floyd, the Who, Australia's Easybeats, and the Kinks.

The cover, with Twiggy of the 1960s, who would have been on his bedroom wall, temporarily joining Bowie on his new planet, was originally photographed for *Vogue* – Bowie would have been the first man on the cover. He was wearing a mask, made up of his own face, designed by Pierre La Roche. The photograph was never used, so photographer Justin de Villeneuve gave it Bowie to use as he saw fit. The *Pin Ups* cover made it clear that even as he was singing songs of the past, written by others, and murdering the galactic, gallivanting Ziggy, he had not relinquished his grip on the perverse-sublime, on an occult sense of his own appeal, and whatever he was seeing, it wasn't what everyone else was seeing. He was still intent on pulling everything into the present, where life was always beginning. He was staring way beyond the rest of us to the very limits of drama and daring us to join him. He was standing out.

As he raced through himself to get to the heart of himself, raging with ideas and theories, wishful thinking and sheer nerve, breaking apart and putting himself back together again, with a sense that what he was doing at any given moment was crucial to his life's work, there is a charged sense that for all the indulgences he had the composure and discipline necessary for the supreme vanity that fascinated him. He was interested in surfaces, but knew that they were superficial and false. He was after the truth, which was deeper, and elsewhere. He was interested in appearances, and how they were a kind of skin, but he was more interested in what lay behind appearances, the invisible self, and the spirit. He was interested in the imagination, which is always elsewhere. He was interested in David Bowie, and where exactly he was. To some extent, he was still a teenager, in love with fads, in love with himself, but wondering what on earth he was going to do with himself.

54.

He is attending a party at the Café Royal in London on 4 July to mark the end of the tour, and Ziggy Stardust – who cannot be killed, because he never existed, and so this creature becomes immortal, always at Bowie's shoulder, a not necessarily evil twin with special charms, but sometimes like a dressed-up dancing bear that just won't let him move on. It's attended by rock stars, peers, collaborators, and is nicknamed 'The Last Supper'.

55.

He has a ghostwriter, Cherry Vanilla, part of Mainman, his 'extraordinary' PR. The columns she writes on his behalf during 1973 and 1974 for a teen-girl magazine called *Mirabelle* become a form of ghosted autobiography, as he retires, comes back, travels the world, conceives *Pin Ups* and sets up *Diamond Dogs*. He gives Cherry the freedom to write what she wants, because 'she has such a great sense of humour and imagination, and I told her to make things up about what Ziggy/Bowie was up to and publish it'. At the start of the run, there is a sense that she is at least chatting to Bowie about what he might want in the column. By the end of the run, it is more obviously Cherry making things up, and placing herself in the columns, someone who Bowie is a fan of, on the way to her own pop career – just to the outside of Debbie Harry, of the Runaways – which begins with the Police as her backing band.

In the first few columns, you get a hint, filtered through the teenybop filter – so that he is another pretty boy, where the other Bewlay brother is David Cassidy – of his adventures in pop, as he starts to slip away from view, behind the scenes of his own construction. He is becoming more and more intermittent, seen only through the narrow prism of rock-writing, through the musical productions, the tours, the films, the chat-show interviews, the sensation-seeking documentaries, the statistics and scandals. There is more of David Bowie on show, on sale, but less a sense that there is anyone there, apart from what is shown, and made up from within, and carefully shared out. He turns up when he has to, to record, perform, promote, but he sinks more and more into his own thoughts and his own unreal world, and he skips away from revealing anything concrete. He is unreliable; there is no way to tell for sure what is really going on, and how much is staged.

Elsewhere, somewhere, there is the Davie Jones who first thought of David Bowie, and he is a very different proposition, and one that all but disappears. Cherry's chatty columns, as cosmetic as they are, become a final sighting of the transformation between one and the other, and she is one of the ghosts that replaces and represents him as he pursues his dream combination of presenting his work that processes his endless, roaming, fatalistic thoughts and privacy. The story of Bowie becomes more and more the story of his work, and his mind, and whatever can be made out from the traces left by ghosts.

56.

He is writing in her column about 'The Last Supper' at the Café Royal:

> Oh, what a night it turned out to be. Mick Jagger, Lou Reed, Jeff Beck, Lulu, Spike Milligan, Dana Gillespie, Ryan O'Neal, Elliott Gould, Ringo Starr and Barbra Streisand ... everyone looking so lovely in their sparkling evening clothes and colourful make-up ... dancing, sipping champagne and tasting delicious salmon and big fresh strawberries and cream. The disc jockey played lots of really good soul and rock 'n' roll records, and the dance floor was absolutely packed all night. Mick and Bianca and Angie and I were all dancing together to 'Honky Tonk Women' – I got a little off balance in my high heels but managed to stay upright for a few more songs. Most of the evening I spent answering everybody's questions about my decision to stop touring and concentrate on movies and recording.
>
> When we made our entrance, Angie in a brand new chartreuse and brown knit ensemble by Freddie, me in my ice blue iridescent Freddie suit, they announced us over the speaker system, and everyone stood up and applauded. I loved the sound of it but in this instance I felt a little blushy and embarrassed – like the groom at a wedding reception. Angie held my hand tightly throughout, and gave me confidence (she always does). They had a big velvet covered king's chair for me ...

57.

He is not sure what to say to Russell Harty, a closeted but very camp gay chat-show host treating Bowie either as a young slightly backward child or a possible debauchee. Bowie explains to a suspicious, or very enchanted, Harty that he is a storyteller, and a collector. 'I collect people and ideas.' He is in costume to the point of comedy drag, with one large dangling silver earring, and shiny red hair – possibly closer to an over-powdered and lacquered middle-aged landlady in a working-class pub in Lancashire than a creature from another planet. It's hard to keep the illusion going all the time, especially in a world that always wants to bring things down to earth.

58.

He is already making a comeback – every day a comeback, another entrance into the life of a star – after his absurdly grand theatrical retirement at the Hammersmith Odeon. He hosts and presents a surreal cabaret show, his magical mystery tour, an end-of-the-pier summer show where the end of the pier stretches into the imagination, recorded at the completely redesigned Marquee Club in Soho where once he was a minor act hacking away in the dense rock undergrowth.

Now he is playing the superstar, the pop hero, promoting his trip down memory boulevard *Pin Ups*, and arranging his kind of television show for the American *Midnight Special* series, which further rearranges pop history a little more to his taste now he has the time-travelling power. *The 1980 Floor Show* – his comeback is naturally in the future, skipping ahead through the decade, giving the Sixties an anti-nostalgic twist – features Marianne Faithfull dressed as a nun holding a skull, the Cher to his Sonny as they perform 'I Got You Babe'.

Singing 'Sorrow', as the man who can sing sad like no one else, David Bowie serenades Amanda Lear, muse, confidante and protégée to surrealist Salvador Dalí, and Roxy Music's *For Your Pleasure* cover model in skin-tight black leather dress and pet panther on a leash, who Bowie liked to say was born a male, an ideal date, to meet in the shadows, which he still finds the time to visit, and exchange points of view. The Troggs perform 'Wild

Thing', and an act Tony Visconti produced, Carmen, perform some *glamenco*, a racy, dotty fusion of glam attack and flamenco flamboyance. The audience includes Angie in luminous green chiffon and son Zowie in striped beige trousersuit babysat by Freddie Burretti, Tony Visconti and wife Mary Hopkin, Cherry Vanilla, Dana Gillespie, Lionel Bart and Wayne County. Many of those attending or performing at the recording would now have their own reality television shows.

59.

She is writing in his column dated 10 November:

> I see lots of you in the papers wearing your new Bowie hair-cuts, and while some look really attractive, some are just not carefully adapted to your lovely little faces. You must be careful to choose your hairdresser with great care and detail. It really doesn't matter how much you spend, either. It could be that your own best buddy has the taste and talent to do it better than the most expensive hairdresser. Unless you have very together and turned on friends, though, you'd best trust a professional.

60.

He is using their column to give make-up tips:

> Most of my make-up comes from a little make-up shop in Rome which imports fantastic intensely coloured powders and creams from India. All are made from natural fruit, root and vegetable dyes. I also use white rice powder from the Tokyo equivalent to our Woolworth's. For the circle on my forehead I usually use a German gold base in cake form which I get from a special make-up store in New York. Sometimes I outline the gold circle with tiny gold rhinestones which are stuck on with eyelash glue. I used to shave my eyebrows off,

only lately I've taken to waxing them off. There is different make-up for off stage. Funny how times change – if I had made a remark like that a few years ago, everybody would have been very shocked at the idea of a man wearing make-up off stage, but now it seems to be commonplace. In fact, the whole way a man dresses, the clothes they wear and their appearance has really changed considerably over the past few years.

61.

He is being profiled on a BBC TV magazine show that resolutely refuses to believe that this is something to be taken seriously. It's the kind of report that marvels how someone who a year ago was an unknown is now, they somehow know, worth half a million pounds a year. Deciding there is a difference between an actor getting ready for a theatrical role and a trivial pop star about to entertain silly, fixated youngsters, the narrator metaphorically rolls his eyes as he explains how Bowie employs his own full-time make-up girl to paint his nails silver. 'He spends two hours before each performance caressing his body in paint and turning himself into a bizarre self-centred freak. It is a sign of the times that a man with a painted face and carefully adjusted lipstick inspires adoration from an audience of girls aged between fourteen and twenty.'

We see some of these girls outside a theatre in Bournemouth on the windswept south coast, some of whom are beginning to crudely attempt to look like the object of their adoration, and needing a lot more advice on how to do it. Some are in tears, because they missed seeing him going through the stage door after waiting for hours, and it's ruined their life. The unsympathetic interviewer tells them, well, he's just a man like me, even if his crotch is diamond-encrusted. They sob some more, until they cannot stop. A few hours later, their sobs will turn to screams, because he is not a man after all.

62.

He is, a long way from Bournemouth, because he cares, or because
he's stealing energy, or searching for inspiration, sorting out and
celebrating the gloriously demented Iggy Pop. He produces – or sort
of redecorates – the third Stooges album, 1973's *Raw Power*, when
Iggy is on the verge of total collapse, and his group are all over the
wretched place. Maybe he was just promoting the obscure, wasted
but exciting idea of Iggy, like some sort of conceptualist impresario, Ziggy as manipulative, star-spotting puppet master, allowing
a short, brutal avant-shock masterpiece to materialise years ahead
of its time. Bowie doesn't do much but remix the master tape and
shift the balance of the voice around, but he somehow shrivels
the Stooges' traditional place-shattering distortion to singed skin
and bone, and Iggy sweats, bleeds and issues threats on the rim
of destruction. Iggy remains hard-core cult, but on the 1977
'Berlin'-based *The Idiot* and the harder *Lust for Life*, shadows/
apprehensions/blueprints of *Low* and *"Heroes"*, Bowie publicises
and partners the idea of an 'Iggy the sophisticated'. A little poet-
ically introverted, a little healed, but still het-up and nomadic, a
savaged soul singer and feral punk hero turned depraved but perceptive existential entertainer. It does no harm to the myth of Bowie
that he locates and to some extent sponsors Iggy the raging, ragged
star, who from then on remains restless, radiant icon.

63.

He is creating and speaking through Ziggy the possessed fantasist, and then it escapes his control.

• • •

In 1973, you'd put together a definitive prog rock collection – Emerson Lake &
Palmer's *Brain Salad Surgery*, Genesis's *Selling England by the Pound*, Gentle
Giant's *In a Glass House*, Yes's *Tales from Topographic Oceans* and Camel's

Camel – and a pretty good heavy-metal collection – *Sabbath Bloody Sabbath*, Led Zeppelin's *Houses of the Holy*, Alice Cooper's *Billion Dollar Babies*. *The Dark Side of the Moon* and *Tubular Bells* were lording it over the charts, Queen and the New York Dolls were debuting, Can were imagining *Future Days* and Faust had reached number *IV*, Bowie was now sealed inside the livid skin of *Aladdin Sane*, having saved the pitted skin of Iggy Pop on *Raw Power*. He was also represented that year by a cheeky re-release of 'The Laughing Gnome', which reached number 6 in the UK charts, while 'Life on Mars?' was single of the year two years after it first appeared and reached number 3, as did a single from *Pin Ups*, 'Sorrow', and a peep into the future perfect past, 'Drive-In Saturday'. Dawn, Peters and Lee, Sweet, Wizzard, Little Jimmy Osmond, and a whole chunk of Gary Glitters were getting the number 1s. Roxy Music were *For Your Pleasure* and *Stranded*, Mott the Hoople were becoming *Mott*, and Roxy's Brian Eno was making a solo break for it with the foaming *Here Come the Warm Jets* and the droning *(No Pussyfooting)*. On King Crimson's *Larks' Tongues in Aspic*, Robert Fripp was playing the sort of guitar building up to the guitar he played on *"Heroes"*. Elsewhere, the leading LPs by solo males were Lou Reed's *Berlin*, Tom Waits's *Closing Time*, John Martyn's *Solid Air*, Gram Parsons's *GP*, John Cale's *Paris 1919*, Hugh Hopper's *1984*, Neil Young's *Time Fades Away*, Kevin Coyne's *Marjory Razorblade*, Marvin Gaye's *Let's Get It On*, Stevie Wonder's *Innervisions*, Fela Kuti's *Gentleman*, Bruce Springsteen's *The Wild, the Innocent & the E Street Shuffle*, and Todd Rundgren's *A Wizard, a True Star*. Some might say, well, what about Elton John's *Goodbye Yellow Brick Road*? Bowie spent ten weeks in the album charts, five each for *Aladdin Sane* and *Pin Ups*, surrounded by Elton John, Led Zeppelin, the Faces, Peters and Lee, the Rolling Stones, Status Quo and Rod Stewart. *Aladdin Sane* was the second best-selling album of the year, pushed back by the soundtrack to *That'll Be the Day*, but *Hunky Dory* (9th bestselling), *The Rise and Fall of Ziggy Stardust and the Spiders From Mars* (12th), *Pin Ups* (14th) and the re-released second David Bowie renamed as *Space Oddity* (44th) showed how much people were catching up with him: popular by smuggling in ideas, images and perceptions that were unlike anything else around him in the charts.

1974

'I've never responded well to entrenched negative thinking.'

64.

He is twenty-seven. The world is pulling itself apart. Britain is crumbling, facing strikes, power cuts, blackouts, the Heath Conservative government is suggesting a return to wartime conditions and banning floodlights and illuminated advertisements. Television programmes are switched off at 10.30 at night.

65.

He is introducing his new album with the words: 'And in the death as the last few corpses lay rotting ... Any day now – the year of the Diamond Dogs. This ain't rock and roll – this is genocide.'

66.

He is piecing together *Diamond Dogs* from leftovers, scrapped thoughts, chopped-up remnants and sundry debris from other projects, aborted concepts, frustrated experiments, images remaindered from a dumped musical version of Orwell's *Nineteen Eighty-Four* as if it featured Fagin's Victorian gang gone apeshit in *A Clockwork Orange* future, a cultural hullabaloo which is all echoes. He is assessing culture around him in order to critique it through prophetic warning. He is raising a red flag, issuing warnings of decay by describing it in its own terms.

He is jaded with the whole Ziggy fiasco, or he is playing

Ziggy being jaded by having to go through the motions. He has absorbed the 1960s idea personified by the Beatles that each record you made enacted a considerable artistic move forward, so that you were encouraged to keep in mind how in four years they had moved from *Meet the Beatles* to *Sgt. Pepper*. He believes in the idea of the vinyl album as way of constructing a distinct work of art that can be as specifically riveting as a painting, as three dimensional as a sculpture, as packed with incident as a film, as intense and open to interpretation as a dream. Each step must announce change, a change increasingly hard to achieve in a 1970s world increasingly filled with newcomers challenging you to stay relevant.

Ronson is gone, because he won't and can't keep up with Bowie's insatiable need to keep up with the ebbs and flows of both commercial and marginal modern pop. Bowie could take from anywhere in order to refresh his work, but a rock-solid Hull rocker like Ronson couldn't bring himself to check what was happening in soul now that it was experimenting with the recording studio, in the early stirrings of disco as it started to play with the length and arrangement of a song, in where the great R & B of the Sixties had headed in response to the more conceptual parts of rock. Bowie was keeping up with where American music was and where it was going, and he could see more than Ronson that it was a clue to becoming American enough to gain American fame.

Without Ronson, the guitars, played mostly by Bowie, shrank and drizzled into a different set of shapes and textures, a drift towards another way of using the guitar, which in disco was pushed to the back, or to the side, and which in electronic music was almost entirely being replaced. The skin-tight macho riffing Ronson had set Ziggy into, as perfect as it was for the elevation and revelation of Bowie, was now as old-fashioned and frayed around the edges as Ziggy was. Because things move quickly in pop, the Spiders from Mars were yesterday's news two years on from being strange tomorrow; but they were a figment of Bowie's imagination, and he could jump from the wreckage without being harmed, leaving them to crash in the dust like all the groups he had ever been part of.

Bowie tentatively proposed a whole different way of playing the guitar, with a brittle, thoughtful attack, one which would be a more noticeable influence on the post-punk music he inspired like Joy Division, Wire, Siouxsie and the Banshees and Public Image Ltd; guitar was a stab, a tear, a cry from the deep, a different way of claiming and inspiring energy, almost at times used to express loss of energy and uncertainty, to calm things down, to undermine pomposity. The guitar playing is more of an emotional release than a lot of his vocals; he could afford to free himself without giving too much away.

If androgyny is as much a mental process as a physical one, this guitar playing reflects that in-between-ness and both-ness, that elusive convertible otherness, rather than the stacked-up macho power chords, which conservatively cling to the rigid, binary world. These new guitars would create a different sort of scenery, more in tune with how he found and arranged his words, and theories, the general tone of breakdown and apprehension, and the improvisational style he was using to assemble his songs. This was the Rolling Stones in a devastated London sunk into the Velvet Underground that recorded *Live at Max's Kansas City* and the Can of *Ege Bamyasi*, a murky combination of distraction, perforated groove and general disquiet, where glam had gone to rot.

The *Diamond Dogs* music was put together more like a montage, in layers, sound as memories and false memories of his favourite music, and idealised favourite music, put together in a slightly wrong way, so that the music's version of the Rolling Stones was warped and full of holes, almost comical, but deadly serious.

It was almost as if, spotting their decline, their Ronson-like unwillingness to keep up to speed with what contemporary pop, rock and soul was doing in the studio and out in the world, he was creating a fantasy template for their future. He was experimenting on the sagging body of the Rolling Stones, who for some reason continued to occupy his thoughts, anxious about their decline because it might predict his own if he got stuck too much in the clichés of Ziggy he once played with and which could easily trap him.

Diamond Dogs was like a dreamlike demo of the Rolling Stones album David Bowie would produce where he gave them the concept, the songs, the musical style, gave Jagger his character – a jacked-up prophet of revelation, lost, lonely, tender, doomed, his fame a fleeting illusion, buoyed only by his own intensely articulate, erotic brilliance and a diagnostic reading of where and how the world is going mad – and then slammed it into the existing, decaying model. Visconti is back to mix it, understanding the sort of scenery Bowie is looking for, and how it should be lit, and framed; in the way that Bowie can follow up specific albums that are released years apart – sometimes in reverse order – this one is like a follow-up to *The Man Who Sold the World*.

It meant that out of all this fantasy, dread and monolithic stories of madness and personal and universal crises came a fantastic pop song, the bizarro Rolling Stones of 'Rebel Rebel', with another one of those tremendous Bowie opening lines that jolts you into an amazing new scene where reality is split down the middle and then slammed back together: 'you've got your mother in a whirl'. It then issues – from the reigning king of teenage dynamics, pregnant with insanely precise insight and a clear understanding that for all the apocalyptic thinking you mustn't forget the sex – a dead-eyed, dragged-down manifesto for what great pop must keep doing, compressing radical otherness and a rejection of the mundane into addictive entertainment. He was anticipating by looking back and picking up signals from the future the punk that was not far off, and already lurking down certain New York streets, the ones you'd use as a backdrop, with dogs barking from derelict windows, for the action of *Diamond Dogs*.

67.

He is Halloween Jack, but just for a flash. Weaned on Ziggy and then Aladdin Sane there is now a need to assume that Bowie is moving from alter ego to alter ego, each one burying Davie Jones further and further into the lost illusion of his past. Sometimes there is really no such character, just a costume change, a line in a song, a whiff of smoke, or a piece of PR held up to the endlessly reflecting mirror of the media.

68.

He is in New York in April and seeing shows by the Temptations, the Spinners and Marvin Gaye, and also Roxy Music and Todd Rundgren's Utopia, where he went backstage after the show. Somewhere among that emerges the blueprint from where his music goes next.

Anyone looking for the American David Bowie, after pondering for a while the incongruous more discreet shape-shifting claim of Joni Mitchell, might consider Todd Rundgren. After a low-key 1960s when he was just out of his teens missing various points but hinting at genius, he was skilled, energetic and perceptive enough as a producer, musician, writer, singer and almighty cultural sponge able to draw influences from all corners of music and enthusiastically keep up with the explosion of pop textures and styles in the early 1970s.

He loved a meandering nine-minute suite crammed with what some might perceive as philosophical bullshit, was obsessed with mid-Sixties British pop, would be infatuated with other pop singers to the point of stalking – with Bowie it was Jagger and Syd Barrett, with Todd, Carole King and Brian Wilson – was prone to apparently derailing a successful career with ambitious, idiosyncratic production experiments, just to ensure he didn't 'fall into that formulaic Elton John thing', and would get carried away with his own savant genius and pioneering zeal – high on the dangerous idea that too much knowledge can keep you sane, or send you mad.

He was as fascinated as Bowie, both being boys brought up on the Beatles, with effecting a paradigm shift not only in the structure of a song but the concept of an album, but with still being pop. He produced others, using up a generous surplus of energy and ideas – Meatloaf, Hall & Oates, Patti Smith, XTC. His faceless almost featureless Utopia band could be a hint of Tin Machine to come. He could switch in a musical moment from catchy to cerebral to the mind-meltingly sweet to psychedelic circus to entertaining sing-song to Broadway to cabaret to gimmick to headbangingly loud to soul ballad to electrifying fairy tales to madcap experimentalism to smooth melodicism to sound collage to the utterly enchanting to the oddly timed to the neo-prog to melodramatic power ballad to heavy metal show-stopper to space age to 'heroic' sentiment.

Bowie would also have noted Rundgren's ability to create a black-influenced blue-eyed soul – where white acts enacted deep soul feeling, originally used to describe the white soul of the Righteous Brothers – by processing his love for gospel, Stax and Motown without sacrificing his conceptual inclinations and without it seeming to be a parody, or a condescending, mock-hip, tambourine-shaking pseudo-soul. Also, Todd's blue-eyed soul, among everything else he was trying and doing, was where he found his occasional chart hits. It was part of his restless, often distracting, experimenting with pop history, with merging styles and creating imaginary hybrids, but it was also commercially successful.

69.

He is taking *Diamond Dogs* on a monstrous American tour with expressionist rock and roll sets the size of his and Defries's self-belief slammed together, extravagantly dramatising the demise of urban civilisation, as if he can take his own dreams on tour. He is being profiled for a BBC documentary that will be called *Cracked Actor*, his every move followed as he drifts through California as though Ziggy has become zombie. The documentary is trying to make sense of Bowie's hold on people's imagination, reporting on his fans as much as Bowie, who are buying into his aura as though he is a godless priest explaining how to explore and reimagine their potential selves and how to live a life without ever being bored.

Gaunt to the point of skeletal, skin as white as paper, eyes blank as obsidian mirrors, lips thinly purple-blue, if he were filling in a teenybop magazine questionnaire he would now say he weighed 90 pounds – light enough to be carried by a woman – and was seven feet tall. He plays to perfection the role of distracted actor/singer/ conceptualist/star/rootless hermit on the edge of being on the edge of self-destructing, either because he is truly about to collapse, crushed by his own ambition, imagination and appetite, on a tour of taking drugs that is taking him into his very own outer space, or because he is giving the BBC crew exactly what they want.

It is another performance, and he understands the ramifications of being in control even if the role, or the reality, is that he is completely out of control, or maybe madly craving more control and having to freak out to get it.

He knows that these moments will be remembered, and be as much a part of the myth as a song, sleeve or show. He chooses his words very carefully; even this out of it he is within himself. If he is expected to play a fragile, stoned, existentially indisposed pop star with followers who more than love him, who completely identify with him, who see themselves in him, because he is so other, and so beautifully unspecified, then he will make sure he does it well, or does it for real. He says:

> If I've been at all responsible for people finding more characters in themselves than they originally thought they had then I'm pleased because that's something I feel very strongly about;

that one isn't totally what one has been conditioned to think one is; that there are many facets to the personality which a lot of us have trouble finding and some of us do find quickly.

He mimes to Aretha Franklin in the back of a luxury limo, where he is most at home, seated inside the hushed and blackened-out temporary security of stardom. He traces star-like patterns in the air with his hand, and drinks milk straight from the carton, which has become his main source of nourishment in the compact space capsule of fame and addiction he has entered. Perhaps it is the milk that makes him so white; the other part of his diet is red peppers, which must have an effect on the colour of his hair.

There are mirrors to check what remains of his reflection, which might give him a clue as to the state of his sanity, and as always there is smoke, that sublime link with his past, the lingering connection with his mum and dad and what was once home. He clings to his cigarettes, because they structure the day, give it a comforting rhythm, and they keep him alive, and somehow help him fight his fear of death. To stop smoking would change the meaning of his life.

He rehearses the songs that will become part of *Young Americans* because as cracked as he is, he is still hard at work, resisting slipping into a creative slump that would be far worse than coming over a little, or a lot, disassociated, in a BBC television documentary, which of course does his reputation as out of this world shape-shifter whose genius might be a form of psychosis no harm at all.

It also turned out to be an audition for a film role that also did his reputation as spaced-out starman no harm at all, one that cinematically sealed the image of him as a self that goes on changing, of a mind free from base human notions of masculinity and femininity. For such a work of fiction, of monumental make-believe, this film becomes a key part of the biography of Bowie, another centre in a story filled with centres, but one that can be placed at the very centre of those centres, as if it contains the most clues about the truth of who David Bowie is, that genius of deception tentatively connected to the real world.

He will over time become as much 'The Man Who Fell to Earth' as anything else; this becomes the best way to describe his otherness, how he appears so different, because he came from somewhere else, and was suddenly here, with some gifts for humanity, having learnt to speak almost too carefully, almost knowing how to act natural, and walk normally. In some ways his first movie is more a documentary than *Cracked Actor*.

The film director Nic Roeg – who had taken Mick Jagger beyond himself as rock star or profoundly self-conscious human in *Performance* – was preparing a film about an alien outfitted in human skin forced to come to earth to save his home planet. His home is being destroyed by a series of nuclear wars and suffering from an endless drought. Only four hundred of his kind survive. His lone job, having made a perilous journey to earth in a rudimentary spaceship, is to amass a fortune using the advanced technological knowledge of his species, build a more solid space ark, and return to his home planet to bring the survivors back to earth. The residents on his planet have learnt all they know about humans from television broadcasts they pick up. Their understanding is a little off. They believe they will be welcome.

As he, Thomas Jerome Newton, goes about his business, curiously observing humans and being closely observed for signs he is a dangerous visitor from the stars, he watches telepathically as his wife and two children weaken and die, or he imagines that they do. Bowie as Newton can look sadder than anyone, for a world that has gone missing, or never even existed. He's apparently immortal, and everyone around him ages as he stays the same age. The film was based on a book by Walter Tevis in 1963 at the height of the Cold War and the Cuban Missile Crisis, when the world was faced with imminent destruction.

Roeg was the lead cinematographer on David Lean's *Lawrence* of *Arabia* and *Doctor Zhivago* before his first film *Performance* with Donald Cammell, mixing and merging the artistic and criminal worlds, and then *Don't Look Now*, mixing and merging horror and mystery. He requires an actor to play the alien misfit with potentially no signs that he is an actor. Peter O'Toole is a promising possibility, because he has the elegantly dazed quality of moving through life without knowing where the fuck he is, but is still essentially an actor, and he would come across as an actor playing an alien. Roeg is committed in his films to eradicating this visible join between pretence and reality.

He is shown shot, skinny Bowie slipping between the cracks in *Cracked Actor*, and immediately realises that Bowie would find it harder to act human than he would to become a creature from another world. Which is actually what he needs – not an actor trying to play an alien, but an actor trying to play human, as if that is the most alien thing of all.

Bowie moves like no one else, because in a way he is always miming his feelings, anxious, or relieved, that words won't be enough. His acting – his overall performance – is all about movement. The fact he has no acting experience in films is an advantage. He could of course act in a fashion, because in the real world, outside of a distinct frame, he was acting all the time. He was acting himself again and again. He was acting all the time to make up for some deficiency in his sense of himself. 'I could immediately tell he was different from other pop stars,' said Roeg. 'He seemed to change his personality every other performance.'

Roeg flies to New York to persuade Bowie to take the role. He arrives at Bowie's apartment at 2 p.m., and is told Bowie is still in the studio and offered a sandwich. Bowie turns up seven hours later. Roeg is still patiently waiting. He has a lot to think about, he is never bored. Bowie is amazed he is still there, assuming he would have left. Before Roeg can begin his carefully prepared pitch, Bowie has told him he really wants to do the film, 'if you'll have me'.

Roeg tells his studio executives Bowie will do the film. 'But it took me seven hours to persuade him!' Bowie wasn't sure about the script, but was impressed and flattered that Roeg waited for him for so long, and soon realised that Roeg had a formidable intellect, a wonderful, fiercely playful mind, and could play the part of teacher he had recently been missing. He loved it when, rarely, he came across someone who could teach him a thing or two about how to mix and merge art and time, and make him think.

Roeg said that he and Bowie didn't particularly discuss how Bowie was going to play Thomas Jerome Newton, but that he was the part as soon as he arrived on set. The studio executives visiting to get a glimpse of their glamorous star were anxious that he seemed a little ... odd. He had, after all, contractually promised a drug-free shoot. Roeg replied, 'He's playing an alien. How is he supposed to act? Like he's Gary Cooper?'

Bowie plays Thomas Newton – Tommy, Tom – by playing himself. Or one of his selves. He is gentle, polite, private, remote, generous, scared, suffering in exile, but endlessly fascinated by his environment, enthralled by television, gripped by alcohol, and in his own way incredibly influential as artist and scientist. His precarious English accent, learnt from studying others, is as far removed from his original south London as his new hair colour is from its original dusty blond, learnt from studying others, but is perfect for that of an alien who has learnt English by studying random television shows. He makes an album under a pseudo-nym – The Visitor – described as 'poems from outer space. You won't know the language but you'll wish you did.'

He doesn't really fit in, but he has the knowledge, ambition and understanding to become one of the most famous, noto-rious, loved and misunderstood names on the planet. He has achieved everything, but it doesn't mean anything. Power and wealth only increases the gap between him and humanity. He has lost the world in which he could savour those successes.

He's being held captive in a prison of luxury trapped inside his fake skin.

He never makes it home. He wants to so much, but things don't work out. His family are so far away. They might be dead. There's nothing he can do. He's pulled down to the level of the ruined humans around him. He's waiting for a future that will never come. He falls to earth, like an angel, or a sinner, someone destined to be on their own. He needs help.

Bowie gets frustrated in an interview on set when the fact that Newton is from outer space is constantly brought up, as if this means he is only interested in things from space, or could only play an alien because he's obsessed with aliens. He is not wanting to end up the eternal alien. People send you funny things in the post and speak to you in silly words and expect you to behave like a Martian.

He implies it might only be an illusion that Newton is from another planet, that his memories of another world are not real. He told Steve Shroyer and John Lifflander in the December 1975 edition of *Creem* magazine:

> Actually I'm not interested in space, you know, it doesn't do much for me. I've used it in some of the things I've done because it makes ... it's a macrocosm, sort of a backdrop to set things against without tying them into something too specific. My character is ... essential man, man in his pure form who's corrupted or brought down by the corruption around him. But it's never definitely said where he comes from, and it really doesn't matter. I mean, he could come from under the sea, or another dimension, or anywhere. The important thing is what happens between the people. It's a very sad, tender love story that evolves over a long period of time. It's the story of a man who falls in love and becomes an alcoholic. (Laughing) No it isn't quite that simple.

While filming in the New Mexico desert during a burning hot July and August, Bowie brings his own portable library of

400 books packed into trunks for his train journey. They were selected from his own much bigger collection, which he would lend to cast and crew. He is always educating himself. 'I get carried along on tides of enthusiasm.'

Roeg remembers him as being incredibly studious, apart, but amiable. 'He had fantastic concentration and an amazing kind of self-discipline. He kept himself to himself so that people started to think of him as this mysterious "other". He was just being himself.'

70.

He is full and empty on *David Live*, which had a working title of *Wham Bam Thank You Ma'am*, almost too colourful for what is effectively a contract-fulfilling technical souvenir of a gradual transformation, as the Diamond Dogs tours begin to become the Philly Dogs and/or Soul Tour, where those lookalikes expecting Ziggy, and sundry attachments including the Spiders from Mars and hard rock, will walk out, faced with a new arrangement of the music and approach, and of Bowie – with tidy side parting, fresh face and neat, boring white suit. The lookalikes have missed the point. He is not going to copy himself, and he is always on the move, so to be truly a copy, you don't copy. The hero worship is not what he thought it would be. He probably didn't think of it having consequences beyond just being liked.

David Live is a blurred blueprint of a blurred pop star shedding skins, changing clothes, hair, sound, style, mind, logo, becoming a near American, to see what will happen, where all is blurred, acting like his now greatest space and glam age hits were part of an invented soul history, as if Ziggy and diffusions were the missing link between Wilson Pickett and Prince, as well as between F. Scott Fitzgerald and Philip K. Dick. There are no limits to where he will take a genre, because there is no limit to his imagination, and he studies style and genre not to copy it or recreate it, but to break it up and put it back together again in another place. He's feeling his way forward by imagining as always different histories, and setting himself inside them.

71.

He is suspicious of his manager, a long way from his wife, his child, the idea of Haddon Hall as a new Bloomsbury scene is long gone, he is living in the anonymous, well-heeled centre of London, he is inside his work, processing what he has to process, because his mind won't stop thinking, thinking about thinking, and he needs to keep going, and one good way to keep going, to work into the night, because he has got so much to do, is to take cocaine. At first, it keeps him going. Then, it keeps him needing more to keep keeping going.

72.

He is seeing what happens when he gives himself to the artist and illustrator Guy Peellaert who in 1973 had published *Rock Dreams*, in collaboration with ever-prescient Nik Cohn, which turned rock history into the kind of romantically diseased and displaced fantasy that Bowie could appreciate. One where everything was made up, time was twisted, myths invented, beliefs exaggerated, rebellion celebrated and the marshalling of facts was irrelevant. It was as though rock music as a history had been forgotten, or over-remembered, and was being dreamt up again based on little evidence but a few fantasies and wrecked memories, and with the belief that this is how it should be: a great, voluptuous 'what if the history had been like this'. What if rock actually is as dangerous as the believing romantics wanted it to be?

It was kitsch hallucination of rock as psychic myth rendered in a photo-realistic way, dreams where there was little cheer. The hidden sleaze of rock and roll as blistering under the surface over at the BBC's corrupt dream of pop, *Top of the Pops*, was rendered in a series of intensely unsettling images. Ian Anderson of Jethro Tull as sick clown drooling over a young girl. Cilla

Black knitting in a deserted street as a mysterious Rolls-Royce approached.

The Rolling Stones were represented as Nazis being entertained by pre-pubescent girls, which was grotesquely accurate as a representation of the relationship between rock stars and their fans, and enhanced the flagging reputation of the group. It probably gave them a few extra years of maverick energy. Mick Jagger asked Peellaert what he was thinking, but he was hired to do the cover for the Rolling Stones' *It's Only Rock 'n Roll*.

Bowie wanted the mind who could do that, and openly steals Peellaert from the Stones. The artist takes a pose based on an all but naked shot of wild, surrealist cabaret singer Josephine Baker from 1926 and turns Bowie into a hybrid of emaciated, watchful, controlling Ziggy and lounge lizard hound-beast in his enriched, hyperreal colours that were part fantasy and part dream truth. Ziggy had mutated this much, beyond human, beyond reason. He was now a real freak, half star, half incubus, looking straight at you not to welcome you in a wonderful new world but warn you what horrors were behind you, and ahead of you.

The hound's exposed genitalia caused RCA some problems; even though the gatefold sleeve meant that Ziggy's generous fantasy penis was on the back of the sleeve, RCA in America panicked and had it removed – a censoring castration that left depraved Ziggy genderless, which was possibly more disconcerting than Ziggy showing his cock.

73.

He is interviewing and being interviewed by William Burroughs, who taught him to listen, whose rhythms and methods in attempting to write a new mythology for the space age he would borrow, especially on *Diamond Dogs* – his techniques of using cut-ups of words, scrapbook orientations, the generating of new memories and dreaming. This wasn't done to be difficult or complex, or to adopt the cool of Burroughs, but to find a new way of transmitting what he wanted to say. He'd done a similar thing before he was fully aware of Burroughs's approach.

These techniques were a way of teleporting the listener from one place to another with a vivid awareness of the moment of transition, which helps shatter rigidity. New meanings can come out of the rearrangement of the same words. You can find new connections and intersections and the leaps in logic, the jumps through time, the sudden shifts in tone have the quality of a dream.

Bowie often eagerly took on the role of publicist for certain writers, musicians and performers, and he was definitely a great publicist for Burroughs and his viciously absurdist take on society, constructed with the intention of saving mankind.

Burroughs's drug addiction, overcome at forty-five, was his central subject. He believed that writing came before speaking. One of the science-fiction writers who influenced him the most was H. G. Wells of Bromley – 'still one of the best'. An avant-garde iconoclastic icon, homosexual rights pioneer and the man who accidentally shot his second wife dead in 1951, Burroughs was on the cover of *Sgt. Pepper's Lonely Hearts Club Band*, and was an important character to be associated with in terms of boosting your cultural stature, from beats to hippies to punks to grunge. Mick Jagger wanted to make a film of his 1959 book *Naked Lunch* with him taking the role of Burroughs's alter ego, Inspector Lee of the Nova Police. Bowie was rumoured to be involved in one attempt to film the book – it was eventually taken on by David Cronenberg. *Naked Lunch* – a title accidentally arrived at by Jack Kerouac, after Allen Ginsberg mistakenly read Burroughs's 'naked lust' as naked lunch – was one of the last books in America to be the cause of an obscenity trial.

Soft Machine and Steely Dan took their names from his books. Bob Dylan invited him to come on his 1975 Rolling Thunder tour. When he lived in London between 1966 and 1974, he lived in Duke Street SW1, near Piccadilly Circus where the rent boys hung out in the toilets of the Underground station, a ten-minute walk down Bond Street from where Bowie was lodging with manager Kenneth Pitt. J. G. Ballard once described him as very difficult to get to know unless you were homosexual, which Ballard wasn't, and a drug user, which again Ballard wasn't.

Bowie gives Burroughs the Bowie he thinks he will want, and they each steer the conversation towards what they think will interest the other. Bowie explains Ziggy Stardust as ending up with a black hole that invades earth in the form of infinites who cause the end of the world. Bowie says he made the black hole into people, because it would be difficult to represent a black hole on stage. Burroughs drily replies, yes, 'A black hole on stage would be incredibly expensive. And it would be a continuing performance, first eating up Shaftesbury Avenue.' They talk about love, sex, the media as our salvation or our death, dreams as inspiration, porn, energy forces, the insidious, asexual Warhol, image, America, China and Mick Jagger, who Bowie describes as incredibly sexy and very virile, but ultimately like all rock stars not nearly as strange as the audience.

They both agree that they are very good liars. Bowie admits he doesn't know if he tells lies, or just changes his mind. He decides it's between the two, it's both, that he has things he has said that later he must defend or elaborate on, and he says, well, I didn't mean anything, and anyway, I've changed my mind. 'You can't stand still on one point your entire life.'

74.

He is talking to the famous American chat-show host Dick Cavett, with an accent so self-consciously almost facetiously English it sounds like one of the last, warped remnants of the British Empire. He is looking as though he has only just managed to put his skin on in time. And as though he might have been raised by insects.

The interview is recording a month before the end of the 1974 tour which segued from the *Diamond Dogs* monster to the marginally more manageable Philly Dogs Soul show, and apart from anything else Bowie is worn down to the bone. He is clinging on to a black cane – in place presumably of a constant drag on his life-saving cigarettes – which he seems to need to balance even though he is sitting down. The easy thing to say is that he is stoned, so high the cane might actually be made of lead to weigh him down, but he is also clearly exhausted. He attempts to swirl the cane like a degenerate Fred Astaire, the entertainer even in the middle of a nightmare.

In performance with his group, he is as energetic as ever, but as soon as he is in conversation, the life force deserts him. He just about has skin, but he might have nothing inside. He looks as though he belongs to Dr. Caligari's travelling carnival.

His ability to give who he's talking to the best version of what they expect is extremely distorted by lack of sleep and whatever legal and illegal medication is making him both slow and quick, sharp and lost at the same time. Cavett wants him to be eccentric rock star, a partner in strange but manageable excess to Mick Jagger, another peculiarly attractive Englishman known for playing fanatics and shape-shifting isolationists, and he does his best, but one of the consequences of the state he's in is that he has forgotten most of his lines. He doesn't want to let Cavett down, but he's clearly having trouble swallowing, and possibly breathing. His intuitive attempts at some flirting shrivel up into nervous twitches that just about stop short of turning into a fit. Cavett wonders about his mum. What does she feel about him? What does she tell the neighbours? He says his mum wouldn't tell the neighbours he was hers. They don't talk much, he says. 'We've come to an understanding.' Bowie doesn't look entirely convinced that he ever had a mum. He came into the world a different way. It looks as though he was the result of a coupling between a ghost and a sewing machine.

It could be said that there are not many people who in the same year can swing between Dick Cavett and William Burroughs – let alone be illustrated as a hybrid of end-of-the-world rock-star freak and monster dog, be shadowed by a documentary crew looking for cracks, and work on an album as great as *Young Americans*, which is only scratching the surface – and come out of it all looking in any way healthy and in control. He looks and acts just like you would expect a rock star under constant pressure to act and behave, but without actually completely losing his mind, and the drugs are only part of the formula that sends him trembling this far out to the edge. Somewhere inside, he knows this. It's all part of the show he has bought into, for now. He turns up for the performance even in this state. Eventually he'll get some sleep.

This is what people sometimes want from their rock stars. To be shown that leading the life can be this much of a risk. The highs are fantastic. The lows can threaten your life. You are worshipped for being someone you never really were, and then you feel yourself slipping into the role.

He giggles boyishly when Cavett asks what he thinks he will be like when he's sixty, perhaps out of relief that despite the wear and tear, the lack of connection between his skin and his bone, between the time of day and his appetites, the physical consequences of living on smoke, milk and scattered vegetable matter, the mental consequences of needing artificial help to sustain his stamina, he is about to make it to twenty-eight. He has almost got through the year of being twenty-seven, the year when rock stars like Bowie are threatened the most, as they disappear into the preposterous, precarious routines of living the dream, which is as nightmarish as it is exhilarating when you push it this far. The entertainer's life, with its chronic call for nocturnal vivacity, is notoriously debilitating. It can easily end in an accidental, or violent, or voluntary death. In the previous few years, the rock-star casualties, the deaths and breakdowns, were piled high. The grim reaper was eyeing Bowie. He survives, even if he almost needs a wheelchair.

• • •

I had a job in a bookshop, and by 1974 I could buy the following records. It was all I spent my money on. David Bowie's *Diamond Dogs* had enough angles, approaches, alleyways, highways, crossroads, predictions, intersections that you could take that would lead you into the following, as if it was both at the centre of all this, but also somewhere in the distance. But it was on the route either into or out of: King Crimson *Red*, Brian Eno *Taking Tiger Mountain (By Strategy)*, Robert Wyatt *Rock Bottom*, Neil Young *On the Beach*, Richard and Linda Thompson *I Want to See the Bright Lights Tonight*, Velvet Underground *1969: The Velvet Underground Live*, Van Morrison *Veedon Fleece*, Frank Zappa *Apostrophe (')*, Joni Mitchell *Court and Spark*, Sparks *Kimono My House*, Peter Hammill *The Silent Corner and the Empty Stage*, Leonard Cohen *New Skin for the Old Ceremony*, Queen *Sheer Heart Attack*, Kraftwerk *Autobahn*, Funkadelic *Standing on the Verge of Getting It On*, Gram Parsons *Grievous Angel*, Bob Marley & the Wailers *Natty Dread*, Tangerine Dream *Phaedra*, John Cale *Fear*, Cluster *Zuckerzeit*, the Residents *Meet the Residents*, Henry Cow *Unrest*, Monty Python *Monty Python Live at Drury Lane*, Lou Reed *Rock 'n' Roll Animal*, New York Dolls *Too Much Too Soon*, Bob Dylan/the Band *Before the Flood*, Can *Soon Over Babaluma*, Ivor Cutler *Dandruff*. Bowie didn't have a UK number 1 single even with 'Rebel Rebel' but Slade, Mud (twice), Suzi Quatro, Alvin Stardust, Abba, the Rubettes, Ray Stevens, Gary Glitter, Charles Aznavour, the Osmonds, David Essex and Barry White did. Bestselling albums were by the likes of the Carpenters, Elton John, Rick Wakeman, Mike Oldfield, Slade, the Bay City Rollers and Wings – but David Bowie's *Diamond Dogs* for all its sleaze, damned magic realism and debauched, collapsing apprehension spent four weeks at the top, replacing and then replaced by The Carpenters' *Singles 1969–1973*, giving an idea of just how much something like Bowie stood out at the time. *David Live* made it to number 2 in the UK and number 8 in America, despite spiteful reviews, and a cover image of Bowie between corpse and creep that freaked out Bowie himself, although it correctly captured the glam guru Bowie mutating – or melting – into what was coming next.

1975

*'In the absence of willpower the most complete collection
of virtues and talents is wholly worthless.'*

75.

He is losing himself, but there will be another one along in a few minutes.

He is liking fast drugs. Nothing that slows him down.

He is thinking that his consciousness is shifting from sensation to sensation, from perception to perception, from idea to idea, in endless succession.

He is searching for the Holy Grail. Each man is his own priest, and lifts therein the Cup of the Grail, and calls down the Flame of Fire, which is the Holy Spirit.

He is getting a little trouble from the neighbours.

He is dressed in brown plus fours and braces, his short red-orange hair tucked into a cloth cap. 'This,' he explains in rapid cockney, 'is my up-all-night look. Please note pallor of skin and trembling of hands.'

He is saying that there will be a political figure in the not too distant future who'll sweep this part of the world like rock and roll did. 'You probably hope I'm not right. But I am ... I always am.'

He is blaming his addiction on government control.

He is thinking, I am one of the most important people in the world.

He is saying well it seemed like a good idea at the time.

He is saying of Los Angeles – where he stayed up for days on end and felt his soul, and sperm, were being stolen from inside him, felt his mind being destroyed by madness – that 'it is a place that should be wiped off the fucking earth'.

He is realising it could never be a home only another stage.

He is realising how a city can make you do terrible things.

He is living for a hundred years in one night.

He is rearranging the pattern of ash in his ashtray.

He is staring so hard at the ashtray he is forgetting it is an ashtray.

He is consulting an invisible mirror.

He is drawing something awful on the carpet.

He is missing someone he is not entirely sure he even knows.

He is watching his entire life fall apart and all he can do is blankly stare.

He is letting the pain in his work interfere with his life.

He is being approached by people who because it's him think it must always be zoo time.

He is seeing people fall from the sky.

He is treating the phone as an instrument of shamanic possession.

He is building large sculptures in his living room next to the TV set.

He is living in a constant state of panic.

He is drinking a glass of milk but it might be milk plus; milk plus vellocet or synthemesc or drencrom.

He is like a child who can do what he wants.

He is thinking he can change the channel on his television without using his remote control just by using the power of his mind.

He is taking so much cocaine, says Mick Ronson, 'that I wish he could be in this room, right now, so I could kick some sense into him'. Visconti says he is taking so much 'it would kill a horse'.

He is shooting a million dollars through his face into his body.

He is lying about and smoking and drinking champagne.

He is reading a book that begins: 'Yes, I certainly was feeling depressed.'

He is looking for an angry fix.

He is measuring his life out in single lines.

He is covering the windows in black felt.

He is hallucinating he is already being turned into nostalgic memorabilia, part of an endless anniversary culture, marking things out in years, decades, centuries.

He is dancing with the devil, but her feet are quicksilver and she turns his into mud.

He is being told by Dr. Caligari's somnambulist that he will die at dawn.

He is wondering if he is the son of a king.

He is passing through a cavern of mirrors and breaking into a million pieces and is being attacked by hundreds of quasi-human characters, some of whom look like Ziggy, Aladdin Sane, Halloween Jack, the cracked actor, the Thin White Duke, half man half dog, they're coming for me, Terry, they're coming for me, I'll see you soon.

He is thinking he will sink into a needle and spoon existence, or bounce off the walls of a psychiatric hospital.

He is not sure what was defeating him, but he sensed it was something he could not cope with, something that was far beyond his power to control or even at this point comprehend.

He is pushing a slender blonde onto the couch and stripping them expertly.

He is seeing past, present and future as coexisting layers.

He is receiving a letter from someone claiming to be his long-lost mother.

He is a ghost wanting what every ghost wants – a body.

He is getting his instructions from street signs, newspapers and pieces of conversation he snaps out of the air, wondering who he is working for.

He is loving to play weird.

He is feeling small – like a cheat.

He is thinking there will be an endless horror movie in his head for the rest of his life for ever and ever amen.

He is thinking when you build your life around one thing you risk losing everything at a stroke.

He is thinking he is being possessed by demons who see him as their ticket out of hell.

He is thinking he can see the face of evil which is the face of total need.

76.

He is reading a classic of occult literature, *Psychic Self-Defence*, written in 1935 by the Welsh-born occultist, writer, teacher, psychologist, artist, psychic and ceremonial magician Dion Fortune, who changed her name from Violet Firth. She lived from the mid-1920s in a spiritual community she founded in an old officers' mess at the foot of Glastonbury Tor, which she called the hill of vision. When she died in 1946, she was buried in Glastonbury Cemetery.

Psychic Self-Defence was a detailed self-help manual on how to protect yourself from paranormal attack both while awake and in your dreams, including psychic vampirism and haunting, not just by lighting candles, saying a prayer or enacting a ritual with a circle of salt.

Places of concentrated unseen energy, Fortune suggests in *Psychic Self-Defence*, can lead the sensitive to subliminal observations. In the opening chapter she writes: 'There are beings that live in the invisible world as fish live in the sea. There are men and women with trained minds, or special aptitudes, who can enter into this invisible world as a diver descends to the ocean-bed. There are also times when, as happens to a land when the sea-dykes break, the invisible forces flow in upon us and swamp our lives.'

Another of her books was *The Mystical Qabalah*, where she wrote, like a mystical semiotician, 'Symbols are to the mind what tools are to the hand – an extended application of its power.'

Fortune was also a member of the Order of the Golden Dawn, a ritual magic group exploring how to communicate with angels and demons whose members included Aleister Crowley – a professed admirer – and W. B. Yeats. Bowie mentions Crowley and the Golden Dawn in 'Quicksand' from *Hunky Dory* – back when the flirtation was more a matter of friendly rivalry with Crowley obsessive Jimmy Page.

Psychic Self-Defence was an influence on David Lynch and Mark Frost as they were conceiving the more supernatural elements of *Twin Peaks*. Mythological details reappeared in the extreme, and extremely cryptic, post-Frost prequel *Twin Peaks: Fire Walk with Me* from 1992 that charts the last seven days of troubled teen beauty queen Laura Palmer, as though the murder mystery could be solved by considering the earthly manifestation of spirits.

Bowie played another of his great shadow selves in *Twin Peaks: Fire Walk with Me*, the 'long lost' Agent Phillip Jeffries, missing for two years, who inexplicably abruptly materialises in the Philadelphia office of the FBI, crossing over from one dream into another. He attacks security cameras, and refuses to talk about Judy, a secret name only he seems to know – 'I'm not going to talk about Judy,' he announces, with the delivery of an inimitable vocalist who sang mystery better than anyone, and who could be paying tribute through Lynch's fascination with Oz to Judy Garland.

He mentions the man from another place, and describes a meeting of the demonic members of the Black Lodge – an idea that came from Fortune – before disappearing again. It was a dream, he explains, not explaining anything. We live inside a dream. The stories I wanna tell you about ... Eventually there would be a 'Black Lodge' bar along the Berlin street where he used to like to drink on his emotional holiday in the city, inspired by but not themed after *Twin Peaks*.

77.

He is on alert. He's becoming seriously damaged, triggered by scents, stains and shapes to imagine the devilish worst, or his natural sensitivities – the openness to ideas and what lurks beneath the fabric of reality that made him such a distinct artist, the unformed feeling that we are here for some unknown higher purpose – are multiplied into hallucinatory supernatural distress by the cocaine psychosis. Dion Fortune writes that a sense of fear and oppression is very characteristic of an occult attack, and one of the surest signs that herald it. 'It is extremely rare for an attack to make itself manifest out of the blue, as it were.' The ultimate message of her book, after explaining various ways of using esoteric magic, ancient wisdom and mystical techniques to fend off evil forces, was to get some outside help.

78.

He is incredibly still in bed after a night before that went through the roof, to the furthest, fastest, darkest side of staying awake, one night of a forgotten high and low too many perhaps, and someone close has placed a mirror near his nose and mouth, to check he is still breathing.

79.

He is.

80.

He is being taken to a mirror by someone close who he trusts who cares for him the most and they are saying to him, 'Look at us both. If you continue to be the way you are being at the moment, you're never going to see me again. You're not worth the effort.'

He is putting a cigarette in his mouth. He pulls on a finger. Then another finger. Then the cigarette.

He is thinking of his son.

He is wondering how to come off the monster.

81.

He is firing his manager Tony Defries, sending him a telegram to inform him that his services are no longer required. 'I think he overdid it. He did a lot of things too early and tried to overkill everything.' Brilliant, relentless, king confidence man, probably what was needed for a few months to break Bowie big time into the big time, because he pushed so hard he would at times operate at the boundary's edge, as if pop music was a kind of black market, one big closing down sale. He was not there from the beginning, he will not be there at the end.

At the conclusion of a long legal dispute and numerous lawsuits, counter-suits and injunctions, to break the stalemate so he can escape the iron grip, Bowie accepts that millions of dollars of future earnings are heading to Defries, who was from the real world of money, not the unreal world of fantasy and performance. Defries receives 50 per cent of royalties on all albums from *Hunky Dory* to *David Live* – owning half of all the great transformations – and 16 per cent of all future Bowie albums until 1982. All expenses come from Bowie's percentage. In the movie version of this story Bowie breaks down in the negotiation room, slamming his fists into the table, and then spends days howling at the moon.

The intimidating framework of superstardom that Defries helped construct is broken down, as if Ziggy has finally left the building, loyal to Defries rather than Bowie, taking the glitter costumes, the bodyguards, the sub-Factory faux-mystique. Bowie says, 'I'm free.' He blames what he saw as the darker spirit of Defries for a considerable period of pessimism.

'I feel mentally strong again.'

82.

He is smiling and the fear flies away in little pieces of light.

He is thinking, all history is fiction, deceit after deceit in the service of truth.

He is leaving a trail, leaving scattered signs to follow, his life is a psychic paper chase.

He is saying to a fan on the set of *The Man Who Fell to Earth* – 'I hope you have a glorious death. Live your life the best you can while you are here, and when you die, your death will be as glorious as your life.'

He is returning from the filming healthier than he's been for years.

He is ready to face the music.

83.

He is moving on almost for the sake of it through 1975's *Young Americans*, which meticulously approximates soul music, proto-disco and slick funk with a seductively indifferent attention to detail, so that it is soul music without a soul, to represent the doomstruck era of Nixon, but packed with feeling, detached and intimate at the same time, deluxe and ascetic, generic and avant-garde, a coolly frantic, nicely ironic commentary on the unbearable lightness of fame.

He seems to have come out of character, slicked the hair down, shed the costumed conceptual distance, but in fact has gone even deeper into someone else, as androgynous as ever in terms of his fluid thinking, using funk as a kind of ready-made found object to juxtapose with existential pleading, surreal social commentary and autobiographical purging, on the way to writing the greatest song of all time. He is stretching the credulity of his listeners.

It's inevitable as a showman influenced by great American showmen that he would alight on this form of extreme show-manship. His album centred on the treacherous sinking sensation of fame to be had from inside America. He is commenting on the state of America, on his state in America, by examining the form of a very contemporary indigenous American music, and creating a kind of seductive discophonic richness that is designed for the charts without appearing a blatant mix of the obvious and the obvious.

Young Americans becomes another watchful, vivid re-boot, so that he might begin again, filled with everything he has done, because he's stuck with all that, but emptying out much of the recent paraphernalia so that he can make up a new set of equations, glue together a new collage of experiences and declarations, and find new ways of turning inner tension, desperate moments and his place in the world into song. He was using the sound to present his thoughts, and for him albums were becoming a new thing, a way to create new worlds, and contain his latest thinking.

He called it 'plastic soul', which didn't mean inauthentic – it was flexible, adaptable, and treated black music not as something to merely steal from, destroying its power and history, breaking down its passions into something safely palatable to a white audience, but as an energy he could complement, and compliment. He's not copying, definitely not blacking up; he is extending the vocabulary by placing soul in a new context, and extending his own vocabulary. He doesn't give up his own particular elements – the residue of glam, the meta-Vegas exuberance, the cocaine zest, the lounge weird – because that would be rude and patronising, a real pretence.

He is saying in an interview: 'I just use music to achieve something I have in mind, an idea or a feeling I want to get across. But I'm not one of those people who treat it as something sacred. You've got to play around with it or it gets to be a dreadful bore.'

84.

He is saying in an interview, 'I don't study rock much, and I'm not a follower of anything much,' but then in an interview it would always depend on who he was speaking to, what he thought they might want from him, always trying to give them what they wanted, to please them, what mood he was in when he was talking, what state of mind, and sometimes that would mean saying the opposite of what he was actually thinking.

He could talk a lot in interviews, but it didn't mean he was giving much away; he held up a mirror or two in the face of whoever he was talking to, preferably he would smoke as well, it's part of his breathing, and he could hide behind the mirror, which had a mirror on the back as well, and drift off into the smoke, and play yet another role, and let the interviewer talk to themselves, and have confirmed what they thought all along. Not that he's got anything to hide.

'Bowie was never meant to be,' he will say, to satisfy the needs of his interviewer. 'He's like a Lego kit. I'm convinced I wouldn't like him if I ever met him, because he is so vacuous and undisciplined.' If he is asked whether he is doing it for the money, he replies with a smile that is no smile, a laugh that is itself part of a show, 'Good Lord, of course I am.'

And he will give them the final words they love to hear. 'There is no definitive David Bowie.'

He would seem relaxed, and easy-going, laughing at jokes almost in synch with the punchline, but ultimately he never let the interviewer truly relax, and get to know him. Perhaps that was something he learnt from Andy Warhol, and refined after meeting William Burroughs, who didn't have to act crazy, because he was so far out for real and could just play the perfect straight man. He has been taught by the best in terms of how to invent, and protect, himself, and develop his personal myth. Not that it keeps you safe.

Bowie could deftly reveal his intelligence, lightly reveal his sense of humour, his vulnerability and sometimes a flinty flicker of his insolence, a smear of mysticism, a quick shot of self-deprecating snobbishness, a flash of his 'malevolent curiosity', his hard-earned status as a permanent outsider allowed on the inside, and leave it at that, so that so many holes had to be filled in to complete him as a person. He let others make him up. He didn't want to interfere with the fiction too much. It was all part of how he was constructing a biography of himself – allowing himself to be turned into a series of found objects that could be put together in order to find the plausible story of David Bowie.

He changed a little in how he performed in interviews, from the 1960s intense, needy sweetheart, through the hot, warm and/or cold, charming, confessional man with a racing mind, a dangerous, collapsing, hounded, addictive, wasted, recovered, contemplative, reformed mind in the 1970s, to the cheeky, chuckling down-to-earth friend to everyone in the 1990s, but it was always essentially the same script and the same oddly formal routine where he kept a kind of aristocratic distance.

It was a duty, almost a contractual obligation, and he always completed the task perfectly, however mad or sane, patient or impatient he was, and came out of it having added just the right amount of detail and hype to what would become his biography, his sense of grand illusion, his carefully constructed public image, a career counted out in transformations, losses, and recoveries, headlines, images and rewrites, his life revolving around his work, which would paradoxically put a highly decorative but blank screen between him and any troubling truth.

85.

He is writing 'Fame' with John Lennon and Carlos Alomar in forty-five minutes.

> I guess Lennon defined for me how one could twist and turn the fabric of pop and fill it with elements from other art forms, often producing something extremely beautiful, very powerful and imbued with strangeness. Also, uninvited, John would wax on endlessly about any topic under the sun and was over-endowed with opinions. I immediately felt empathy with that. Whenever the two of us got together it started to resemble Beavis and Butt-Head on CNN's current affairs debate show *Crossfire*.

86.

He is thinking fame is a trick. 'Fame can take interesting men and thrust mediocrity upon them.'

He is writing another song in a couple of hours and then complaining: 'Another song. That's the last thing I need. I write an album a month as it is.'

He is twitching with energy. He's fidgeting, jabbing a cigarette in and out of his pursed lips, bouncing lightly on a stool behind the control board in a makeshift demo studio, staring through the glass at Iggy Pop.

He is saying, 'I really, honestly and truly, don't know how much longer my albums will sell. I think they're going to get more diversified, more extreme and radical right along with my writing. And I really don't give a shit . . .'

He is a recording instrument. He is not an entertainer.

He is leaving a living hell, which for a time was at the dark demented edge of the deep blue Pacific Ocean.

He is saying I'm bored, bored, bored.

●   ●   ●

1975 was the year Bob Dylan made sure you knew exactly who Bob Dylan was with *Blood on the Tracks* and where he's been with *The Basement Tapes*, Patti Smith said look at me too with *Horses*, Dr. Feelgood issued a stripped-down threat to the dragons of prog pomp on *Down by the Jetty*, Brian Eno invented or 'invented' a future music with *Discreet Music*, 'thought' of another on *Another Green World* and with Robert Fripp thought of 'another' on *Evening Star* – pre-echoes of which part of the future Bowie was about to relocate – Kraftwerk found *Radio-Activity*, Bruce Springsteen was *Born to Run*, Neil Young was behind the shades with *Tonight's the Night*, Bob Marley and the Wailers were *Live!*, Robert Wyatt thought *Ruth Is Stranger Than Richard*, Parliament were making a *Mothership Connection*, Joni Mitchell was discovering *The Hissing on Summer Lawns*, Willie Nelson was a *Red Headed Stranger*, Richard and Linda Thompson went to *Pour Down Like Silver*, John Cale was with *Helen of Troy*, Burning Spear hailed *Marcus Garvey*, Kiss were *Alive!*, Henry Cow with Slapp Happy were *In Praise of Learning*, Peter

Hammill's *Nadir's Big Chance* was a surreal blueprint for post-punk, Gavin Bryars was reporting on *The Sinking of the Titanic*, and Elton John made another album. David Bowie's *Young Americans* was easily in my top 5 of that year even with all that going on, and probably along with *Horses*, *Blood on the Tracks* and Joni, the one I played the most. In a year of strange number 1s, as if the way was being prepared for the urgent arrival of punk, including outright novelty hits by Telly Savalas, Don Estelle and Windsor Davies, Typically Tropical and Billy Connolly, and neo-novelty songs by the Bay City Rollers, Pilot, Mud, Rod Stewart and Art Garfunkel, 'Space Oddity' made it to number 1. From this we can take a measure that Bowie was six years ahead of his time, and from the music he was making that year, still approximately six years ahead. For number 1 of the year it was up against 'Stand By Your Man' and the year of odd 1s ended well or not so well depending on your point of view with 'Bohemian Rhapsody'. Elsewhere, there was 'No Woman, No Cry', 'Autobahn', 'Love to Love You Baby', 'Never Gonna Give You Up', 'The Hustle'. Outside the charts, just plain outside, Pere Ubu's '30 Seconds Over Tokyo' and Television's 'Little Johnny Jewel' issued another warning. Bowie was on top of it all, and taking heed of the warnings, and issuing his own, in the form of funk, with 'Young Americans', 'Fame' and 'Golden Years', now thoroughly knowing his way into and out of a chorus, on the inside of the pop world and yet still on the outside, all of them right up there with singles of the year, many of which were opening up new musical futures, but also in the charts, and pulling stranger music towards the charts to join him.

1976

'Searching for music is like searching for God.'

87.

He is touring North America on the Isolar tour to support the *Station to Station* album, it's how he earns a living, and he has Europe on his mind, where he thinks he will be able to see things in a new way. He performs on a bare black stage under a white cathedral of light. He's chain-smoking Gitanes – 'I don't have to be doing this. I'm doing you a favour. I could be at home just smoking my cigarettes' – and the support act is made up of a playback of Kraftwerk's 'Radioactivity' and a showing of Salvador Dalí and Luis Buñuel's short 1929 film *Un Chien Andalou*, where two dreams meet, Dalí's hand covered in ants and Buñuel slicing an eye with a knife which famously becomes a razor blade in the film. He starts the show wearing a piece of cloth covering his face, and during it sings Brecht and Weill's 'Alabama Song' from their 1930 opera – or musical drama – *Rise and Fall of the City of Mahogany*, a savagely satirical warning of decadent times, set in a new city based on nothing but pleasure, a Sodom or Gomorrah where anything goes and all appetites are catered for. Singing 'Alabama Song' from a parable about the destructive power of capitalism was a way of commenting on his own self-destructive period. It's one of his favourite pieces of musical theatre – along with Benjamin Britten's *Peter Grimes* and *The Turn of the Screw* and Sondheim's *Sweeney Todd* – the sort he always sets his heart on producing himself.

88.

He is moving to Switzerland, in the hills above Montreux, and while he is working Angie is preparing their new house, which he describes as his first home.

89.

He is reducing the monstrous, bloated Mainman staff to a small, mobile and efficient unit that work completely for and with him. One of the Mainman staff survives, the French-American multilingual Corinne Schwab, known as Coco, who soon becomes a constant companion, almost a carer in his worst moments, worrying about his weight, reminding him to eat, shielding him from extreme fans, sharing his most intimate spaces, which are becoming the back seat of the twenty-foot chauffeured limos and his bland hotel suites. He would increasingly look after his own business affairs with a combination of lawyers and business advisers, and always Coco as his ultimate steadying force, close collaborator and constant counsel. Angie is not concerned and explains to anyone who asks that she is not worried he will ever fall in love with someone else while they are apart. 'He's incapable of loving anything other than his work, anyway.'

90.

He is greeting his backstage guests after a performance at the Los Angeles Forum on 8 February: Rod Stewart and Britt Ekland, Alice Cooper, Ringo Starr, Ray Bradbury, Linda Ronstadt, Carly Simon, Henry Winkler and Steven Ford, son of Gerald Ford.

91.

He is not present as *The Man Who Fell to Earth* is premiered at the Leicester Square Odeon on 18 March. Guests include Lionel Bart, James Coburn, Lee Remick, Rick Wakeman, John Peel and Amanda Lear.

92.

He is visiting Berlin during a day off in the German section of the Isolar tour.

He is fascinated by the dramatisation of power as practised by the Nazis and Hitler's favourite architect Albert Speer's plans to make Berlin the biggest city in the world and the capital of a 1,000-year Reich.

He is saying to an obsessive Swedish reporter that he believes Britain could benefit from a fascist leader.

He is arriving in Britain at London's Victoria Station after being away from England for two years. He waves to the crowd who have come to greet him from the back of a limo. A photograph of the event seems to imply he is giving a fascist salute.

He is getting carried away with the idea there is no line between art and life.

He is saying a bunch of reporters asked a load of ridiculous political questions and he gave them a load of ridiculous answers. 'I am astounded anyone took it seriously.'

He is learning that there are some things you cannot play in real life.

He is forced to take a new direction.

He is being described in the *Daily Express* as looking terribly ill. Thin as a stick insect. Corpse pale. He might even scare the nervous. He's apparently flirting with fascism. 'Strong I might be. Arrogant I may be. Sinister I am not.'

He is saying,

> What I'm doing is theatre, and only theatre. All this busi-
> ness about me being able to raise 7,000 of my troops at the
> Empire Pool by raising one hand is a load of rubbish. In the
> first place the audience is British, and since when will the
> Brits stand for that? What you see on stage isn't sinister.
> It's pure clown. I'm using myself as a canvas and trying to
> paint the truth of our time on it. The white face, the baggy
> pants – they're Pierrot, the eternal clown putting over the
> great sadness of 1976.

He is told that rock and roll had been good to him. 'Well, I've
been good for rock and roll.'

93.

He is feeling the need to be clean.

He is overworked.

94.

He is fighting with Angie, about more or less everything from
child care via the latest state of the many love triangles to who
among the pair of them needs the most care, and he is fighting
with his new post-Defries management. Angie and management
become a constant crisis, because he is impossible to live with and
impossible to manage, or because he cannot choose very well,
or because he can only maintain that level of intimacy with any
form of partner for a certain amount of time. It gets nasty with
Angie, and nasty with his management.

95.

He is being described by his latest fallen manager: 'David can be very charming and friendly and at the same time very cold and self-centred.'

96

He is finishing *The Idiot* with Iggy Pop with the final mixes being done at the Hansa studio in Berlin.

97.

He is starting work on what becomes *Low* in the thirteenth-century Château d'Hérouville, in the Val d'Oise region 30 kilometres north of Paris where the Bee Gees had recorded *Saturday Night Fever*. It was also the location for a number of porn movies including *Kinky Ladies of Bourbon Street*. Bowie was concerned it was haunted, and refused to sleep in the master bedroom.

He compiles the sounds and songs that will be mixed in Berlin; the Berlin it came to represent is of course a state of mind, a stage of being, a plunge into another reality. Berlin is not described on *Low*; he describes a Berlin in his mind, which is close to Lou Reed's *Berlin*, which was written and recorded seven years before he actually visited. Reed did not need to go to Berlin to know Berlin, a microcosm of a divided world, a perpetual incompleteness, always in the process of becoming, where people are trapped by mental as well as physical walls. Locations are not important. The Bowie and Reed Berlin then becomes a part of the real Berlin and the tangled dream; because the city has always been built and designed by individual imaginations, based not on stability but change, and projection.

98.

He is going through great waves of ecstasy and despondency.

99.

He is fleeing the heat of an unnamed crime, an unbearable situation, quitting a scene gone bad.

100.

He is in a state of withdrawal.

101.

He is at work in the studio which becomes his sanctuary from business, relationships, and the intrusive outside. It is where he can construct other worlds, recover a form of necessary innocence, and surprise and delight himself with fresh ideas and unexpected connections. The studio is the purest way he can be inside his mind, where everything he is really exists, and this then becomes music, which for a while can be a new form of protection from the pressures and entanglements on the outside.

102.

He is on assignment in a new part of the world. 'It is necessary to travel. It is not necessary to live.'

He is moving from where he was losing his life to where he feels as though all he is doing is earning a living.

He is moving from the very edge of America, where he was about to fall off, to a city in the middle of a vast plain stretching all the way into Russia.

He is feeling the need to be reminded that creative boundaries exist primarily in order to be negotiated, breached and redefined fluidly.

Hc is wishing Brian Eno was in Iggy Pop's group.

103.

He is living near Tempelhof Airport next door to a gay bar
round the corner from where Marlene Dietrich was born,
where he becomes a regular eating bean soup and drinking
Scotch, reflecting on absence and presence. Things can never
be made to reappear again no matter how deep you dig.

He is thinking that a story about a person in a city inevitably
becomes a story about the city itself.

He is living in a city that is a memento you could wander
around in for years.

104.

He is riding a three-gear Raleigh bicycle in peasant cap,
scraggly beard and baggy windcheater around Berlin in the
summer, the other side of Hollywood hell, but in parts a vision
of hell, grey and spectral and anonymous, but he's feeling
closer to where he needs to be. He rides up and down the road
to recovery, which is also known as Schöneberg Haupstrasse,
he rides to Kreuzberg, to the Exil restaurant, to the Paris Bar
near the Zoo Station, to the Brücke Museum in Grunewald
where original expressionist art sits waiting for him to take
nourishment. He rides through a film of ruins, through
yesterdays echoing everywhere, and to the Hansa studio near
the Wall where it overshadowed the Potsdamer Platz, in pre-
war days the commercial heart of the city, now surrounded
by watch towers and barbed wire, staged to feel deserted and
open to question and filled with the ghosts of history.

He is crossing the Wall at Checkpoint Charlie and eats at the
Ganymed restaurant in East Berlin, where Brecht once dined.

105.

He is having an impact as a musician, as a brand, as a sign of the times, that is as great as Dylan and the Beatles, his influence as an otherworldly pop star actually greater, and if you just want one example of what he got up to as this erudite pop combination of shaman, singer, thinker and shameless self-promoter holding up a mirror to himself in order to interpret the outside world, then *Station to Station* is as good a place as any to start. It is a mesmerising album, one of Bowie's best, which is saying something, as he made many, most of them during the 1970s, that were sold as entertainment but contained the moving detail and mysterious, transformative depth of art.

It may well be one of rock's very greatest, as a comment both on where the smart, neurotic artist who made it was, psychologically, creatively and commercially, but also where rock music itself was, on its compelling journey from Sinatra, Presley and the Beatles to Prince, Jay Z and Kanye, from the Velvet Underground, the Kinks and Kraftwerk to Madonna, Nirvana and Nine Inch Nails, from Joni to Cat, from Joy Division to Radiohead. It is one of those Bowie albums, like *Hunky Dory*, or *Ziggy Stardust*, or *Low*, or *Lodger*, or *1. Outside*, that are at times my favourite of his – did I mention *Aladdin Sane*, *Diamond Dogs*, *The Next Day?* – because they demonstrate with such élan what a sparkling, mischievous mind he had.

It came between the Americanised, fictionalised and highly stylised soul-funk slickness of his high-on-life *Young Americans* album and the estranged, challenging Euro-bleakness of the low *Low*. He's not thinking of a particular direction, or style. He was fast approaching thirty, which at the time within pop and rock was mostly unprecedented, with very few role models to get some cues from about how to age, not just performing your hits but how to continue in an evolving research and development mode. Jazz was where the precedents were set, but not in terms of mixing the explorations with the nature of stardom that had become part of his methodology.

He needed to keep himself interested, as though he feared that once he lost interest, in himself, and what he was doing next, that madness he sensed at the edge of his vision might creep a little further into his psyche.

The music started to appear when he was working on Nic Roeg's *The Man Who Fell to Earth*, which ultimately seemed perfect for the lost, distracted, preternaturally bright and, post-fame, close to haughty, all-powerful seeming, but transparently disjointed Bowie. *Station to Station* was a soundtrack that never was to the movie, as Bowie was strangely not asked to compose the film's music, or if he was didn't finish it in time. Roeg just wanted the cracked, emaciated Bowie that was falling apart in real life, the wired, burnt-out pop star wonderfully closely resembling the stranded, baffled but brilliant spaceman from a dehydrated future who was part newborn innocent, part ancient guru, part conceptual businessman, part inventor/magician, part completely shattered.

Playing an alien, having believed or pretending to believe a little too much in his own publicity that he was some sort of alien himself, having lost sight of his real self after years of relentless shape-shifting, Bowie constructed a new dubious character he hoped might protect him, the Thin White Duke. Inside six years, since the late Sixties, he'd been goofy, psychedelic music hall singer, warped novelty specialist, surreal folkie, risqué glam-rock starman, cosmic wizard, apocalyptic androgynous dog-man and blanked-out white soul man sarcastically flirting with the pleasures and pressures of American-enhanced superstardom. Now, he would play a ghostly, narcissistic, deceiving, amoral, cocaine-obsessed existential adventurer, for all the chaos in his life still a creature of communication and communion, anxiously yearning for deeper meaning in a superficial, chilling world.

His restless, crazily inventive drug-assaulted and hedonistic personality had disintegrated to such an extent he would confess he barely remembered making *Station to Station*. Even in a waking coma he can create great theatre, or perhaps it is great theatre because it captures that unique to him in the mid-1970s combination of alertness and trance. He managed to drift or plummet into rock star chaos and Hollywood dread but still have the wit to send back messages, a poetic reporter on the writhing details of an altered state to – nearly – the very end.

Bowie would kill off the damaged, demented Thin White Duke a little quicker than he killed off Ziggy Stardust, just in case the nefarious Duke took over like Ziggy appeared to. The soundtrack to this character showed Bowie withdrawing in a final blast of tortured extravagance from his fascination with the expressive, penetrating showmanship of American soul and turning to more enigmatic and forward-looking, but more obscure, European music, especially German avant-garde electronic rock out of Can and Neu! influenced by experimental musicians and theorists like John Cage, Karlheinz Stockhausen, Steve Reich and Terry Riley and the American west-coast experimentalism of Grateful Dead.

Young Americans, containing hits such as 'Fame' and a guest appearance by John Lennon perfectly playing a Beatle beaten into a new shape because he'd left the Beatles, features Bowie somewhere between living and leaving the dream. Lennon does his version of Bowie as much as Bowie does his version of Lennon, affectionately competing for rights.

Young Americans was the calculatedly commercial Bowie response to achieving the American fame and glamour he had set his heart on. He was, though, becoming so successful he was peering into some form of the middle of the road, a fixed place Bowie wasn't ready for quite yet if ever. Part of him set his heart on a virtual Las Vegas world, but he never relinquished his artistic yearnings. He was never really in the mood to cash in on a particular style when it had established him as a commercial success, even if all that attention was what he had been craving in the first place.

He took the risk, down to arrogance or an untreatable addiction to his experimental tendencies, of seeing whether he could try something less obviously commercial and still win people over. Could he maintain his appeal without having to carry on climbing into undignified costumes as he hit his thirties?

He had an eye on punk, as well, which was reducing the flat-footed pomp and bombast of numerous pointless rock acts to uncool rubble; some would never recover their original hard-earned cool. Bowie was perhaps the only rock star that didn't get chronically undermined, even destroyed, at least critically and culturally, by the intolerant emergence of punk.

The early Seventies work, those parts coming out of the Velvets, Iggy, and various esoteric outsiders, had helped set up a difference, but punk could easily have made all that look ridiculous – it was the albums from *Station to Station* to *Lodger*, travelling through their own externalised zone, that erected a force field and kept him immune from the toxic effects. By the time of *Lodger* in 1979, he had found himself close to where the adventurous extremes of punk had gone, easily – but what a move it was – finding himself filed and belonging among Gang of Four, Wire, Joy Division, Public Image Ltd and Pere Ubu, music representing the dislocation of the times.

He soon slipped through a side door, to yet another, less volatile something else, but even as commercial, or as mixed up, as he got during the 1980s, in the long run, the albums he made in the second half of the 1970s, discreet, but still fantastically simulated soundtracks to the culture, conflict and strain of the times, to a mind breaking and repairing itself, closest to what he would have wanted 'Bowie' to sound like if it were a genre, ensured an enduring artistic legacy.

So strong was the force created by this sequence he could still revert to crafty novelty, straight commercial strategies, dilettante trials, blockbuster greatest-hits tours, random, never quite breakthrough film roles, and even his experiment at being in an ordinary group, Tin Machine, in the 1980s, and, ultimately, still not lose his cool, even if it was only ever 'cool', another act, another stage. Everything becomes a reaction to the fact he has been here, making this music, and making the music he makes next because of it. From then on his job becomes one of addition and subtraction, adjustment and re-adjustment, playing himself against himself and his own developed history.

The movement that helped him conjure up this critical aesthetic immunity began with *Station to Station*. Working with the young engineer who had helped him come up with the synthetic funk sound of *Young Americans*, Harry Maslin, he was on his own in a way, without the sympathetic help of Tony Visconti or Ken Scott, who had learnt to understand his ways. He has settled on a central rhythm section – Carlos Alomar on guitar, George Murray on bass, Dennis Davis on drums – that will stay with him into his European period, and keep the experiments anchored in the dislocated groove he'd worked hard to establish.

He had to feel his way towards a sound, which adds to the sense of distance, of a music emerging from a new set of conditions. It sounds like Bowie because it is Bowie, but remains removed from a specific genre or style. It is the sound using rock instruments and a recording studio of a crashed mind working out where to go next, feeling the comforting pull of the past, but instinctively preferring the unknown pull of the future.

It formed a synaptic link between his eruptive pop star years and the stateless, experimental era, and was a resplendent example of how Bowie used music and the construction of a conceptual framework, however loose, as a kind of psychic quarantine. Maybe he was worried after almost being fixed in space and not allowed to change after his first hit 'Space Oddity', which for a while was all it seemed people wanted from Bowie.

Station to Station – feeling hunted, his memory cradicated by constant change, he was moving from place to place, hotel to hotel, character to character, fixation to fixation, charade to charade, happy to be homeless yet still searching for a home, feeling a tragedy he felt was just within the reach of everyone – was where he faced his demons, and made a kind of baroque soul music where it is not quite clear if there is a soul involved.

It retains the gelastic post-disco groove of *Young Americans*, shards of the recent elegantly simulated funk, some of the insecure grandeur of *Aladdin Sane*, and the singer he played was some strung-out descendant of the modish Soho crooner, the hard-rock madman, the delicate folkster, the cabaret tart, the leper messiah. The impressionable nuttiness and tense humour of 1967–1971 is filtered through the frazzled, exile on surreal street guitars of *Diamond Dogs*. There are decaying traces of the kinky folk, screwy metal, insolent space-opera glam, solemn space crooning and cabaret melodrama he'd passed through in the early 1970s, but he was already crossing a remote border into his less obviously commercial next territory – abstracted European electronic music.

It's another new Bowie, bleached of spirit, broken by sensation, detached eye still on the prize, crawling out of the wreckage into the wilting post-geographical light. Out of this collision of remnants, fusions, vamps, paranoia, superstitions and sickly speculation emerged another new set of genres. It's the music of a nebulous man who cannot remember making it, who might not have been there as it was bent into the shape of his mind by Maslin and his musicians, until the material had its own volition, but who must have been absolutely convinced at the time it was all epic, dramatically beautiful and thrillingly sentient. If he'd died at that point, or lost his memory forever, and his music needed his memory, to recast experience, technique and knowledge, he would have already written the greatest song of all time, but not yet have written his very best.

106.

He is telling the musicians in the studio that he has a new song he wants them to play that he hasn't written yet.

107.

He is talking about 'Station to Station', the title track that starts as though Bowie is lost in some deep, dark train of thought, like some imaginary opening credits are rolling, and is a total ten-minute-long demonstration that few understood how to begin and structure an album as brilliantly as Bowie, still with Mingus on his mind, immediately establishing that he's part of a mystery that needs to be solved, eventually introducing himself as though he is part detective, part fantasist, part rock manager and part witch.

The album then contains echoes of everything Bowie had done, or was about to do, which is why it sticks around when-ever the thought has to be, just to slow things down sometime, what is his best album? Previous characters he'd conceived and ghosts and lovers of Bowie re-dream themselves in a very dif-ferent landscape, somewhere between Amerika and an endless, hopeless desert, swinging from knowing exactly where they fit in the scheme of things, to having no idea, capable of being deeply romantic, flawed, scared, superstitious, numb, crazed, cryptic, triumphant, cold, heroic, desolate.

He sings an immortal love song he wrote for Elvis, 'Golden Years', which confirms that he has cracked funk, can spin, snap, groove and click like a deranged falsetto master, so he'll revel in his genius a little longer, or maybe for a thousand years, and in this context, Elvis is the other Bewlay brother. He sings a song, 'Word on a Wing', as though he's close enough in some dream he's having to touch God, who might also be the other Bewlay brother. He sings a voodoo hymn dedicated to the dark magic of the TV screen, which he can see will suck everything inside it

until we're all stuck in a reality on the other side. He takes over
a song taken over by Nina Simone, 'Wild Is the Wind'.

'Stay' it was reported from within the studio was recorded
in a cocaine frenzy, and comes complete with guitar interplay
that if you could snort would keep you awake for days. Nothing
can quite get inside, from the outside, the experience of taking
a certain drug under certain circumstances while recording an
album, which takes incredible concentration and commitment to
get right, but sometimes needs enormous artificial stimulation,
than hearing the controlled, end result of the music being made
while the drugs were being taken.

Station to Station becomes the tunnel, the cavern, through
which Bowie crawled – spent, emptied out, done with the
temptations and devastations of America – from fraying,
eaten-up pop-star decadence to the three classic made-in-a-real-
or-imaginary Berlin albums he released next.

He fell in love with the wonderful nonchalance of Berlin,
the lovely almost lazy extravagance, its history of individualist
spiritual cosmopolitanism, artistic flair and serpentine sin, its
own self-contained underground communities, the wall that split
it in two, the effortlessly found hiding places on a landlocked
island within a separated country, the city of smoke where
chain-smokers never die out. He could disappear, and after all
that appearance since Ziggy, he craved the nothing and nowhere
of being nothing and nowhere, but not a nowhere like Bromley,
a nowhere that was hiding something magnificent, that perhaps
only came out at night, behind blank closed doors at the end
of a nondescript road you couldn't easily find, daring you to
discover it. It is a perfect city for Bowie to move to as it exists
between recurrent collapse and confusion on the one hand – his
Los Angeles state – and urgent clarity of vision and mobility of
thought on the other.

On *Low*, *"Heroes"* and *Lodger*, Bowie and close collaborators Brian Eno and Tony Visconti with his latest studio

mini-orchestra including Robert Fripp, sometimes accidentally, sometimes following an exact set of instructions, created a stark, pulsating post-pop, forward-scanning soundtrack to personal and historical tensions where Bowie broke out into the wider spaces of the universe, a no-man's-land almost completely out of sight of Major Tom, Ziggy and Aladdin Sane. Here, the only space he was interested in was the space he could stare into and think without distraction.

On this informal expatriate trilogy, Bowie refrained from entering the worlds himself, and losing himself in all the offbeat theatre and topsy-turvy hyperbole. There was little hype anyway, certainly by the time of *Low*, which sounded about as commercial as Stockhausen to his aghast record company hungry for more Bowie teen-trapping trendsetting pop. As with Lou Reed's indignant conceptual provocation *Metal Machine Music,* also on RCA, it sounded like a record that belonged more on the label's classical division, Red Seal.

He didn't quite abdicate his hard-earned knowledge of how to conceive a far-out melody to remember, but the music this time was bordering on the inert, where the concept appeared to be a general mulling over his own cheerlessness, none of it garlanded with self-mockery or irony. A study in pessimism, it appeared to take the apocalyptic worldview he had turned into a thorny, galvanising cartoon during his glam and post-glam years to very non-rock and roll limits; the motto might well have been 'as bad as things are right now they might just get worse', not exactly a great selling point.

Perhaps, of course, he wasn't in a selling mood, not after he had discovered that his contract with Defries meant he was effectively working for him. Defries was the Warhol in this relationship, the dead centre of the business, and he was just a factory worker, and would be for six more years.

What better than to frustrate someone looking for more relentless royalties than to construct a downbeat anti-pop, and include on an album by a well-known pop singer actual instrumentals?

This was part of his therapy, really, taking the heat off, releasing the pressure, and finding the space to locate a sound unique to him, rather than found in various other places and bolted together, and analysing what actually separates a good song from a great song. This thinking process led to the song '"Heroes"', built out of experimental methods and an openness of mind, put together more like a painting than a song, striving to incorporate new modes of observation, where words and images were strewn throughout like the accumulating symbols of a dream, but ending up one of his biggest hits, an actual, uplifting anthem, heading one day to almost being the world's anthem.

It was a great example of how Bowie did not need to be obvious and repeat himself for something he wrote to end up being used in an obvious way in the outside world as a straightforward pop song, a love song, a pleading for peace, a yearning for togetherness that can end up embracing the listener with its apparently orthodox precision. It could only have happened if he had gone as low as he did, if he'd fled America, and the charts, and lost himself a little, or a lot, come close to committing rock and roll suicide. If he'd stuck to a formula, he would never have found himself in the right place with the right people and the right impulses to think of such a song and to be able to phrase, project and present it still as an enthralling, idiosyncratic, intriguingly damaged crooner, but with the restless soul of a true adventurer who took seriously if a little reluctantly and abstractly his role as spokesperson for those persecuted and preyed on by menacing forces.

Station to Station was where he recovered himself, or at least enough of himself that he could continue his search for new views and schemes, and new experiences which lead to new knowledge, and the kind of unusual, unforced, untethered new pop music he craved, and worlds of his own he could visit, and introduce others to, but not stay in. He never wanted to settle, however much pressure there was on him to do so, and when he was at his most troubled and traumatised was the moment when he most wanted to escape the shackles of classification. He wanted to establish a reputation not as skilled dressing-up dilettante but musical vision-ary; the first stirrings of a consideration that what came next, after the stardom and the troubling sometimes ugly aftermath, was to begin organising his legacy, which would be the reality of who he was for longer than he would live, however long he lived.

The dream was to have hits, and the financial protection that came with them to continue experimenting with his art and his presence, without having to settle into the risk-averse, solid-as-a-rock middle of the road, which by its very nature rejected disconcerting, marginal extremes and the inevitable inconsistencies of unflagging experiment. And if he was to engage with the middle of the road, and exploit that for a while – for more protection – it would be on his terms, for his still experi-mental reasons, not because he was being forced into it.

108.

He is finishing *Low* at the end of the coldest of Berlin months, November, and he has been absorbed into the migrant space of Berlin, and begun to leave traces of his own. He needed another space to employ the roving energy of his imagination. He has charted the outline and movements of himself in a defamiliarising mirror; replacing the self, drawing a self-portrait in alien space, a spatial self-portrait. A meeting point – between Bowie and the city, Bowie and Eno, Bowie and Visconti, Bowie and his mobile instrumental models – is realised in terms of movement.

• • •

In 1976, a year of transition, David Bowie's *Station to Station* was the best album of the year, not just in my mind. This was when there was also the Ramones' debut, Stevie Wonder's *Songs in the Key of Life*, Jonathan

Richman and the Modern Lovers, Bob Dylan's *Desire*, Patti Smith Group's *Radio Ethiopia*, Flamin' Groovies' *Shake Some Action*, Joni Mitchell's *Hejira*, the Upsetters' *Super Ape*, *Blondie*, Blue Öyster Cult's *Agents of Fortune*, Jackson Browne's *The Pretender*, Burning Spear's *Man in the Hills*, Bootsy's Rubber Band's *Stretchin' Out in Bootsy's Rubber Band*. The UK number 1s, with 'Save Your Kisses for Me' the biggest-selling single of the year, were screaming, punk, come and save us, beginning with 'Bohemian Rhapsody' and then going through a lot of Abba, the Wurzels, Demis Roussos, and ending with Chicago's 'If You Leave Me Now' – an American number 1 as well – Showaddywaddy's 'Under the Moon of Love', and Johnny Mathis's 'When a Child Is Born'. 'Anarchy in the UK' trashed the charts with proper radical rock style among the Cliff Richards, Bostons and Bay City Rollers and Nick Lowe's 'So It Goes', Blue Öyster Cult's '(Don't Fear) The Reaper' and Junior Murvin's 'Police and Thieves' might have been single of the year at any other time. Bowie didn't have much of a singles year; he was in transition himself but *Station to Station* achieved one of his highest American chart positions, reaching number 3.

1977

*'When I was eighteen I thought that to be a romantic
you couldn't live past thirty.'*

109.

He is celebrating his thirtieth birthday in a nightclub with
Iggy. The black-walled nightclub Chez Romy Haag belongs to
29-year-old Dutch transsexual pioneer Romy Haag, another
Capricorn, another mirror for him to look into, another life
to get inside, another set of influences to steal from, another
someone to piss off Angie – who says all he did in Berlin was
sit around in nightclubs pretending he was watching the rise of
Nazi Germany – another someone to help him, and get stoned
with and talk for hours. Another way of dealing in love. Her
autobiography was called *Eine Frau und mehr* (*A Woman and
Then Some*). Some say she was the reason he went to Berlin in
the first place, and risk the tension in the air and the real and
abstract threats of the divided city when really he was needing
safety. Some say she's the muse for everything that happens
during the Berlin years.

110.

He is imagining he has found his *Cabaret*, his own Sally Bowles,
made up by Christopher Isherwood in the book and backed up by
Bob Fosse on film, which never existed for real, but which is part
of the history of the city. Many things never actually happened
to or in Berlin but are remembered as though they did, because
so much did happen there. It's a place to get lost in time.

111.

He is finding his thoughts are being given a curious motion.

112.

He is in a city that makes itself host from the Huguenot
immigrants in the late seventeenth century, to the thousands
of young men from West Germany in the Sixties and Seventies
who flocked there as the status of Berlin resident exempted
them from military service, to guest workers from southern
and eastern Europe. The influx means it is always in flux.

He is enjoying how in Berlin, unlike New York and Hollywood,
no one seems particularly delighted to see a famous face.
They're almost disappointed, like it might spoil the city.

113.

He is sending a letter to *Melody Maker*, firmly but politely
asking for a printed correction to their suggestion that he
manages Iggy Pop. 'Iggy looks after his own business affairs.'

Iggy is saying that all they did in Berlin was a lot of coke and
compete with each other to find the best-looking transvestite
with the best-looking stocking-covered calves.

He is using Berlin as a theatre of dreams whereas Iggy has
come to shoot drugs in the heroin capital of the world. The
night hours carry a scent of secrecy, a whiff of the forest and
the vagabond life.

He is playing keyboards for Iggy on his *Idiot* tour, but it is a
secret, and no one is quite sure until the show begins whether
he will be part of the band. Even when he is, he stays in the
background, happily playing a member of the group.

He is flying for the first time in five years, travelling to America with Iggy. 'I think the aeroplane is a really wonderful invention.' He claims he has lost a lot of his fears recently. Fear of flying, fear of elevators. 'Fear is not a word in my vocabulary any more. I am a man of great inner strength and courage these days.'

114.

He is in New York seeing Devo – a mixing and merging of the Mothers of Invention, the Monkees, mad scientists and Moondog – and gushing like a fan 'this is the band of the future'.

He is recording the album *Lust for Life* in Berlin with Iggy. He comes up with the riff for the title track whilst watching television and playing around with a ukulele.

115.

He is saying he likes Berlin because of the friction, transforming the uncertainty of the times into artistic energy. Grey plaster crumbles off nineteenth-century facades riddled with bullet holes. Large areas of wasteland are common, especially the nearer you get to the Wall. The Reichstag stands empty, a mausoleum to a nation that no longer exists. The buildings are ruined, standing against a clear blue sky vivid enough to absorb sin. He can rub against the city, and things happen. He couldn't write any more in London, New York, Paris or Los Angeles. 'Berlin has the ability to make you write only the important things ... the rest you don't mention ... you remain silent ...'

He is drifting like an unknown expressionist artist into the lowest abandonment of the individual who feels misunderstood by society.

116.

He is living in Berlin full time, living quite a spartan life, well below his means, living out the student years he never had perhaps amidst a joyless sea of flats, and feeling good about being on the edge of something.

117.

He is arriving with Iggy at the opening of the SO36 club on Oranienstrasse in the damaged wild south-eastern part of Kreuzberg near the Wall, the centre of the decade's militant protests, beginning as an artists' squat. The club was based in an abandoned building and took its name from a now defunct postcode. It's become an alternative institution now, listed in Frommer's. As Bowie arrives, one bubble of action clashes with another, one real Berlin fuses with a more unreal one. The activists, squatters, punks, nomads and sensation seekers watch him arrive in their midst wearing an expensive shapeless suit and looking like 'a toothpaste salesman'.

118.

He is at his lowest ebb.

He is getting into a very peculiar state when he is in the recording studio.

He is accepting his own internal exile.

He is arriving home at six in the morning after a night's recording and he would break an egg into his mouth and that was his food for the day.

He is finding his name among the graffiti on the Berlin Wall where East and West uniquely face each other, where locals go for a piss, the last two letters of his name scratched into a Swastika. This does not amuse him.

119.

He is intending to put his next album together inside a three-week time limit.

120.

He is part of a power trio with Brian Eno and Tony Visconti. A different sort of power trio. The power is not to do with volume, or strength, or riffs and energy; this is a spiritual power trio, and each one is a producer, using the studio as their main instrument, with a different approach to what it is a producer does. It is an electronic power trio, an estranged power trio. The producer, from Phil Spector onwards, has in effect been the person who created pop music, who turned songs and music into finished, amplified and organised items that were a combination of emotional product, fixed memories and sonic sculptures. The producer encouraging, demanding and exploiting an improvement in technology was responsible for the accelerated changes that there were in the sound and style of pop and rock.

The power trio that worked using parts of Europe and mainly Berlin as a base were perhaps the only known example of three producers forming a kind of group, and working together as a trio, with the help of a cast of musicians, which combined each of their talents and approaches. Visconti brought in the practical skills of making a pop and rock record that sounded familiar but brand new, with a tremendous amount of up-to-date technological knowledge and an uncanny ability to turn the studio and its increasingly sophisticated way of manipulating sound into a distinct whole. More prosaic and practical than the other two, but just as much committed to the idea of locating and fixing the unfixable, a certain sort of unlikely mental magic.

Each has a marvellous, raw intelligence, and they become

close friends as well during recording, which also has a way of feeding into the music – that it is coming out of a very intense, close working relationship where they are pushing each other to discover more about themselves and how they work. Recording with Bowie becomes a social event.

For Bowie, there was more of a reconfigured jazz mentality, a performer's attitude, in terms of organising a session, hiring the musicians, imagining an end point, spontaneously developing ideas, generating material and concepts and creating the right conditions within which to perform. As aware as he is of other music, and other reference points, he tries to get himself into such a state that all other music does not exist; he is making it up from scratch for his own purposes. He is designing his own history.

For Brian Eno the role of producer is an artistic one, about creating, and sometimes disrupting, conditions that produces various pieces of material that can be used in the building up of a piece of music that will sometimes be a song, sometimes instrumental, sometimes a bit of both. He functions as a number of things when he is producing, from an aesthetic consultant, to a psychologist and abstract motivational coach, to a liberator of ideas.

He is not the official producer as part of this cryptic power trio, he is guest star, or soloist, or member of the orchestra, but he operates in much the same way he did as part of Roxy Music – interfering in a more conventional pop process from within with a musical mind that was trained in the stark arts of avant-garde music. Bowie and Eno share a love for the Who, and various marginal pop genres, but the Elvis or Little Richard for Eno is John Cage, who encourages the making of music from the point of view of it not being about sound, or harmony, or rhythm. Music is another artistic method of generating and articulating ideas, and giving them as much permanence as you want them to have.

After Eno left or was ejected from Roxy Music, for interfering too much, he sang some of his own songs for a while, imagining what his version of Roxy Music would be like, the history of pop tumbled up into a whole different set of shapes, edges and contours. He gradually stopped singing, so that by the time of *Another Green World* there is a combination of songs and songs without words. *Low* is a follow-up to that album as much as any by Bowie.

At the same time as he was making these post-Roxy, rewired Roxy albums, where he was the new Bryan Ferry, he was also distilling his non-pop musical thoughts into a repetitive music carefully shaped into shapelessness influenced by theoretical and practical ideas from Erik Satie to Steve Reich and Morton Feldman that he called 'ambient'. He was also as hungry for new musical ideas, and new states of mind, and as horrified by becoming a cliché, as Bowie. He was collaborating with various German electronic musicians on ideas that would renew his ideas about pop and his ideas about the recording and treatment of sound in the pursuit of unprecedented atmosphere and depthless calm.

Eno encourages Bowie to leave behind the deformed chronicling and intense reportage he had been doing, the storytelling he thought was the centre of his work. He urges him to leave behind narration and find a more abstract way of expressing his emotions and articulate psychological atmosphere. He didn't have to be the singer-songwriter any more, not now the music could be put together in such a different way. It becomes a new direction, but not a forced one, and one that frees him from having to directly engage with characters, and their stories, but which still refers back to things he had done earlier. It's still having some chords, a melody, and having some words, a poem or a few lines, and finding a way to put them together so the two things become a third thing, but Eno has applied a whole new set of thoughts to how to achieve a difference in first the music, secondly the words, so that the third thing, the finished piece, becomes something completely new.

Low and *"Heroes"* are also a projection of what Roxy Music would be like if Eno took over and hired David Bowie as singer, or what Roxy Music would be like if David Bowie took over and hired Brian Eno to re-join. Where Eno went next – to Talking Heads – meant they too were a new model of Roxy Music, and the album he made with David Byrne, *My Life in the Bush of Ghosts*, is as much a follow-up to *Low* and *"Heroes"* as *Lodger*.

121.

He is preferring to be in a room with the diffuse electronic collage, modern-art German groups Can, Neu! and Cluster – where the listener can feel part of a dream, and yet fixed to the real – than the ordinary, hoofing, mind-numbed showmen Mick, Rod and Elton. He would now rather be a member of Kraftwerk, divining the computer future, than a member of the Who, dragging the Sixties with them. After a greatest hits album, *Changesonebowie*, charting how Bowie the beguiling entertainer had caused a crisis of his own making, by making people expect glittering, predictably charming things from him, 1977's *Low* is Bowie controlling things with the rest of his spiritual trio, and the thoughts of hedonistic adviser Iggy, voluntarily falling off the edge of the pop screen, where a needled, prehensile masterpiece could be compiled. We hear him occupying a spiritual centre of his own. We hear the sound of the end of the world that Bowie was scandalously sensationalising a few years before, which then becomes the magnificent sound of the beginning of a new world, because however far out Bowie gets, he's got another record to make, other experiments to pursue, and he's still following those early blueprints he introduced as pre-star, and then star, and then superstar. A time machine sent from *Hunky Dory* lands on *"Heroes"*, where there is the agitated Visconti/Eno/Bowie *Low* pressure, and songs without words, moods pulled inside out, worlds and selves falling apart, and star-Bowie gravity, and pop-Bowie levitation, and songs produced out of textures, hollows, gestures, syllables, tones and pulses, lingering in a state of probability and uncertainty. Visconti called it the positive outcome of the darkness of *Low*, not least because it was recorded in a better studio. It's *Low* on heat.

122.

He is deciding to put the word heroes into inverted commas, so that the title of the album is *"Heroes"*. There was, he said, no intended concept to the album, so he picked the one song on the album that had a story. Because it has a story, about lovers, about a secret romance, that might be Tony Visconti's, that might be Bowie's and Romy Haag's, it becomes the single that the record company were so startled was lacking on *Low*. It needed a visit to the depths of *Low*, into a new research and development lab, a time spent in low profile, to find the mental energy to conceive *"Heroes"*.

The album was a collection of pieces put together with Eno, Fripp and Visconti that could have been called *The Sons of the Silent Age* from the song that imagines a soul-music soundtrack to a silent movie. The inverted commas around "Heroes" make it seem as though there is a little irony about the idea of believing in such a thing as a hero. He's keeping his distance. In time, as the song became loved, and taken into other states, and situations, the cooling idea of the inverted commas, that barrier between it being a little too sentimental, melts away.

123.

He is using a lot the Oblique Strategies designed by Brian Eno with the artist Peter Schmidt in the making of *"Heroes"*. These cards containing aphorisms suggesting possible creative action were based on Chinese I Ching or Book of Changes and the chance-controlled compositions of John Cage, where he would consult the I Ching about decisions needing to be made in the composition of a piece of music, and use the answers to compose. It was the latest stage in the artistic development of a composer who was from an early age as ferociously disillusioned with conformity as Bowie, and saw society as the greatest impediment an artist can possibly have to creating good art. Art, he decided, was everywhere, and the centre is wherever an individual decides to pay attention.

In his 1937 lecture 'The Future of Music: Credo', Cage discusses his vision for the direction of contemporary music: 'I believe that the use of noise to make music will continue and increase until we reach a music produced through the aid of electrical instruments which will make available for musical purpose any and all sounds that can be heard.'

Cage had been using the idea of chance since 1951, what he called 'an exploration of non-intention', as a way of escaping individual taste, memory and personality, and also as much as possible other artistic and musical influences. He used the hexagrams of the I-Ching and the rolling of dice to make decisions about which scales to use in a piece, which chromatic transpositions to concentrate on, which instruments or sound sources to use, which notes of pitches to play next. Eno was interested in how Cage fused philosophy and composition, and turned it into the Oblique Strategies, enabling the artist to see new perspectives when they feel blocked and uninspired.

It produces a kind of tethered chaos, which in a way is at the heart of the recording process itself where chance is constantly being synthesised with rigorous discipline. Artistic choices are reduced, or intensified, to asking a question, and seeing what the answer is, and see if it rings some bells or not.

For someone like Bowie who used his music to change himself, and who had moved to Berlin to discover new things about himself, this was the perfect technique to use. It was not something that could be particularly explained, because to some extent it was a way of making music that could be kept vague – which suited him as well – but which he could still be driven by. It was not a scientific method, an infallible way of writing songs, but an obsessional one, which is what made it work for him. He could combine it with how he worked with his musicians, throwing chords and structural ideas at them and letting them jam those thoughts into a working structure.

Cards include messages such as: Don't be afraid of things because they are easy to do; How would you have done it; Ask people to work against their better judgement; Use an old idea; Is there something missing?; Be extravagant; Would anybody want it?; Reverse; Trust in the you of now; Work at a different speed; Always first steps; Use filter; Ask your body; Question the heroic approach.

124.

He is appearing on the cover of *"Heroes"* photographically shadowing painter, printmaker and sculptor Erich Heckel's 1917 woodcut portrait of fellow artist Ernst Kirchner. The same image inspired the cover for Iggy Pop's *The Idiot*. Heckel had moved to Berlin in 1911 having formed the idealistic, communal Die Brücke – The Bridge – a revolutionary group of German expressionist artists six years earlier in Dresden. Kirchner and Heckel admired the dynamic simplicity of African sculpture and Polynesian carvings as well as the psychological intensity of Norwegian expressionist Edvard Munch, resisted the conventions of then traditional painting, and aimed for an agitated, anxious, even threatening boldness. The sombre quality of a series of eleven woodcuts reflecting a desolate, forbidding world that Heckel made after the Die Brücke group ended in 1913, including one in particular called *Young Man*, were a strong influence on Bowie as a painter. The manipulating of space, the abrupt cropping of the frame, the compression of figures into tight areas, the general sense of oppression and tension all became an influence on *Dr. Caligari*.

125.

He is being asked if his new approach to writing music means it might not be as commercial as his pop songs of the early 1970s and mean it might not sell to the satisfaction of his record label. 'No shit, Sherlock,' he grins in reply.

126.

He is appearing on *Marc*, a television programme for Granada TV in Manchester hosted by his old friend and competitor Marc Bolan which is officially a children's show, with jolly cartoon inserts, going out at 5 p.m. teatime. Marc presents it as a cross between kindly wizard, scatterbrained sweetheart and lapsed hipster, as though his years as pop star had made him possessed by a general sense of mind-altering cosmic jive. Bowie of 'Berlin' appears on the final show of the series, free of the past, as focused as a grown-up, coolly dressed down in faded denim, leather belt around his hips, with anonymous straight fair hair, designed for black and white, whereas Marc was still trapped in the feather boas, glam satin and corkscrew hair, a brightly coloured twilight zone of his own making.

Bolan had helped his relatively recent reappearance as pop star by featuring in his show some of the new punk groups that were as inspired by him as much as, if not more than, Bowie – including Generation X and Eddie and the Hot Rods on the show Bowie appeared on. There was also during the six-part run Showaddywaddy and the Bay City Rollers – Granada television producer Muriel Young has produced their similarly rickety series – and at the other end of some sort of spectrum, the one that Bolan spanned between 1967 and 1972, Hawkwind.

(I visited the set a couple of times, where Marc playfully teased me for being so nervous and tongue-tied in his presence. I played him new local Manchester group Buzzcocks, who he thought as undeniable pop expert were bubblegum punk, and also chatted briefly with him about Bowie. 'He's always getting the blues, man,' Marc chuckled, as if this was something that never happened to him, and is what made the difference between the pair. Bolan's reluctance to allow his real feelings to stray into and stain and steer his music perhaps contributed to it stagnating inside a dying fantasy.)

After witnessing Marc becoming a pop star first, Bowie then achieved what Bolan never could and became a pop star in America. The pressure of trying to break America, the logical next step after peaking so dramatically in Britain and most of the rest of the world, ended up breaking Marc. He became so distracted working out how to do it that he lost his grip on British stardom, failing to refresh his particular formula and extend it outwards and elsewhere in the way Bowie could. Bowie could even make critically and commercially successful music without using Tony Visconti, which mostly eluded Marc once the original glam momentum faded. Bowie could report metaphorically in his music on his mental and physical state and incorporate allegorical ways of reflecting the state of nations and other worlds in ways that Bolan couldn't.

Bolan found it difficult to escape the glue of the boogie, the fuzzy halo of hair. The glitter was stuck to his face, like a mask that he couldn't remove. He couldn't absorb as much outside artistic and theatrical influence and process it as ingeniously and progressively as Bowie. In the end, he lacked the experimental and non-rock part of the aesthetic that could constantly reform and deform the obvious, crowd-pleasing part, which soon ceases to please the crowd if it doesn't develop.

He tried to match Bowie's conceptual ambition as his place in the British charts became less secure after 1973, tried to slip into other musical states as apparently effortlessly as Bowie could, the blue-, or grey-eyed soul and the unexpected, rarefied hybrids, but could only watch helplessly as Bowie conquered the might of America as the Seventies' equivalent of the Jesus-beating

Beatles. As Bowie crashed into the classic status of rock star casualty, somewhere between acting it out and suffering it for self-destructing real, he was somehow still producing albums as vivid and visible as *Young Americans* and *Station to Station*. Marc produced entertaining, often lovely, but increasingly insular anagrams of *Electric Warrior* and *Slider*.

Marc slumped, became bloated, his fine features distorting into a sadly non-elfin-like bulbousness, where the curls just looked like desperate question marks, while Bowie's reaction to the dangers of fame and keeping it or losing it was to deflate into a more severe, romantically attractive hollow-eyed soul-bruised skin and bones. In the competition of most successfully cataclysmic rock and roll breakdown, without actually dying, Bowie won.

They had entered one of their occasional periods of being friends again. Coming together first of all in 1964 as finely drawn dancing mods with model poise mad for more prowling the streets of Soho and attending endless auditions, looking for the right door to walk through to find the golden star. Then in the late 1960s, as gentle guitar-strumming gurus of peace and love sprinkling moondust and cosmic vibes over their wide-eyed followers, separating after 'The Prettiest Star'. At the time, Marc's wife, June, considered Marc far too superior to be giving Bowie the gift of his guitar playing.

Both were now materialising in a post-chaos setting, and almost seemed set to collaborate on new music, writing something together about the madness they had been experiencing. On the *Marc* show, Bowie solemnly sings in the nowhere vacuum of a television studio his new song "Heroes", which starbursts in sublime slow motion into the glare of a kiddies' show like a psalm suddenly solemnly sung at a seven-year-old's birthday party between pass the parcel and the birthday cake. They duet together, Bolan in singlet pouting like it's still 1971, Bowie in dark glasses concentrating like he's on the other side of time.

At the end of a song that goes nowhere but a giggling end, Marc, overwhelmed by the situation, trips over a wire, and falls off the stage. There was no time for another run-through, so the ragged conclusion is broadcast as it happened, two misfit brothers making a little mess. Bolan's the younger by nine months, but on this showing Bowie looks both older, as in more in control, but also younger, as in fresher, with more life in him. The show ends with the toothiest of Bowie smiles, watching as Bolan falls to the floor of the studio.

Bolan dies nine days later in a car crash in south London returning in the early hours from a West End party thrown by Rod Stewart, so this televised laughter as they shared the same microphone was how their friendship ended in TV reality. Bolan loved cars as erotic, exotic objects of desire and speed, and featured them in his songs, but he never learnt to drive, fearing the worst possible outcome between his soft flesh and the car's lethal metal.

His girlfriend Gloria Jones was driving the purple Mini that crashed into a tree on a dangerous curve as they drove home to East Sheen. She survived with little injury; he was crushed. His death kept the death of internationally famous opera artist and ultimate diva – La Divina, the divine – Maria Callas off the front pages of the UK papers.

The funeral is a few days later, attended by Rod Stewart, Alvin Stardust, Steve Harley, members of punk pioneers the Damned and Eurovision Song Contest winners Brotherhood of Man, Tony Visconti and his wife Mary Hopkin, Bolan's ex-wife June keeping a low profile, and hundreds of fans in satin scarves, T-shirts and 'Marc is God' badges comforting each other. Keith Moon, Elton John and Cliff Richard send flowers. Marc's record company sent a huge white swan made of carnations, which gives the particularly bleak funeral a whimsical lift of fantasy.

Bowie arrives in shock ensconced in the secure star limbo of long limo, wearing dark glasses and grey fedora, sweeping into the ceremony and out again in a man who fell to earth circus blur of tabloid-chased fame. While he was in London for the funeral, he goes to Brixton to look at his first home, but he doesn't take a look inside.

The final *Marc* show was broadcast eight days after the funeral. The credits featured Marc Bolan and David Bowie as hosts.

Both were morbidly scared of and fascinated by death. If one of the races between the pair with their intense fan's awareness of the nature of myth and immortality was who would have the tragic early rock and roll death, in a car or plane crash, in drug overdose meltdown, producing the eternally young corpse, joining the most elite and stupid of clubs, Bolan won, and lost.

127.

He is celebrating Christmas, because he believes; after all he has a mother who once helped him believe and a young son. He is appearing on the latest edition of Bing Crosby's annual Christmas show *Bing Crosby's Merrie Olde Christmas*, looking as though he has just wandered along a corridor, or stepped out of a limo, after singing with Marc, for his duet with Bing, over the other side of pop history. It's actually four days later, 11 September, in Elstree north of London, and there's a little flashback element as other guests on this English-themed Christmas special include Ron Moody, born the same day, and Twiggy, of the *Pin Ups* cover.

Bowie is apparently initially reluctant to take part because he does not like the song he is asked to sing with Bing, 'Little Drummer Boy', eventually persuaded when the show's writers hastily conceive of a sweet little counterpoint entitled 'Peace on Earth'. After an hour's rehearsal, Bing and Bowie are ready.

Maybe he consulted Oblique Strategies, and got a card that said Emphasise differences, or Courage!, or Remember ... those quiet evenings, or Go to an extreme, Move back to a more comfortable place, or Listen to the quiet voice. It was a chance to promote "Heroes", and Bowie never got too big for his promotional duties.

Bing is his mother's favourite; Bing certainly resembles his neat, orderly, weirdly brittle father. David looks on his Sunday best behaviour; as if as he said the cocaine years were like a journey into space, and after the dangerous adventures on different worlds were over he returned to earth, and got out of the spaceship feeling and looking fairly healthy, even if his sense of time had been damaged, and a few years either added to or knocked off his expected lifespan.

It's not Ziggy with Bing, the great combination of white bread and offbeat the legend claims. It's two singers from either end of the history of recorded music meeting in the middle of time to compare and contrast a form of singing that isn't that far apart, ultimately, in terms of technically mastering timing, phrasing, vocal understanding, the role of the microphone, which Bing was the first to use as a musical instrument. It is Crosby that first exploits the miracle of magnetic tape in order to record his radio show, and free him of the fixed nature of presenting it live.

The Nazis had developed the use of audio tape recording to broadcast their propaganda across different time zones. After the war, the victorious Americans discovered the technology, and it was introduced in America first of all on Crosby's show. It's the very beginnings of the kind of fluid, time-shifting sound recording that Bowie, with Visconti, Fripp, Eno and co., had just been exploiting and extending. They had been doing this within 500 yards of the Berlin headquarters of the Nazis where the magical idea of tape as a way to supervise and rearrange time, and flexibly insert it into media, and to control the masses, first appeared.

Bowie gracefully acknowledges the master, the mentor of Elvis, who set the whole notion of amplified singing in motion, paying tribute to Bing's role as innovator, master of artifice and populariser of jazz, as much as clichéd, cardigan-wearing, golfing

family entertainer – he's a combination of the inventive and the
accessible Bowie deeply respects. Somewhere in the middle of this
unorthodox collaboration the subtext is that the power of entertainment is a curious thing. It is a truly surreal event, because
of its looping historical resonance as much as the generational
oddity of the coupling.

Introducing David's guest spot, Bing soothes a dumbstruck
Twiggy about what she is now going to hear. His introduction
dissolves into Bowie singing an echoing, aching "Heroes", which
at the time still sounded more apprehensive and doomed gothic
romance suited to Bing's make-believe castle, and the imaginary
snowy ruins on the outside, than chiming anthem of universal
togetherness. Bing understands, though, introducing it with real
appreciation of its gravity and its ambiguous tenderness, even if
he didn't write or even listen to the words he spoke; on the other
hand, inside, he really does understand that a baton has been
handed on between generations of recording artists. He had only
a month to live; Bowie as the great predictor of death. Bing's
intro falters a little, he forgets a word or two, but just about gets
across what he wants to say: 'Loneliness, just as painful, just as
beautiful as they ever were. Whether you're a novelist, a poet or
even a songwriter, it's all in the way you say it . . .'

The still, understated and beautiful Bowie mimes in a pre-
recorded sense, cut out of expressionistic black, direct into
camera, what might be his greatest song – or 'song' – when it
was just another sonic and lyrical experiment that had not yet
uncoiled and insinuated itself into the popular imagination and
which might yet go nowhere. Simultaneously, he is shown in
neat grey two-piece earnestly miming in a Marcel Marceau sense
the meaning of the song, the lovers against the wall, Bowie and
Romy, fighting for love, and freedom. He acts out the love story,
even a passionate kiss, like some European street entertainer
hoping for a few coins to be dropped into his hat. Still with the
sad clown in his heart, he marks out the wall with his hands in

the way the classic mime artist describes a box they are trapped inside, as if to say, the wall is not really there.

128.

He is releasing the *"Heroes"* album a week before young East Berliners at a rock concert in Alexanderplatz are chanting 'Down with the Wall', something that will not happen for another ten years.

129.

He is leaving Berlin, and leaving the walled-in Berliners a hymn, which is a sign of his rebirth, and becomes a part of the city's own rebirth, and which doesn't exactly eventually knock the Wall down, but imagined a world where it was not needed, and needs to be sung when it is, and comes to symbolise the significant end of a divided city.

• • •

If you want albums that summed up a new world of meaning in rock in 1977, and how far things had come since 1974, then there was Television's *Marquee Moon*, Wire's *Pink Flag*, Kraftwerk's *Trans-Europe Express*, *The Clash*, Elvis Costello's *My Aim Is True*, *Suicide*, *Talking Heads: 77*, Sex Pistols' *Never Mind the Bollocks, Here's the Sex Pistols*, Iggy Pop's *Lust for Life* and *The Idiot*, Ian Dury's *New Boots and Panties!!*, The Damned's *Damned Damned Damned*, Richard Hell & the Voidoid's *Blank Generation*. Fleetwood Mac with *Rumours* and Pink Floyd with *Animals* carried on as normal; Bob Marley and Culture were occupied in their own battleground, Peter Gabriel and Peter Hammill were in worlds of their own, Brian Eno was still imagining the future with *Before and After Science*, but it was two Bowie albums, *Low* and *"Heroes"*, which proved that he alone of anyone who had made it in the mainstream in the early 1970s could keep his up-to-date and up-to-speed wits in a new contemporary setting, and cast himself forward, sounding further out than most at the time, into a future, where music would be called post-rock, and then actually be post-rock, and then actually be in the past, present and future at the same time. Singles of the year were by the Sex Pistols, Buzzcocks, the Ramones, Elvis Costello, the Stranglers, X-Ray Spex, the Adverts, Talking Heads, Alternative TV – but Bowie was among them with "Heroes". If you weren't partial to the new world, the singles of the year were by Foreigner, Fleetwood Mac, Aerosmith and Al Stewart. The chart number 1s were cut off from this change, filled with David Soul, Abba, Brotherhood of Man, Kenny Rogers, Manhattan Transfer, finishing off with Paul McCartney's 'Mull of Kintyre'. There was enough Bowie momentum, and enough glamour about the look of the album and the content of the songs, and the presumption he was still inhabiting a science-fiction character, despite the dubious transformations on show, for *Low* to make it to number 2 in the UK album charts, stopping just short therefore of being perhaps the most experimental pop album ever to make number 1. Despite the myth that it was the most uncommercial of Bowie records, because of the extremist sonic and emotional outlook, it reached higher than *"Heroes"* later that year, and even in America for all its un-American tone, it stopped just one short of the top 10, whereas *"Heroes"* failed to enter the top 30. The single didn't even make the top 100, and stalled at 24 in the UK. To some at the time, it seemed weary and forlorn, and somehow out of focus. It would take time to grow on the world.

1978

'I don't have stylistic loyalty. That's why people perceive me changing all the time.'

130.

He is narrating a wonderful performance of Sergei Prokofiev's symphony for children, *Peter and the Wolf*, with the Philadelphia Orchestra conducted by their internationally famous Hungarian music director, Eugene Ormandy, a favourite interpreter of Bartok, Shostakovich and Sibelius who had started working with the orchestra in 1936, the year Prokofiev wrote his unexpected masterpiece. Each character in the story is represented by a different instrument – flute for bird, oboe for duck, clarinet for cat, French horns for the wolf, a curt bassoon for Peter's grandfather. The blast of the hunter's shotguns is played by the kettle drums. Hero Peter gets jaunty strings.

What began as a whimsical, unstuffy way to attract children to classical music had become a classic that attracted many notable performers to narrate – Ralph Richardson, John Gielgud, Basil Rathbone, Eleanor Roosevelt, Sharon Stone, the classical world enjoying the association with a star from outside their world, the star enjoying a little touch of class. Winnie the Pooh – his voice, Sterling Holloway – even did it.

Ormandy had no idea who Bowie was, and was a little worried when he discovered he was a rock singer with a strange, difficult reputation. They never met – Bowie recording his voice in New York in 1977 and it was added to the previously recorded performance – but it became one of Bowie's strangest, loveliest collaborations.

RCA were clearly looking for a certain aloof, measured English voice, because they asked Alec Guinness and Peter Ustinov who turned them down, before it was pointed out that they had an artist signed to their label already who was English and spoke English as though he were acting it out.

'What happens when a world-famous maestro teams up with a pop-rock dynamo?' trumpeted the promotional material, but what the orchestra and conductor got was not the gaunt, vampiric rock star failing to pronounce the easiest word that they might have seen on *The Dick Cavett Show*, but a relaxed, obliging, almost anonymous actor who dearly wanted to do it as a present for his six-year-old son. As much as any of his records or films it proves what he often said about what he did which sometimes seemed a distraction – that he was acting, and each thing he did was another part.

He delivers a powerfully beguiling and good-hearted performance, relishing working with such a significant orchestra and Ormandy's rich, romantic conception of sound, to the extent it might be the very best version to hear, and perhaps takes the form of a disguised follow-up to the moods of *David Bowie* and *Hunky Dory*.

He has been a children's entertainer; it's not much of a challenge to do it again, and he brings to the project, both because he is doing it, and in how he does it, a hint of something daintily psychedelic that suits the music and the concept. Boris Karloff had done it, and he did not do it as Frankenstein's monster, and Bowie does not do it as Ziggy, Aladdin Sane or the Thin White Duke. If anything, he does it as Davie Jones, but a Davie Jones that has been watching from within what his own creation has been doing, and has learnt a lot from him about timing, persuasion and illusion.

He plays it differently for each character – suddenly stern as Peter's grandfather – and as the little bird, Bowie plays the he as a she, because, bringing a certain expertise in transformation to the project, who's to say what the truth is in this sort of fable?

In a year when it seems there was no Bowie studio album, in a decade when they usually seemed to come at least once a year, in fact, there was a great Bowie record. A half-hour of gorgeous fantasy in its own way as subversive and engaging as any record he made during this speeding, splintering decade that started as a rush into rock and roll stardom and ended up as an escape from its destructive pull. It was as though, as well as giving a gift to his son, he wanted to leave some unfiltered charm and a discreet work of art in the middle of all the intensity. The kindly Narrator can be added to Major Tom, Ziggy, the cracked actor, the Thin White Duke, Jareth and company, another role he adopted as he stretched himself every way he could on the way to his final role.

131.

He takes a part in Marlene Dietrich's last screen appearance, *Just a Gigolo*. He does the film as a favour to director David Hemmings, a living symbol of the 1960s after playing Mordred in *Camelot*, Dildano in *Barbarella*, and definitive swinging fashion photographer in Antonioni's study of the times, *Blow-Up*, and because of Dietrich. She films her two days of work in Paris, the city she slowly dissolves into, and Bowie's work is all filmed in Berlin. The two never actually meet, but she recruits him for her crew of gigolos, and explains the secret of life. 'Dancing, music, champagne; the best way to forget, until you find something you want to remember.'

Dietrich, of Berlin and *The Blue Angel*, silent movies and Las Vegas, cabaret and object, cowboy and sinner, mind reader and top hat and tails, schmaltz and transcendence, make-up and wigs, Lang and Hitchcock, Welles and Wilder, a complete belief in her own magic, finishes off her film life in a film with David Bowie that for him is 'all his thirty-two Elvis movies in one go' and for her is a $250,000 pay cheque for two days' work. It's as unsuccessful as his meeting with Andy Warhol – to some extent they were also in different studios when they met – but it means he is attached to such a legend, as if two dreams try to mate, but do not fit into each other. This is how he studies, though. From afar, which can sometimes be as near as he needs to be, and up close, which can sometimes be across the universe, but still as near as he needs to be.

Kim Novak is also part of the cast, so Bowie becomes part of a history that includes: girlfriend of Sammy Davis Jr., the redhead in *Picnic*, the showgirl in *Pal Joey*, the possessed Madeleine in *Vertigo*, a witch in *Bell, Book and Candle*, and the nightclub girl helping addict Frank Sinatra kick his habit in *The Man With the Golden Arm*.

It becomes his second acting role after *The Man Who Fell to Earth*, and he plays talentless Prussian lost soul Paul Ambrosius von Przygodski as though he actually is a duke, with the same sort of blurred precision, remote and noble with a hint of someone who has been worshipped and/or ignored for centuries. At the same time as he's helping Brian Eno at the weekend mix one of the greatest warped novelty albums of all time, *Are We Not Men? We Are Devo!*, he is speaking lines such as 'I may be a gigolo, Fraulein Kaiserling, but I'm not a whore.'

• • •

Bowie was in the middle of his very own flow, looking deep within, checking his own pulse, sometimes barely finding it, but he still had his antennae up when it came to knowing where things at the leading edge were flowing. He didn't want to drift as far away from where things were happening as he had in 1967, and at the same time he didn't necessarily want to drift too far away from the charts, as he had been before *Ziggy Stardust*. The albums of 1978 were Kraftwerk's *The Man-Machine*, Steve Reich's *Music for 18 Musicians*, Wire's *Chairs Missing*, Talking Heads' *More Songs About Buildings and Food*, Pere Ubu's *The Modern Dance*, Devo's *Are We Not Men? We Are Devo!*, Brian Eno's *Ambient 1: Music for Airports*, Magazine's *Real Life*, X-Ray Spex's *Germfree Adolescents*, Pere Ubu's *Dub Housing*, Buzzcocks'

Another Music in a Different Kitchen, Patti Smith Group's *Easter*, Public Image's *Public Image: First Issue*, Annette Peacock's *X-Dreams*, Siouxsie and the Banshees' *The Scream*, XTC's *Go 2*. There was Bruce Springsteen's *Darkness at the Edge of Town* at the top of many critics' lists, and also *Peter Gabriel* (2), Culture's *Africa Stand Alone*, Ry Cooder's *Jazz*, and others still wishing punk and post-punk hadn't become so distracting, or even never existed, would have been taken by the Who's *Who Are You?* and the Rolling Stones' *Some Girls*. Apart from the dream aside of *Peter and the Wolf*, Bowie was simply on *Stage*, his second live album in five years, a steady, almost deliberately neutral record – after some nostalgic Ziggy show business on side one – documenting the transition from *Young Americans* and *Station to Station* to *Low* and *"Heroes"*. It presented the fixated, flattered Bowie who had been Ziggy and co., and the stressed, attention-seeking fabricated young American, but also the self-conscious stardom-jettisoning conceptual European in the clothes of a straight man playing with machines, pals and spectral futures, acting like *Station to Station*, *Low* and *"Heroes"* were as much sliding templates for epic arena rock as they were shadowy alleyways, suggestive signposts and informative footnotes on the way to post-punk, electronica, goth, new romance, ambient, techno, glitch and beyond, to the streaming collapse of genres.

Music was moving so fast, so the singles of the year were now by Buzzcocks, Public Image, Elvis Costello, Magazine, the Clash, Subway Sect, the Cramps, the Fall, Scritti Politti – and in another zone by Sylvester, Bee Gees and Rose Royce – so that he might easily be wrong-footed and fall off the stage, into the lap of Mick, Rod and Elton. The exhaustion, fear and general disorientation that had generated the creative tension on *Low* and *"Heroes"* might now really drag him away from the fast-developing and re-coalescing post-punk and electronic world he was existing in parallel to, and to some extent influencing, and dispatch him into the has-been arena that for most rock acts faced with the new world had been inevitable.

1979

'I wanted to prove the sustaining power of music.'

132.

He is drifting away from Berlin, the city as a place, but there'll always be Berlin in Bowie, and Bowie leaves his traces, and the routes he followed.

133.

He is finding the key to his flat in the pocket of a dingy dirty yellow overcoat where anyone could have found it. He smokes some marijuana and watches some old silent movies on the TV, no sound, just words on the screen, which don't particularly seem to fit the action on the screen. He scans some books that are on the table, looks at the TV, looks at the books, looks at the TV. Iggy's wearing different-coloured socks and girls' underwear. He's taken some acid. He walks up and down the hallway dealing with what's happening in his head, which isn't helping his mind or his body. He tries to get Bowie's attention, but Bowie's only got eyes for the TV. He stomps off in a sulk. Bowie is working although you'd never know it looking at him. He's watching the action on the TV, looking at some pictures in a book. He's switching channels, looking at books. Changing channels, turning pages. Turning, changing. He's in the business of finding things, and then indexing what inspires his interest.

134.

He is divorced from Angie, who finally got fed up with him being in at least two places at once, which takes the kind of months in court he's used to when he's challenging management. The rise and fall of David and Angie Bowie coincides with the rise and fall of Ziggy Stardust, as though Angie was actually really married to Ziggy, and as soon as he was only really a shadow of his former self, she also found herself a shadow in David's life, losing touch until it was like it never happened.

135.

He is using the recording studio as a time machine which now materialises as *Lodger* where there is a touchy punchline to this so-called Berlin trilogy, this scenic, simulated triptych of dispossession. It all goes to show he's in his element when he's a little bit out of this world and his mind. After all he has been through in the Seventies, from sheathed skin and bone boogie man to temporary Berliner, he washes up as advanced, piercing and conceptually smart as pop gets, full of himself, nameless, all-knowing, at a loss, re-set, ready to start again, for another album that could be called, simply, *David Bowie*, for another beginning, one more debut reboot, and, finally, a new decade, and new real and imaginary locations to discover, and true and invented tensions to experience.

He's still using Oblique Strategies, and the spiritual power trio of Visconti, Eno and Bowie, the involuted supergroup, are still following the instructions, shifting the emphasis from guitar to electronics, but the instrumentals remain under the skies of Enoland, and 'Boys Keep Swinging' and 'DJ' are follow-ups to 'Rebel Rebel' as much as *Low*'s 'Sound and Vision'. In 'DJ' he makes no bones about his place(s) in the world: 'I've got believers believing in me.' Same too in smeared, leery triple drag in the video for 'Boys Keep Swinging', where Bowie recreates the drag performances he would watch at Chez Romy Haag in a set based on the club, and feature Romy's signature wipe of her lipstick and snatching off of her wig. On 'Red Sails', the song that ends side one, he affectionately marvels at his own need for adventure and epiphany: 'Boy, I really get around.' Sometimes he ends up in the wrong town. The visitor has become fantastic voyager round a planet he can't get enough of.

The time of the trio seems to be able to just about span a trio of albums, before Eno loses interest, and spies other opportunities for extending sound, and experimenting with musical history. Their time apart as co-workers will be sixteen years: Bowie's time apart from Visconti, twenty-one.

Bowie discreetly now seems to belong wherever you look, but as a musician, which in the end took him over in the 1970s, he was especially at homeless home with the post-punk works that were altering the entire trajectory of the sound of rock. At the time, when the patterns hadn't settled, there was a definite loss of lustre, a perforated ghostliness that returned him to the displaced, disabused melancholy that had been on show a decade earlier in the months before *The Man Who Sold the World*. He'd lost a large amount of what can be described as the casual audience, but that's ultimately temporary; he gives so much to these songs they are injected with a life force that will send them deep into the future, beyond their time, beyond fashion, for when the world is ready. Not so much that they are ahead of their time, but they can belong in any time.

The fact that Bowie, while still being Bowie, a radiant star so recent it was still very much in the air, was also making a cult album of deep appeal only for those continually fascinated with wherever he was and whatever he was doing made it even more intriguing. So forgotten was it for a while when his best was considered, and when his lost moments were catalogued, it made it one of those albums I would definitely confess at times was my favourite Bowie record. It was seen, seductively, to be even more difficult and opaque than *Low*, before that album was discovered as a sign of life, of confidence in the future, not moody disillusion.

Lodger was where the experimental and endless mental and metaphorical wandering, the setting sail for some unknown other place, seemed to combine with the theatrical pop star post-glam action and his still smart critical awareness, however blurry, of where music was heading at the time. And of all those 1967 musicians he was once adrift from, none would sound as contemporary twelve years later, as sure of themselves, as in the moment and influential, on the verge of sealing such a flowing, flowering set of legends.

136.

He is making an appearance on *Saturday Night Live*, and working out how he wants to play it, with a lot of the eyes of America on him and in the mood to explicitly play up those transgressive sides of him that Middle America hates and fears. *SNL* is filmed in a New York of Mudd Club, Studio 54, Danceteria, and Max's Kansas City, where dance is being taken over the edge of rhythm, to the beginning of a whole new history, as Bowie always predicted, and punk and post-punk is part of a swirling scene, producing all manner of permutations. Bowie has helped make all this happen, and wants to help it go further.

While in Berlin, Bowie's heard all about Klaus Nomi, fan of Elvis and Maria Callas, who imagines vaudeville on Venus, Mickey Mouse from Mercury, opera from Oz, and who sang arias after work at the Deutsche Opera where he was an usher. In New York, as Klaus Nomi – an anagram of Omni, for Universal, from the science-fiction magazine – he's performing Camille Saint-Saëns in experimental punk cabaret nightclubs wearing a transparent cape. His voice sails through the octaves from high to low, from deep down to uncanny falsetto, creating a sound that devoted fan Morrissey described as the sound of a man trapped in a little girl's body. He poses in the shop window of Manhattan fashion centre Fiorucci's for hours without apparently blinking, terrifying passers-by when there's a sudden little sign of human life behind the black lipstick, pale mask and performance art mime.

He's from an alternative universe that's emerged because of everything Bowie did between 1969 and 1974, from mime to the end of the world, Weill between Brecht and Broadway, and Marlene Dietrich between Germany and America. Bowie instantly recognises a fellow traveller through the boundless space of performance, another connoisseur in the art of giving a voice to the body, of the giving and taking away of faces.

137.

He is meeting Klaus and his friend and Fiorucci colleague Joey Arias, who, he tells Bowie, has a voice like Billie Holiday and shares his own brand of crazy. They meet in the lobby of the RCA Studios off Sixth Avenue. They are going to perform three songs from across Bowie's 1970s for the *Saturday Night Live* performance, 'The Man Who Sold the World' from the beginning, 'TVC 15' from the middle, and 'Boys Keep Swinging' from the end. Davis, Murray and Alomar remain the fluid, forceful rhythm centre of his band, joined by Blondie keyboardist Jimmy Destri. Martin Sheen was the host, promoting his latest film, *Apocalypse Now*.

He's using the homo superior triptych of 1970s menace, mutancy and the mystical to think ahead to a 1980s where pop becomes a trans-national visual extravaganza because of MTV, and while he's at it, with the help of Nomi and Arias, make room for a new transgender species – a flash hint of a possible next step in the progress of evolution. Why not? Change can come when you most expect it.

Arias tells the man who comes to get them from the lobby that he is so excited to meet David Bowie. The man who collects them has a beard, smells a little off, and is wearing ill-fitting polyester trousers and funny shoes. The man laughs, and Arias to his embarrassment instantly knows that he has blundered and that this is David Bowie. Bowie spends hours talking with them over lunch, saying it's a shame he never met them while he was in his Ziggy years.

With the money they get given for costumes they buy some Thierry Mugler dresses tight enough to display all their wares, and Bowie gets excited when he sees what they've bought, and wants to join in with them. He loves their determination to have the time of their lives, and decides not to wear the planned suit that will set him in with the band. He rejects the conventional rock-group daywear for something a little more in the spirit of an occasion.

The first costume made up for 'TVC 15' is nicknamed 'the Chinese airline stewardess outfit' finished off with grey high heels, and the second for 'The Man Who Sold the World', an oversized plastic tuxedo that binds his legs together so he has to be carried on stage. The costumes come through Bowie's mind and memory from Sonia Delaunay's oversized designs for Romanian poet and Dada mastermind Tristan Tzara's 1921 play *The Gas Heart*, featuring characters called Mouth, Nose, Eye, Ear, Eyebrow and Neck.

He'd been thinking about his own proposed musical play on *Saturday Night Live* as including his own Mouth, Nose and Neck, Bowie, Joey and Klaus, all jockeying for position, and throwing his voice and the voices of Klaus and Nomi into their own statement on how identity is used as an ordering and controlling tool. Such thoughts are at the scrambled heart of Dada, and also at the divine heart of show business. From the spaces in between spaces, where Bowie likes to work, animated by his sudden encounter with the incredible Nomi, his view is that *The Gas Heart* is as alive and significant as anything by Shakespeare. Tzara called it 'the greatest three-act hoax of the century'. Bowie was going to issue a three-song response to the hoax, with the haywire zeal of someone committing their own beautiful hoax.

For the filming of the show, later in the week, Bowie has performed a little magic, and Joey now recognises him as David Bowie. The screams that follow him as he enters the building help with the identification, as does the production staff exclaiming, 'Bowie is in the building.' When Bowie is in this mood, inside one of his most flamboyant 'what if' bubbles, excitement crackles in the air.

Joey does Klaus's make up, Klaus does Joey's, and they both do Bowie's. The performance is more than a hint of where Ziggy Stardust would have gone if he'd lived to see the end of the decade and married Romy, where the Rolling Stones could have gone if they'd paid attention to the free advice Bowie was giving them with *Diamond Dogs*. For the final song, 'Boys Keep Swinging' – a lusty TV message to stray love Romy – the trio become half human half semi-naked puppets, and there's a flash showing of the non-male penis of Bowie that got taken away from the *Diamond Dogs* cover.

It joins the *Top of the Pops* 'Starman' as one of the great pop on television moments, with the thrilling impact of a what if you mixed vaudevillian gaiety with the colossal eccentricity of an exorcism; anyone who saw it can never forget it, and they think about all sorts of things from sex to desire in a very different way after.

Klaus looks forward to further collaborations and signs a record contract with RCA records, who think they have a new Bowie, or at least a new Ziggy. He adopts the Bowie adaptation of the plastic Dada tux and enlarged bow tie as his own look, and Bowie has used it up anyway. He releases two albums adored by a select few, taking in a history of music from Henry Purcell's aria 'Death' from the opera *Dido and Aeneas* to Chubby Checker's 'The Twist' via 'Ding-Dong! The Witch Is Dead', and he continues developing his crown-seizing solo performance and an ability to contort and distort pop, cabaret, opera and his aura into new shapes and sizes. Jean-Michel Basquiat and Keith Haring are true believers.

In 1982, lesions start to appear on Klaus's neck that will eventually lead to complications caused by what was not then widely known as AIDS, and he dies on 6 August 1983 aged thirty-nine as one of the first to have to deal with the horror. His life and body increasingly thin out, as if flesh is falling off, the solidness of existence gradually evaporating, until there was nothing left but a shell, the haunting echo of one life turned into a great, defiant performance, and a final leaving of the stage that was everything to him, a saving of the performance of his life to the very, very end.

He never got the call from Bowie to continue any arrangement. The scintillating *Saturday Night Live* showing off, an entertainment in a world of its own, was all the magic Bowie needed from the union. Sometimes it's all over in one fabulous night, desire fulfilled, desire destroyed, which finishes with one of the greatest ever post-action smokes of a cigarette, the spirit of another randomly encountered shadow across time being inhaled deep into the body, and never leaving.

•　•　•

Pink Floyd didn't want the new breed to have it all their own way and in 1979 there was their *Wall*, as if they were creating a protective barrier around themselves, because the critics, certainly in my part of the world, were looking more towards Joy Division's *Unknown Pleasures*, Talking Heads' *Fear of Music*, Gang of Four's *Entertainment!*, Wire's *154*, Public Image Ltd's *Metal Box*, *The B 52's*, *This Heat*, The Pop Group's *Y*, XTC's *Drums and Wires*, *The Specials*, the Human League's *Reproduction*, the Fall's *Live at the Witch Trials*, the Slits' *Cut*, *The Raincoats*, Michael Rother's *Katzenmusik*, Swell Maps' *A Trip to Marineville*, the Residents' *Eskimo*, and Neil Young was reporting on the changes from his point of view on *Rust Never Sleeps* and

Live Rust. Motörhead and AC/DC were making sure the trajectory all wasn't heading one way, as were Earth, Wind & Fire, Chic and Michael Jackson. Bob Dylan, Tom Waits and Ry Cooder were as stubborn as ever. The number 1s were by Ian Dury, the Police and Blondie as much as Cliff, so a form of change had happened, and with cut-price aliens Tubeway Army having two hits there was a sense of nostalgia for the space age, science-fiction David Bowie, a yearning for his obvious, play-acting weirdness, not his knowing, aesthetic, art jumping weirdness. The best singles of the year were by the Specials, Clash, Gloria Gaynor, Public Image Ltd, XTC, the Pop Group, Echo and the Bunnymen, the Cure, Joy Division, Orchestral Manoeuvres in the Dark, Blondie, but I voted 'Boys Keep Swinging' pretty high as well, and its abrasive exuberance, drag spectacle and sexually shuffled video made Tubeway Army a little more cute than singer Gary Numan hoped.

1980

*'Sometimes I think my head is so big
because it is so full of dreams.'*

138.

He is still in the 1970s even as time ticks on, and there's a new decade ahead, the last one before the computers take over, and more and more people can start operating on reality, not just the artist and musicians.

139.

He's summing up his 1970s with *Scary Monsters (And Super Creeps)*, which created the climax to the decade, setting up his shadows, ghosts, spacemen and showmen for a dramatic end-of-show encore, and was another kind of debut, in the way he originally made *David Bowie* twice, another go even after everything he's just done in ten chaotic, magnificent years at programming and structuring his thoughts, influences and memories, at becoming a one-man fusion of eras and attitudes. The greatest hits of an alternative 1970s Bowie, a sensibly resplendent montage summary of some 1960s and 1970s time and space travel brought back from a parallel universe.

140.

He is rehearsing in July to take over from Philip Anglim in a Broadway production of *The Elephant Man*, based on the life of Leicester-born Joseph Merrick, 'a despised creature without consolation'. As a youngster in Bromley, Bowie had a typical half-repulsed, half-tantalised teenage interest in freak stories and stories of people with misaligned and mutant bodies. The Elephant Man becomes one of the great icons of Victorian freakery, a natural source of material for Bowie, ever-curious about the matter of appearance and identity.

Merrick's body became distorted by unsightly growths of flesh and bone, and he was transformed from ridiculed, hideous side-show freak to privately housed object of equally voyeuristic but less harrowing upper-class and aristocratic observation.

The Elephant Man by American poet and playwright Bernard Pomerance was originally produced in 1977 at the Hampstead Theatre in north London and then in repertory at the National Theatre. Pomerance had recently read a book called *The True Story of the Elephant Man*, and his play, originally titled *Deformed*, also using the notes of the Doctor Frederick Treves who rescues Merrick, helped generate new interest in the previously marginalised Victorian Londoner, and the human, spiritual being behind the appearance. (Treves mistakenly called Merrick John.) This led to David Lynch's 1980 film version, not based on the play. For the film, John Hurt was made up in a process that took six hours to resemble the original deformed shape of Merrick.

In Pomerance's play, from his original instructions to avoid the distraction of prosthetics, the grotesque features are left to the imagination. The actor playing Merrick is encouraged to use facial expressions and body manipulation to suggest the severe nature of his twisted body and a head the size of a man's waist – not the size of Bowie's waist.

Bowie begins his time as Merrick in Denver at the end of July, his first appearance on stage in a conventional theatre production. Previous actors had played the role nude. Bowie insists on wearing a dhoti covering little but his groin as his costume which creates folds over his thin frame that further imply Merrick's diseased lumps and humps. Doubters and the indifferent are impressed by how he can act, and this is the first chance since the late 1960s he's had to continue the kind of non-pop work he was doing with Lindsay Kemp.

A role that requires a considerable amount of non-verbal movement is ideal for someone trained in mime and the illusions of pop stardom. Playing superficially ugly, but deeply human, disabled but graceful, melancholy but courageous, a bright mind trapped in an impossible body, Bowie, always challenging 'the norm', was interested in how to represent Merrick as an example of 'other' – not as an object, or a martyr, but as an example of redefined humanity. Merrick is also an audacious master of self-invention, turning himself into someone out of almost nothing that appears human.

It's further research for Bowie into the idea that consciousness can have an identity and presence that is nothing to do with appearance or gender, and that can be both part of a physical presence, as well as separate. There is a subjective self – an individual humanity – and then the objective self, facing outward, which are subject to what others think and their fears, actions and desires. The body should not dictate a reaction to the person's essential spirit, which lies outside and beyond body and appearance.

The play travels to Chicago, and then to Broadway to run through to the early days of January 1981. John Lennon in his last interview with BBC disc jockey Andy Peebles two days before he was shot in New York, a short walk from the theatre where it is playing, talks about Bowie, and the Elephant Man, as he has front-row tickets with Yoko to see the play. They were due to go the day after he was murdered.

I must say I admire Bowie for his vast repertoire of talent the guy has, you know. I was never around when the Ziggy Stardust thing came, because I'd already left England while all that was going on, so I never really knew what he was. And meeting him doesn't give you much more of a clue, you know, because you don't know which one you're talking to. But …

and, you know, we all have our little personality traits, so between him and me I don't know what was going down but we seemed to have some kind of communication together, and I think he's great. The fact that he could just walk into that and do that. I could never do that.

John Lennon was shot by Mark Chapman, who had been to see *The Elephant Man* while he was in New York on what was meant to be a holiday – Bowie once said that he also had a ticket for the same show as John and Yoko, also in the front row, so that in the performance of 9 December there are three empty seats right in front of him. Chapman also reputedly had Bowie in his thoughts as a possible target – the ultimate moving target suddenly very vulnerable with his whereabouts and working hours known as he worked in a New York he loved because he could be so mobile, and relatively invisible. A target that was really the shape of fame. Bowie would explain:

> I have worked out a very coherent New York lifestyle and there are two ways of walking down the street – I really buy that one. You can walk down the street wanting to be recognised and you can walk down the street not wanting to be recognised. This is especially true of New York and to a certain extent, most of America. The most you get is, 'Hi, Dave, how's it going?' It's very neighbourly. They don't get as excited at meeting you as they do in London, which is still a bit star conscious. Here you see Al Pacino walking around or Joel Grey jogging. It's quite easy to do that, it's great.

There is no chance of any extension of his time on Broadway as the Elephant Man. The death of a close friend close by didn't necessarily make a difference to what he was thinking; but oddly for someone so theatrical the theatre doesn't work for him. He cannot become someone else as easily as he can when he is in control of his own work.

The project was a way of studying another mind, another time, another life, from as within as he can go under the circumstances, and with the circus that comes with him he's perceived, patronised and pampered as the weird rock star indulging himself in a Broadway role he's nowhere near qualified for.

It is impossible for him to do it without drawing the kind of attention more to do with being David Bowie than being the actor experimenting with a complicated role that involves the kind of intrigue about the self and a relationship with the outside world that fascinates him. In a way, he too becomes the freak in a sideshow, goggled at because he is not like anyone else, because he's larger than the production, not because he is disappearing into another who is not like anyone else.

In films, it's the same to an extent, but not with an audience there with him in the room, right on top of him, watching him as David Bowie, crowding him out, trying to climb inside his mind, interfering with his timing, getting in the way of allowing real magic to happen. The magic that cannot happen when there is close scrutiny. He was in the way of the actual point of the play.

He had been asked in a television interview, by Tim Rice of *Jesus Christ Superstar*, if he would like to go back on stage after the role was over. 'Not particularly,' he abruptly admitted, before politely going on to fulfil promotional duties as diligently, neutrally but generously as ever by expressing how much he had learnt in a few weeks, and how he hoped in the time he had left to experiment a little with the role.

The idea of playing the Elephant Man was all he really needed, taking into his imagination and his thinking new ideas about the connection between body and spirit. The thinking he did about who Merrick was and how he behaved as a human being so different he was almost his own species had more impact on his mind than the demands of the performance.

He investigated what someone so isolated was thinking and feeling, because he was so different, an equivalent to how Bowie was so different. What it means to be so different that inevitably you will be lonely, and adding that to his sense of what it is to be alive. The actual act of acting became a different thing, less important to his developing mind. The acting was more about his relationship with an audience, and his heavy fame, in a place that was somehow too fixed. Acting this way he can't forget that his name is David, which strangely he can do when he's playing himself.

The curtain came down on his theatrical life for the last time on 3 January 1981. Another retirement. He walked out of the theatre and headed south down Broadway in the direction of Soho. Hardly anyone else was around. He once sang that you can walk around New York while you are asleep in your bed. Perhaps that is what he was doing.

He is as alone as he is in his dreams. He now has the power to step into the dreams of others, from one to another in a moment, because he has found a way to belong anywhere, transported by song.

• • •

It was not known at the time but vinyl was in its final few years and albums and even singles would soon be replaced by a completely different format which itself would only last for about twenty years. At the time, the idea of the album and the single seemed absolute, as fixed as the sea and the sky. The album mentality would be hard to disregard, but the historical and cultural conditions that created the sound, content and structure of the rock album were coming to an end. In 1980, the albums of the year were by Joy Division, with *Closer*, which spoke a language learnt from listening to albums such as *Diamond Dogs*, *Low* and *Lust for Life*, Talking Heads, the Beat, Black Uhuru, Holger Czukay, Ry Cooder, Peter Gabriel, the Cramps, Magazine, Suicide, Cabaret Voltaire, Grace Jones, Lou Reed, the Teardrop Explodes, Echo and the Bunnymen, Siouxsie and the Banshees, Tom Waits, X, the Sound, Prince, Swell Maps, Harold Budd/Brian Eno . . . a very different place from ten years before, but Bowie was in both places at once, and already aware of a new set of future styles, and we were almost taking it for granted. He is having a number 1 single with the pop spiritual 'Ashes to Ashes', where he brings back to life Major Tom, who exists as much as anyone in his real life, and looks back over a life within the 1970s, which has now died away, leaving him with a very new life, a very different position, but feeling the same as he ever did. Once more, he has to begin again, but brings more past, more experience, into the next incarnation. He finds himself haunted by his own music, and his own life. 'What I like my music to do is awaken the ghosts inside of me. Not the demons, you understand, but the ghosts.'

8

VOODOO POWER

1.

While I was working as an artistic adviser to the *David Bowie is* exhibition at the Victoria and Albert Museum, I was asked by Geoff Marsh, one of the curators, if I could attempt to write a book in a weekend, while sitting near the ticket desk by the cloakroom in the high-arched entrance area of the museum. It was a part of the events, talks, showings and debates that were running alongside the exhibition itself. The words I typed would be shown on a screen, so that people could come and watch my progress; and possibly see me fail. The loneliness of the writer turned into an installation.

It seemed like a risk worth taking, and one way of at least beginning such a book if not finishing it. It would seem that the enormity of the task of writing about Bowie, who is this one thing made up of millions of things, and of millions of responses to those millions of things that are all the same, and all different, is to create an environment within which to work, and then set a deadline. It's like being given thirteen hours to fight your way through an impossible labyrinth while faced with various challenges and crises.

I turned up for work one Saturday morning in April 2013 and began to write.

9.55 a.m.

Notes for a book about David Bowie to be written by me in a weekend in the Grand Entrance of the Victoria and Albert Museum as a kind of temporary writer in residence at the *David Bowie is*.

First of all, I must explain more fully where I am and what I can see around me, to fully capture the moment, the reality of how for whatever reason I have ended up in the position of being expected as one version of an expert on the ways of Bowie to complete a book in a weekend. This situation is perhaps the equivalent of me going to work, from ten to six, and this is my wonderfully grand and hushed office, filled with glossy marble, monumental columns and the larger than life light of the gods.

I am sat to the side of the Grand Entrance, and opposite me, hanging down many metres from the vaulted cathedral-like ceiling is Dale Chihuly's alien-dramatic Rotunda Chandelier. Made in Seattle in 2001 from tangled, convoluted blown glass and steel, it could easily be a representation of something David Bowie would have worn at some point in 1973 to represent his subversive show-off mind. On the other side of the ticket and information desk are the ghostly Medieval and Renaissance Galleries, 1350 to 1600, known to V&A staff as the Med and Ren. I had been warned not to enter these galleries before I began work, as I would be arrested. I took this warning seriously.

To my left, hanging below a majestic golden gothic altar, three large, tinted photographs of David Bowie overlook the ticket and information area. He seems to be licking his fingers with something that is not quite relish, not quite pure, deviant flirtation, looking both out of place and very much at home in the spectacular entrance, mocking the very idea he should be hanging in such a place, making it very clear this is exactly where he belongs.

Some will come to worship at the altar, and some will come to register their distaste, that a mere rock star has been given such exalted, truly iconic status.

11.14 a.m.

Adrian Deakes, a Performance Education Manager from the learning department of the Victoria and Albert Museum, passes my desk and tells me that he has been doing a study project with pupils from the secondary school in Bromley where David Bowie went as a youngster in the early 1960s. It was Bromley Technical High School when Bowie attended as David Robert Jones; it is now Ravens Wood School, although Adrian says Bowie would still recognise it as the school he went to, the same halls and corridors, and, no doubt, similar smells and sounds. 'The same view,' says Adrian, 'over the playing fields to the large white houses beyond, the house opposite the school entrance, proudly stating "built in 1875".'

The 2012/13 teenagers were very taken when they visited the exhibition and heard the young Bowie, someone previously not that familiar to them, a distant rumour at best, how when he talked he sounded just like they did. He has travelled so far away from that time and place, through so many other times and places, sometimes to the other side of space, experiencing the illuminating, and deforming, white heat of fame, but he was still there, with them, for them, close by, as relevant as anything in their lives, ultimately, more so. They have made a film about their experience getting to know about someone they were delighted to discover actually went to their school. They have called the film 'David Bowie is one of us'.

'David Bowie is a person who did exactly what HE wanted to do,' said one of the students, Jack Gordon, 'now look where he is . . .'

11.23 a.m.

There are those who are treating me sat at my desk as a kind of information desk, as some sort of museum guide, asking where the lifts are, where the Ladies is, where indeed 'Is' is, and once or twice they decide I might even be a psychiatrist or, perhaps, on the other side, a patient in need of treatment. Someone who wishes to be known only as Helen and is very alarmed when I asked her real name lives around the corner in South Kensington, and seems to use the V&A as her local, a convenient place to visit when she is bored at home or the builders are in. Maybe she comes here to forget all the things going on around her. In just a few minutes she fills me in on her life, her husband in Geneva, her kids. She asks me directly what is it about David Bowie, then. 'Why are you so interested?'

She had an accent that turns out to be part Polish, which makes her question sound a little sinister, like the pair of us have just entered a demented detective mystery directed by Roman Polanski. I mean, she says, he was beautiful as a young boy, but what was that film *Labyrinth* all about? David Bowie showing off how well-endowed he was and starring in a film alongside a baby and a bog of eternal stench?

As far as she was concerned, nothing he had done that was great could ever make him recover from this most peculiar affair. It turns out she is critical of the exhibition itself. 'Pretentious, no?' she decides, in a way that intends to make it difficult for me to disagree. I make a defence of the very idea of pretentiousness, that without it there is no possibility of creative ambition, of the kind of risk-taking that can lead to genius, to genuinely important solutions to aesthetic and ultimately social problems. She abruptly dismisses this line of thought, and says she has to nip back home to take delivery of some new radiators for her kitchen.

Later, fortysomething Wendy from Sussex gives me more of a

fan's view, and tells me about an amateur performance she had seen in her local hall just a few days ago that almost seems like she made it up. It was a musical about someone called David Jones, who is not David Bowie, but who identifies very closely with Bowie, was born on the same day, and dreams of being as successful. The more successful Bowie becomes, the more of a failure David Jones becomes, losing sight of himself as he obsesses over Bowie, and he turns to drugs and crime, falling so far into grubby lonely obscurity it seems all that is left is death. I cannot quite work out what happens next, except that he is saved by hearing 'Rock 'n' Roll Suicide', and there is a relative form of a happy ending, and a band comes on and plays some of Bowie's greatest hits.

For Wendy, more than Helen, who I realise is probably more of a Med and Ren person, David Bowie has changed her life, and she tells me of the experience she had at school as she was growing up that I recognise – how you could tell looking around at what some fellow pupils had done to their uniforms, or their hair, or make-up, just the way they walked, who were the Bowie fans, outsiders on the inside of something they felt was special, and who were not. You could see minds opening in the way a skirt or blazer had been given a little personal, home-made touch of colour, in how their hair had been treated, twisted, touched up.

More and more visitors of all shapes, sizes and ages pour through the Grand Entrance on their way to experience the dispersed, concentrated traces of David Bowie haunting various sectors of the museum, and many of them, like Wendy, look like they are making a pilgrimage, into their very own past, shared with their very own Bowie, when everything was possible, or a future they still believe in, that can still, surely, be about change, for the better.

12.23 p.m.

And then someone comes up to my desk to ask me to fix their phone. And then someone comes up to my desk to ask me to turn the music down – there is a DJ in the entrance, playing music by and inspired by Bowie, which just happens to be some of my favourites, from Magazine and Joy Division to Philip Glass turning *"Heroes"* into a monumental minimalist symphony made of blown glass and steel. It all sounds perfect to me. She is livid; her world is falling apart, shattered by the decadence of these rude intruders into her calm, collected and soothing sanctuary.

I do not want to be too rude and suggest that of those in the museum she is on the older side, but she is not shall we say the type who will talk of the moment she first discovered David Bowie. She has yet to discover Bowie. She is right now not in the mood to ever discover Bowie. She wonders what all this clowning about is actually for. 'We don't expect this racket in here!' she explodes during the particularly sensational and for some legendary Mike Garson piano solo on *Aladdin Sane*.

I toy for a moment with trying to explain why the music should not be turned down or off but UP, especially during this particular beautifully berserk solo, a capsule history of free jazz for those who have never experienced it, which is joyously harmonising with the light pouring from the skies into the vast entrance, but decide she looks in the mood to have me deported if I oppose her in any way. Bitterly disappointed that I am in fact of no use to her, she charges off to search out those in control who might get rid of this horrific noise, so that she can enter the Med and Ren, and appreciate all those quiet, settled centuries without Garson's startling piano.

A few minutes later a young lady in a scarlet Bowie wig wearing cut-off denim shorts draws the attention of everyone in the Grand Entrance by dancing the slowest, look-at-me-but-don't-look Moonage Daydream daydreamy movement to 'Moonage Daydream', as though this is actually a happening, a wonderful breaking through of decades of tightening formality, and I think that by now the older lady not wearing the scarlet wig and threatened by Garson's piano is planning her own counter-revolution, or feeling that she is sitting in a tin can far above the earth.

The changes began forty odd years ago in small halls in small towns around the country by Bowie and his company of mavericks and showman militants have eventually reverberated all the way through to the moored, supervising spaces of the Victoria and Albert Museum. I watch a five-year-old girl walk past my desk with a red and blue Aladdin Sane flash painted across her eye, which looks exactly right, and it seems like the Ziggy-zonked outsiders led by their glorious, pacesetting and inspirational ringleader still believe they can make a world of difference.

12.53 p.m.

A story about David Bowie from 2004; someone who wishes to remain anonymous tells me about seeing him during the recording of a television programme in Los Angeles, and how as he walked along a corridor towards the studio, the people all along his route separated to let him through, because they were in the presence of a real star, actually, something wilder than just a mere real star. They could tell he was a real star, or the next stage up and beyond, not least because also appearing on the show was Marilyn Manson, there with his then girlfriend, the burlesque dancer and actress Dita Von Teese. 'He just looked pathetic next to Bowie,' my witness says. 'Like someone had covered him in cheap Kiss make-up and then thrown a bunch of metal studs at him.' Her abrasive comedienne friend, not known for being sentimental, was introduced to Bowie, and before she could think of anything cool to say, immediately burst into tears.

1.36 p.m.

I have a suggestion box on my desk. It is there so that visitors to the museum, most likely those that have come because of David Bowie, can offer their own thoughts and memories. Perhaps their words will be of use to me during moments when I am having trouble working out what to write next. Writing a book in this way, sat at a desk surrounded by people who can observe, disturb and inspire me, means that I do not have to go out into the world to research, but the world can come to me, without me having to make it up too much. It will be the world of David Bowie filtered through fans that happen to be here this weekend.

I have had printed on these cards three questions, which I hope people will find interesting – essentially, I am asking what they found most interesting about Bowie, when they were first aware of him, and how they would describe themselves.

1.46 p.m.

At first, I thought no one was going to fill in the cards. Maybe they find the questions a little uninspiring, but then suddenly, there is a rush of filled-out cards placed into the box on my desk.

My favourite thing about David Bowie is: him

I first knew about David Bowie in: 1974–75, I drove all the way to Memphis from New Orleans.

I would describe myself as: Geisha=arts person and future Diamond Dog

---

My favourite thing about David Bowie is: the looks/the texture of his voice

I first knew about David Bowie in: mid 70s, the plastic soul into Nic Roeg era

I would describe myself as: under his influence even now

My favourite thing about David Bowie is: Low

I first knew about David Bowie in: 1972

I would describe myself as: inquisitive

My favourite thing about David Bowie is: his innovation, charisma, his presence, awesome performer, songwriter, vocal second to none

I first knew about David Bowie in: 1972, school days, we would take turns to buy the latest album and meet up to listen to it.

I would describe myself as: massive fan. Always in awe! I catalogue my collection in html pages. How sad is that?

My favourite thing about David Bowie is: The constant changes

I first knew about David Bowie in: Early 70s when my aunty used to sing and dance along and frustrate my gran.

I would describe myself as: trying to keep up . . . (that short lass from Wigan that works at the college according to Stephen.)

My favourite thing about David Bowie is: the way he inspired my girlfriend.

I first knew about David Bowie in: listening in my girlfriend's car in 2011

I would describe myself as: a garage and grime DJ. 'I put on a (very messy) free party (rave) in a forest in a Welsh valley last weekend. We'd been playing garage and techno and house all night but put on some Bowie at dawn and it took everyone to another place. I'll remember that all my life.'

My favourite thing about David Bowie is: The beguiling myth that penetrates through time. The layers and layers to uncover and discover. Fearlessness. He goes for it.

I first knew about David Bowie in: 1983. 'Let's Dance' was massive. Then I heard 'Life on Mars?' and had to buy Hunky Dory. I cried. I bought everything else slowly over the years.

I would describe myself as: A cross between Thin White Duke and Queen Bitch, from the Channel Islands.

My favourite thing about David Bowie is: his ability to always look forward and never get stuck in one character or period

I first knew about David Bowie in: my college years, when I first heard 'Life on Mars?'.

I would describe myself as: a fan of the ever-evolving, ever-changing, always brilliant David Bowie

---

My favourite thing about David Bowie is: sexless. Male/female I mean

I first knew about David Bowie in: when he married an African-American model

I would describe myself as: ignorant of British stars – a black American on holiday

---

My favourite thing about David Bowie is: His music and his gay announcement in 1971

I first knew about David Bowie in: 1969 – 'Space Oddity'

I would describe myself as: Holly Johnson x

My favourite thing about David Bowie is: The fact that he can't remember making his best album

I first knew about David Bowie in: Arguments over how to pronounce his surname correctly

I would describe myself as: Time Magazine's Person of the Year 2006 (the year they gave it to 'You' meaning everyone . . .)

My favourite thing about David Bowie is: he still sounds the same now, forty years on

I first knew about David Bowie in: 1973, when I became a teenager

I would describe myself as: 50 + + young when I listen to Bowie, I am transported back

---

My favourite thing about David Bowie is: his cheekbones

I first knew about David Bowie in: 1976

I would describe myself as: inspired by the beauty of the cult of Bowie

My favourite thing about David Bowie is: his flamboyance, his song writing ability and appearance

I first knew about David Bowie in: 1996 when I was four years old and my mum sang 'Space Oddity' to me

I would describe myself as: a steampunk mod girl

My favourite thing about David Bowie is: his old cheekbones

I first knew about David Bowie in: The soundtrack of the TV series Life on Mars

I would describe myself as: an art student!

My favourite thing about David Bowie is: that no matter who you talk to they can relate to him

I first knew about David Bowie in: 2012 (I'm 16)

I would describe myself as: having no idea of who I am, but that's ok

My favourite thing about David Bowie is: not being afraid to be who he is

I first knew about David Bowie in: Labyrinth

I would describe myself as: someone who is afraid

And here, taking me a little by surprise, is an unexpectedly common way that many fans found their Bowie: through the *Labyrinth* film that Helen from Poland and around the corner from the museum found, as many did, so preposterous, the moment where Bowie seemed related to Kermit and played the Lord of all he surveys as a cross between evil clown in a fright wig and spoilt, spiteful big kid, as a flaky mix of dreamboat and beast. A collaboration between George Lucas of *Star Wars*, Terry Jones of *Monty Python*, Jim Henson of the Muppets – and David Bowie of David Bowie – it celebrates the importance of the imagination, and of finding ways to keep it alive with a mixing and matching of Wizard of Oz, *Alice in Wonderland*, Peter Pan and Grimm.

It all depends when you come across Bowie as Jareth in *Labyrinth*. If you see it at the right age, with an open mind, and no knowledge of who David Bowie is – so in effect, he is Jareth – then the effect is similar to coming across Ziggy Stardust. There's a bewildering sense of wonder. As Jareth, he's wearing the same sort of skin-tight tights stacked with very visible energy that made young boys – and girls – swoon in 1972, and singing some haunting songs about worlds that are falling down – and dancing, or moving around his self-consciousness – that can lead you into a secret retreat.

You are coming across pure, seductive Bowie, a believer in all forms of magic, taking his role very seriously because he understands the cathartic importance of fantasy, and illusion. He was intrigued by the idea of mixing creatures, humans and songs with a voyage through a dangerous maze, as if that is the essence of his whole life. He turned down the offer to play a Bond villain in *A View to a Kill*, the role that went to Christopher Walken as a watered-down version of the Thin White Duke: he knew this was by far a better villain to play, much more realistic for all the nutty hair and leggings, and he can stage-manage far more trickery and even wickedness. And Jareth makes better use of his malicious, weirdly spectral smile than a Bond villain.

For those older and apparently more knowledgeable of his ways it is too close to 'The Laughing Gnome', to *Peter and the Wolf*, and his sweet introduction to the *The Snowman* where he revealed himself to be the grown-up version of the boy in the animated film. This is the Bowie who had as a part of him the eternal family entertainer, the man who can appeal to every age group as more than just a rock star or even actor. He simply wants to get under your skin, perhaps just for the sake of it, to make him feel better. The believer in Bowie as a rock god or an ingenious and manipulative postmodern artist gets worried when there is this kind of suggestion that actually all he is doing is searching out what is ridiculous and laughable in humankind, committed to nothing more than encouraging us all to discover our own individual clown, the one that has grown up within us but that we ignore.

He is perhaps after all simply the mime artist, the court jester, keeping his own thoughts totally blocked off. He climbed into rock and made it his own with a few clever self-marketing psychodrama tricks, but at heart he is simply The Actor, sniffing out life's rules through self-serving spiritual quests, presenting possibilities in an ever-changing masquerade where no one role is more or less important than another. Another performance, another tent, another set of lights. The show must go on until there is nowhere left to go.

In terms of where people arrive at Bowie, so much had happened in the 1970s that some, locked into their age group and their generation, find it hard to imagine that for many, a first contact with Bowie is yet to come. They cannot consider a world where you don't come across Bowie for the first time as one of these 1970s inventions. But for those not yet in their teens in the 1980s, those not coming across pop music, they have yet to hear the name David Bowie, and yet to hear and see him. They have yet to have their moment. They have yet to begin making up their David Bowie, and becoming a part of their collaboration. There are plenty of Bowies still to come beyond the 1970s where people first found him, and he found them. All of them the same, however different.

For many, even if they don't know it initially or ever, Bowie as Jareth in *Labyrinth* is still the bi-Man Who Sold the World, Ziggy, still Sane, the Diamond Dog, the dissolving Berlin nomad, Major Tom the junkie, the radiant pop star, still that energy, or at least, it shows ways to find that energy, to begin a relationship with Bowie that isn't harmed by it beginning there. You find him, and you can feel him finding you, whatever it takes. 'Obey me', he says, 'and I will be your slave.' He is always playing an image of desire, on his way to capturing as many people as possible, as part of his quest to find a place to belong.

On the morning of my second day at the office – the chandelier opposite me now seeming to writhe and squirm as if it came to life during the night, when all was closed, and it is now settling down into today's frozen shape, different from yesterday, with perhaps some of its glass tentacles having stretched out during the night to make intimate contact with the Bowie photos hanging nearby – the first person to talk to me is on her way to a day of film screenings.

The films are all connected in some way to the spirit and history of Bowie, starting at a surreal eleven in the morning with Dalí and Buñuel's *Un Chien Andalou*, which Bowie used as the support act, or guest spot, on his 1976 *Station to Station* tour. Twenty minutes later, she will be watching Hans Richter's hypnotic avant-garde mixture of film and psychiatry, *Dreams That Money Can Buy*. At 13.30, the highlight of her day, and one of the highlights of her life – the first time she will see *Labyrinth* on a big screen, albeit in the Hochhauser Auditorium, a steep-banked lecture theatre buried deep inside the V&A a little like the permanently decaying black hole that is buried deep inside Dr Who's Tardis.

Only Bowie can take you from the diabolical slicing of an eyeball, via a favourite film of David Lynch about a man who has the power to create dreams and then sells them, to a slightly jaded gothic glitter goblin who juggles crystal balls, lives with talking worms and a pirate dog, and can shape-shift into a barn owl. Bowie lurks amidst Dalí the charming, opportunistic and surrealist showman/conman doubting his sanity, battling his own limits as a human being and possessing a weird fascination with Hitler; the slightly sinister, indefinite dreamer and salesman of dreams; and the mischievous, bullying clown toing and froing across psychic borders and weirdly expressing things through physical gesture.

The woman on the way to watch the films is another fan who found Bowie, and all that was on the other side if you kept going, through Jareth. She first saw *Labyrinth* when she was sixteen, in 2001, and it was actually her eight-year-old sister who made her watch it. Her sister loved the Goblin Battle, and had already been taken by the atmosphere that Bowie inhabited, and brought with him, into the film, and she used the word 'pierced' for when she first spotted Bowie as the all-powerful Jareth. 'His eyes!' she swoons, right in front of me. 'I was captivated.' She tells me how she appeared dressed as Aladdin Sane in a flash mob the museum had promoted on the Friday opening of the Bowie Weekend I now find myself part of. She came second; perhaps if she had come as

Jareth complete with what became known as the Bowie Bulge she would have won, but she seems happy enough.

She mentions how lots of people she knows either came to Bowie through 'Starman', or through Jareth. It seems to me it's the girls who found their Bowie through the Jim Henson film, and men who are now of a certain age and are vinyl wistful who found him as a starman. Jareth seemed to have been a way into sex for an entire generation of girls, and any others rendered speechless by a groin with a life of its own.

Because, as I am working, as an installation in the Grand Entrance, what I am writing appears on the large screen behind me, quite a few people are noticing that the word *Labyrinth* keeps popping up. They are drawn to the word, and all it clearly stands for, and appear to materialise in front of me, slightly reticent members of a cult less talked about and amplified than the cult that developed around Bowie putting his arm around the shoulders of Mick Ronson and the holier cult that developed around the 'Cygnet Committee'.

This brings forward more fans who found Bowie through the film, and this little form of informal market research confirms that those who discovered Bowie in the early 1970s tend to be male, and now made up mostly of memories, and those who discovered Bowie through the goblins tend to be female, and reticent perhaps because they are used in the world of forums to being slightly condescended to because they are more on the goblin in a silly wig side than the riff-mad spiders from mars.

One of this shy cult, wearing a Goblin King T-shirt, so possibly one of the leaders, tells me how she feels that some more hard-core Bowie fans are angry with those who followed the Labyrinth, viewing the symbolism, escapism and fantasy of that world as somehow inferior and tackier than the fantasy world that folded out from Bowie in the battered Britain of 1970s, because it was rooted only in its own fantasy rather than being connected to a real world, because it wasn't authored by Bowie himself.

The rock fans were perhaps disturbed and unimpressed by the fact that the pure, more anarchic idea of Bowie was compromised because it came packed inside ideas and urges associated with Henson's Muppets, the narrow-minded preoccupation with myth of producer George Lucas, and the crackpot post-Python zaniness of screenwriter Terry Jones. Maybe some of the cynics know that Michael Jackson was briefly considered for the role, and so Bowie was second choice. As I write this, the member of the cult, not so shy after all, returns, keen to make sure I take the telling of the *Labyrinth* seriously. I am now under its spell myself, and have spent all of Sunday morning following my own exploration of the Labyrinth. Perhaps this fan has put me under the spell, as she seems to know that I will still be writing about the film.

I can now ask her name: Rachel. Her timing is perfect. I am just writing about Jackson and Jones, and she can tell me that Jackson, and others such as Sting, were not seriously considered for the role, and Henson wanted Bowie, his fantasy of the perfect rock star, for years. He knew he understood how to play Jareth; it was about much more than just bringing in a rock star name. You had to be a genuine trickster as well.

She can also tell me, her fan knowledge now getting a chance to be fully released, to compete with all those stories about Bowie from the early 1970s, that Jones was taken off the film at one point because he was making it too funny, but Bowie was not as pleased with the script when the Jones elements were removed. Jones was asked back. She doesn't think that people consider it a funny movie, and doesn't think of it as scary so much as full of suspense. She thinks also that the songs were his best between *Scary Monsters (And Super Creeps)* and *1. Outside.*

For her, the appeal of the film was instant – the young lonely girl, Sarah, feeling estranged suddenly immersing herself in a fantasy world, with the mighty, unstable creator of the menacing Labyrinth needing her to believe in him, to give him the power he craves. She wouldn't quite put it like this, but there is no doubt that the rickety, appropriated levels of fantasy set up by Henson, Lucas and Jones and then amplified by the history and charismatic and shamanic sophistication of Bowie combined to produce something peculiarly intoxicating

Jareth's existence actually depends on Sarah; I am learning this about the Labyrinth, and the reasons why young girls seem so attracted to this creature and creation of Bowie's, which probably parallels the reasons why all those teenage boys became so besotted with Bowie in the early 1970s. It is about sexual fascination and transition, as much as those Seventies' teenage fans of Bowie, now grown up with families and lives more solidly rooted in reality, would prefer not to think of it that way. Jareth/Bowie gives you power even as he seems to be turning your world upside down and ushering you towards the terrific and terrible next stage of your life.

As someone now says, telling me about how her children at eight or nine are utterly entranced by *Labyrinth*, reminding her of the time she was, it is ultimately because Bowie makes the scary but not nightmarish Goblin King completely, darkly sexy, and you respond to that even if you don't understand that this is what you are responding to. He beckons you into this new world, and this world is sex – before you know what that means, the way there is shown to you.

After the showing of the film, someone, not a member of the shy cult, more someone who would remember Bowie in the 1970s, reports that his feeling was that Bowie had his tongue in his cheek, and was perhaps exploiting his experience as a manipulator of desires and dreams, having fun with playing the idea of old-time glam icon with a hint of resigned, roguish menace, and that it was just another way of finding something amusing to do in the 1980s, where he didn't feel he belonged. He referred back to his loved 1970s persona inside a children's adventure fantasy, repeating some of his old tricks without it looking like he was repeating himself.

The DJ in the Grand Entrance plays 'Five Years' by Bowie, and this makes me realise that in my world, in my bubble, I have two hours to finish what may be a book, or a 'book', the end of one world, and it might be time to start thinking about what the end might actually be. I have two hours ... that's all I've got.

Usually, when writing, on my own, there would be no contact with others. Usually, looking up from my keyboard after writing a word, or a sentence, or a paragraph, there would be no one standing there, either waiting to talk to me or just viewing me as an installation, or a museum guide, who can tell them where the bookshop is, or where the exhibition begins. I would look up, and nothing would happen. Here, in my temporary office, this surreal studio where I have ended up having a series of out-of-body experiences, when I look up, there is often someone standing in front of me, with a question, a story, a memory, or, perhaps, just a need to know where the toilets are.

Perhaps one of these people who sometimes surround me, not sure, like me, whether this is a book or a 'book', will give me a clue about an ending, whether there can be such a thing as an ending. All the way through the weekend they have been giving me clues about what this book is, other than being, essentially, a book about Bowie, about the *David Bowie is* exhibition, about reaching some sort of conclusion about what he actually is, or at least is not.

When I look up, break away from the words on the screen, because I cannot think of the next word, or know only too well what the next word is and cannot bear the suspense, there is someone to help me with my next thought, and the next word. Perhaps that is what this book has become, an unusual collaboration, between me, the writer – usually alone, in an unsteady relationship with my mind, and a dubious screen, with the content of whatever it is I am writing – and those who just happen to be passing by, and who just happen to have something to say that does have some relevance to what it is I am doing. These people, if they will forgive me for describing them as such, have a lot on their mind.

During the weekend, there have been those who have helped me with the next word, or thought, or story, those that have made the book become a lot more about the Jim Henson film *Labyrinth* than I imagined it would be when I started, those that urged me to write about less obvious Bowies, from periods and places not often written or talked about. There are those who talk of a David Bowie riding around on a pink bike in the 1960s delivering grass for a mate called 'hippie Jim', those that remember the Tin Machine Bowie playing a small venue in Liverpool in the early 1990s, walking out onto the stage and opening the show simply by switching off a fourteen-inch portable television that had been placed on a stool, those that expertly discuss a Bowie from so early on in the 1960s, he was seriously rehearsing the idea of being a blues musician, those that want to make a claim for the influence of Peter Hammill on Bowie, of George Melly, why does no one talk about that, those that met him on a plane, he was so lovely, those that want to talk more about Mick Ronson, or Angie, or Visconti.

A couple of hours left to go to solve the problem of the labyrinthine dream of David Bowie, and I haven't even got to the 1980s yet. There are those looking at me as I try to find an ending, standing in front of the screen, looking at what the ending is going to be. Will there be someone who is my saviour, so that when I look up, they give me the ending?

2.

I was a little stunned, as fan for over forty years and writer about him for almost as long, when I was asked to be involved in the Victoria and Albert David Bowie exhibition, even though at no point was it ever made clear if Bowie himself had asked for me to contribute, or it just seemed that way, because I wanted it to be that way, and fantasised like the teenage fan I once was and really still was that Bowie had himself requested my involvement.

I received a call out of the blue from Bill Zysblat, his business manager, who told me at the beginning of the call to sit down. I did as I was told, wondering for a few moments if I was actually in trouble about something I might have done but couldn't remember. Had I put some of his lyrics into an article and not credited him?

Bill asked if I would be interested in helping out Bowie. There was a project Bowie was involved in that he thought I might have some thoughts about. My first reaction was the cheek-reddening shock of a fifteen-year-old that Bowie had any idea who I was. I remember being shocked enough when he once mentioned the Fall, amazed that he knew of a group I saw play their first-ever show. That seemed close enough.

I was asked to contribute to the exhibition at a point when it had been in preparation for a few months. The implication never written down or specifically stated was that Bowie wanted to ensure that the exhibition didn't end up being too Hard Rock Café in the way it presented items, a display for decorative collectibles, memorabilia and the more obvious gold disc paraphernalia of rock and roll. It might be too Wikipedia in how it covered the story, a little too clear-cut and sterile, and it needed to be more, say, inventive, unstable, multilayered art happening than bolted down rock and roll groovy, fixated more on the imagination and how his worked than hanging guitars on the wall and dressing mannequins in costumes.

It was never denied or confirmed that he was pleased or not pleased with the direction it was taking or not taking, or whether he sanctioned the exhibition title *David Bowie is*. I never knew for sure whether he liked the title, whether he approved of the subsequent effect the title had on the shape of the show, supporting my own feelings that it should not be called, blandly, 'The Exhibition', or if he had read the manifesto I had written proposing the idea to the V&A, or even if he really cared.

I took his silence as a possible yes. Sometimes during the

production of the show his silence meant a possible no, but, it was decided, not in this case. His charm worked in mysterious ways.

The exhibition was something he particularly wanted to do, of more interest to him than a knighthood as an acknowledgement of his ideas and achievements from within the establishment. He was anticipating that this was the beginning of a way someone like David Bowie could continue touring the world as a living entity even after he had died.

The contents of his vast archive provide raw material for all kinds of biographical interpretation of his psychological energy and artistic ambition, so he was ensuring that the amount of work he had put into turning himself into someone you couldn't help but notice was not likely to be underestimated.

The exhibition contained hundreds of clues about who and what he was that should be satisfying to those loving Bowie because he was a life-changing sex-changing species-changing glam rock star determined to make an extreme impression but also to those intrigued if not entirely convinced by Bowie because he was a hyper-active self-assertive aloof overrated unashamedly pretentious performance artist with a potentially alienating even self-indulgent taste for the possibly nonsensical avant-garde. Each object, however small or boring seeming, had an important story to tell, all a major contribution to how the idea of Bowie is pieced together, not so much as a man, a human being, but as an aesthetic force. Each object had a physical place in the museum, but also a mental place in Bowie's memory, and his presence, selected from his own private church of Bowie, invited visitors to literally bask in his aura.

He was offering or encouraging the existence of his own alternative to the congealed, over-the-top, moonstruck and repetitive view of what he was, that it was all just about great riffs, quirky anthems, outlandish costumes, space age pizzazz, rock star pomp, cracked acting, arcane symbolism and crazy puzzles.

He was making a case that while to some extent he can be neatly fixed into scholarly gallery place, with the academic establishment equivalent of a lifetime's achievement award, the story was still moving forward, and changing, and always should. The history itself was still changing, and in his own way, he was ensuring that it turned out more as he would like, once he was more definitively from the distant past. It was all part of how he was taking as much control of his own past as he could so that it didn't get entirely taken over by those, lovers or haters, who could turn it into something he wouldn't recognise, or at least appreciate.

As the exhibition was planned, commissioned, designed, debated and built, there was no sign of him, no communication, but he was always on and in the minds of everyone involved, and the exhibition was both nothing to do with him, and everything to do with him, another remaking of the idea of Bowie, based on what others think, which in the end is what matters most as long as that thinking is based on his reasoning.

It is an exhibition about the momentum he has created over the years, founded on a collective response to his work that he to a greater and lesser extent continues to manipulate, and ultimately his contribution to the exhibition was to add unexpected fresh momentum by releasing of all things new music. He had timed the release of singles and an album to regenerate the reputation of David Bowie, so that this would not be merely a ceremonial exhibition romanticising a star in decline, a celebration of a grand, faded myth, the expected accessible arrangement of familiar image, effect and anecdote. He re-materialised as an up-to-date version, still in control as everything slips out of control, of the original performer that ended up deserving such epic, glorifying attention in the first place.

He did not curate the V&A exhibition, as much as the museum hoped he would, articulating his own restless, wide-ranging history from the inside, occasionally even turning up for in-depth meetings to check on the designs and take part in some general brainstorming. They were sure when they began their venture that they would get to work closely with Bowie, and a little confounded by his almost ghostly non-appearance, his lack of direct instruction, the constant no visits. Sometimes it seemed as though there was no Bowie there, just a space that everyone filled with their own ideas of who and what he was, inventing an idea of Bowie because somewhere there had to be Bowie.

In the distance, you felt the guidance of Coco Schwab, the last link with Mainman, his unshakable main supporter since the 1970s, but even that support and advice was delivered as enigmatically as Bowie's. The two stayed loyal to each other to the end of Bowie's life.

The exhibition was something he seemed not to be involved with even as he ensured it worked on his demanding terms – how to make something that by its very nature was nostalgic still seem to be about new possibilities and the creation of a future – which were never clearly stated and certainly never written down. This was how he would tour the world in the future: as an epic, mobile piece of history belonging in the great monuments of the world, which he turned into a theatre, filled with fantasies that he brought to earth and set down in the time he liked to mess around with, seeking the made-up worlds of the future, entertaining fans even as he confused and confounded others, incredibly present, completely invisible, perpetuating his myth wherever he actually was, or wasn't, in the world.

The curators were stunned, saddened, disappointed, appalled when it was made clear that it was me – a dull rock journalist, a mere critic, essentially yet another overexcited fan – who was going to be, as someone close to Bowie put it, 'Bowie's represent-ative on earth', or at least, his representative inside the V&A in partnership with his latest art director, Jonathan Barnbook. At my first meeting with the curators, Geoff Marsh and Victoria Broackes, it was clear they did not think they needed any help from a critic who thought he could work on something so tech-nical and demanding, and they were probably right.

Geoff, detecting that even in my mid-50s I perhaps still believed in Bowie, perhaps a little too much for the ultimately sober academic setting they required, asked why it mattered to me so much. I said something about how this was a fantastic opportunity to create a template for what was going to increasingly happen as rock music moved into history, this institutional way of remembering and presenting the ideas of the great, iconic performers and keeping the immediacy of their work in some kind of contemporary motion in years and decades to come without it being only about nostalgia and memorabilia.

Geoff didn't look too impressed with my answer, perhaps deciding, well, that was the answer of an ignorant critic with absolutely no idea of the complexity of mounting an exhibition in a historic building like the V&A.

In the end, we came to a compromise, the kind perhaps Bowie was hoping for between the undeniable honour of being set inside such a museum, and a hint, even a hint of a hint, of something that still subverted the idea, and treated it with enough irreverence for it not to seem like he had completely submitted to a rigid manifestation of the establishment.

Bowie's contribution was that he made available his personal archive, detailed evidence he kept about what he has been up to since he was a teenager plotting his escape from traditional, depressing post-war suburban limitations. The fact that he has kept just about everything from invoices, articles, sketches and blueprints to glitter jumpsuits and stage plans for arena tours proved how much he organised his own destiny and anticipated – willed into being – its importance. He was the first student of David Bowie; and, at the end of his life, as he contemplated his own life for the last time, coming to his own conclusion about what it had all meant, he was still studying.

The exhibition, the first of its type, because Bowie liked to be first at everything, was high on the 1970s and 1980s and edged close to being a hi-tech memorial acknowledging his time as both arena being and Berlin private investigator, as if this were Bowie's final act, the ultimate inventing of his past, which however quiet he became he was always working on.

In fact, the quieter he was the more he was working on his legacy, and working out to organise it from his perspective in terms of how he and it would be remembered. He once said the last song he would want to sing at his last-ever show would be 'Ziggy Stardust', which was the Shirley Bassey inside him, loving a perfect theatrical climax, but the last pieces of music and the last images he would want released would reflect more the still evolving, speculative artist, and be a reflection of what had happened to him as a thinker because of everything he had done, facing the moment when he would not be able to think any more. He'd thought a lot about what it would be like not to think any more. A lot of that thinking went into some of his greatest vocal performances; trying so hard to imprint himself so deeply into existence he could never be separated from it.

9

DIVINE SYMMETRY

David Bowie is a history of pop music

Taken from the 1967 David Bowie debut, Edwyn Collins's version of 'The Gospel According to Tony Day' declares it a better song than any on the Beatles album released the same day. Mercury Rev trip all over 'Memory of a Free Festival' from the planet-high second David Bowie album and, showing why the song made the world a stranger place, there's 'Space Oddity' by Natalie Merchant, Seu Jorge, The Langley Schools Music Project, the Flamin' Groovies or Tangerine Dream. From *The Man Who Sold the World* you're face to face with Lulu, Simple Minds or Nirvana for the title track, and Tori Amos cuts religiously deep into 'After All'. *Hunky Dory* becomes Streisand's satanic 'Life on Mars?', Shawn Mullins's sweetheart 'Changes', Stone Temple Pilots' darling 'Andy Warhol' and Dinosaur Jr.'s sunken 'Quicksand' and the Bad Plus make spontaneously natural Peter Noone's blank 'Oh! You Pretty Things'. Because *Ziggy* spawned glam and goth, there's Bauhaus for the title track, Culture Club for 'Starman', Brian Molko for 'Five Years'. *Aladdin Sane* is tenderly kissed by Bowie authorities Ian McCulloch, 'The Prettiest Star', and Morrissey, 'Drive-In Saturday', and from *Diamond Dogs* Bowie addicts Heaven 17 accompany Tina Turner the reigning acid queen on '1984' and Rickie Lee Jones adores singing 'hot tramp' during 'Rebel Rebel'.

Beck thinks about the greatest song of all time singing 'Win' from *Young Americans* and the Cure think the same thing with their version of the title track. Bowie wanted Elvis of Las Vegas to sing 'Golden Years' from *Station to Station* and make it his best song ever, but he gets Marilyn Manson instead. *Low* alone just for the group who named themselves Low, but then also Sea and Cake's sultry and Matthew Dear's seedy 'Sound and Vision' and the *'Low' Symphony* of Philip Glass. For *"Heroes"* the *'Heroes' Symphony* of Philip Glass, obviously Blondie v Nico, but then hear Robert Fripp, the man who played guitar on '"Heroes"', take it on and on with King Crimson, and TV on the Radio take it over. Billy Mackenzie cruises through *"Heroes"* singing 'The Secret Life of Arabia' and then arrives on *Lodger* with all the sleazy theatre of 'Boys Keep Swinging', passing by the post-punk swingers the Au Pairs, piercing skin with 'Repetition'. The neo-aristocratic 'Under Pressure' is turned by Xiu Xiu into a crumbled hymn. M. Ward goes no-disco slow around the trembling edge of 'Let's Dance' like he knows what the greatest song of all time is.

And then the posthumous tributes start to appear ... Hear Anna Calvi move all over the not-a-pop-star space of 'Blackstar' on Jherek Bischoff and Amanda Palmer's deeply felt *Strung out in Heaven* string quartet tribute to David Bowie, which also stars 'Space Oddity', with Neil Gaiman, 'Ashes to Ashes', 'Heroes' and 'Life on Mars?'.

10

LOOKING FOR CERTAINTY

*'In the 1980s, it was like people were adapting to a
new way of life, another level of society, coming to terms
with chaos being the structure of reality.'*

The musical momentum of the 1970s continues for a while,
spilling over into the first few years of the 1980s. The
Changestwobowie compilation commercially summarises his
1970s changes in 1981 and hastens the separation from his
contractual ties to RCA, and that evocative, spinning space age
orange.

His songs are already being loosened from their moorings,
and beginning their own individual new life, separate from their
original contexts and intentions – a ten-track compilation of
tracks fragmented into a new collage, so many sparkling fishes
out of water, so many examples of how glamour casts spells,
songs taken from *Aladdin Sane*, *Hunky Dory*, *The Rise and Fall
of Ziggy Stardust and the Spiders from Mars*, *Diamond Dogs*,
Low, Scary *Monsters (And Super Creeps)*, *Station to Station*
and *Lodger*, plus the non-album single 'John, I'm Only Dancing',
when Bowie beautifully managed to put getting the jitters and
seizing the moment into a song.

The genre of this music really should be Bowie, but the official
Wiki-labelling drily, dully needs to span art rock, glam rock,

funk rock, soul and new wave, the grooves he seemed to follow and set up but none of which really hit the target. It's all a part of what he does, but the terms are as useless as the ones used to chase Miles Davis through his amorphous musical changes. No mention of glam gospel, biosoul, interzone, sophistico or paranoid pop, which might get us closer.

The single to promote this collection is 'Wild Is the Wind', with Bowie confidently and not a little grandly playing the greatest ballad singer of his generation, with immense technical precision, an unnerving, inspiring power, and more or less saying goodbye to that particular role, as though he is making another more oblique retirement. Even in the middle of one appearance, he is enacting another disappearance, always flinging himself, and us, into and out of space. There is always more going on than the mere song. Even when he seems less active than the manic 1970s, he's challenging us to keep up with him.

Because he can't help himself, he will make a comeback as the greatest ballad singer of his generation in 1998 when he collaborates with Angelo Badalamenti who has been asked to select a song and singer as part of a centennial tribute to the songs of George Gershwin. Badalamenti is a classically trained musician who's arranged for Shirley Bassey and then became the bizarro alternate universe Weill to Lynch's Brecht when composing the music for David Lynch from *Blue Velvet* to *Twin Peaks*. Badalamenti chooses 'A Foggy Day (in London Town)', set in the fog that some still think was hovering over a quaint London in 1998.

Bowie hears the backing track that has been sent out to find a singer. He knows that foggy London from when he was a kid in the 1950s, the Clean Air Act having only been introduced in 1956 after the Great Smog of 1952. He knows the song has been sung by, among others, Fred Astaire, Frank Sinatra, Ella Fitzgerald, Billie Holiday, Doris Day, Shirley Bassey, Judy Garland, Petula Clark and Tony Bennett. Bowie wants to be part of that list, and make a reconnection with the London where he started his travels, and where he's now a stranger. He calls Badalamenti where he's working in a New York recording studio, and stakes his claim as the man to sing it. Badalamenti can't think of a reason why not. Hours later, Bono is calling to stake his claim. He's told the news. 'Well,' ponders Bono, 'he can sing good as well.'

Charles Mingus set out his own version of 'A Foggy Day' after the colossal opening piece on *Pithecanthropus Erectus* that helped stimulate Bowie's passion for the extended apocalyptic suite, so that side one goes from the rise and fall of man to the feel of a modern city, where life goes on. Mingus does it as a street scene with emphasis on radio-like sound effects, and sets it in San Francisco because he's never been to London.

Badalamenti with a sense of Mingus on his mind turns 'A Foggy Day' into a brooding suite with some musical additions of his own, and this could be on some imaginary compilation where it follows on from the savagely ravishing 'The Width of a Circle' that opened *The Man Who Sold the World*. Bowie is recapturing a London, now as much a figment of his imagination as Berlin, where he found out what it was to be lonely and lost, in a city that once threatened to totally absorb him. There's sunshine, though, penetrating the fog.

It's this form of unmoored, moonlighting performance that produces many of the great Bowie moments over the next couple of decades; he's completed one of the most intense sequences of albums there is in any form of music, at the level of Bob Dylan, and he's contributed so much of his life force to a collection of songs that have taken on a life of their own, and now the details come less rapidly, less fixed, in a non-linear, episodic, often non-musical way that we can now see heads all the way to his final album, his carefully controlled artistic and theatrical endgame.

He wasn't only made up of his great album period; even in the more fractured, less conspicuous years that followed, when his presence is often distant to the point of invisible, he is still working on what will become his legacy, even as he slips out of focus, and out of the way.

Other aspects of what he did took over from the constant release of albums, and collaborative albums, and the live albums and compilations. The 1970s were his album period, and during the next few decades there would be a constellation of mini-periods, a sequence of overlapping activities whether acting, play-acting, speculating, writing, guessing, reflecting and guesting that constantly generate and regenerate the momentum of David Bowie so that at the end of his life all that energy can be released.

'Blackstar' can follow 'A Foggy Day (in London Town)' on this imaginary Bowie compilation called *Our Play is Done* charting how he moved across a life of music into a ghost town of the mind. There are many songs where it could go next, but there's always '"Heroes"'.

Another lovely one-off, 'Absolute Beginners', released in 1986, set in another London hallucination, could also follow 'A Foggy Day' on this compilation as the song that in another dimension is as loved as '"Heroes"'. It has the same emotional power of a modern standard. At Glastonbury in 2000 he performs it between 'Life on Mars?' and 'Ashes to Ashes', three of his most melodramatic expressions of how he tells a story of a life in stories that always contain worlds of their own tinged with feelings of sadness and loss.

For a song embedded in what was regarded by some as his dark, hopeless period, in the middle of almost officially his two least-liked albums, it is in a formal sense one of his classics, one of those Bowie songs that lets the listener orientate themselves in his sometimes chaotic, untethered world. There is no chance of it being put inside inverted commas. In this song, he's absolutely sane, and he absolutely loves you.

It was written for Julian Temple's brave, doomed attempt to remake the movie musical for the MTV era based on Colin MacInnes's novel recording the impact of pop culture in 1958 west London, ahead of the swinging Sixties it anticipates arriving. This was when the word 'teenager' was not yet widely used, and was a very early look at recording a new world of modernity that was forming around youth and black voices and the anxieties around youth, race and nation at the time. It was published three years before Anthony Burgess's *A Clockwork Orange*, both books a reaction to Teddy boys and what was coming next, but was more a celebration of youth, their music and clothes, and the insider slang based more on the jazz and beat of the time is aggressively echoed by Burgess's more invented futuristic slang.

Temple's ambition was to transfer to the screen a mixing of the experimental and the realistic, the documentary and the dreamlike fictional without being particularly faithful to the more journalistic grain of MacInnes's book. To invent a territory where teenagers of the time were already being covered in the kind of glossy style magazines like the *Face* and *Blitz* that emerged in the 1980s.

Unforgivingly perceived at the time for its sloppy unevenness in the way it jumped from the serious to the playful, the comic to the tragic, and set its 1950s Soho inside a 1980s Soho, the film anticipated the logic-chewing, colour-saturated musicals of Baz Luhrmann. It also predicted how Quentin Tarantino would use music and song to distort time, place, genre and story in his worked-up cinematic love letters to movies. *Absolute Beginners* was over-hyped as 'the future of British cinema', ridiculed for what were seen as its excesses, and has never really recovered.

Bowie seems in yet another dimension performing the song, one he would rarely visit so unashamedly, where Bruce Springsteen and Paul McCartney take over from Lou Reed and John Lennon. It's as though he were able to conjure up, out of nowhere, a combination of studio experiences to produce a song that seems as experimentally put together as '"Heroes"', but with more orthodox results.

In a 1958 article, an early example of pop criticism, a stage before Nik Cohn, MacInnes was talking about how English pop singers – Tommy Steele and Lonnie Donegan – were gradually capturing a place in the pop market. Nearly thirty years later, this has led to David Bowie, with his own assured place in the pop market, reaching number 2 in the charts with a song for a film based on MacInnes's novel that had a few premonitions about the intense difference teenagers allowed to make their own choices would make to the world.

Written and performed with a group of musicians Thomas Dolby was using at the time, and produced by Alan Winstanley and Clive Langer with something of the melancholy tone they and Elvis Costello brought to Robert Wyatt's version of 'Shipbuilding', it is a tribute to the sort of emotional, uncomplicated pop music Bowie never got round to writing. He seemed set up to do so in the late 1960s; the 1970s, and all that, and his own hyperactive mind, got in the way. It's also an exercise in writing the perfect love song to be played over the end credits of a film and extend the fantasy for a few more wonderful minutes. A love song about a love song, about the power of film, where the singer dreams of a love song that can fly over mountains, sail over heartaches and laugh at the oceans. Bowie's still being clever, but also unashamedly comforting as well because not to be would mean it was a failed experiment.

He isn't faithful to the idea that the film is set in the 1950s but makes a mid-1980s-sounding music because when you heard music in the 1950s, you wouldn't think, that's 1950s music. It would simply be music from the present; the here and now MacInnes was very interested in portraying. Bowie captures the rough, splendid essence of the 1950s as he remembers or dreams it; where all the songs seemed about love, where the smooth brass of jazz still lingered in mainstream pop, where animated doo-wop was a perfect embodiment of the strange and the invigorating, where teenagers were new heroes in new, self-invented clothes escaping a dismal past and heading into the unknown. It's all filtered through his knowledge of what was about to happen, and the skill he has picked up at being able to express memory through melody.

The unnamed nineteen-year-old protagonist in MacInnes's novel introducing us to the alluring new subcultural world of London's youth would be about the same age as his extremely non-conformist half-brother Terry was when he was introducing Bowie to lesser-known sights and sounds, helping him enter new worlds and deep layers of history that might yet control and prevent madness.

Terry had been a patient for years at the notorious Cane Hill psychiatric hospital built on a hilltop near Croydon almost cruelly overlooking London, with its own ballroom, water tower and chapel – to create 'normal Sundays'. It was a home at times to over two thousand inmates. He was still stuck there by the 1980s, as the widespread use of these brutal Victorian-built complexes for the treatment of the mentally ill was coming to an end. He would be one of the last to experience such an enclosed, unforgiving regime in the name of healing – or hiding away – before those like him were tipped into the outside, often to fend for themselves.

A dismal, monumental place of suffering and endurance, it seemed long abandoned even before it was over a century since it first opened in 1883, finally shutting down completely in 2008. It is now a community of regimented Barratt homes known as Cane Hill Park. The asylum's motto was 'Aversos Campano Animos' – 'I bring relief to troubled minds'.

Forty-seven-year-old Terry, who resembled his half-brother enough for it to be noticeable to those that knew they were related, died in January 1985, a few days after Bowie's thirty-eighth birthday, completing a violent act of suicide he had rehearsed a few times. He scaled a high wall in the middle of a raging storm that led to a staff shortage allowing him to escape the asylum unnoticed. He made his lost way to isolated Coulsdon South Station, and laid down on the tracks in front of a speeding express train that was running a few minutes late.

Bowie didn't attend the funeral, explaining he was worried his presence might cause an inappropriate tabloid scene – the tabloids were on the case, sensing a problem that might crack the infuriatingly impenetrable Bowie wide open, accusing him of indifferent treatment, leaving his half-brother to rot while he gallivanted as safe, secure and rich rock star. Bowie sent flowers, adopting a line from the end of *Blade Runner*: 'all these moments will be lost, like tears that vanish in the rain'.

Bowie said at the time he sang the sonorous 'Absolute Beginners' that he wished he could be in this kind of love with someone, but there is definitely some love, and real loss, making it into the song. He's singing a song for Terry, who helped give Bowie his beginning.

Bowie is entering an alternative zone based on those turbulent late 1950s, imagining another world where Terry was fine, life was 'normal'. London was as open as it was petty and small-minded. A time and place where Davie Jones wasn't so savaged by anxiety that he too was living on the edge of reality, always on the verge of toppling into what was still called madness even in the early 1980s when Terry was still locked away, because there was no other solution.

He's singing a dream of the kind of less tense, less distressed music he might have made if he didn't have the shadow of Terry always there, the constant fear of losing control, of having to make a choice between staying with all the madmen or perishing with the sad men roaming free; this love song-loving Bowie was always there, among all the shadows keen on ruling, and ruining, his psyche, which is why there was always a big-hearted pop element lurking in even his more dark, savage songs. Here it takes over.

It is a sophisticated reading of the innocence of discovering love, film, music, life, travel, and there's just a hint around the edges of where all that romantic innocence can end up. It took Bowie eight years to make a more direct comment on suicide, of somebody, if not Terry, on one of those songs often described during this officially fallow period, as 'his best' since 'Ashes to Ashes', or 'Absolute Beginners', a 'return to form' – 'Jump They Say', from *Black Tie White Noise*. This single was another way in for many to David Bowie, their first contact, with an MTV-friendly Mark Romanek-directed video playing with various Bowie selves and shadows, and a vivid, abstracted solo by his playful, adventurous, equally as sly and restless experimental trumpet-playing namesake Lester Bowie.

Bowie, like Bowie, knew how to use the past to make a future. D. Bowie is using L. Bowie, a one-man history of jazz trumpet, to create a memory of his own way in to jazz, via Terry, in an early 1960s London where jazz music was making its way into rock through the likes of Georgie Fame, Jon Hiseman and Graham Bond, and changing British music.

There was some mostly tabloid disquiet that it had taken David Bowie so long to make any sort of artistic reference to the suicide of his half-brother. Speaking as someone who took over twenty years to make any direct reference in my writing to my father's suicide, first of all, eight years is not a long time at all. Secondly, the event, the change in your life, will always be in the work you do immediately afterwards, however much, coldly or not, cowardly or not, you push it away and do not seem to acknowledge it. Not long after Terry's death there is 'Absolute Beginners' – and his songs for *Labyrinth* – which suggests there was an emotional reaction, if not as cataclysmic or dramatically self-conscious as some might have expected. He always keeps his distance, and issues reactions to moments in his life he might use as material a few steps removed from the obvious.

Twenty years after MacInnes was discovering the early aspirational workings of the teenage mind, some examples of the teenager, now inventing themselves a long way beyond London,

had crashed hard against their own cravings to distance themselves from stale mainstream culture. The innocent good times
have been twisted into nihilism. The absolute beginners had
become the absolutely wasted.

The soundtrack to Uli Edel's raw, unsettling 1981 *Christiane
F.* reflects the years in and around Bowie's Berlin, as if this is one
sunken, broken place where the music belongs, where the ruins
aren't romantic, they're crash sites, deathtraps and graveyards.
Once Bowie's music started to be used in movies and television, it
gained extra new life; each song could start to change its identity
depending where and when it ended up, at what dramatic point,
in the past, present and future. Time is shifted and shuffled,
brand-new associations are made, Bowie keeps changing shape.
Bowie now begins to seep and flow far and wide in this way; in
how others use him and respond to him.

In *Christiane F.* music from the late 1970s is used as the
soundtrack to a film set in the mid-1970s, the desperate true
story, unsentimentally told, of a young West Berlin teenager
living in drab social housing infatuated, or infected, by the songs
and appearance of Bowie. She plunges into a surreal nightmare
of heroin addiction and prostitution at a time when the city was
at its most sordid and depressing. The history has it that Berlin
is where Bowie went to find an escape from his own addiction;
the musical representation of his withdrawal and deliverance is
used as a backdrop to a complete personal collapse, and a disappearance under the surface of a city of spirits and ruins that can
damn you as well as save you.

Christiane, innocent at the beginning, crashes vein first into
lowest-depths depravity. Bowie is featured throughout as a kind
of dream fix running parallel to the heroin; the two ways of
making a dismal, violent life more interesting or palatable. His
other-worldly image is scattered Che Guevara-like around the
streets and subways of Berlin, somewhere between Big Brother
and big brother. He's watching you. He's looking out for you.

He's embedded in the texture of the film, and he's being marketed outside it. The whole idea of Bowie is becoming something else; the *Aladdin Sane* flash, one of his most resonant veils, is already living a life of its own, becoming a signpost for a whole different way of thinking and remembering.

It's after the delicious rush of seeing Bowie live that Christiane first sniffs some heroin, 'just out of curiosity'. After this tumble down the rabbit hole, it's Alice in hell. This is the other side that Iggy went looking for during his Berlin period, the vice-ridden metropolis, human bodies jerking like lightning through the apocalyptic disco-rock night, downtown in the city of nightly neon ecstasy, while Bowie searched on two wheels for art, history and the route to a clearer mind, and conducted a rejuvenating undercover love affair with another shadow of his own being, another existential mirror he could check his own reflection in.

In the film, a gang of unruly teenagers run riot through a shopping centre to the sound of '"Heroes"', which is part of the story of the song itself as it travels upwards and onwards through different levels of perception and reception. You can place it in so many different settings, and it will shine with new meaning. It is made to exist in other places, and generate new responses; every second there is a suggestion of a new direction you can take into and from the song. It comes alive in the other Berlin of *Christiane F.* and adds new incidental atmosphere and feeling to the living essence of Bowie, and predicts how '"Heroes"' can flow into so many other surroundings and grow in power.

The combination of concert footage and a cameo from a larger-than-life Bowie and the ruthless documentary style coverage of heroin-taking made *Christiane F.* a cult film, and one of the most successful German films of all time. The savage reality of taking heroin to elevate or escape wretched existence is given a treatment mixing and merging the roughly glamorising with rancid, horrific desolation.

The real Christiane Felscherinow, who survived the carnage

portrayed in the film, remembered going to see the film in 1981, having been told Bowie and entourage would be at the showing as well. She takes a lot of cocaine to deal with meeting him, shaking when the car pulls up with him inside to take her to see it. A friend she brings along for support collapses as soon as she sees Bowie, although Christiane is surprised at how weak and insignificant he actually looks – 'like my father' – compared to the aloof, apart, pop star image.

In July 1981, Bowie records 'Under Pressure' with Queen, who had made pumped-up rip-roaring success out of the sort of framed, distancing theatricality that had once made critics suspicious about Bowie, and to some extent still did. Their mock metal could seem as mouthy but eccentric as Bowie's on *The Man Who Sold the World*. Together the two acts who love acting-up construct a song that doesn't relinquish the theatre and the posing, but instils it with a form of nebulous dynamic protest that assures the combination of camps doesn't sink under too toothy melodrama.

It's a luxury enhancement of the discophonic direction Bowie took on *Young Americans* filtered through the distressed spiritual nature of the Berlin years, with Queen playing the role of his band with ravishing studio-chiselled elegance, and Bowie playing the role of guest star with exhilarated panache.

Queen haters who were Bowie lovers were torn at the time, as the man who had just been *Low* and *Lodger* should not be singing with someone who for musical snobs, or realists, of the time was a corny pop music equivalent of Bruce Forsyth. But as *Low* as he'd gone, or perhaps because he's gone so *Low*, Bowie was never put off by the thought of some impeccable song and dance. Any chance to put on a show, with no fear of appearing trivial. Such a fear could hold you back, and separate you from the emotions of people.

Sometimes with Bowie, it's Bassey with Roland Kirk, for the sake of the 'what if'. This time it's Bassey with Presley, and it's no less a glorious 'what if'. The pair of them inspire each other to new heights of pure performance, which is all the song might be about – the competition to excel that Bowie always loved, never afraid of setting himself up with the best at what they do, so he can absorb some of their powers, even steal them, or just enjoy watching and learning from them at close quarters. Bowie had a much more sophisticated and flexible reading of the ultimate nature of musical integrity than the rock critics of the day, and knew exactly how he could reach people without sacrificing artistic substance. He had his own ideas where the boundaries of artistic taste were – pretty much anything but country – and resisted anyone patrolling them.

The music materialises under those studio circumstances emerging from improvisation and sticking together scraps of existing ideas that make it difficult to know who came up with what, but Bowie has something that he wants to say, and he's the one bringing the 'pressure' into the song. Or, it was Mercury who was feeling the pressure, or maybe it was all to do with the general sense of having to finish a song. But once you have that word, and the one that's put in front of it, the song can become a classic, spinning round and round the pressure, feeling tense, feeling relieved, feeling high, feeling higher. The pressure becomes a kind of prayer. Hearing the first notes appear in the middle of an innocuous daytime programme drifting along in the background will always put me on high alert, as though I am being watched, especially if I am late delivering a piece of work or a book.

Who knows whether the words are tossed together by consummate professionals as a way of getting into and through the song, with no real intention behind them other than giving Mercury and Bowie something to get their considerable teeth into, the perfect balance of syllable and attack, of rhyme and rhythm, or whether there is a real call to arms, a way of facing up to the darkening prospect of the Reagan and Thatcher years and a collapse of the counterculture that the clairvoyant Bowie can see coming in the way he saw the tensions of the 1970s coming. After the relative outburst of freedom, and then the kaleidoscope collapse, what next?

It's an example of the sort of energy from a combination of energies that can be generated in a studio context without any particular direction, which ends up working because the protagonists are at the height of their powers, and each and every one of their instincts for where the song should go and what it needs to achieve are perfectly in tune. It could end up as nonsense, as an awkward mix of styles and manners, but in this case the result is totally in focus, and the bass line is the perfect expression of this focus, the fluid, confident sound of an amazing temporary compatibility between minds, of a connection between the rapturous and the ominous.

The song is a fulfilment of that gift Bowie had for sounding joyous and uplifting while issuing a series of warnings about imminent collapse and disarray; taking pop and making it truly sing with a vague but transcendent, indecisive but precise power that can be interpreted in so many different ways, depending on the wishes, needs, experience, location, age and sensibility of the listener. It can also change meaning over time; make sense of different tensions and events that happened long after it was written, because it wasn't written about anything categorical.

Even if you're passionately in favour of Freddie Mercury and his combination of hard corn and euphoria, you would not have expected to see him make a move from 'Under Pressure' to Brecht, with Christiane F. and Bing Crosby along the route from one to the other. He is never caught between, or in, so many different worlds. No one travels like Bowie.

At the end of 1982, Bowie's duet with Bing on 'Peace on Earth/ Little Drummer Boy' is climbing to number 3 in the UK charts, coming up short behind Renée and Renato's 'Save Your Love', but having more enduring appeal. A few months before, Bowie is appearing as Baal in a BBC production of an Alan Clarke adaptation of Bertolt Brecht's subversive comedy *The Life and Times of a Man Called Baal*, written when he was twenty in 1918 and which he changed in the 1920s, as always seeking to increase the relevance of a work as time passed. It is early Brecht, when his life was hectic and full of furious imaginings. Having experienced indirectly fighting in the trenches of a world war and fighting on the streets, it was written when he was especially distrustful of all forms of idealism.

Clarke, at home with the traditional and the avant-garde, had directed British classics such as *Kes* and *Cathy Come Home*, and was a committed populariser of Brecht's work. He originally had his eye on Steven Berkoff to play Baal, but Bowie's reputation since his performance as *The Elephant Man* brought him to Clarke's attention. It was a perfect match, especially with Bowie's fascination for German expressionism, which Brecht was marking the end of. Bowie identified with how Brecht was interested in provoking an audience into new decision-making, a desire for further knowledge, and action. Bowie would also have been sympathetic to Brecht saying, not long after he had written his first version of *Baal*, 'But I keep realising that the essence of art is simplicity, grandeur and sensitivity, and the essence of its form is coolness.'

A bearded, banjo-clutching, intense-looking and very earthy Bowie is on screen from the very first frame. Baal is a lone, angry, messianic, adolescent and heavy-drinking poet idolised by his peers. It's Rimbaud the archetypal forever teen anti-hero, refusing to compromise whatever the cost in terms of personal relationships, public acclaim or physical comfort.

Savage symbolist poet Rimbaud of 'I is another' was ancestor of the beats and godless father of surrealism, the angry young man intoxicated with his own genius, content with nothing on earth or above it, fiercely dissatisfied with his experiences of time and sense. It's a dream of the post-adolescent insecurity tipping into fury and rage that's at the heart of the cliched bad boy rock star. Amoral, anarchistic, anti-authoritarian, anti-social, snarling hater of women but inexplicably attractive to them, Baal spurns and alienates everyone he comes in contact with, leaving destruction in his wake.

It's a long way from Thomas Newton – although they share the same passion for gin – but Bowie can take on this nasty, misogynistic monster, and give the role the same sense of inhuman, timeless detachment it needs; he is not theatrically immersed in the character, playing it as early twentieth century or even 1982; he is placing it inside the inverted commas he placed '"Heroes"' inside, and this gives his performance a different kind of immediate, dislocated power than if was performed by a more trained, conventional actor.

He's bringing rock star charisma into the role without drowning it in vanity or distracting trickery, and without the phallic folly – it's the spaced-out, ambiguous Bowie version of the rock star set deep into his own imagination who has no problem assuming either sex, so it has its own disassociated otherness that suits Brecht's early attempts at what becomes 'alienation effect'. Bowie plays Baal as much inmate in a mental institution as heady, big-headed rock star, and if he is a rock star, it's the rock star as a god of fertility, Baal the half-bull half-man-god focal point of pagan idolatry. He looks ready to bite the face of God.

It's a brave part to take on, because it is inevitably next to impossible to identify with Baal and his hard, rootless and rotten existence, but Bowie was never swayed by the idea he should choose sweet, lovable roles in order to please the crowd. He prefers adding uncomfortable texture to his image through the choice of unsavoury, unstable or deeply flawed roles. He's the great collaborator who also understands the benefits of collaborating with fictional characters who can give his image, and his own image of himself, extra complexity and additional allure. He teleports into other fictional spaces and stories; he's stepping through dreams.

Baal, however cruel and perverted the character, however dis-
likable, even repulsive, allows Bowie to have his own allegorical,
time-shifting punk years, and adds the depth and degeneracy to
his state of being that he likes in order to balance out the Bing
and Queen. He never stays in the light, he never stays in the
shadows.

He was, though, keen to say in the *Radio Times* about playing
the wanton and abusive rebel, possibly under pressure to cling to
some recent therapy: 'I think these days I'm a lot more optimistic
about the human condition. I think there is a resolute wave of
indignation building up in people to the conditions they've been
put in. I've got complete faith in the human spirit to pull ourselves
through. I don't think Baal has that at all.'

He recorded the five pieces of music from the production with
Tony Visconti in the same Berlin Hansa studio which Brecht's
music partner Kurt Weill used. Weill was an experimental crowd
pleaser fond of a high–low stylistic mix and heavily indebted
to Stravinsky, mixing baroque traditions, opera and operetta,
choral music and jazz into an exalted and mental dance music,
free, but tightly disciplined, with askew, mechanical rhythms
issuing a warning about Nazi horrors to come.

The genre is always hard to pin down, because the notion of
genre is one of those things Weill is considering in his music and
surreally reworking, which made it a big influence on Bowie from
1967 onwards – the mixing of a lyric with a style of music that
it doesn't seem to belong to, the constant but sincere adopting of
musical drag. Weill was committed to creating a 'new genre that
will deal with the utterly different expressions of life in our time
in an appropriate form'.

Weill was an entertainer, who didn't only want to write 'music
for the mind', but felt in 1936, with what was coming around
the corner that he spotted very early in Berlin, 'the stage has a
reason to exist today only if it aspires to a rarer form of truth'.
Bowie was always expecting that around the corner were dark

things, and that art could see it coming, and imagine solutions and conceive emotional resistance.

Bowie and Visconti modelled their *Baal* arrangements, instrumental textures and small theatre band line-up on Weill. Weill didn't write the music for this set of Brecht texts, but Bowie sees it as entirely reasonable to pay tribute in their musical organisation and atmosphere to him. Weill could be mentioned in the same sentence as Hindemith and Schoenberg, or as Cole Porter and Sondheim, even as though based on a shot or two of Louis Armstrong he has already heard Eric Dolphy and Charlie Mingus; a brilliant German classical composer who transformed himself into a brilliant Broadway composer, a strikingly original mind mixing and merging the theatrical and the orchestral.

Bowie singing these songs in this way throws light and meaning onto his more familiar songs. They become part of the way you can piece Bowie together, from across each area of interest, to create a picture of his mind and his way of working. *Baal* for instance is a way of joining *David Bowie* the first with *Low* and *The Elephant Man* with *Ziggy*, of The Visitor with the *Peter and the Wolf* narrator – taking what he does out of the time and place it is in and rearranging the order to connect moods, themes, theories and obsessions.

It becomes the *Baal* EP, another of these miscellaneous moments between the *Scary Monsters (And Super Creeps)* album of ceremonious conclusion, and the shameless, brightly coloured opening up of *Let's Dance*, as he runs out his RCA contract, and puts together in conceptual limbo an abstract sequence reflecting how far and wide his mind can roam.

These random, one-off asides, tributes, guest appearances, commercials, genre deconstructions and projects, a continuation of *Peter and the Wolf* and *The Elephant Man*, can mean as much as the main pieces in the long-term construction and maintenance of the multilayered idea of Bowie, and which actually look ahead to where and how he operates over the next few decades – where the albums will now become the asides to the more varied, unorthodox other work he does as actor, collaborator, observer and innovator in other, less specific areas. After the long 1970s, there is now a new way to track his thinking, set adrift from it simply being about albums, which become different sorts of projects, and which leads all the way to the staging of the finale after the *David Bowie is* exhibition.

In the 1970s he was entering and leaving all manner of men, women and creatures, minerals and mysteries, forces and fads, becoming other and another as if it was both easy and a disease, keeping secrets and spinning yarns, but even though what happens next is widely considered to be the end of such shapeshifting, he becomes among other presences, and absences, fictions, and spirits, 'heroes' and villains, real lives and dreams: Nikola Tesla and Pontius Pilate, Andy Warhol and the boy who knew and flew with the Snowman, the Goblin King and Philip Glass's first symphony, an Internet sailor and a Wall Street speculator even innovator, moustachioed hitman, cellist vampire, comedy foil to Ricky Gervais in *Extras*, himself imitating himself in *Zoolander*, Agent Jeffries in Lynchland and Major Jack Celliers in *Merry Christmas, Mr. Lawrence* confessing he wishes he could sing in the intense all-male world of a Japanese prisoner-of-war camp. Each role, each event, each aside and repositioning is in its own way as alive as one of his 1970s albums.

In the words for his songs, he established a zone all of his own that is not poetry and not song lyric but somewhere new between the two, and in his acting he occupies a different space as well, one he's always in control of however flimsy the film around him, locating an expression of character and being that adjusts the idea of David Bowie as much as a great song, video, or album. He can lose himself but still be himself, and he's clearly inside the Andy Warhol he brilliantly brings to flawed, fantastic real life in Julian Schnabel's *Basquiat*, understanding exactly how Warhol became a genius at drawing and generating attention for himself and others, and how he could both have feelings, and none at all, be caring, and careless.

It's all about Warhol, and you can learn as much about how Warhol operated from watching Bowie's combination of a loving impersonation, critical analysis and a vaudevillian send-up as from a biography. But you can also learn a lot about Bowie, his ability to turn a performance in the middle of a film into an isolated work of art, to be both an observer and the observed, the subject and the object, which makes him perfect to play Warhol.

He fills in the blanks of Warhol, with the sublime skill of someone who is always filling in his own blanks. He transmits someone who is both deep and shallow with his own expertise at merging the deep and the shallow. He knows exactly how to pin down a ghost, and exquisitely frame smoke, and register irrational single-mindedness as a kind of virtue. You're watching Warhol, but you're also watching Bowie, neither of whom in many ways actually exist, and one feeds the other.

He slips in full aristocratic drag into Martin Scorsese's dream-like and spiritual life of Jesus, *The Last Temptation of Christ*, as the enigmatic, shadowy Roman governor Pontius Pilate coolly cross-examining this shabby and deluded cult-leading revolutionary. He quietly tells Jesus, 'It simply doesn't matter how you want to change things. We don't want them changed.' Bowie plays a troubled, ambivalent human being who has become an invented myth.

Bowie's changes in the next quarter of a century are not about being the rock star; and sometimes they are. Everything, though, is connected, and it all becomes a part of the life of his work, which incorporates the textures and histories of those he plays, plays with and comes in contact with. It increases the power of the living, human thing his work is becoming, so that it necessarily includes unparalleled complexity that he brings with him from all the places and playgrounds he passes through – from the nice to the nasty, the charming to the cold, humble to haughty, political to inhuman, the tormented to the fun-loving, failure to swaggering, silly to transcendent, the normal to the freakish, the freaked out to the fearless. All those roles he plays, the way he deals with himself as a brand and an industry, how he presents himself through the media, it is all a part of how he anticipated the future in different ways to when it was solely musical.

As an image, a process, he continues; he pieces himself together in a different sort of way, using his own considerable past, and his very presence begins to permeate culture and collective memory in ways that wouldn't be obvious for decades.

In 1982, he's hired by odd film-making couple director Paul Schrader and producer Jerry Bruckheimer to write the theme song to *Cat People*, the follow-up to their first ultra-stylised collaboration *American Gigolo*. The intensely literate, speed geek Schrader wrote the screenplay for Martin Scorsese's *Taxi Driver* and later for *Raging Bull*; Bruckheimer saw Hollywood more as a system for generating power, fame and wealth. Bruckheimer packaged Schrader's obsessive, twisted reveries on violence, sex, fate, forbidden passion and the history of film itself as flash, trashy Hollywood treats overdosing on glossy style, so they were a hybrid of superficial hard-sell and crusading and/or campy intellectual pretensions.

Loosely linked to the original 1942 *Cat People*, it features girl and brother played by Nastassja Kinski and Malcolm McDowell with their own mix of the silly, the solemn and the 'are you sure?' turning into leopards when aroused. Schrader intended to link incest with fear of loss of virginity, bestiality, lycanthropy, and bondage and films the story as hyper-real audacious myth. Bruckheimer had to work hard to sell that. Where Blondie were hired as the fashionable pop finish for *American Gigolo*, David Bowie is hired as grand enchanter to sing *Cat People*'s theme. He wrote the lyrics to soundtrack designer Giorgio Moroder's luxurious, Euroamerican drum and synthesiser soundtrack.

The film begins like something from *The Man Who Sold the*

World; aeons ago when the world was a wind-blasted burnt orange desert littered with bleached skulls, and giant tree-dwelling leopards ruled the world, a few feeble, robed humans made a deal with the monstrous beasts. They offered their women to please the leopards. The leopards did not slaughter the women. They mated with them. The creatures created in this ancient legend live today as the Cat People. Moroder's theme plays, and Bowie doesn't fully materialise until the end, and has little to do with the film that's just played but plants an idea knowing in his own way it might light a fire in those who see and hear it.

It does light a fire. Another hyperactive, referential and reverential film student and idiosyncratic music fan Quentin Tarantino was disappointed by how the song seemed too good for the film, which even for him was too hammy. He eventually performed some shape-shifting cut and paste himself, placing it in his 2009 violent comic fairy-tale *Inglourious Basterds* haphazardly set in a fictional Second World War. He builds an entire, blazing twenty-minute revenge scene around it, something he claims he decided as soon as he saw *Cat People*. The reality of the Second World War is assaulted even more as a 1982 Bowie song from another film fantasy, and the wider fantasy of Bowie and his own re-contextualisation of time and place, allows Tarantino to go montage mad in a huge way and set logic, and history, and his own story, on fire.

He collaborates with his own version of Bowie by using a Bowie song in an apparently inappropriate way to pay gleeful tribute to how Bowie dissolved distinctions between high and low culture, and rearranged historical truth to suit his own play-ful and sincere artistic needs.

Bowie's spirit becomes mixed up in another highly distinctive work, part of another fusion of entertainment and hype, reaches another audience, but he does not need to make a direct contribution. This provides clues about the progress of Bowie through the next three decades, and how he saw his work as being a joint effort between himself, the audience and the unpredictable actions of chance. He didn't have to turn up as much as he had in the 1970s; and he could turn up in increasingly different ways. He alone knew where it might all be heading.

(Bowie songs in films, taken elsewhere, into other settings, because they can take the change, and be changed as they make changes, take Bowie the author and his audience elsewhere. These appearances, these indirect collaborations, are other ways that his songs are marketed, promoted and distributed, recreated and remade, their associations continually regenerated, intensifying their life force through their attachments to other fictions and realities whether they come during or over the end credits: 'Space Oddity' in *The Secret Life of Walter Mitty* and *Mad Men*, 'Moonage Daydream' in *Guardians of the Galaxy*, 'Let's Dance' in *Zoolander*, '"Heroes"' as part of a medley in *Moulin Rouge*, 'This Is Not America' from *The Falcon and the Snowman*, 'Young Americans' in *Dogville*, '"Heroes"' in *The Perks of Being a Wallflower*, 'Golden Years' in *A Knight's Tale*, 'Life on Mars?' and 'Rebel Rebel' in *The Life Aquatic with Steve Zissou*, 'Modern Love' in *Frances Ha*. His name and voice adds steel and weight to the most frivolous of projects. As his songs are used more and more in films and television there is a generalised production of his image that is beyond his control, and yet still within it. It's a part of how his work is becoming a consciousness of its own.)

In his words for *Cat People* Bowie uses the same thousand years to set the song inside that he used with 'Golden Years', which in Tarantino's cartoon Nazi world becomes linked with the Thousand Year Reich. Maybe that's how long the 1970s seemed to last in Bowie's mind. To some extent, they still weren't over.

He finally could step outside RCA, and into world-class major label EMI, for superstar money, and *Let's Dance*, his first album for his new label released in 1983, is consciously constructed as the smart, efficient work of a superstar singer with a superstar producer knowing how to play to a superstar audience.

Tony Visconti is ready to resume duties, but Bowie is coming out of Queen-land rather than Berlin and *Baal*, or even 'Ashes to Ashes', which provided one myth-making finale to his 1970s, and to a study of sadness and dread that threaded through his songs. He's coming out of *Cat People*, which, as much on the basis of Moroder's methods, was an American hit.

The other member of the spiritual power trio, Brian Eno, made *My Life in the Bush of Ghosts* in 1981 with David Byrne, two comedians in the guise of straight men having the time of their lives, broadcasting flat-out American craziness from the thundering depths of the African jungle, conjuring up a world where the Middle East was at the centre of civilisation and the West was a strange freak show in the eerie, fading distance.

Nice work if you can get it, but Bowie has been talking up optimism even when he was sinking into the mire of *Baal*, and he made a darting visit on *Lodger* to the imagined lands and intertwined cultures Eno and Byrne are exploring which satisfied immediate cravings. The alliances with Queen and Moroder have challenged him to see what happens if he consolidates his position as central pop visionary. Perhaps Freddie showed him the size of his latest royalty cheque.

It's time for a change of direction; he has done the juxtapositions, he's had the total freedom to find himself, he's escaped the shadow of Defries, Angie of the early 1970s has gone and now he has to shine a light on where he has ended up. Look, I'm alive, I've made it through. I've escaped by the skin of my topsy-turvy teeth, and now I am someone again. It's time to work with someone new. There's something about a fresh start; another chance to make an impression, another chance to take on the world.

Even as it appears he has a difficult 1980s, he is still making fresh starts. Then again, looking at it from a different direction, *Let's Dance* is more of a conclusion to his run of 1970s albums that began with *The Man Who Sold the World*. He puts a glowing exclamation mark at the end of the run, and ensures, for financial, conceptual and ego reasons, that he will be now be thought of internationally as a rock star. It will trap him as the singer David Bowie, but free him up as the artist David Bowie.

He decides Nile Rodgers is the man for this job. For Bowie, the more experimental thing to do, now he's left behind his student years and reconnected with the music industry, is collaborate with a producer who has not yet established superstar credentials, but, Bowie knows, soon will. After all, he will teach Rodgers as much as Rodgers teaches him. Rodgers plus time with Bowie equals, a year down the line, the smartly packaged Madonna's *Like a Virgin*.

Rodgers had been one of the masterminds behind discotopian dreamers Chic and Sister Sledge, who wouldn't give up their music not now no way no how, generating cool, calm and collected disco anthems with New York style. Disco as power generated by outcasts, the overcoming of persistent social borders, celebrating love, dance, escape, party, good times among bad, an expression of a desire for different sorts of people to come together. Disco had died of its own disease by 1983, but only the name. The inventions and social forces that led to it continued in other places and guises. Bowie, out on his own, had already given it mutant form throughout the late American to Berlin years, with the central rhythm section maintaining dreamlike, and murkier, links with modern dance music however far removed the overall form and structure went. Bowie was always mod enough to need flawless, scenic groove.

Disco died, and then there was the afterlife. The Sugarhill Gang rapped over a sample of Chic's 'Good Times' with the bass line that became a celebrity, and it started to become hip-hop. As house it got abstracted and stripped of the lush. It also developed as a commercial proposition, part of all kinds of new overlapping interchanging hybrids where boundaries could still be pushed.

'Let's Dance' is a deluxe fantasy of the mainstream potential of pop music, the latest knowing refinement of where the fluid crossover between black and white has reached, designed by two practitioners who slip and slide between the two forms as if they occupy the same territory.

There is nothing downright alien, there is nothing fishy, the music is not pitched at an oblique angle; there is no explicit sign of a consultation of the Oblique Strategies, unless the cards said make it more sensual, don't be frightened to display your talents, don't be afraid of things because they're easy to do, don't be frightened of clichés, make a blank valuable by putting it in an exquisite frame, try faking it! There are different ways of achieving a masterpiece.

What Bowie hadn't done since his early 1970s success, oddly, was make an album as a singer being produced, actually allowing himself to be treated as an object that someone else can turn into the fantasy. He's still co-producer, he's still the auteur, but his main role is to become the artist being produced. He allows, within reason, Rodgers to make the model, the sonic image, and Bowie does nothing to scare him off.

It's a follow-up to *Young Americans*, perhaps a version of the one record company executives might have expected instead of *Station to Station* and definitely what they wanted as a follow-up to *Station to Station*. It's an idea that he had perhaps incubated for years, and not wanted to do while he was still supplying Defries with more bonus royalties, or because the pop environment wasn't in the right shape, or he wasn't.

But then, his mind wasn't running in chronological order, as though he already knew that eventually people would make up their own running order, their own story and biography. At this point in time, this was the perfect album to make; he would claim the same even for those that many would rate as his least successful, for those that seem like afterthoughts, or stopgaps.

As with *Young Americans*, conceived at the beginning of

disco, it seems he's taken off the mask, and announced 'This is me', but this is still another mask, it's still strategic. He's still getting inside the head and skin of someone else, and speaking just like them. It's still about adventure, a love of chance, and a pure desire for intensity, still removed from so-called life, still a manipulation of himself as a work of art, but rendered with the help of Rodgers as the most accessible, untwisted pop he's ever done. It's so much on the opposite spectrum to *Low* it could have been called *High*. It didn't mean this was what he was; this was where he was at the time.

He wasn't ready to establish any kind of continuity in 1975, and needed a considerable detour before he's ready again to take on a hybrid of black dance music and his conceptual pop, and a structured, uptown early 1980s update of the early 1970s Bolan boogie. Dance as the simple solution to the deepening problems of the world and the mind and our powerlessness faced with the irresistible forces of law, celebrity, war and unregulated capitalism.

If he's feeling disconnected, he sure knows what to do. Shake it. Let's dance to the song playing on the radio. The fact that the first two words you hear in the title track is 'let's dance' from the absolute master of an opening line to a song says it all. No messing; here's the invitation. He smuggles his darker, more playful mentality into the party in discreet ways; in how he sings the two words 'serious moonlight' as if he's just smoked a cigar with Presley and Nietzsche.

At the time – let alone in 1975 – it was still unusual for a so-called rock act to dabble with what seemed the shallow world of disco, or dance. The two sides hadn't yet fused as they would so definitively by the end of the decade. In the margins, exploratory white musicians flirting with funk and dance could seem a little militant; for an expensively sponsored rock star it could seem like mere indulgent tourism. Bowie remained the hybrid of explorer and tourist, of historian and futurist, taking from and re-staging whatever enigmas and events had fascinated him since he first started listening to pop.

He shows Rodgers a photograph of Little Richard in high-living red-suited action from the 1950s as part of his brief for the album, and Rodgers, being a thoughtful, surreal marketing man himself, gets the point, and understands the aim of the project. Create a product from the past that seems like it came from the future, or vice versa, and create a soundtrack for the point where one meets the other.

It's still a placeless place, rooted mostly in Bowie's imagination, as much as 'Space Oddity' or 'Subterraneans', but it is meticulously organised, and Rodgers gives this fantasy a hard-edge, lucid modern radio-friendly sound. Bowie keeps his side of the commercial bargain by carefully staying within certain accessible limits when it comes to detailing the grooves and tunnels of his mind, articulating an unsentimental optimism, effortlessly recording intense moments of emotion. The plastic soul of *Young Americans* is perfected, he doesn't have to rely so much on metaphorical bravura to compensate for the lack of more conventional methods of persuasion, and he has his eye on a wider audience, without proclaiming new direction, new style or new manifesto, simply by being Bowie, pop star, here in the now.

Bowie and Rodgers hit their target. It gives America, especially, the image of a charming, eccentric British rock star they could commercially cope with, conservatively decadent, nicely aristocratic, absolutely not fretting about the end of the world. He completes his extraordinary tour of duty that began in Haddon Hall and ended up slap-bang in the middle of MTV, even if some consider it was all over after the first three tracks, 'Let's Dance', 'China Girl' and 'Modern Love'.

To many, those born after his debut album who come first to Bowie through *Let's Dance*, and the big-time Serious Moonlight Tour and sunny Australian videos that promote it, this establishes their central idea of what Bowie is, a more or less middle-of-the-road singer very adept at appealing to the mass audience with hints of a kinkier range that never really makes itself felt. If anything a male Madonna, sometimes as efficiently blonde and bouncy, perhaps a part of some British equivalent of the Rat Pack with Mick, Freddie and Robert Palmer, even Phil Collins.

The goofy, dad-dancing duet he does with Mick Jagger in July 1985 for Bob Geldof's Live Aid will consolidate this particular radio- and MTV-friendly Bowie. Their loving, high-living version of Martha and the Vandellas' once moderately incendiary Marvin Gaye-written 'Dancing in the Street' now turned into souped-up cheerleading song for the entire world was recorded in four hours during the 'Absolute Beginners' session with Langer and Winstanley.

After his dalliances with Lennon and Mercury in the exotic, exclusive country of fame, here he is sparring with Jagger to see who wins the battle of the stars as if he is on a cruise through the main tourist sites of pop culture, having preposterous experiences only he can gain access to. It's another thrilling sense of connection for this Bromley boy to the cultural energies of the world.

Duetting with Jagger was some kind of dream destination, but this is not Honky Tonk Stardust. In the equally hastily knocked together video they wear floppy 1980s versions of the dashing Mr. Fish daywear that caused such a fuss in the late 1960s. They play a sweet game of chase in and out of an abandoned building, with what is a combination of mild sexual tension and well-disguised embarrassment. You might be able to predict that Jagger could end up here even after singing 'Brown Sugar' and 'Ruby Tuesday'; it's harder to imagine this is where the Bowie of 'Quicksand' and 'Warszawa' will end up, even after the mating with Mercury.

Their energy is adorable, and does the job. It's for charity, it's number 1 for four weeks during the summer, reaches number 7 in America, and it becomes a party favourite.

For those who only know Bowie this way, as a smiling, dancing, very clean and willing-looking member of the ageing rock
establishment, it will be a surprise, even a shock, if and when
they find their way to other Bowies, later and earlier, stumbling
across a stray example of another time, another face, piecing
together their own chronology, finding what he's done with madness, drag, 1984, Berlin, Burroughs, space, and his vivid dreams
and personal fears and fixations. When Kurt Cobain first hears
'The Man Who Sold the World' on the radio, and can't wait
to find out who performed this song, which sounds too madly
modern and too much from a dream to belong to the late 1980s,
he refuses to believe it is the same singer he's seen merrily skipping around and shaking butts with Mick Jagger.

After *Let's Dance*, it's no surprise that finally the inspiration, the
locating of new experiences, dried up, at least when it came to
making whole albums. There's a collapse, after all that moving
on and around. There was the unloved, distantly twinkling
Tonight and *Never Let Me Down*, as though any featured new
character was based on the phoniness of the yuppies, on the
polite, or desperate, idea of satisfying his legion of welcome new
fans – potentially easily distracted by other singers – by sticking
around for while at being vivacious, light-hearted blond pop star.

There are financially focused, stadium-sized expressions of
sheer (will) power, and then he seemed to be withdrawing from
the grand, busy pop stage, now crowded with others trying out
ways of stealing, combining, remixing and styling themselves on
the way to either mind-changing originality or mere displays of
fantastic, conniving and financially rewarding energy.

He'd planted a constant stream of songs, albums, hits, stunts,
faces, blueprints, dares, claims, diagnoses, collaborations, projects,
fictions, quotes, spectacles, dramas into the twentieth-century
entertainment landscape like they were sculptures, installations,
exhibitions, advertisements or commandments. He'd thought of

the self as a set of pure improvisations from one minute to the next. He'd not finished yet, he was still in the picture, but all around him the world had if not caught up with him then caught on, and MTV was one punchline to his recent transactions, Boy George, Morrissey, Pet Shop Boys, Prince, Michael Jackson and Madonna becoming others, among many others. There was competition for attention. To quote Stravinsky quoting Jimmy Durante, everyone was getting into the act. He'd done extremely visual music before there was MTV, whether it was song and dance or charged with a surrealist spirit; in a way he helped lay the ground to make it a possibility that there could be non-stop music videos giving pop music a different image-based energy.

He distantly observed and mirrored – sometimes projecting his credentials, voice and star presence inside – the very scenes, crazes, personality disorders, glitz, programming and movements he originally provoked. And if he does try to take part, he is drowned out by the amount of music, the amount of artifice he has inspired. He's elbowed out, like he was when he began; working hard, but finding too many others in his way. It offends his imperial sense of entitlement. He leaves that stage as quickly as possible.

He perhaps selected the Oblique Strategy card that said 'Do something boring', and decided he was tired with all his faces, voices and legacies. Perhaps, if he was in some ways back to square one in an unforgiving world he helped fabricate, he reverted to what he did in the 1960s, which was find a group, and simply become their pragmatic lead singer, and try to find the new slipstream without sacrificing his own dignity.

He hid in deadpan plain sight as a self-conscious no one special inside a quotidian art rock group, Tin Machine featuring David Bowie on plain, just-doing-my-duty vocals, Reeves Gabrels on guitar, Tony Sales on bass and Hunt Sales on drums. For many, Tin Machine didn't seem to have a heart, and they laboriously soldiered on for a while, as if this was a critical commentary on some of the more automatic, regimented elements of the decade.

New music for a dull world. Go through the motions. Get lost.

Or: Follow the trend for guitar noise and words about personal and universal crisis that come in code; if there had been a noise revolution in rock in the 1980s as symbolised by Sonic Youth, he'll take that as the 1980s equivalent of the 1960s R & B he was once flirting with as just another face in the crowd. Perhaps that was where the young were looking for the blurred, blurring world between the real and the surreal; maybe this was the new psychedelic, where the loss of innocence/coming of age now was. He could do that; perhaps they could do with him. Maybe he thinks he's found the perfect new scene: dissonance and structure, the mutability of bodies, opening up the channels between paranoia and identity. He can do that. Maybe it was his response to Margaret Thatcher saying 'there is no such thing as society'. Something repetitive and reductive in the face of cold, relentless political mechanism.

Perhaps he was making himself as blank as he felt. Climbing inside the Machine for safety. Cutting his way out of an old identity. Being seen to do something, but just trying to make it through to the next stage, whatever and wherever that was. He talked of the 1980s as being a time of numbness – even if it was just his own – where people were coming to terms with chaos being the basis of reality.

Tin Machine was his numbed reacting to this numbness. It was a kind of camouflage, a movement made up of no movement, but which was all he could do under the circumstances. Some of the reaction to the group is extreme, as though Bowie, now he's stopped apparently being the Bowie some thought he was, is coming out as a sort of fraud. Surely he was suffering from a light concussion. Later he would suggest that as soon as he hit forty in 1987, right on cue, he had a mid-life crisis.

Tin Machine in particular were a form of collapse that confused and disappointed people, winded by how he had seemed to wilfully make himself an ordinary member of an ordinary band who were following not setting a trend. It seemed to contradict the very essence of Bowie; but that was a Bowie they had made up in their own mind, which they couldn't have made up without him doing what he did in the first place. If he had nothing to say, he still wanted to say it in his own way. If it was an update to where he had been in the 1960s, on the outside of where he felt the action was, not being able to break inside, because it wasn't his decade, at this point it seemed like he might not have another decade where he would belong.

The album in 1992, *Tin Machine Live: Oy Vey, Baby*, with a title response to U2's *Achtung Baby*, as awful as his pre-Spiders from Mars group names, sealed off the much-derided Tin Machine project, where it seemed an engineered version of David Bowie had been co-opted by a corporate entertainment state ordering him to make efficient, macerated sonic works of art that have no point and yet throb with strict purpose. He wasn't being inspired by William Gibson; he was disappearing into one of his stories.

There was the flicking off of various switches, the showing of respect for the limits of the imagination, a moving enough hint that everything is a process without end. It was a very different way of challenging himself from ten years before, but then so it should be. It wasn't the diminishing of radical powers that is the typical assumption of the ageing artist, and especially the ageing rock star. He was being expected to repeat the riffs and novelty, but he knew that to continue in the same way would have looked as unexceptional as Tin Machine, but more poignantly the act of a has-been.

It was impossible for Bowie to make a *Ziggy* or a *"Heroes"* or a *Scary Monsters* even if he had made the equivalent-sounding collection filled with equally sounding songs, because he was older, with other things on his mind, because rock was a very different place, it had settled down, and there was no place for the equivalent shock to the system, only versions of them, and replays, by those more interested in the business of rock than the art. He could never again be emblematic of the times in the way he had been, to the frustration of certain fans. To those who wondered why he wasn't writing songs like the good old days, he replied in 1995, 'In 1972, "Starman" was a shock. Everything is now a known quantity. Anything now is merely another colour in the tangled network of information that we exist in now.'

His albums in the 1980s were as ahead of some of his other records because they were already from a future world where rock and pop would become the establishment; there could be very few moments as artistically dramatic in the mainstream, only commercial recreations of the artistically dramatic that were almost immediately co-opted by the mainstream. The revolution was over; it was the era of evolution, adjustment and the beginning of a post-vinyl momentum that would stretch to when music went digital, and it could all happen at once.

Some consider what happens next to Bowie as rock musician a kind of abandonment compared to his 1970s work, a desertion, even a sign of artistic impotence. His relative inactivity though is the natural extension of where he has just been, placing in the inverted commas of *"Heroes"* the idea of the work of art, of the modern performer, of the way a rock performer grows old. His mind doesn't slow down.

Suggesting he was never again as good as he had been was a very rock way of seeing and judging things, and ultimately he was not a rock musician. Or not only a rock musician. He used rock as part of his performance, incorporated the processes, schedules, media, but he was so many other things as well, which is what made him so different. He was a performance artist more than a rock musician, an actor who had presented himself as his characters in the real world, breaking away from the fixed stage onto stages of his own devising.

As he made a series of records that faded into the rest of the pop world either as pop successes or relative flops, becoming simply part of the parade, there was no sense of what he should and could be doing from the disappointed or underwhelmed, only what he was not doing. Even a new kind of Bowie could not have had a similar impact as both pop star and provocateur; in the MTV and compact-disc era, there were new stars as influenced by Bowie as anyone else as visual conceptualists and musical dramatists, but the finished product, the eventual impact, could not be the same. The music was not as charged and reactive as Bowie's and the context, the times, had changed. Tin Machine were a symbol of the breakdown, into a world where rock was ordinary, obvious, non-subversive, bland, however noisy, violent and superficially galvanic. Bowie was still on the pulse of something, but this time noting and reflecting a different time, both for him and pop music. By its very nature it had to be predictable, even if Bowie being so predictable was in itself not something anyone saw coming.

He finds the love he seemed to be hoping for in those unguarded love songs, vivid contrasts and warm melodies of 1986, meeting 35-year-old Somalian entrepreneur, activist and first black supermodel Iman Abdulmajid in 1990, previously married to American professional basketball player Spencer Haywood.

Someone who in her own right is distinctive and famous enough to be generally known by her first name, she was described by Yves Saint Laurent as his 'dream woman'. She's got an agile, challenging mind, speaks four languages, and gets under Bowie's skin, into the spaces in his brain and body craving something other than being David Bowie having to be David Bowie, where there is still, patiently waiting, aghast at some of what he's been witnessing, a Davie Jones. She also gets onto his skin, a tattoo of her riding a dolphin on his calf with the serenity prayer underneath, from one of his drawings. There is no doubt in a Bowie world where there is usually always doubt: he absolutely loves her. 'You would think that a rock star being married to a supermodel would be one of the greatest things in the world. It is.'

David Bowie breaks up the band, but not before he proposes on stage in Paris and gets publicly married to Iman in a ceremony in Florence perfect for coverage in *Hello!* magazine like he's been getting wedding planning advice from Rod and Mick. (Iman uses *Hello!* to make statements about her life, her way of keeping secrets, hiding her real life behind the gush and gloss.) This pushed it beyond doubt, or played with those who were doubtful, as, for a wedding, it had a postmodern quality. Guests included Yoko Ono, Bono, who was late having missed his flight, and Bowie's mother, Peggy. Once he is married to Iman he becomes closer to Peggy until her death in a St Albans nursing home in 2001.

Brian Eno, who also attends, makes it part of an illustrated lecture he delivered at the Sadler's Wells Theatre in 1995 entitled 'Perfume, Defence and David Bowie's Wedding'. Eno admitted he wasn't sure if the wedding was for the readers of *Hello!*, or for those who were attending. 'It was lovely,' he concluded, 'and I was totally confused.' (In April 2016, as the last track of his latest record *The Ship*, Brian Eno sings 'I'm Set Free', a song written by Lou Reed from the third Velvet Underground album. He hasn't sung a pop song in such a way since the 1970s, and the song becomes a sensual spiritual, as much a secular hymn as the song he wrote with David Bowie, '"Heroes"'. He said it was a song he had wanted to cover for twelve years, but never found the right place for it. He sings Lou Reed, whose group the Velvet Underground showed both him and Bowie that you didn't have to be a musician or an artist, you could be both, conjuring up ghosts from his own past, and from Bowie's. He places the song between Brian Wilson, Roy Orbison and Kraftwerk and his own ambient music, and it seems clear there is another reason he is singing the song.)

Bowie finds a new enthusiasm for making albums under his own name, as though Tin Machine did their job as rescue vehicle and carried him to a new shore. He doesn't seem to have been there before, but he finds his own footprints, and signs of his previous life scattered around like ruins from other ages to decipher. He begins to look to his own past to make up a future, but not in ways that will see him go glam. He begins to rewrite his own traditions, remake his history and revisit his collaborators, and somehow glance ahead to the kind of music he would make in years to come, a process that will carry on until his last album; after Tin Machine there's a new album period, but one that accepts his new position as being less vital, less required to be so damned in and of the moment. He starts to make his own moments inside his own world, and make plans outside for a future he sees before many others where being a rock star will be as common as a tin of soup.

He makes an album of songs based on music he had written for his marriage ceremony and comments on the idea of partnerships, including the one with Mick Ronson, who would die the year his eighteenth album *Black Tie White Noise* was released (1993), the one with its producer, Nile Rodgers, and the abstract ones with Scott Walker (teacher), Morrissey (protégée), Madonna (copyist) and the house music that had emerged from Kraftwerk colliding with black underground club music, and therefore the traditional, troubled alliance between black and white music. There's also the loose partnership with Lester Bowie reactivating the jazz that has always been a part, however silent, of the way he approaches his music.

It's an intimate, intricate gift for his new wife, a complex exploration of race relations and fusion music, a record about energy – creative, conceptual and cultural – and it recaptures the forward-looking album energy that the 1980s engulfed. It didn't become a clear comeback, or a glowing relocation of cool, or a definitive new 'debut' – it acted as a clarifying fusion of the cryptic, doubtful 'Berlin' Bowie and the commercial, comforting *Let's Dance*, as if he was now following up earlier albums not only one at a time. The general, rock, view was that Bowie certainly had not run out of ideas.

Those looking for Bowie's best work since the 1970s, since 'Ashes to Ashes', since *Baal*, were looking in the wrong direction. It wasn't going to be like the music of his past. It was going to be more like the music of his future.

Perhaps the final decade of the twentieth century is where he was blankly staring at from the cover of the *Space Oddity* album, when it was difficult to work out what was real and true. He doesn't invent any more new genres – the ones he helped invent themselves spiral off into new genres, so he can claim an interest in those, and whether it's lad-locked Britpop or instrumental electronic music, Bowie's a prime source – but he's still alert to changes happening around him, because of him, and working them into his own new music. The one man many is reborn, if less lauded.

On 1995's dense, demanding *1. Outside* he plays evidence-gathering Holmes to Eno's chance-arranging Watson trawling for clues in a multilayered mystery about the murder of art, or art as murder, or the murder as art. On *1. Outside* and the avant-nostalgic soundtrack to *Buddha of Suburbia*, he strongly suggests he prefers his own music when it juxtaposes meted-out atmosphere and an attack on continuity with strange domestic beauty, more space-shifting *Berlin* than space-age boogie. He prefers his music to exist in a state where it seems to forget the time around it. The more it can do this, he thinks, the longer it will last.

1. Outside is numbered 1 because it was intended to be part of a five-album series that reacted musically to what was happening at the end of the millennium. It was the Bowie and Iman wedding that got Eno and Bowie talking about a new project. It's ahead of its time in the way it imagines what comes next after the vinyl-era concept album; but it's either two minutes ahead, or two thousand years. The next four inevitably never materialised.

Both records contain extensive sleeve notes, *The Buddha of Suburbia*'s a state of the musical nation address with a few glimpses about his writing processes and 'a desire to relegate the straightforward narrative to the past', and *1. Outside* a detective story/invented art history called *The Diary of Nathan Adler, or The Art-Ritual Murder of Baby Grace Blue*, which is described as a 'non-linear Gothic Drama Hyper-Cycle'. Mixed up with a story it would take ten hours to tell in a film, and actually just to explain in conversation, are some glints of autobiography ... 'I suppose you can never tell what an artist can do once he peaks.' Maybe he's just speculating like the intelligent deceiver he is, appearing to suggest that the creation of a work of art, or an album, is itself a kind of crime that needs solving.

He was in the middle of a writer period, acting very nicely as an inquisitive journalist with interest in art, music and fashion. He reviews books for Barnes & Noble. He's looking for something, new adventure, new values and new knowledge, maybe some tips, and he gets to see yet more other worlds, to compare with his, where people get to do what they want, and then promote it. He enthusiastically and thoroughly interviews Britartists Damien Hirst and Tracey Emin, anti-modernist artist Balthus and polite prankster and most successful American artist since Warhol, Jeff Koons, for *Modern Painters*, where he becomes a member of the board; strung-out trip-hop nomad Tricky for *Q* magazine as if he's beginning a science-fiction story; and fashion designer Alexander McQueen in an affectionately joshing, elderly uncle way for *Dazed & Confused*.

Even when he's interviewing someone else, there is a sense he is interviewing himself; his presence is the more interesting. Even when he is being interviewed, when he is playing the familiar role of alert, compliant interviewee, he is control of proceedings, and it can come across as though he is interviewing himself.

He sort of interviews Jarvis Cocker for an edition of the *Big Issue* edited by Damien Hirst, even though it is officially Jarvis interviewing Bowie. Hirst chooses a theme for the pair: smoking. The two have a fine chat about chasing satisfaction, trying again and again to reach another temporary nicotine high, Bowie charting his move from Gitanes to the perhaps less toxic Marlboro Lights. Thinking of how much he has smoked in his time, and the clear connection that has been made between cigarettes and death, Bowie admits that there has never been a time when he didn't think about death.

> Well I think I still do a lot of drugs, you know: caffeine and smoking and I'm probably addicted to television and certain kinds of newspapers and art. Addiction comes in all sorts of forms, but the ones that were physically damaging, not so much to me but to the people around me, they had to go firstly. Then there's cigarettes. Once Iman and I start having children I think they will have to go too. Do you really stand by the idea of living for a long time or do you instead want to fill a shorter life with maybe more interesting things? One makes a compromise between the two actually.

He wrote a fractured piece in response to Julian Schnabel's *Basquiat* film where it seemed not just the sentences but the words could be read in any order: 'Your chance is not the same as my chance.' Art, he decides, is sorcery burrowing its invisible tunnels in every direction. He was made into Boz, the hero of a computer game called Omikron: The Nomad Soul, giving his likeness and voice to a space adventure game where he is rendered as a combination of space age rock star member of the Dreamers and techno-spiritual revolutionary leader, an electronic being who lived inside the Internet. As he said, he didn't think it was enough any more to only make a record. These were some of my favourite Bowie moments in the 1990s; not necessarily his albums, but around the edges, in his writings, his appearances, his thinking and his preparing for his future, and the wider future.

•   •   •

Those looking for a new, groundbreaking and conceptual Bowie only through his music missed some of his more futuristic acts in the 1990s. They were looking in the wrong place for the equivalent of a Ziggy or a Thin White Duke, for how he was trying to find the future. They should have been looking at how he set a trend for securitising intellectual property. They should have been noting how Bowie could see that the excitement of 1970s glam was now in the new fragmented, centreless world of the Internet. More than excitement, here was the revolution, and nothing would be the same again. Which side were you on? 'The absolute transformation of everything that we ever thought about music will take place in the next ten years,' he said at the end of the twentieth century, 'and nothing is going to be able to stop it. I see absolutely no point in pretending that it's not going to happen. I'm fully confident that copyright, for instance, will no longer exist in ten years.'

In February 1997, the year after he played Andy Warhol in *Basquiat*, with the prospect of how to monetise music set to become a considerable problem to the record business, he conceived a solution with his business manager Bill Zysblat that meant selling off the royalty rights for ten years to twenty-five albums he owned that were published before 1993. This meant not having to wait for the money to come in over time, and never know how much that was going to be; it all came in one extraordinary go.

He received $55 million for these Bowie Bonds, all of it from the Prudential Insurance Co., quite some fiftieth birthday present to himself. As someone whose record sales were never consistently platinum level it was an astonishing amount of money. He didn't have to go public, and sell himself direct on the stock market; the deal was done through a third party, Bowie remaining as elusive as a financial player as he did as celebrity. Owners of the bonds could cash in by licensing the use of his songs; taking the control from Bowie on where the songs would end up.

A capitalist stroke of genius, which in itself seemed pretty non-rock and roll, and a first in entertainment, it offended those who saw it as a complete sell-out, a betrayal of some sort of artistic worth that should be maintained in a music that began as a symbol of the counterculture. Bowie actually was thinking of his music as a work of art, and in that sense it was worth a considerable amount; art, after all, the world of iconicity, auctions and masterpieces, was really about money. He sent his work, as if it was one well-known, and highly desired piece, to auction. He knew that music was no longer a 'replacement for the church'. It was becoming a huge, sterile shop, a huge selection filled with different styles to satisfy all tastes.

From the point of view of the art world, Bowie saw it as being completely natural that his work would be worth millions, like a single Picasso or Warhol canvas, with a clear value outside of the relationship between the buyer of his records and his music. It didn't destroy the essential integrity or the challenge of the work; it didn't devalue the actual impact the songs had on those who heard them. They still existed in their own reality, their own ever-changing history.

I don't really understand the details or ramifications of the deal – it's another Bowie labyrinth I have to decipher inside a few, precious hours – but the deal was as much a work of art as anything he did. He abstracted the very peculiar economic rules of the music business that meant in the last part of the twentieth century, possibly for only a few anomalous decades, popular songs became incredibly valuable. The writers of successful pop songs earned vast amounts of money purely through having their songs played. It was an extreme overcompensation for how the early blues pioneers and hack pop songwriters were ripped off and their songs undervalued. Bowie, once an exploited victim himself of business ruthlessness, turned the generation of income through writing songs into an artistic statement. It was seen as greed, or a trashing of his songs' beauty and meaning, but it was a way of using the greedy money world to create a surreal act.

Because he was in the unique position of being able to do so, he produced another of his tricks, and found a way to put a value on the imagination and on the dreams of song-writing artists.

It was a different way of looking at and valuing music, exploiting the very fact that the songs of David Bowie existed in many different places, and added worth and weight to other products, companies, entertainments and systems. He could see one system coming to an end, and conceived of another in a different sort of conceptual collaboration to the one he had with his guitarists, drummers and producers. It was a great illusion that created instant wealth in a rock world that was entering a different dimension. Others tried to follow, but no one had the same level of success.

Anticipating a communications revolution meant Bowie was the first major-level rock musician to release an online-only single, in 1996, and he was experimenting with CD-ROMs and cybercasts of shows by 1997. He could already see how the Internet offered a direct route to his fans, a way of communicating with them in an instant, and how it could become a vast interactive version of the late 1960s idea of the Arts Lab. If he had been shrewd, visionary capitalist with the Bowie Bonds, here he was technological visionary imagining a radical new way of sharing ideas, music, images, messages, writing, reviews and artworks. He was already beginning to search for what the unique would be now that making music and releasing it was about to become a torrent of the ordinary, an orgy of the average.

On 1 September 1998, an Internet service provider, BowieNet, became a part of the idea of David Bowie. You could enter the Internet through an ambitiously designed David Bowie website using new plug-ins like Flash where you got access to a detailed history of Bowie, complete access to the Bowie archives of photographs, videos, diaries and audio tracks, a members section with chat rooms, forums and message boards, and an area with Bowie-sanctioned recommendations and links to other sites. There was a journal where Bowie, or a ghost of Bowie, adopted the light, cheery, genial next-door-neighbour tone that was used for his *Mirabelle* columns in the early 1970s.

There were plans for it to become a news, sport and entertainment site, and you could get your own Bowienet email address and, controversially, as if it might be a bit Big Brother, or Big Bowie, sign up to a Bowie bank and get a Bowie credit card with his picture on.

At the time it was almost like a science-fiction fantasy of a future where people relied on such sites for most of their daily interactions, and you could connect your whole life to it, and make that the centre of your reality and become a part of the entertainment. There would be constant contact with what Bowie optimistically imagined would be the better part of the consciousness of the planet: a beautiful joining up of brains, locations and experiences.

It made little sense at a time when the Internet was in relative infancy. He was predicting a world where people would create and share versions of themselves and could invent a new identity, or identities. He was even predicting a world where stars and celebrities would communicate through new technological formats their feelings about trivial, and profound, things. In 1999, he told a quizzical Jeremy Paxman on *Newsnight*: 'I think the potential of what the Internet is going to do to society – both good and bad – is unimaginable. I think we're actually on the cusp of something exhilarating and terrifying.'

BowieNet was ahead of its time, Bowie getting as sincerely overexcited about the plans for this project as he did with *Outside*, and never became the revolutionary portal blending virtual reality, arts club, behavioural tips, fleeting thoughts, music venue, hallucinatory transformation, fractured memories and social media Bowie hoped for.

Bowie fans were always suspicious that their notoriously capricious leader wouldn't maintain his enthusiasm, and by 2006 it was over, Bowie learning enough to know what to do if he ever made some new music. Running your own site and acting as the host and always being there, and accessible, was too much of a hassle, requiring almost office-hours regularity.

At the beginning he was so keen on this new model that he would host erratic, often fairly chaotic live web chats where Bowie, or a hired Bowie, played everyone's funny, gossiping friend, even contributing himself with the user name 'Sailor'. Your view on the name depended on your personal take of Bowie – for some it was a reference to the camp 'Hello Sailor', for others it was from the sailors fighting on the dance floor in 'Life on Mars?', there were the sailors in the Jacques Brel song 'Amsterdam' that Bowie would sing, the sailor in 'Red Sails' from *Lodger*, and there's a Sailor in William Burroughs's *Naked Lunch*.

Eventually, the Sailor – who once reflected how in another life he could be walking around Bromley with his grandkids – got bored, and sailed off into the distance, leaving a community without a guide who talked among themselves for a while, before getting the point.

He'd like to put out an album a year like in the 1970s, but he's finding the business sluggish, which is one reason he looked for a new, different form of the old-style record deal. The records don't come as fast as they did in the 1970s. *Earthling* in 1997 is the wide-eyed Newley fan with a developing evangelical taste for where electronica mutated into drum 'n' bass – efficiently abstracting stability – fed through the numb but primed *Low* mind transformed into the Nine Inch Nails admirer obsessed with other worlds.

The album *hour*s . . . in 1999 is another of his occasional trippy 'debuts' where he corrects some thoughts, and remakes his mind, and re-works music that he and Reeves Gabrels had written for the civilisation of 'Omikron' where his electronic spiritual ally 'Boz' existed. It was the correct, unflustered way of leaving the fancy, ferocious twentieth century he so ingeniously plundered.

Those that discussed Bowie – through the rock filter, through a conventional chronology, always worried about 'age' – as having lived for two decades in some sort of aesthetic wilderness greet these last two records with relief, as if he's emerged from the dark, featureless tunnel he disappeared into after *Scary Monsters*. It was as it had been with one of his past idols and surrealist tutor from afar, Bob Dylan, whose later work, after a difficult 1980s when he lost track among all those videos and rhythm machines, grew stronger as he got older, shed a few shadows, and headed towards an extraordinary punchline.

There is the talk again of it being emotional, honest and even unusually autobiographical, of there being a removal of the masks, of the role-playing, as though any kind of record first of all by Bowie as part of his overall work and second of all made in a recording studio as a piece of constructed sonic theatre can be free of role playing and illusion. Ultimately all his records are autobiographical, but not so much of a life, but of his ideas. Or: all his words are autobiographical and all of them are fiction.

He'd been meeting up with old friends, finding new associates, still on the hunt for the greatest song of all time, and made plans for the post-record industry world, guarding his space, protecting the brand and taking his time. He remained discreetly fond of a bipperty-bopperty hat, not-necessarily-true pasts and a costume that marked out certain territory.

In the early twenty-first century, a few more switches are turned off, some switched back on, hits repackaged, ego transcended, stardom safely filed, theories sifted, possible last words considered, new ways to say the same thing considered, further acknowledgement of a self constantly changing in response to context. With Tony Visconti back for more, 2002's *Heathen* fabricates an imaginary follow-up to a few of his classic albums, somewhere between the happy H for the love and kink of *Hunky Dory* and the hollow 'H' for the exile, manufactured reality and distinct accent of *"Heroes"*. There's a couple of tracks he might have put on a second *Pin Ups* album, including the Modern Lovers' 'Pablo Picasso' which can now go next to his 'Andy Warhol'.

Reality is a New York record, made there in 2003 with a feel and love for living there, the speed, beat and sound, but as much a conceptual, fluid New York as the Berlin of before, places that belong in his mind that leak into each other, places he goes to continue work on the illusion of fixed identity. *Reality*'s a fantasy follow-up to the never made follow-up to *Scary Monsters*, largely regarded as the most confident record he has made since then.

The title track is a classic example of Bowie giving everything and nothing away; cutting up the riddle of his life, or inventing a story using his experiences for effect, another game of duplicity. Talking about building a wall of sound to separate him from a 'tragic youth', hiding among the junk of wretched highs, speeding from Planet X to Planet Alpha, struggling for reality ... it might have been him summoning up the 1970s. He's looking for sense but getting next to nothing.

He might have been playing around, seeing if anyone was paying attention. But admitting that singing about 'my death' is more than just him singing a sad song, like when he was young and taking on Jacques Brel as an act of bravado, tells some kind of truth about where he is in his life, and why his songs are now confronting an end that is getting at times too close for comfort. There was always death in his songs, but never as a reality that had to be faced.

Reality proposes a possible final album title, but hints at further revelations, other permutations, looking towards a final kind of settled down, sorted out, seriously revealing, ultimately fluctuating 'David Bowie' debut, another start, but possibly an ending, composed of many selves, beyond reality, and the empty spaces around it, where he can finally be himself, reaching an absolute that can give him peace of mind.

For a while, he seems to have finished with *Reality*.

• • •

From 1987, he had topped various accounts with open-air festival appearances and constant large-scale tours – Glass Spider,
Tin Machine, Sound and Vision, Outside, Reality – that reflect
his affection for arranging himself and his golden repertoire
into accessible, often magnetic, show-business shapes. It's the
glam rock star equivalent of Bob Dylan's endless tour as a way
of dealing with the past and staying ahead of it, an awareness of
how in a world where recorded music is increasingly generic and
unspectacular it is touring that remains the only unique situation; Bowie's travelling fair is more dramatic and unwieldy, and
it's never as constant, but it's one way through the uncertainty
of the times where he can maintain the illusion of the rock star,
and keep himself occupied doing one of those things he loves the
most: performing. Even if he has to repeat himself, and keep selling himself as someone who sincerely believes in his own fantasy,
pretending to maintain the intensity from venue to venue, station
to station, he has a little light Dylanesque fun rearranging some
of his old classics, and maintains his grip as a master illusionist,
the clown who crossed over to the rock side, the artist who created a pop star, a copy of a copy of which there is no original.

However experimental his new music might become, however
trapped he might get working out what kind of new music, or
no music, to make, and however interested he gets in extra-
curricular activity of interest only to a minority, he can't shake
off the habit of needing an audience looking up to him and marvelling that he is who he is and has visited such lands. He sang
on *Reality* that he was back where he started from, and that was
regularly playing David Bowie the spectacle with a sort of radiant
straightness in front of a constant thousands of people, some of
whom were seeing him for the first time, and he was getting more
of that feeling he was addicted to, that there was still the same
question coming from an awed audience that had been asked
since 1972: who *are* you, what are you, what is *your* secret?

It is while on one of these large touring shows where it seems his hectic, addictive 1970s, and all the touring and promoting, finally chases him down. Reality caught up with him, as sober as he now was, beyond even the Marlboro Lights, as healthy as he now seemed, power returning to his voice after a late twentieth century dip, a sprightly 57-year-old looking charismatically pop star ageless as if he had no real past, despite the apparent facts. He could do this in his sleep now: project his dreams as a sur-real, seductive song and dance man with razor-sharp timing who could cut deep with just a glance, with a repertoire of songs that leap across time filled with lines and melodies that are fantastic to sing and have helped turn him into legend.

He's on one of those tours that take him to another and another and yet another cold, massive, concrete and metal arena in a major capital city, with a light show honed to perfection, and he's singing a song about death and the passing time, because most of his songs are. He's in pain, soaked to the skin with sweat, he can't finish the song. He's helped off stage, returns to finish the show, and a mis-diagnosis that it is only a trapped nerve means he travels to the next show, a festival in Germany. He completes a tentative show with 'Ziggy Stardust', so it becomes the last song he sings on tour as David Bowie, and as soon as he leaves the stage, he collapses. This time, at a local hospital he's diagnosed as having a blocked artery in the heart, and undergoes emergency surgery.

At various stages between 1984 and 2004, as he sometimes lost what he called 'the trade winds', and faced up to the tricky prospect of becoming an ageing rock star destined to disappoint almost simply by getting old, his preferred route might have been a period of artistic silence, a formidable absence, almost in a Marcel Duchampian sense. Retire from the active nature of making art, and suppress your presence to such an extent it becomes its own powerful identity. Certainly after he married Iman, he was constantly considering separating himself from always having to be David Bowie.

He could spend the rest of his life, the New York era, as a relative recluse doing his equivalent of Duchamp spending the decades playing chess, making occasional observations and comments from sublimely isolated afar, allowing secrecy to be his one main contribution to his myth. A complete withdrawal from the art and business of making art within business. Silence, until he could finish off his work, his life as art. The idea that the end of artistic activity is not the finish but freedom.

In those years between his heart attack and *The Next Day* and the *David Bowie is* exhibition, there was a version of this. The heart attack compelled him to slow down, and make the most of living in New York, the best city for a restless traveller to end up if they have to end up anywhere, with enough in walking distance of a Manhattan home to feel constantly in touch with a wider, shifting world. It was Iman's city and he knew he could better disappear into the rhythms and attractions of New York than London. They live there, almost in plain sight but hidden, and in the countryside around Woodstock, New York State, where he's surprised by how much he takes to the mountain air. The beautiful outdoors ...

He lived a family life, travelling less like a 'Lodger' accumulating extreme, random experiences and more like a down-to-earth tourist, enjoying the sights as a stylish, even fit, but vague-looking man in his sixties. He would often slip into London and Scotland without being noticed, making good use of Luton Airport. He would accompany Iman to her social events and premières with the regal bearing of a consort he often displayed when on duty for himself, especially when he was being interviewed on the BBC.

'I'm very at ease, and I like it,' he said in one of those interviews where he's giving away a version of where he might be and what he should be thinking, as if reading out lines written before. 'I never thought I would be such a family-oriented guy. I didn't think that was part of my make-up. But somebody said as you get older you become the person you always should have been, and I feel that's happening to me. I'm rather surprised at who I am, because I'm actually like my dad!'

In 2000 his second child, Alexandria Zahra Jones – Lexi – is born, and the combination of being father and husband in the city he loves pulls him further away from the constant busy-ness of the past forty years. Lexi starts to accompany them on some of their trips; when in London, he takes her to look at Haddon Hall in Beckenham, where he wrote 'Changes', 'Life on Mars?' and 'Quicksand'. The family visit the *David Bowie is* exhibition at the V&A for a private tour one Sunday in May 2013, and it's like seeing more sights, it's another kind of city break. But Bowie is the city. Bowie is a visitor to his own history, taking photos, marvelling that this is where he's been, and this is what he built. Lexi begins to get an idea of how many versions of someone and something her dad has been, and how many hair colours he'd had. She becomes the latest student.

He'd been to all the parties he needed to go to, done all the interviews to supply everyone with enough facts, and misdirections, to satisfy or frustrate immediate needs. He could walk to wherever his new favourite groups were playing – Arcade Fire, TV on the Radio – and play along not so much as an impresario or critic but simply a fan. Most of the time he has the pleasure of looking without being seen. He sings 'Changes' with solo piano at a New York charity show with Alicia Keys in 2006, the last song he sings in public.

Whether he planned for it to be this way in his sixties or not, he has more time to work on the status of David Bowie as a presence, as a new kind of force. The silence, the remoteness, combined with the constant activity of the Internet in compiling and indexing his work promoted him in new ways. The Internet was creating a different sort of reality, and Bowie had always been ready for that.

The different sort of reality in the 1980s wasn't to his taste, the one in the 1990s seemed too neurotically anxious about the coming millennium and blocked the future out, and the 2000s were not yet fully immersed in a new reality that was soon going to affect the very nature of how we communicate with each other. The Internet was becoming his kind of reality, and one that would end up producing the conditions where he could manipulate things to suit his own desires and plans as he had done in the 1970s.

He had taken a major part in the invention of a musical form unlike anything before, changed the direction of popular music, and sustained his creative energy through all sorts of demands and dilemmas for over a decade, and effected such change it needed a substantial pause for thought before he made his next move. His thinking had been based on a set of systems that he had altered so much he would now need to reconfigure how he fitted in to where it went next, if at all.

For a while, he had nothing new to exhibit. The old, though, was becoming new by becoming part of a new reality, his songs were constantly moving through film, television, memory, history and the Internet. And when he did have something new to show, he managed to deceive everyone.

THE TRUTH IS OF COURSE THAT THERE IS NO JOURNEY. WE ARE ARRIVING AND DEPARTING ALL AT THE SAME TIME.

The years 1947 to 2016. A strange, intense time to be alive, and to think about being alive. From just after the end of the Second World War, when reality had been broken into pieces and needed a considerable amount of repair and realignment, through the accelerating impact of rock and roll and pop culture, to the beginnings of an emotionally violent communications revolution promising or threatening to change what it means to be human. The Internet is breaking reality into pieces, the result of a different sort of war, one that may well end up being between humans and machines – pop music created the soundtrack to this battle from the very beginning, being the result of a collaboration between humans and machines where sometimes the machines intensified the human and sometimes seemed to be taking over.

If you were in awe of the universe, all the pain and pleasure, as Bowie would admit he was, always working on his own map of its dimensions, daring to disturb it, then there was no better time to be alive, and feel its immensity and odd, intimate power, and its weird, constant presence in the mind.

Bowie started out in music catching up with a new breed of

British musicians fusing their home-grown instincts and influences with the sound of black American blues and jazz, and ended it producing music as influenced as anything else by the studio methods, sonic eclecticism and conceptual playfulness of elusive, devious black entertainers like Kendrick Lamar, D'Angelo and Kanye West, whose own music and controversial public intellectual power was influenced by the generation-defining, shape-shifting and marketing perceptiveness of Bowie. He had prepared the way for such a multilayered, self-centred presentation of self, mixing the traditional with the experimental with the new-fangled and the futuristic, and a certain sort of mad, insecure ambition. He could still make the release of an album an event – especially with what came just a couple of days after its release – but not many others now could. He knew that the release of an album had become so mundane, and that for those who still wanted to operate as musicians and pop stars there needed to be a new way of producing An Event, something that stood out from everything else, and got people talking about a person or group at a time when everything was being talked about and everyone was looking for attention.

He started playing home-grown skiffle on home-made instruments in post-war austerity, and ended making a sophisticated internationalist electronic music embedded in the shared Internet. No other musician could claim to be as in the musical moment at both ends of the spectrum, to have had the artistic courage to keep up with where technology, innovations and the audience had moved over a fifty-year period, so that his music and imagery was as part of the times in 2016 as it was in the early 1970s, both commercially and creatively.

Blackstar was a flickering sequence of sounds, pulses, tone colours and instrumental gestures made by Bowie leading his latest Miles Davis-esque ensemble, the most orthodox jazz line-up of all, although he wasn't making jazz but as always using its strategies to help compose songs – this collective featured New York jazz players including the pianist Jason Lindner and saxophonist Donny McCaslin. This group knew the strained, storming blackness of Kendrick Lamar's *To Pimp a Butterfly* as much as the sunshine mini-pop symphonies of *Pet Sounds*, its Tim Buckley, Aphex Twin, Neu!, Roxy Music, the Soulquarians, Stevie Wonder, the Necks and Godspeed You! Black Emperor as much as its Andrew Hill, Keith Jarrett, Charlie Haden and Vijay Iyer. This was music reacting to the existence of other music from a variety of times and spaces, and reacting to how the very best music is always a matter of life and death, of keeping certain flames burning.

I've always found it fascinating that rock musicians who came to new music in the early 1960s and in the years afterwards mostly never seemed to move on from their original influences, so that their early work is compelling, urgent and radically new, and their later work stuck in the same place. As Bowie found with Mick Ronson in the mid-1970s, there is an almost superstitious fear of keeping up with new music, of changing with the times, a sense of panic and despair that they have lost their original magic. Maybe most rock musicians have a year or two of youthful genius, and then the inspiration dries up and there is nothing left but repetition and nostalgia.

Bowie, a fan of new music from across centuries, was always listening and feeding his findings into his latest work. He was always learning, and always wanting everyone to learn together. Sometimes it didn't work, but led to something that did; for what turned out to be his last work, his closing argument, everything gels.

He willed it into being as he guided the recording of the music while suffering the most punishing and dehumanising effects of chemotherapy, which apart from anything else clearly focused his mind. 'How long?' he once wondered, thinking about how many years he had left to live, 'and what do I do with the time I have got left?' He was working out the answer in his last songs.

Blackstar, his last record, *was* a kind of end-of-career 'Best of' except that it was a new collection combining the best elements of Bowie's music. It was the best of the ways he put his music together. He's up to his old tricks in a new sort of way. He still wants to hear tomorrow coming, even if tomorrow isn't what it used to be.

There was his ability as a singer-songwriter to string words and syllables together, sometimes as he admitted merely 'to jolly the music along', to create so much space for interpretation and insight, so he climbed into the mind of the listener who could then climb into his mind. As always, as from the very beginning, he mixes delightful, almost ridiculous nonsense and wordplay – here directly acknowledging a prime source, Anthony Burgess's *Nadsat* slang from *A Clockwork Orange* – with remarkable clarity of thought, clear meaning with nothing of the sort, saying little but saying so much, letting his listeners get from the songs exactly what they want, according to their personal version of Bowie. He's communicating something even before it is understood.

There's melancholy as a form of exhilaration, ghosts of other songs and characters, a weakness for the sensational, glimmers of the supernatural, daydream, trance, faith and passion all existing on the borders of waking thought. He was always pushing against something, and here he's out to slay dragons, which are closer to him than they've ever been, and more hideous than ever, and he's always facing up to the demons, the pressure of life and now death and searching even at this point this late in life for another true, beginning place. His mind is alive even as his body is failing; seeing more and feeling less.

There's his need for a great producer – and here it is as it should be Tony Visconti – to ensure that the sound of the music is itself pure, physical pleasure, the very best example of how the recording studio, another fading aspect of the making of rock, created this fifty-year period of scintillating electronic illusions.

There's the singing, the sound of wistful thinking, the vitality within weakness, still stretching his wings, everything however macabre or whimsical delivered with radiant confessional honesty.

There's even his fondness for the ceremonial-seeming, multi-levelled ten-minute suite, which works as a procession of episodes, stitching together numerous sources, as if the music is there to chase away dread and uncertainty, and he's on the verge of touching the next world. Sometimes he was play-acting the end of the world; now it was for real.

The ten-minute title track shares its title with an Elvis Presley song – *when a man sees his black star/ he knows his time, his time has come* – and its title and abandoned atmospheric eeriness echoes one of Bowie's favourite pieces of music, 'Black Angels' by George Crumb from 1970, subtitled 'Thirteen Images from the Dark Lands'. It's a soul-ravaging string quartet containing the power of the wildest heavy metal which presents a free play between the polarities of good and evil, itself quoting Schubert's *Death and the Maiden*, alludes to Tibetan prayer and was written to 'portray the journey of a soul'.

On 'Blackstar', to the extent Bowie was forced to deny the song was about ISIS, he pursues his fascination with the vague, enormous and menacing nature of evil, and courts the spirit of his darkest mentor Aleister Crowley, the grand degenerate adorer of the irrational, who once said, 'Every man and every woman is a star.' Crowley also confessed to anyone who happened to come across his words that: 'The joy of life consists in the exercise of one's energies, continual growth, constant change, the enjoyment of every new experience. To stop means simply to die. The eternal mistake of mankind is to set up an attainable ideal.' Bowie took his ideas from far and wide, from Bing Crosby and John Cage, Aleister Crowley and *Viz*, T. S. Eliot and *Peaky Blinders*.

Blackstar was another example of how Bowie made his music thinking not like a rock musician, stuck in time, in a groove, always yearning for the old times, happy days, but thinking like an artist. He kept listening, looking, absorbing, stealing, adapting, right to the very end, fighting ultimately for the sake of it to achieve some kind of harmony with the universe and his place in it, to make his last artistic statement as vivid and powerful as any he had made during his so-called golden age.

To do that he had to make sure people were paying attention, and the way he manipulated circumstances to recapture that time when he was the centre of attention was a final sign of his powers of seduction. He had said that once he was past fifty, he was well past the age when he was acceptable. 'You are forbidden access. You won't get the coverage you like in music magazines, you're not going to get played on the radio or television. I have to survive on word of mouth.' He made word of mouth work for him; the Internet had turned the whole world into word of mouth. Everything was up for grabs.

He grew as a pop star during a period when the idea of being the rare beast, the one-off, the sole occupier of a certain brand new territory was vastly important, and *Blackstar* was his own tribute to that idea at a time when old thoughts about what was important about music had disintegrated.

And it was a piece of genre-liquifying work that, like Kanye, or Beyoncé, needed some other, new word to describe it, reflecting the ways these expressions materialise on a screen, and how they get heard about, shared out and distributed, something better than 'visual album'. Something perhaps inspired by Bowie, whose sudden unannounced appearance with 'Where Are We Now?' triggered a new theatrical way for the last few roaming superstar entertainers to appear with their product and make it seem special now that music is made mechanically too available – call them genies, perhaps, something, to show that they are different entertainments, different vessels, to what the LP was.

Maybe they're 'egos'. Have you heard the new 'ego' by Madlib? Or they could be called 'dimensions'. Maybe they're just 'releases'. A release of mood, emotion, time, rhythm, anger, lies, fear, confusion, stardom, glamour, belief, fragility, secrets, guile, martyrdom, secret knowledge, conceptual ingenuity, sheer self-possession. You can now work in multi-dimensional space, stretch yourself through and all over time, and intrude into everyone's lives not only with songs and sounds but with your face, image, passing thoughts, spontaneous gestures, and random claims.

Blackstar also became an Instagram series of fifteen-second dramatic interpretations, *Unbound*, compressed abstract images written by Carolynn Cecilia in response to the musical atmosphere, phantom characters and word clusters that Bowie generated. Bowie, never afraid or frustrated by the new, a long-time lover of the fragmented and the cryptic, reacted positively to Snapchat and Instagram, the way it created the possibility for the transmission of dreams and illusions as banal or meaningless as these could sometimes be.

He was interested in how the shape-shifting post-contemporary world constantly throws up new cross-border, largely unprecedented free-form venues, stages, territories, avenues, links, networks, systems, communities, collaborations, strategies, commodities, technologies, puzzles, hybrids, signs where the ideas of old and new as well as high and low real and unreal young and old male and female were being completely dislodged.

The release of *Blackstar* was a work of art about how the very idea of thinking is changing, and how Bowie was at an age to have seen that transformation begin, and to be both grateful he'd lived through a time when the solo artist could demand attention, and disappointed that he wasn't going to participate in the communal sharing of ideas and dreams across a new form of time and space. He knew that in terms of what was about to happen to entertainment, and the reality it responded to and shaped, he was living in the equivalent time to the black and white movies. He was Charlie Chaplin.

He was leaving one world as another took shape, and he had done all he could to contribute ideas to what that new world would be – and produced plenty of examples of what it was like to live approaching and during those changes.

In the 1970s, Bowie was working so quickly and so presciently as though there already was an Internet, an MTV, Google, Twitter,

Instagram, a distortion of the generation gap, a realignment of gender divisions, a gathering invasion of androgyny, a knowledge that popular culture and the magic-seeming power of fame were central to how people would organise their existence and connect with each other. He was already thinking in the way people would as the concept of linear time broke down, and everything would start to happen at once, and could be replayed in any order. The multimedia reality of the world itself would become surreal, cubist, postmodern, and deconstructed – open to limitless interpretations of meaning, never anchored in one significant place.

He let the world catch up with him, and then finished off his life's work with an intrepid flourish, making it appear as though he was exactly as here and now as he had been during the 1970s when, as he once said, for a few years he was the very definition of the rock star. At the end, he made a beginning. It was always what he was most interested in. That, and forever.

He's in the dark of the cupboard, wondering if it's time to come out yet. He's thinking of what Elvis sang in his 'Black Star' – There's a lot of livin' I gotta do/ Give me time to make a few dreams come true/Black star. He's frightened by the total goal. He's thinking of what T. S. Eliot said hell was – a place where nothing connects with nothing. He's floating in a tin can. He's riding his bike down to the shops in Bromley. He's looking up at the chimneys of Haddon Hall. He's doing the clap thing in 'Space Oddity'. He hears Mingus sawing and plucking his double bass and making the sound of progress. Ziggy played guitar. He's wearing his Alexander McQueen Union Jack jacket. He's sex object and prophet of doom. He's standing by the wall. He's walking unnoticed through New York carrying a satchel wearing a flat cap. He's answering his last email, still wondering what's happening next. Wondering what in the world is happening to me. A final photograph. A last pose. A last wander nowhere in particular. He said, life really is as short as they tell you it is. Some last hours with his son. Always remember you're unique just like everyone else. Let's drink to that. There's a feather on the back of his hand waiting to be blown away. He is smoking his last cigarette. A last look in the mirror. Sails of oblivion at his head. A last, lingering look into the eyes of Iman. A last feel of her cool fingers. He sings his line in the 1997 Children in Need version of Lou Reed's 'Perfect Day', originally the B-side of 'Walk on the Wild Side'. A perfect day, where he forgot himself. The gods forgot they made me, so I forgot them too. Books were among his gods. They made him a different man. He takes them with him everywhere. Wherever he is going next he will need something to read. He counts down a list of his 100 favourite books:

Interviews with Francis Bacon by David Sylvester

Billy Liar by Keith Waterhouse

Room at the Top by John Braine

On Having No Head by Douglas Harding

Kafka Was the Rage by Anatole Broyard

A Clockwork Orange by Anthony Burgess

City of Night by John Rechy

The Brief Wondrous Life of Oscar Wao by Junot Díaz

Madame Bovary by Gustave Flaubert

Iliad by Homer

As I Lay Dying by William Faulkner

Tadanori Yokoo by Tadanori Yokoo

Berlin Alexanderplatz by Alfred Döblin

Inside the Whale and Other Essays by George Orwell

Mr Norris Changes Trains by Christopher Isherwood

Hall's Dictionary of Subjects and Symbols in Art by James A. Hall

David Bomberg by Richard Cork

Blast by Wyndham Lewis

Passing by Nella Larsen

Beyond the Brillo Box by Arthur C. Danto

The Origin of Consciousness in the Breakdown of the Bicameral Mind by Julian Jaynes

In Bluebeard's Castle by George Steiner

Hawksmoor by Peter Ackroyd

The Divided Self by R. D. Laing

The Stranger by Albert Camus

Infants of the Spring by Wallace Thurman

The Quest for Christa T by Christa Wolf

The Songlines by Bruce Chatwin

Nights at the Circus by Angela Carter

The Master and Margarita by Mikhail Bulgakov

The Prime of Miss Jean Brodie by Muriel Spark

Lolita by Vladimir Nabokov

Herzog by Saul Bellow

Puckoon by Spike Milligan

Black Boy by Richard Wright

The Great Gatsby by F. Scott Fitzgerald

The Sailor Who Fell from Grace with the Sea by Yukio Mishima

Darkness at Noon by Arthur Koestler

The Waste Land by T. S. Eliot

McTeague by Frank Norris

Money by Martin Amis

The Outsider by Colin Wilson

Strange People by Frank Edwards

English Journey by J. B. Priestley

A Confederacy of Dunces by John Kennedy Toole

The Day of the Locust by Nathanael West

1984 by George Orwell

The Life and Times of Little Richard by Charles White

Awopbopaloobop Alopbamboom: The Golden Age of Rock by Nik Cohn

Mystery Train by Greil Marcus

Beano (comic, 1950s)

Raw (comic, 1980s)

White Noise by Don DeLillo

Sweet Soul Music: Rhythm and Blues and the Southern Dream of Freedom by Peter Guralnick

Silence: Lectures and Writing by John Cage

Writers at Work: The Paris Review *Interviews* edited by Malcolm Cowley

The Sound of the City: The Rise of Rock & Roll by Charlie Gillett

Octobriana and the Russian Underground by Petr Sadecky

The Street by Ann Petry

Wonder Boys by Michael Chabon

Last Exit to Brooklyn by Hubert Selby, Jr.

A People's History of the United States by Howard Zinn

The Age of American Unreason by Susan Jacoby

Metropolitan Life by Fran Lebowitz

The Coast of Utopia by Tom Stoppard

The Bridge by Hart Crane

All the Emperor's Horses by David Kidd

Fingersmith by Sarah Waters

Earthly Powers by Anthony Burgess

The 42nd Parallel by John Dos Passos

Tales of Beatnik Glory by Ed Saunders

The Bird Artist by Howard Norman

Nowhere to Run: The Story of Soul Music by Gerri Hirshey

Before the Deluge by Otto Friedrich

Sexual Personae: Art and Decadence from Nefertiti to Emily Dickinson by Camille Paglia

The American Way of Death by Jessica Mitford

In Cold Blood by Truman Capote

Lady Chatterley's Lover by D. H. Lawrence

Teenage by Jon Savage

Vile Bodies by Evelyn Waugh

The Hidden Persuaders by Vance Packard

The Fire Next Time by James Baldwin

Viz (comic, early 1980s)

Private Eye (satirical magazine, 1960s – 1980s)

Selected Poems by Frank O'Hara

The Trial of Henry Kissinger by Christopher Hitchens

Flaubert's Parrot by Julian Barnes

Le Chants de Maldoror by Comte de Lautréamont

On the Road by Jack Kerouac

Mr. Wilson's Cabinet of Wonder by Lawrence Weschler

Zanoni by Edward Bulwer-Lytton

Transcendental Magic: Its Doctrine and Ritual by Éliphas Lévi

The Gnostic Gospels by Elaine Pagels

The Leopard by Giuseppe di Lampedusa

Inferno by Dante Alighieri

A Grave for a Dolphin by Alberto Denti di Pirajno

The Insult by Rupert Thomson

In Between the Sheets by Ian McEwan

A People's Tragedy by Orlando Figes

Journey into the Whirlwind by Eugenia Ginzburg

At the end of a book about him there is one way through his life:

1953   Bowie family move from Brixton to Bromley
1963   Becomes a professional musician
1967   Meets dancer Lindsay Kemp
1967   Novelty record 'The Laughing Gnome' is released
1967   *David Bowie* the album is released
1969   'Space Oddity' is released
1969   Appears both recorded and live on *Top of the Pops*; father dies of pneumonia
1970   Records a session for BBC, *In Concert*, with Mick Ronson
1970   Marries Angie Barnett
1970   *The Man Who Sold the World* is released
1971   Son Duncan Zowie Haywood Jones is born

1971   Third album, *Hunky Dory*, comes out

1972   Declares to *Melody Maker* readers that he is gay

1972   *The Rise and Fall of Ziggy Stardust* is released

1973   Adopts a new persona for that year's album, *Aladdin Sane*

1973   Back catalogue released helps to make Bowie the best-selling act of the year

1974   US-inspired album *Diamond Dogs* is released

1975   *Young Americans* comes out

1976   Moves to Switzerland

1976   *Station to Station* is released

1976   Stars as Thomas Jerome Newton in *The Man Who Fell to Earth*

1977   *Low* comes out, in the same year as *"Heroes"*

1978   Appears in the film *Just a Gigolo* alongside Marlene Dietrich

1979   *Lodger* is released

1980   Angie and David are divorced

1980   *Scary Monsters (And Super Creeps)* is released

1981   Seminal German film *Christiane F.* is screened

1983   Achieves success in America with *Let's Dance*

1983   Appears as Major Jack Celliers in *Merry Christmas, Mr Lawrence*

1984   *Tonight* comes out

1986   Appears in cult classic *Labyrinth* as Jareth, the Goblin King

1986   Writes theme for *Absolute Beginners*

1987   *Never Let Me Down* is released

1988   Appears as Pontius Pilate in *The Last Temptation of Christ*

1992   Has a role in cult David Lynch TV series *Twin Peaks*

1992   Marries for a second time, to model and entrepreneur Iman

1993   *Black Tie White Noise* and *The Buddha of*

Suburbia are released in the same year

1995   *1. Outside* is released

1996   Portrays Andy Warhol in the film *Basquiat*;
inducted into the Rock and Roll Hall of Fame
by David Byrne (he does not attend – Madonna
accepts on his behalf)

1997   *Earthling* is released; Bowie Bonds created

1998   BowieNet is launched

1999   *Hours* is released

2000   Bowie and Iman's daughter Alexandria or 'Lexi' is
born

2001   Has cameo role in hit film *Zoolander*; his mother,
Peggy, dies

2002   *Heathen* comes out; curates the annual Meltdown
festival, inviting, among others, Badly Drawn Boy,
Coldplay, Harry Hill, Luke Haines, Peaches, Philip
Glass, Suede, Television, The Divine Comedy and
The Legendary Stardust Cowboy

2003   *Reality* is released

2004   Undergoes surgery after suffering a heart attack

2006   Appears as Nikola Tesla in *The Prestige*

2013   Surprise album *The Next Day* is released to
coincide with *David Bowie is* at the Victoria and
Albert Museum

2016   *Blackstar* is unveiled, days before Bowie's death.
He is cremated and his ashes discreetly scattered.
There is no fixed resting place. Posthumously
awarded the prestigious Board of Directors Tribute
Award from the Council of Fashion Directors of
America. Celebrated and reinterpreted by s t a r g
a z e as part of the 2016 Proms season at the Royal
Albert Hall.

Inside the cupboard it's the darkest it's been. Surely it can't get any darker. He feels someone lean in and look into his eyes and ask, 'How is it in there? What do you see in there?' He hears himself say, 'Nothing.' And a voice says I just wanted to say thank you. Thank you for everything. He looks up and the light floods back into his face. 'Really?' And then he sinks back into a black void, set free to find a new illusion.

And that was that, and then there was

•

MY THANKS

Iain MacGregor at Simon & Schuster for opening the door

Martin Bryant for copy-editing

David Godwin for wisdom

Philippa Sitters at David Godwin Associates

Jonathan Barnbrook

Paul Kobrak

John Wilson

Caspar Llewellyn Smith at the *Observer*, Lucy Tuck at the *Financial Times*, Sarah Crompton at the *Daily Telegraph* and Jo-Ann Furniss at *Arena Homme +* for commissioning pieces about David Bowie, parts of which made it into this book

Geoff Marsh

Victoria Broackes

The Victoria & Albert Museum

The Morleys, The Mitchells, The Donnellys and The Levys

Madeleine Morley for inspiration

&

Elizabeth Levy for brilliance, patience, occasional therapy, reminding me to breathe and for being with me at all times during what was simultaneously a sprint and a marathon

• • •

INDEX